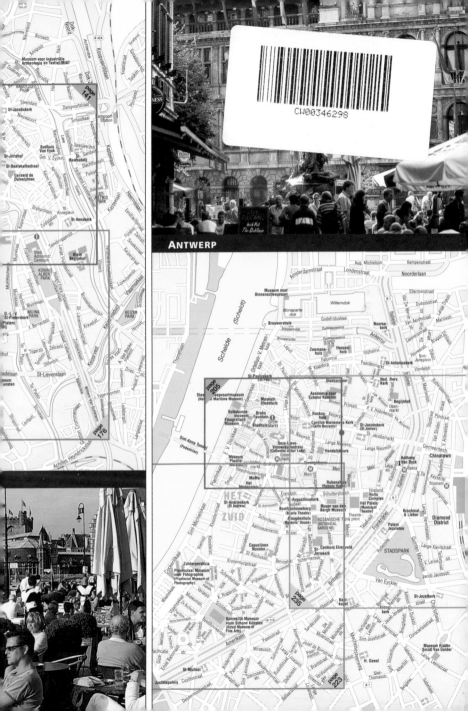

ANTWERP

INSIGHT **CITY GUIDE**

# BRUGES, GHENT & ANTWERP

Part of the Langenscheidt Publishing Group

2

## ❊ INSIGHT GUIDE

# BRUGES, GHENT & ANTWERP

*Editor*
**Carine Tracanelli**
*Art Director*
**Klaus Geisler**
*Picture Editor*
**Hilary Genin**
*Cartography Editor*
**Zoë Goodwin**
*Production*
**Kenneth Chan**
*Editorial Director*
**Brian Bell**

### Distribution

*UK & Ireland*
**GeoCenter International Ltd**
The Viables Centre, Harrow Way
Basingstoke, Hants RG22 4BJ
Fax: (44) 1256-817988

*United States*
**Langenscheidt Publishers, Inc.**
36–36 33rd Street 4th Floor
Long Island City, NY 11106
Fax: (1) 718 784-0640

*Australia*
**Universal Publishers**
1 Waterloo Road
Macquarie Park, NSW 2113
Fax: (61) 2 9888 9074

*New Zealand*
**Hema Maps New Zealand Ltd (HNZ)**
Unit D, 24 Ra ORA Drive
East Tamaki, Auckland
Fax: (64) 9 273 6479

*Worldwide*
**Apa Publications GmbH & Co.
Verlag KG (Singapore branch)**
38 Joo Koon Road, Singapore 628990
Tel: (65) 6865-1600. Fax: (65) 6861-6438

### Printing

**Insight Print Services (Pte) Ltd**
38 Joo Koon Road, Singapore 628990
Tel: (65) 6865-1600. Fax: (65) 6861-6438

©2006 Apa Publications GmbH & Co.
Verlag KG (Singapore branch)
*All Rights Reserved*

*First Edition 2006*

# ABOUT THIS BOOK

The first Insight Guide pioneered the use of creative full-colour photography in travel guides in 1970. Since then, we have expanded our range to cater for our readers' need not only for reliable information but also for a real understanding of the culture and workings of their chosen destination. Now, when the internet can supply inexhaustible facts, our books marry text and pictures to provide those more elusive qualities: knowledge and discernment. To this end, they rely on the authority of local writers and photographers.

#### How to use this book

*Insight Guide: Bruges, Ghent and Antwerp* is carefully structured both to convey an understanding of the city and its culture and to guide readers through its sights and activities:

◆ To understand Flanders today, you need to know something of its past. The first section covers the region's history and culture in lively, authoritative essays written by specialists.
◆ The main Places section provides a full run-down of all the attractions worth seeing. The principal places of interest are coordinated by number with full-colour maps.
◆ The Travel Tips listings section provides a point of reference for information on travel, hotels, shops and festivals. Information may be located quickly by using the index printed on the back cover flap – and the flaps are designed to serve as bookmarks.
◆ Photographs are chosen not only to illustrate geography and buildings but also to convey the moods of the city and the life of its people.

his writing (he updated the original *Insight Guide to Venice*) and his photography, which is also featured in this book. The restaurant reviews in the book and the restaurant map were written and selected by all three.

The Travel Tips chapters for all three cities were compiled by **Derek Blyth**, Brussels-based writer of *Flemish Cities Explored*, which covers historical walks throughout Flanders, and a contributor to *The Bulletin*.

The essays on art and architecture, the people of Flanders and the photo feature on the Symbolist movement were written by **Antony Mason**, who has an extensive knowledge of all three cities. The mouthwatering essay on Flemish gastronomy and the photo feature on genever was written by **Fiona Simms**, who has also worked on food supplements for *The Guardian* newspaper in London.

Thanks also go to Insight editors **Pam Barrett** and **Roger Williams**; **Ilse van Steen** of the **Tourism Flanders-Brussels** bureau in London; the local tourist offices in Bruges, Ghent and Antwerp; as well as **Sarah Kettering** at **Eurostar** for literally taking us there.

Many of the photographs are the work of **Gregory Wrona**, **Anne and Philippe Croquet-Zouridakis** and **John Brunton**, as well as Insight regular **Jerry Dennis**. Picture research was carried out by **Hilary Genin** and **Helen Stallion**.

The guide was proofread by **Sylvia Suddes** and the index was compiled by **Isobel McLean**.

## The contributors

This new book was put together and edited by **Carine Tracanelli**, using writers and photographers based in Flanders or with specialist knowledge of the destination.

The main three authors for the book were **Katharine Mill**, **George McDonald** and **John Brunton**. Mill, a regular contributor to *The Bulletin*, a weekly English-language magazine published in Brussels, wrote the Bruges Places section. Responsible for the Ghent Places section, McDonald is an Insight favourite, having written the *Insight Pocket Guide to Brussels* and the *Insight Compact Guide to Bruges*, and updated the *Insight City Guide to Brussels*. He also wrote the introduction and history chapters of the book. Brunton is also an Insight regular, both for

## CONTACTING THE EDITORS

We would appreciate it if readers would alert us to errors or outdated information by writing to:

**Insight Guides, P.O. Box 7910, London SE1 1WE, England. Fax: (44) 20 7403-0290. insight@apaguide.co.uk**

**NO** part of this book may be reproduced, stored in a retrieval system or transmitted in any form or means electronic, mechanical, photocopying, recording or otherwise, without prior written permission of *Apa Publications*. Brief text quotations with use of photographs are exempted for book review purposes only. Information has been obtained from sources believed to be reliable, but its accuracy and completeness, and the opinions based thereon, are not guaranteed.

**www.insightguides.com**
*In North America:*
**www.insighttravelguides.com**

## Maps

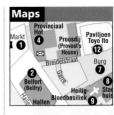

## Travel Tips

# THE BEST OF BRUGES

Unique attractions, bars, boat rides, exciting family outings, romantic hideaways... here, at a glance, are our recommendations

## BEST VIEWS

- **Halletoren**
  The top of the belfry's 366 steps is the highest and most central standpoint in town, with a panoramic view as far as the coast (on a fine day). *See page 65.*
- **Sint-Janshuis windmill**
  The giddy climb to the top of the windmill's ladder on the north-eastern ramparts rewards with a view over the Sint Anna district rooftops and a chance to play the easy game of "spot the steeple". *See page 104.*
- **Canal boat tour**
  It seems like a tourist trap but a boat tour is your chance to see the city from the "swan's eye view", peeking into back gardens and ducking

under low bridges and overhanging boughs. *See page 72.*
- **Peerdenbrug**
  Drink in the heart-wrenchingly romantic view of the prettiest stretch of canal in Bruges from this bridge along the Groenerei. *See page 72.*
- **Rozenhoedkaai**
  The bend in the canal that has inspired poets and novelists for the way it lays the city at your feet: swans, rooftops, the belfry and – if you're lucky – no tourist boats in sight when you click the shutter. *See page 73.*

---

**TOP RIGHT:** exploring the canals of Bruges.
**LEFT:** the Halletoren, Bruges' very own "leaning tower", offers one of the best views in the city.
**RIGHT:** learn the secrets of Belgian chocolate at Choco-Story.

## BRUGES FOR FAMILIES

- **Museum voor Volkskunde**
  Sweet-making demonstrations are held on Thursday afternoons in the old confectioner's shop in the Museum of Folklore. Another of its tiny houses contains an ancient schoolroom with clogs lined up at the back. *See page 103.*
- **Choco-Story**
  Indulge a taste for sweets with the story of where chocolate comes from in this slick, modern museum, for chocolate lovers of all ages. *See page 100.*
- **Groeninge**
  This museum has a children's corner with a playhouse to keep kids entertained while the adults admire Flemish Primitives. *See page 79.*

- **Bike rides**
  A ride around the old ramparts *(see page 85)* or up the Damse Vaart to Damme *(see page 113)* covers a lot of ground fast and helps to get the measure of the districts of Bruges.

- **Sint-Janshuis windmill**
  On a windy day, this old mill goes into action producing flour. It has to be turned round when the wind changes. Not for those scared of heights as the climb is steep. *See page 104.*

## BEST FOOD

● **Chips**
The secret of Belgium's success with its chips is to fry the potatoes twice. This is done to absolute perfection in the caravans outside the belfry on the Markt, where the long queues are not just composed of tourists. *See page 65.*

● **Mussels**
The most succulent mussels of the season are dished up in the classic large black saucepans at Breydel-De Coninck, a stalwart of the Bruges restau-rant scene that knocks socks off the competition in the preparation of Belgian seafood classics. *See page 76.*

## BEST BARS FOR BELGIAN BEER

● **Het Brugs Beertje**
This small sidestreet bar is decorated like a museum and presided over by an owner with an encyclopaedic knowledge of beers. *See page 77.*

● **Staminée de Garre**
Down a tiny alley, this ancient establishment covering two floors has exposed ceiling beams, a wood stove and a convivial atmosphere. Clients are limited to three glasses of its own brew, the extra-strong Tripel de Garre. *See page 77.*

● **De Halve Maan**
A chilled glass of Bruges' famous Straffe Hendrik beer is all the better after a tour of its brewery, a visit to which includes a free drink. *See page 93.*

## BEST ALMSHOUSES

● **Spanoghe**
Slip down the alley on Mariastraat and enter a bucolic micro-universe with a small green by the canal and quaint painted houses. *See page 85.*

● **Sint-Jozef and De Meulenaere**
The doors to each of these lead into the same pretty cottage garden with a small chapel and water pump. Cooing wood pigeons and a languid black cat complete the idyllic picture. *See page 82.*

● **De Pelikaan**
A row of well-restored brick homes built for destitute widows occupies a prime real estate location along the Groenerei canal. *See page 82.*

● **Onze-Lieve-Vrouw van Blindekens**
The alley alongside the church of the same name allows a glimpse into the backyards of this demure housing estate for the blind, nestled between Kreupelenstraat and Kammakersstraat. *See page 91.*

## HONEYMOON IN BRUGES

● **Horse-drawn carriage tour** There's always a queue on the Markt waiting to take a carriage ride, but what could be better than to be transported clattering across cobbles while you imagine yourselves to be the Duke and Duchess of Burgundy making your *Joyeuse Entrée* to the city? *See page 65.*

● **Die Swaene**
The discreet luxury hotel on Steenhouwers-dijk is the ultimate in accommodation for dreamy lovers. Rooms with canal views are highly sought after. *See page 127.*

● **Minnewater Lake**
It's called the Lake of Love, which rather speaks for itself. The bridge at the top gives a lovely view over the glassy surface and weeping willows to the begijnhof and beyond. *See page 83.*

**ABOVE:** waiting for tourists on the Markt, one of the best places to pick up a horse-drawn carriage.
**LEFT:** beers on display at Het Brugs Beertje.

# THE BEST OF GHENT

Here, at a glance, are our recommendations to help you make the most of your trip to Ghent, plus our top tips on saving money during your stay

## BEST WALKS

- **The Old Centre**
  From Korenmarkt an almost straight line takes you past the Sint-Niklaaskerk, the belfry and Lakenhalle, the Stadhuis, and Sint-Baafskathedraal – a whistlestop tour of the city's standout sights. *See pages 141–7.*
- **The Waterside**
  Beginning and ending at Graslei or Korenlei, a stroll takes you along the quays of Ghent's old harbour, along the Leie and the Lieve. *See pages 154–6.*

- **Patershol**
  It won't take you very long to get around this small, atmospheric district, but the chance to peruse its restored 16th and 17th-century houses, while taking in some of Ghent's finest restaurants, will surely persuade you that small is indeed beautiful. *See page 176.*

## HIGHEST AND FINEST

- **Highest towers**
  The "three towers of Ghent" – Sint-Niklaaskerk, the belfry and Sint-Baafskathe-draal – have become an easily recognisable image of the city. *See pages 142, 144 and 147.*

- **Finest guildhouses**
  The best surviving examples are the Gildenhuis van de Vrije Schippers, the Gildenhuis van de Onvrije Schippers and the Gildenhuis van de Metselaars. *See pages 157, 170 and 143.*

## BEST FESTIVALS

- **Gentse Feesten**
  July. Parades, free events. Runs in tandem with Ten Days Off, a festival of techno music. *See page 195.*
- **City Parade**
  June. *See page 195.*

**RIGHT:** the belfry is one of the "three towers of Ghent", which form an almost straight line through the city centre.
**ABOVE RIGHT:** the Graslei is a hub of activity at all times of the day and night.

## GHENT FOR FAMILIES

- **Het Gravensteen**
  Boiling oil and instruments of torture, and the chance to "storm" the battlements. *See page 173.*
- **Donkmeer**
  East of town, this lake with boats for hire is a good place to escape all the cultural sightseeing. *See page 186.*

- **Huis van Alijn**
  While children are finding out about life in Ghent at the end of the 19th century, adults can enjoy the folklore museum's excellent old café. *See page 177.*
- **De Wereld van Kina**
  This natural history museum is designed as a learning resource for schoolchildren, and showcases a model of 16th-century Ghent. *See page 179.*

## BEST MARKETS

● **Vrijdagmarkt**
The best street market in the city, selling food, clothes and other items, takes place on Friday on "Friday Market Square" – and continues on Saturday. *See page 152.*

● **Prondelmarkt**
Anything and everything that's old and tatty makes its way onto the various stalls of this age-old market located on Bij Sint-Jacobs. *See page 152.*

## BEST BARS

● **Old-fashioned cafés**
Among the best of these traditional old bars are: Het Waterhuis aan de Bierkant *(see page 165)*, the tiny but friendly 't Dreupelkot, Ghent's oldest genever bar *(see page 165)*, and 't Galgenhuisje *(see page 165)*.

● **Trendy, modern cafés**
In these cases, "trendy" does not always signify a fickle, "here today, gone tomorrow" style: Vooruit *(see page 165)*, set in the eponymous cultural centre, and Brasserie HA' *(see page 164)*, which has outside tables in summer.

**LEFT:** fine furniture at Design Museum Gent.
**BELOW:** the SMAK museum is mainly devoted to Belgian and international artists since 1945.

## BEST MUSEUMS

● **Koninklijk Museum voor Schone Kunsten**
The Royal Fine Arts Museum probably comes in behind the major art museums of Antwerp and Bruges, but with works by Van Eyck, Rubens, Magritte and Ensor on its roster, it is still a place to see. *See page 163.*

● **Stedelijk Museum voor Actuele Kunst** (SMAK)
Ghent's most adventurous museum displays works by modern Belgian artists like Panamarenko

and Broodthaers, among others. *See page 163.*

● **Design museum**
A mix of classical and cutting-edge design takes the floor inside the elegant mansion and the ultramodern extension that form the museum's premises. *See page 171.*

## BEST PARKS

● **Citadelpark**
The grounds of a 19th-century fortress have been transformed into Ghent's premier park, a rambling and, in parts, somewhat gloomy green place. *See page 162.*

● **Stedelijk Natuur-reservaat Bourgoyen-Ossemeersen**
For some fresh air and an escape from the crowds, Gentenaars head to this huge park on the city's southern edge. *See page 188.*

## GHENT FOR FREE

● **Sint-Baafskathedraal**
You have to pay to see the *Adoration of the Mystic Lamb* altarpiece, but the rest of Ghent's cathedral is gratis. *See page 147.*

● **Sint-Niklaaskerk**
Ghent's second most important

church is an interesting mix of Scheldt Gothic exterior and baroque interior, with free admission. *See page 142.*

● **The Begijnhofs**
Oases of tranquillity in a busy city, the former religious communities of the Sint-Elisabethbegijnhof and

the Klein Begijnhof are worth visiting. *See pages 163 and 176.*

● **Free concerts**
Summer concerts of classical and other music at the bandstands in Citadelpark and on Kouter. *See pages 159 and 162 .*

# THE BEST OF ANTWERP

A brief guide to all that is good in Antwerp, from the museums to the bustling markets, and from the atmospheric cafés to the carriage rides

## ANTWERP NIGHTLIFE

**Café d'Anvers** (15 Verversrui), where techno took hold, is as wild as ever, but you can also party at **Stereo Sushi** (6 Luikstraat), **Bar**

**Tabac** (43 Waalsekaai), **Café Café** (8 Nassaustraat), **Club-Industria** (10 Indiestraat) and **El Devino Danscafé** (6 Nassaustraat).

## BEST MUSEUMS

- **Koninklijk Museum voor Schone Kunsten** Flemish painting from Van Eyck and Brueghel to Magritte and Rik Wouters. *See page 221.*
- **MuHKA** Avant-garde art in a converted grain silo. *See page 228.*
- **MoMu** Revolutionary exhibitions and an extensive permanent collection. *See page 223.*

- **Museum Plantin-Moretus** A patrician mansion incorporating a printing works, publishing house and library listed as a UNESCO World Heritage Site. *See page 213.*
- **Nationaal Scheepvaartmuseum** The Maritime Museum has a dry dock with ancient ships. *See page 215.*

## ANTWERP FOR FAMILIES

- **Antwerp Zoo** One of Europe's oldest zoos, with some 6,000 animals, often housed in stunning pavilions, like the giraffes who live in an Egyptian temple. *See page 241.*
- **Aquatopia** Brand new complex of 35 futuristic aquariums. Everything from sharks and piranhas to coral reefs and tropical rainforest. *See page 261.*
- **Horse and Carriage Tour** Magnificent dray horses pull old brewers' wagons from the Grote Markt around the city centre. *See page 206.*
- **MuHKA** Check out the Contemporary Art Museum's first floor where MUST for Kids includes a playground with art-inspired games. *See page 229.*

- **Boat trip on the Schelde** From the quay on Steenplein, you can take a tour of the port or a day trip as far as Brussels. *See page 215.*

**ABOVE LEFT:** Antwerp is known for its cool nightlife.
**ABOVE:** the city's zoo is one of the oldest in Europe.
**BELOW:** bric-à-brac galore.

## BEST SHOPPING

- **Burie**
(3 Korte
Gasthuisstraat).
This is the home
of the most
famous artisan
*chocolatier* in
Antwerp. *See
page 260.*
- **Philip's Biscuits**
(11 Korte Gasthuis-
straat). The home-baked
cakes and biscuits on
sale here are simply
irresistible.
- **Episode**
(34 Steenhouwerstraat).
This cavernous vintage
clothes shop is packed
with stylish bargain
basement-priced outfits.
- **Phenix**
(20 Steenhouwersvest).
This is a true paradise
of rare art deco and

art nouveau
collectables.

- **Labels Inc.**
(4 Aalmoezenierstraat).
This boutique, just off
Nationalestraat, sells
high-quality second-
hand designer clothes,
often direct from the
runways of fashion
shows. They are not
exactly cheap, but
a good deal less
expensive than the
original couture prices.

## BEST OF RUBENS

The **Rubenshuis** is
an essential visit, but
the home of the great
Flemish artist is not
necessarily the best
place to see his finest
works. The **Koninklijk
Museum voor Schone
Kunsten** has an ex-
cellent collection and
his paintings can also
be found in both the
Plantin-Moretus and
Rockoxhuis museums,

but it is the churches
that have the finest.
Start at **Onze-Lieve-
Vrouwekathedraal**,
which has four master-
pieces, then head to
**Sint-Paulus**, well-
restored after a fire.
Next, visit **Sint-Jakob**,
where Rubens is buried.
Finally, **Sint-Carolus-
Borromeus** has a ba-
roque façade featuring
sculptures by the artist.

## BEST MARKETS

- **Exotische Market**
On Saturday, Theater-
plein is transformed into
a vast food market with
many stands speciali-
sing in Mediterranean
and North African pro-
duce. *See page 238.*
- **Vogelenmarkt**
Held on Sunday morn-
ing, with hundreds of
stalls selling everything
from flowers and
kitchen utensils to
antiques and clothes.
*See page 238.*
- **Vrijdagmarkt**
An auction market
of second-hand goods
that takes place not just
in the square but also in

a host of surrounding
auction warehouses.
*See page 213.*
- **Criée**
Near Centraal Station,
this lively daily covered
market is where locals
come for fresh meat and
vegetables.

## BEST OF ANTWERP'S DESIGN

- **Het Modepaleis**
Beautifully renovated
belle-époque building
that showcases the
creations of Antwerp's
most successful de-
signer, Dries van
Noten. *See page 218
and 213.*
- **Véronique
Branquinho**
(123 Nationalestraat).
The work of this
Antwerpan designer
can be found behind
a striking mirror-glass
exterior. *See page 246.*
- **Walter**
The bad boy of
Belgian fashion, Walter
van Beirendonck has
created a brilliant
design space in a
renovated garage.
*See page 261.*

- **Maison Close**
(139 Nationalestraat).
This offbeat boutique
is the place to discover
the up and coming
generation of
designers.
- **Ann Demeulemeester**
(38 Leopold de
Verlatstraat).
The showroom of
Antwerp's most
renowned female
designer is stripped
back to absolute
minimalism.
- **Verso**
(39 Huidevettersstraat).
Showcases not only
the hippest Antwerp
designers, but also
trendy Italian and
French stylists, in
an impressive belle-
époque building.

**LEFT:** Rubens is commemorated everywhere in Antwerp,
from the Rubenshuis, his house-museum, to cafés.

# THE SOIL OF FLANDERS

**The Belgian region of Flanders supports the theory that you can have too much history – but centuries of turbulence have produced a cultural richness**

The boundaries of Flanders have been expanding and contracting through the centuries, right up to the 1990s – and a few unresolved issues could yet bring changes. The territory has evolved in response to the shifts in the winds of war and the success or failure of dynastic arrangements. There have been periods when Flanders has sunk out of sight, buried under layers of larger states to which it represented little more than an antique title and a faded coat of arms. Throughout the years its rulers have ranged from petty warlords feuding over scraps of feudal turf, to kings and emperors in the Levant during the Crusades. A baby born in Ghent in 1500 would grow up to become Charles V, ruler of the greatest European empire since that of the Caesars.

Places that once were part of Flanders now belong to France and the Netherlands. Lille, Arras and Dunkirk also have Flemish names (Rijsel, Atrecht and Duinkerke); and the southernmost part of the Netherlands' Zeeland province is called Zeeuws-Vlaanderen (Zeeland Flanders). In compensation, places that were once separate states, such as Brabant, now belong to Flanders, which today comprises the northern, semi-autonomous, Dutch-speaking region of Belgium. Five modern-day provinces make up the region. West-Vlaanderen (West Flanders) and Oost-Vlaanderen (East Flanders) have been the heartland of the Graafschap (County) of Flanders since its earliest days. Further east, Antwerpen (Antwerp) and Vlaams-Brabant (Flemish Brabant) both belonged in the past to the Duchy of Brabant. The final province is Limburg.

Flanders is well-endowed with history, and history can be quite an indigestible dish – just look at the glazed expressions on the faces of visitors trying to take in an historical thumbnail-sketch on guided tours. It's not surprising if they get their Burgundian dukes mixed up with their Benedictine nuns. But historical divisions are, to an extent, arbitrary. For ordinary people life went on much as before whoever occupied the Castle of the Counts or the Prinsenhof. Yet these rulers, and the buildings and monuments they left behind, help provide a sense of perspective and continuity across the centuries. ❑

---

**PRECEDING PAGES:** along the canal from Bruges to Damme; Laundry Day street festival in Antwerp. **LEFT:** cycling along the Graslei, in Ghent.

# THE MAKING OF FLANDERS

Flanders has evolved over the centuries, coming under the
rule of various foreign dynasties, and growing rich on the
wool trade. Always prepared to fight for its freedom,
it has now been recognised as a separate region

The recorded history of Flanders begins
with the Roman invasion in the 50s BC –
although by this time Celtic farmers were
already well established in these lands. Julius
Caesar wrote that the Belgae, an alliance of
Gallo-Celtic tribes, fought with great valour
against his legions. Ultimately the Belgae were
defeated and the region was occupied by Rome
for almost 500 years. The conquerors established urban living, built roads and developed
trade. During the 1st century AD, a Gallo-
Roman settlement was founded beside the
rivers Reie and Dijver on the site of present-day
Bruges, and another at the confluence of the
Schelde and the Leie, on the site of today's
Ghent. From a century later come the earliest
indications of a settlement at the mouth of the
Schelde on the site of present-day Antwerp.

## The arrival of the Franks

Following the collapse of the West Roman
Empire, the power vacuum was filled by the
Franks, a confederation of Germanic tribes
who had crossed the Rhine and settled
between the Meuse and the Schelde from the
4th to the 6th century. Around 630, St Amand
founded the abbeys known today as Sint-
Baafsabdij and Sint-Pietersabdij, on the site
of what would become Ghent. Bruges begins
to emerge indistinctly from the mists of the
Dark Ages around the mid-7th century, when
St Elegius (Eloy) preached on the coastal plain

**LEFT:** the mighty emperor Charles V, native of Ghent,
painted by Jakob Seisenegger (1505–67).
**RIGHT:** Saints Elegius and Anthony Abbot preaching.

of Flanders. Chronicles of his life refer to a
Frankish community, the *Municipium Flan-
drensis*, an important town and seat of a
Frankish count, which seems to have been a
reference to Bruges.

During the reign of Charlemagne, King of
the Franks from 768, the Frankish Empire
extended all the way from the Elbe to the
Atlantic and from the North Sea to the
Mediterranean. Charlemagne was crowned
Emperor of the West at Rome in 800. However, his successors were unable to retain control over such a large territory and in 843 the
Treaty of Verdun carved up the empire into
three parts. Flanders west of the River Schelde

joined West Francia (the future France); the territory east of the Schelde became part of the Middle Kingdom, then, in 855, of Lotharingia (Lorraine). The River Schelde became the dividing line between French and German spheres of influence.

## A man called "Iron Arm"

The first certain mention of Bruges occurs in 851 in records of monks from Ghent and by 864 the word *Bruggia* appears on coins of the French king, Charles the Bald, to whom Flanders owed allegiance. Baldwin Iron Arm, whose residence was a castle in Bruges, built in about 850 for defence against Viking raiders, is the first count of Flanders whose name is known. He seems to have been a swashbuckler, eloping with Charles's daughter Judith and responding to his new father-in-law's indignation by threatening to ally with the Normans. The king had no choice but to swallow his pride.

In 868 Baldwin built a fort in Ghent at the place where Het Gravensteen now stands. His successors extended Flanders south to the Somme, and in the 11th century Baldwin V reached eastwards beyond the Schelde. By so doing, the Flemish counts became, from 1056 onward, vassals of the German emperor as well as of the French king.

## BATTLE OF THE GOLDEN SPURS

In the early years of the 14th century, it looked as if France under King Philip IV (Philip the Fair) would complete the annexation of Flanders he had begun in 1297. Emotions were at a high pitch in the Flemish towns. Bruges' craftsmen, led by butcher Jan Breydel and weaver Pieter De Coninck, rose against the local patricians who backed the French. During the early morning of 18 May 1302 the rebels overcame the city's French guards. A bloodbath known as the *Bruges Matins* ensued in which 1,500 Frenchmen and collaborators were slaughtered.

Anyone who could not pronounce correctly the Resistance watchword *Schild en Vriend* (Shield and Friend) – which was, and still is, tough for a non-Dutch speaker to do – was instantly killed.

Encouraged by this success, the common folk all over Flanders reached for their spears. Flemish craftsmen and peasants faced French armoured knights in a battle near Kortrijk on 11 July 1302. The French, who had been confident of a walkover, were decisively beaten. When the fighting ended, the rebels collected 700 golden spurs from the field, and the battle has gone down in Flemish history and folklore as the Battle of the Golden Spurs.

There is a statue of the two Flemish rebel leaders in the Markt in Bruges (see pages 66–7).

## Prosperous trading cities

During the 11th century, development of the cloth trade brought prosperity to Flanders and rapid growth to its towns and cities, especially Bruges, Ghent and Ypres. Bruges also became a trading centre for goods from Italy, France, England, Germany and Scandinavia. Up to the 11th century, ships sailed right into the city on the River Reie, but by its end silting had closed access to the sea. In 1134, flooding created a channel, Het Zwin, from the sea to Damme, and Bruges dug a canal to Damme. Seagoing ships now went as far as Damme and smaller vessels handled canal traffic between the two towns.

In Bruges and Ghent, the weaving industry – which relied upon a steady supply of English wool – flourished. The quality of Flemish textiles was unmatched in Europe. Colourful fabrics from Flanders were in demand as far away as the Orient, but the beneficiaries were the merchants rather than the weavers, dyers and fullers, who earned pitiful wages.

On the political front, Count Charles the Good was assassinated in St Donatian's Church in Bruges in 1127. Thierry of Alsace succeeded him as count of Flanders. He is said to have brought back a relic of Christ's blood from the Holy Land around 1150. An alternative, and perhaps more likely, explanation is that the relic was brought from Constantinople in the time of Count Baldwin IX, who was the first Latin Emperor of Constantinople (1204–5) after the Fourth Crusade had captured the Byzantine capital and looted its treasures. You can see the relic today in the Basilica of the Holy Blood; on Ascension Day the bishop carries it through Bruges in the Procession of the Holy Blood. In Ghent, Thierry's successor, Philip of Alsace, was clearly sending a message to the citizenry in 1180 by building Het Gravensteen Castle, and that message was: "Don't mess with me."

This period coincided with a great influx of wealth from textiles and trade. Bruges was a key member of the powerful Baltic-based Hanseatic League trading alliance, hosting the the most important of the league's four principal *kontore* (foreign outposts). So wealthy was Bruges that when Queen Joan of Navarre visited in 1301, she complained that hundreds of women were as finely dressed as she.

It was also during the 13th century that the concept of the *begijnhof* (beguinage) came into being. These were communities of pious lay women who lived like nuns but who never took the vow of poverty. Over 20 beguinages remain, with the main community in Ghent and the most picturesque one in Bruges *(see page 82)*.

Evidence of the region's wealth during these years was manifest in a building boom, as great Gothic churches and magnificent town halls were constructed.

## Wolf in sheep's clothing

At the start of the Hundred Years' War (1337–1453), Flanders opted to side with France against England, causing the latter to stop deliveries of wool. Trade therefore came to a halt. The people of Ghent – merchants and craftsmen, rich and poor – were in agreement about how to get the economy back on its feet. For this, they must rebel against their rulers and re-establish trade with England.

The rebel leader was wool merchant Jacob van Artevelde. In 1340, he made a treaty with England's King Edward III to protect the weaving trade. Alliance with England meant that trade blossomed again, but the old conflicts

**LEFT:** coronation of Charlemagne by Pope Leo III in St Peter's, Rome in 800.
**RIGHT:** Hundred Years' War battle scene.

between merchants and craftsmen also returned. When, in 1345, Van Artevelde suggested that Edward III's son, Edward the Black Prince, should become Count of Flanders, the weavers promptly murdered him and usurped power in the cities. Their action was condemned by other craftsmen and a civil war ensued which left Flanders bereft of most of the power it had gained. In a battle on Ghent's Vrijdagmarkt between members of the weavers' and fullers' guilds, more than 500 people lost their lives. In 1356, Antwerp, which belonged to the Duchy of Brabant, was annexed by Flanders. It would be restored to Brabant by the Burgundians 50 years later.

## Golden Age of the Burgundians

The counts of Flanders gradually gained autonomy from France, yet Louis de Male accepted French help against a new wave of Flemish insurrection, led by Philip van Artevelde, son of Jacob. Van Artevelde captured Bruges, but was defeated and killed at the Battle of Westrozebeke in 1382. Louis, the last of the counts, died two years later. After his demise, the House of Burgundy produced its dukes. Their seat had been in Dijon until Duke Philip the Bold married Louis' daughter and heir in 1369, thereby pocketing Flanders and ending its independence when Louis died. The dazzling Burgundian century had begun, during which

### THE PEOPLE WHO ADDED POMP TO PUBLIC LIFE

Trades and guilds gained their independence in the 14th century and functioned as political forces until the 17th century. They played an important role in shaping the cities of Flanders. As civic pride and prosperity burgeoned during the so-called Golden Age, the prosperous burghers and guilds of the Flemish cloth towns enriched their cities. Indeed, they built Gothic town halls and tollhouses, guildhalls as well as mansions, cloth halls and municipal records offices. These major public buildings were always clustered around the prestigious main square (the Grote Markt, or just Markt). A town hall – *stadhuis* in Dutch – was the most prominent symbol of

civic pride. The Bruges *stadhuis*, dating from 1376, formed the Flemish model for such buildings, inspiring those in Brussels, Ghent, Leuven and Oudenaarde, where the influence is clearly seen.

During this period, cloth halls and guildhalls were integral to trade, and their architectural quality matched the success of the mercantile Flemish cities. Called a *lakenhalle* in Dutch, the cloth hall served as a commercial centre, meeting place and, on occasion, a place of refuge or political asylum. Some of the finest cloth halls can still be seen in Bruges (where it is called the Hallen; 1240 and later), Ghent (1441) and Ypres (1304 and 1378).

the dukes increased their power and territory by diplomacy, military action and cleverly arranged marriages, adding most of the Low Countries to what became, in effect, an empire.

Philip was succeeded by his son, John the Fearless, who was killed in 1419. The Burgundian title was then inherited by his son, Philip the Good. In 1453 Philip won the decisive Battle of Gavere, ending a five-year struggle by the citizens and guilds of Ghent to uphold their privileges; the city's dignitaries were forced to beg Philip for mercy. He built the Prinsenhof in Bruges, from which he ruled. The court in Bruges patronised distinguished Flemish masters such as Jan van Eyck (1390–1441) and

the Bold, the last "great duke". Today's quinquennial *Praalstoet van de Gouden Boom* (Golden Tree Parade) in Bruges recalls the sumptuous marriage of Charles to Margaret of York in 1468, when a grand tournament and procession was held on the Markt. Charles attempted to create an extensive, independent Kingdom of Burgundy, at the expense of his arch-rival, the king of France. However, he proved too bold for his own good, losing both the Battle of Nancy and his life in 1477.

That same year, the citizens of Flanders forced Charles's daughter and heir, Mary, to sign the Great Privilege in Ghent, re-establishing their civic freedoms. She should perhaps be

Hans Memling (who was born in Germany in 1453 but spent much of his time in Flanders). However, by 1459 Brussels had become the favoured residential city of a powerful realm in the midst of a golden age of cultural enrichment, artistic splendour and political prestige.

### Decline and fall

The fall of the House of Burgundy was due to its overweening ambition. Philip the Good died in 1467, and his successor was Charles

remembered as Mary the Horseless, since it was her fatal fall from a horse in 1482 while hunting in the forest at Wijnendaele outside Bruges that pitched Flanders into the hands of her husband, Crown Prince Maximilian of the Austrian House of Habsburg. The citizens of Bruges – as was by now pretty much routine – rebelled against its new ruler, imprisoning Maximilian in the Craenenburg mansion on the Markt. When he was freed he retaliated by moving the ducal residence to Ghent and by transferring all Bruges' trading privileges to Antwerp.

His successors later extended the vendetta to Ghent, which was equally inclined towards insurgence, continued the commercial tilt

**LEFT:** street fighting between guilds in Ghent in 1340; Philip II the Bold marries Margarete of Flanders in 1369.
**ABOVE:** Burgundian footsoldiers c.1467–77.

towards Antwerp and concentrated political power in Brussels. These measures, combined with the decline of the cloth trade, the closure of Bruges' Zwin outlet to the sea due to silting, and the impact of the looming religious wars, sent the old, proud Flemish cities into a tailspin from which neither fully recovered.

In 1494, Maximilian handed over the Low Countries to his son, Philip the Handsome, who later married Joan the Mad, Queen of Castile, thereby retaining the family tradition of bizarre names and bringing Spain into the Habsburg fold. This laid the foundations for what would become the world empire of their son and heir, Charles V.

## Charles V

The future Holy Roman Emperor and King of Spain was born on 20 February 1500 in Ghent, the son of Philip the Handsome, King of Castile, and Joan the Mad. His father died in 1506, and his mother was confined for the rest of her life. Charles spent his childhood in Mechelen under the guardianship of his aunt, the Archduchess Margaret of Austria. When his maternal grandfather died, Charles was ceremonially declared of age in Brussels, being installed as Duke of Brabant and King of Spain (as Charles I) in 1516. At heart he remained a Netherlander all his life. Writing to his son Philip he referred to the Low Countries as "Our Father Burgundy".

### FLEMISH TAPESTRIES

Flanders' wealth was spun from fine cloth. Skilled weavers transformed English wool into tapestries and clothing. During the Golden Age, Flanders was the most celebrated tapestry centre on the continent. Flemish designs decorated palaces, churches and châteaux all over Europe. Weavers and designers worked together to produce harmonious but technically challenging work, as the religious themes of the Middle Ages gave way to historical tableaux and pastoral, mythological and hunting scenes. The technique combined embroidery with weaving, often incorporating silk, gold and silver thread into multi-coloured designs.

In 1520, Charles received the Holy Roman Emperor's crown. At 20, he was the most powerful monarch in Europe. The Spanish and Habsburg empires he had inherited now extended across Europe from Spain and the Low Countries to Austria and the Kingdom of Naples, and across the Atlantic to the newly discovered Americas. To borrow a phrase, it could be said that Charles ruled from Brussels' Coudenberg Palace over an empire "on which the sun never set".

Needing huge sums of money in order to finance his wars, which included almost perpetual conflict with France and the Ottoman Turks, he viewed the wealthy Flemish cities as convenient sources of ready cash and levied heavy taxes on them. In 1539, Ghent rebelled against Charles, only to herald his return with a humiliating parade the following year. He also borrowed heavily, from the Fuggers bankers in Antwerp, among many others.

As the chill winds of religious discord spread through the Low Countries in the wake of the Reformation, Charles saw himself as "God's standard bearer", believing he had been given such great power in order to defend Christendom against the Ottoman infidels without, and Catholicism against Protestant heretics within. His heraldic device bore the legend *Plus Ultra* (Always Further). He

crown to Philip. Shortly after that he divided his lands by abdicating as Holy Roman Emperor in favour of his brother Ferdinand. Divested of power, he left the Low Countries for ever, retiring to a Spanish monastery in Estremadura, where he died in 1558.

## War with Spain

Rampaging Protestant mobs sacked churches across the Low Countries in 1566, in an action recalled as the *Beeldenstorm* (Iconoclastic Fury). Charles V's way of preventing the forward march of the Reformation had been to have an occasional Calvinist beheaded or burned at the stake, as an example to the

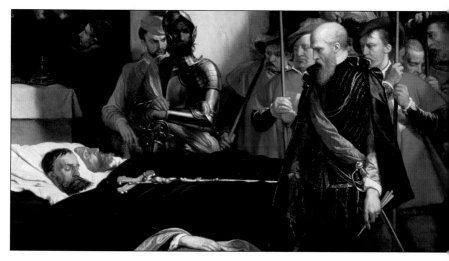

seems to have taken this quite literally, spending most of his reign travelling, on horseback and by boat, from one threatened point in the empire to another. In 1553, worn to a frazzle by a lifetime of almost continuous war, Charles returned to the Low Countries. He made his last public appearance in October 1555, before the assembled estates of the 17 provinces in the Great Hall of the palace in Brussels. He renounced the throne of the Low Countries in favour of his son, Philip. Early in 1556, he also relinquished the Spanish

others. Philip II, a fanatical Catholic, vastly extended the scale of the repression and sent in the much-dreaded Inquisition, spearheaded by the Jesuits, shock-troops of the Catholic Counter-Reformation.

With the religious struggle developing inexorably into a full-scale popular uprising against Spanish rule, he dispatched the ruthless Duke of Alba the following year to suppress it. Alba was the man for the job.

The duke established the "Council of Blood" and launched a reign of terror in which some 18,000 people were executed. In 1568, the two most prominent victims, counts Egmond and Hoorn, were beheaded on Brussels' Grand-

**LEFT:** *Entrance of Charles V into Antwerp*, 1520.
**ABOVE:** last respects to the counts Egmond and Hoorn.

Place. To this day, some Flemish parents still tell their children that if they aren't good, Alba will come and get them.

Philip's actions of repression unleashed a decades-long welter of violence that eventually pushed thousands of Protestants to emigrate, to the ruin of a large number of Flemish cities, in particular Antwerp. It also led to the independence of the northern, Protestant provinces, today's Netherlands. The savage Spanish campaigns during the late 16th and early 17th centuries waged to suppress Protestantism and rebellion in the Low Countries finally set the seal on economic collapse in Flanders.

Leadership of the rebellion was assumed by the Dutch prince, William I of Orange (William the Silent). In 1576 William occupied Ghent. A treaty dubbed the Pacification of Ghent was signed to permit religious freedom in the Low Countries and unite the population against Spain. That same year, the Spanish garrison of Antwerp launched an orgy of slaughter and destruction in the city, recalled as the "Spanish Fury". In 1579, by the Treaty of Utrecht, William secured the independence of seven Protestant provinces of the north (an area that corresponds to most of the modern Netherlands). Protestantism was in the ascendancy, but the war continued.

## Capitulation and control

Philip's moves to maintain control led to further repression and a series of military campaigns. Having sent the experienced general, Alexander Farnese, Duke of Parma, to the Low Countries in 1578 at the head of a large army, Philip was able to force the rebellious southern provinces to capitulate one by one. The Union of Arras joined the provinces that accepted the Catholic king as their ruler. In Bruges, where the Calvinists were strong enough to seize control of the city council for six years, from 1578, and to execute or chase away its monks and nuns, Spanish troops crushed the city's rebels in 1584. Ghent fell to Farnese the same year.

By 1585, Spain had re-established full control in the southern Low Countries. Spanish troops re-occupied Antwerp; the Dutch countered by blockading the River Schelde and the Flemish cities went into steep decline. Amsterdam replaced Antwerp as the chief trading centre of Europe. Many Protestant merchants, artists and craftsmen fled north to the United Provinces, taking their wealth and skills with them. The north prospered while the south gradually stagnated.

In 1598, Philip transferred authority over the Spanish Netherlands to his daughter Isabella and her husband, Archduke Albert of Austria. During their reign, the people enjoyed a more peaceful existence. The gallows and scaffold disappeared, the economy rebounded and a taste for courtly pomp and celebration prevailed once more. Pieter Paul Rubens (1577–1640), court painter to the Spanish regents in Antwerp, captured the spirit of the era in his paintings.

By the Treaty of Westphalia in 1648 that ended the war, Belgium remained under Spanish control as the Spanish Netherlands. The Schelde remained closed to shipping.

## Austrian rule

The treaties signed in 1715 at the end of the later War of the Spanish Succession handed sovereignty over the Spanish Netherlands to the Austrian Habsburgs. Under Empress Maria Theresa, Belgium experienced economic prosperity. But while the Austrian Government in distant Vienna was turning huge profits, along with the Belgian industrialists and city merchants, the common folk fared badly. Low wages, unemployment and social destitution were the lot of a majority of the population – conditions that would eventually bring about revolts.

But while the sun shone upon the rulers and the wealthy, their interests developed in the direction of fine arts and crafts. The gold-and-blue decoration of Belgian porcelain was soon recognised in the finest drawing rooms of Europe. The fashion for lace also reached its peak during this period, and the industry entered one of its most productive periods.

When Maria Theresa died in 1780, her son, Joseph II, who had been co-regent since 1765,

into the fold and the fledgling country was quickly defeated. After just one year of freedom Belgium once again found itself under the Austrian thumb.

## Enter the French

By June 1794 revolutionary France had defeated the Austrians and then annexed both Belgium and the Netherlands, which were combined as the Batavian Republic. The French spent most of the next 20 years knocking down churches, monasteries and palaces, along with much else of the Habsburg regime's absolutist apparatus. Most of the people had had enough of corrupt clerics and

succeeded to the Habsburg throne. His hasty reforms fanned the smouldering resistance to Austrian rule. Encouraged by the revolutionary turn of events in France, the people of Brabant revolted in 1789. They were successful in evicting the Austrians, and on 11 January 1790, proclaimed the "United States of Belgium". However, this union of states did not last long. A new Austrian emperor, Leopold II, sent troops to pull Belgium back

venal aristocrats and gave the demolition their enthusiastic support. But French domination had its drawbacks: for one thing, Belgians were conscripted to serve in Napoleon's campaigns. The River Schelde, re-opened to shipping, was soon closed again by a British blockade. Napoleon did, however, develop the harbour at Antwerp, which – ever ready with an apt phrase – he called a "pistol aimed at the heart of England".

An alliance composed of Austria, Britain, Prussia and Russia, defeated Napoleon once and for all at the Battle of Waterloo in 1815. Many Belgians were to regret the departure of the French, in view of what was decided at

**LEFT:** scene of the "Spanish Fury" in Antwerp, 1576.
**ABOVE:** Emperor Napoleon and Empress Marie-Louise visit the fleet lying at anchor on the Schelde outside Antwerp on 1 May 1810.

the Congress of Vienna. The unification of Belgium and the Netherlands would be perpetuated, but now ruled by the Dutch House of Orange. The Hague and Brussels were nominated joint capitals, but the northern half of the united country, economically the stronger, set the tone.

### Independent Belgium

The patience of the Belgian population was coming to an end, and 15 years later the revolution of 1830 against Dutch rule resulted in a free and independent Belgium. On 25 September 1830 a provisional government was established; it declared independence on

principal industrial nations. This process was supported by a flourishing textile industry centred on Ghent and Kortrijk, an equally successful arms industry, and the expansion of the port of Antwerp. In 1838 a railway connecting Brussels, Ghent, Bruges and Ostend became operational.

Not everybody benefited from the boom; wages were low and working hours long. Female and child labour were commonplace. Social security, industrial safety and Sundays off were a long way from the political agenda. Inevitably, hunger riots erupted. The Industrial Revolution mostly bypassed Bruges, which was nothing more than a quaint, impov-

4 October, and Brussels became the capital. In their search for an appropriate sovereign, the leaders turned to the German Leopold of Saxe-Coburg-Gotha, an uncle of Queen Victoria. In 1831, as Leopold I, he became the first king of the Belgians.

Fired by the taste of freedom, the Belgians went to the forefront of 19th-century Europe. The process began with the construction in 1835 of a railway line between Brussels and Mechelen, the first on mainland Europe, and the rail network became steadily denser as coal mining in the south and the development of the iron and steel industry around Liège raised Belgium to a position alongside the

erished backwater by the time Belgium won independence, and which was to become the poorest city in Belgium. Not until the harbour at Zeebrugge was completed in 1904 and connected to Bruges by canal did the city's economy show signs of life again.

Leopold proved himself unequal to the difficult task of mediator and unifier of the Flemish and Walloons. Although Dutch was spoken by the majority of people, French became the language of government, administration and education. Many Flemings objected to being governed in what they regarded as an alien language. Violence repeatedly broke out, as Flemish nationalists in the north became increasingly vociferous in their call for independence from the French-speaking south.

In 1863, Leopold bought back from the Netherlands the right to levy customs duties on the River Schelde, a loss which had severely hampered the expansion of Antwerp.

## World War I

On 3 August 1914, Germany demanded that Belgium allow its army passage through Belgian territory to attack France. When the government denied the request, the Germans invaded. The Belgian Army put up a spirited resistance, but by the end of the year almost

with little ground gained by either the Germans or the Allies, but with huge loss of life on both sides. Some 180 military cemeteries in and around Ypres are testimony to the bitter, four-year struggle. The city's Menin Gate memorial arch lists more than 55,000 British soldiers missing in action *(see page 122)*. By the time a ceasefire was declared on 11 November 1918, millions lay dead and years of fighting had turned the Flemish soil into a massive graveyard. Mines, weapons and skeletons are uncovered to this day.

Society was very different after the war. The badly damaged economy was slow to recover. There was a brief upswing in the late

the entire country was in German hands. King Albert I acquired a glorious reputation by leading the resistance to the invaders.

The area around Ieper (Ypres) and along the River IJzer in West Flanders, close to the French border, witnessed some of the bloodiest and most extended fighting of the war. Trench warfare persisted from 1914 to 1918,

1920s, but then came the Great Depression of the 1930s. Unemployment rose rapidly, social deprivation was rife and, as in other countries across the continent, fascist groups gained ground and for a while were able to profit from the general unrest.

## World War II

Nazi Germany attacked France, the Netherlands, Luxembourg and Belgium on 10 May 1940. The Belgian Government fled into exile in London, while King Leopold III chose to become a self-styled prisoner at the Royal Palace at Laeken until June 1944, when the Nazis removed him to Germany.

**LEFT:** scene from the last attack of Dutch troops on Antwerp in 1830; they capitulated soon after, paving the way to Belgian independence.
**ABOVE:** the "battle of the mud", trench warfare in Ieper (Ypres), 1917.
**RIGHT:** dogs were used as messengers in World War II.

Flanders was granted special status. Many Flemings belonged to the Flemish movement and supported the German annexation of their land. The Nazis considered Flanders an "area capable of being resettled". This meant that, after the elimination or deportation of all opposition elements and Jews, Flanders could be recognised as a German region.

The number of Belgian collaborators is reckoned to have been considerable, and the king himself was unable to dispel suspicions that he had collaborated. Most collaborators came from the fascist-monarchist movement, which still exists today. But many Belgians showed great courage in their commitment to

the Resistance, protecting the persecuted, and destroying transport and communication lines to hinder the occupying forces. Socialists, communists, liberals and Christians fought side by side, simply as Belgians and anti-fascists.

Many Belgian Jews – in addition to German and Austrian Jews who had fled to Belgium to escape persecution in their own countries – were murdered by the Nazis. But some – calculations suggest about half the number resident in the country at the time – were saved because they were hidden by members of the non-Jewish population. The liberation of Belgium started at the beginning of September 1944, and its success was swift.

## Renewal and reform

Belgium's economic recovery after the war was relatively rapid. Antwerp's harbour had been spared major damage (despite coming under heavy V1 flying bomb and V2 rocket attack after its liberation), and the country's energy reserves were adequate to supply the necessary power.

Leopold returned from exile in Germany and the simmering crisis in relations between the king and his ministers turned into open conflict. In 1950, a referendum was held in order to determine what constitutional rights the monarch should be granted. In Flanders, 72 percent favoured the king's return; in Brussels it was only 48 percent, and in Wallonia just 42 percent. Parliament voted to reinstate the king. There followed a wave of protest in Wallonia, and the king abdicated in favour of his son, who became Baudouin I (Boudewijn in Dutch) in 1951.

Postwar Belgium has been characterised by linguistic and territorial disputes. Since the end of World War II there have been differences in the way the Flemish north and Walloon south have developed. By the early 1950s the first regionalist demands had been heard, with both the Walloon and the Flemish federalists calling for a reform of the centralised state. Constitutional revisions in the 1970s, 1980s and 1990s were designed to give both linguistic groups (Flemish and French) more autonomy in economic and cultural matters. Belgium was consequently divided into three regions: Flanders, Wallonia (which has a German-speaking minority) and Brussels-Capital.

### STANDING UP FOR THE REGIONS

Most political parties in Belgium have a regional affiliation. The national government is currently headed by a Fleming, Guy Verhofstadt, from the Flemish Liberal and Democrat party (VLD), in a coalition that consists of his party, the Francophone liberal Reform Movement (MR), an alliance of the Flemish Socialist Party (SP) and the social democrat Spirit Party, and the Francophone Socialist Party (PS). The Flemish Greens (Groen!) and Francophone Greens (Ecolo) suffered severe losses in the 2003 elections. Groen! didn't win any seats in the House of Representatives, but do have one "co-opted" senator, thanks to an agreement with the SP.

## Flanders today

In 1993, the monarchy changed hands when King Baudouin died. He was succeeded by his brother, Albert II, who has been a cautious, even lacklustre, constitutional monarch, evidently fully aware of the many pitfalls, both seen and unseen, that await a Belgian sovereign, and determined to avoid all of them. Despite his caution, he has won respect for his dogged determination to see things through.

Merely a year after Albert came to the throne, the Belgian constitution was amended both to effect and reflect the devolution of central powers to the regions. This process

developing regional "foreign policy" – should not be underestimated.

Flanders continues to make full possible use of the powers it has in economic, cultural, social and environmental policy. Its greater share of national income is most visibly seen in the generally better shape that Flemish towns and cities are in, compared with the often blighted districts of rust-belt Walloon towns.

Racial tensions have now been added to the sectarian mix. Belgium's highest court ruled in 2004 that the Flemish nationalist Vlaams Blok (Flemish Bloc) party was racist, and

has now gone about as far as it reasonably can, without bringing about the de facto withering away of the state.

It seems likely, however, that there will be further tweaks to the system in the future. There are a number of contemporary politicians who delight in cocking a snook at the Belgian Government from the Flemish regional parliament in Brussels. And the ability of regional politicians to continue pushing their own interests – by, for instance,

forced it to disband. Even before this, the other political parties had refused to allow Vlaams Blok to be part of any coalition, so unacceptable were its policies.

However, the party, under its energetic leader Frank Vanhecke, takes approximately a quarter of the vote in Flanders overall, and a third in Antwerp, so it is not surprising that it quickly re-emerged. With a somewhat modified programme and a slightly different name, Vlaams Belang (Flemish Interest), it continues to push for complete Flemish independence from Belgium and for measures against immigration and existing immigrants, as well as seeking to enlarge its power base. ❑

**LEFT:** taking it easy on the dock of occupied Antwerp.
**ABOVE:** Albert II, King of the Belgians since 1993, in front of a portrait of his ancestor, King Leopold I.

# Decisive Dates

***c.*1000–800 BC** Celtic tribes settle in what is now Flanders.

**57 BC** Julius Caesar's invading Roman legions defeat the Belgae, a conglomeration of various Celtic tribes, in the northern part of Gaul (today's France).

**1st century AD** A Gallo-Roman settlement is founded beside the rivers Reie and Dijver, on the site of present-day Bruges.

**2nd century** Earliest indications of a Gallo-Roman settlement beside the River Schelde, on the site of present-day Antwerp.

**4th–6th century** The Franks, a Germanic people, cross the Rhine and settle between the rivers Meuse and Schelde.

***c.*630** St Amand founds the abbey known today as Sint-Baafsabdij, on the site of what will become Ghent.

**800** Charlemagne, King of the Franks, is crowned Emperor of the West.

**843** The Frankish Empire splits into three. Flanders west of the Schelde joins West Francia; the territory east of the Schelde becomes part of the Middle Kingdom, then, in 855, of Lotharingia (Lorraine).

**863** Baldwin I "Iron Arm", the first Count of Flanders, occupies the Burg castle in Bruges.

**867** Baldwin I builds a fort in Ghent where the Gravensteen now stands.

**1127** Count Charles the Good is murdered. Thierry of Alsace becomes Count of Flanders. Bruges is granted its first charter and building of the city wall begins.

**1297** Philip IV of France annexes Flanders.

**1302** An army of Flemish peasants and craftsmen slaughters the French knights in the Battle of the Golden Spurs at Kortrijk.

**1305** War with France ends in a treaty unfavourable to Flanders.

**1345** In a battle on Ghent's Vrijdagmarkt between members of the weavers' and fullers' guilds, more than 500 people die. Leader Jacob van Artevelde is murdered.

**1357** Antwerp, which belonged to the Duchy of Brabant, is annexed by Flanders (restored to Brabant by the Burgundians in 1406).

**1384** Count Louis succeeded by his daughter Margarete, wife of Philip the Bold, Duke of Burgundy. The Burgundian century begins.

**1400s** Cloth-making declines, but prosperity is maintained by trade and banking.

**1430** Duke Philip the Good founds the Order of the Golden Fleece in Bruges.

**1432** Jan van Eyck paints the *Adoration of the Mystic Lamb*.

**1477** Death of Duke Charles the Bold. His successor is Mary of Burgundy, wife of Habsburg Crown Prince Maximilian of Austria. The citizens of Ghent force Mary to sign the Great Privilege, recognising civic freedoms.

**1482** On Mary's death Low Countries come under the sway of the Habsburg Dynasty. Bruges rebels against its new rulers, imprisoning Maximilian in the Craenenburg mansion; when he is freed he retaliates by moving the ducal residence to Ghent.

**1500** Charles V, grandson of Maximilian, and later Habsburg emperor, is born in Ghent and baptised in the city's St Bavo's cathedral.

**1520** Silting of the Zwin closes Bruges' access to sea. Economic decline begins.

**1539** Ghent rebels against Charles V, only to herald his return with a humiliating parade the following year.

**1541** Mercator draws first map of Flanders.

**1555** Charles V abdicates in favour of his son, King Philip II of Spain.

**1566** Protestant "Iconoclasts" sack churches across the Low Countries. The following year, the Spanish Duke of Alba suppresses the movement. His reign of terror leads thousands of Protestants to emigrate.

**1576** Dutch rebel leader William of Orange occupies Ghent. Pacification of Ghent aims to permit religious freedom in the Low Countries. Duke of Alba takes Antwerp and subjects the city to the Spanish Fury, an orgy of destruction and slaughter, before retreating.

**1585** Spain re-establishes control. Spanish troops occupy Antwerp; the Dutch blockade the Schelde estuary; Flemish cities go into steep decline. Many Protestant merchants, artists and craftsmen flee to the Netherlands.

**1608** Rubens becomes court painter to the Spanish regents in Antwerp.

**1648:** By the Treaty of Westphalia, Belgium remains under Spanish rule as the Spanish Netherlands. Schelde closed to shipping.

**1715** By the Treaty of Utrecht, Belgium passes under the authority of the Austrian Holy Roman Emperor Charles VI.

**1789–90** Pro-French revolutionaries proclaim the short-lived "United States of Belgium"; the Austrian Army regains control.

**1795** French revolutionaries annex Belgium. The Schelde is re-opened to shipping, but is soon blockaded by the British.

**1815** Napoleon defeated at Waterloo. The Netherlands and Belgium form the Kingdom of the Netherlands under William I of Orange.

**1830** Belgium revolts against Dutch rule, becoming the Kingdom of Belgium the following year under King Leopold I.

**1838** Railway connecting Brussels, Ghent, Bruges and Ostend opens.

**1847** Bruges becomes the poorest city in Belgium. Hunger riots erupt.

**1892** Georges Rodenbach's novel *Bruges-la-Morte* is published.

**1904** Work on the new Bruges sea harbour, Zeebrugge, is completed.

**1914–18** World War I. German troops invade Belgium. Battles around Ieper (Ypres) and along River IJzer are among the war's bloodiest. Germans destroy Zeebrugge harbour.

**1940–44** World War II. Germany occupies Belgium. Government goes into exile in London. Germans destroy Zeebrugge harbour.

**1948** Customs union between Belgium, the Netherlands and Luxembourg (Benelux).

**1951** King Baudouin I ascends the throne after the abdication of Leopold III.

**1957** Belgium is a founder member of the European Economic Community, the forerunner of today's European Union.

**1971** Flemish and Walloon communities are given greater autonomy in cultural affairs; this process is extended in 1980.

**1977** Belgium is divided into three regions: Flanders, Wallonia and Brussels conurbation (becoming Brussels-Capital Region in 1989).

**1984** Flanders adopts bilingual Brussels as its regional capital.

**1993** King Baudouin I dies and is succeeded by his brother Albert II.

**1994** A new constitution completes Belgium's transition to a federal state, with considerable powers devolved to regions.

**2002** Euro becomes Belgium's currency. Bruges made Cultural Capital of Europe.

**2004** Nationalist Vlaams Blok (Flemish Bloc) party ruled as racist and disbanded. Re-emerges as Vlaams Belang (Flemish Interest) with a modified programme.

**2005** The government survives a vote of confidence after an unresolved dispute over voting rights of minority French-speakers in Dutch-speaking communes around Brussels. ❑

---

**LEFT:** Flemish victory at the Battle of the Golden Spurs.
**RIGHT:** Belgian Prime Minister Guy Verhofstadt.

# THE FLEMISH WAY

Now one of Europe's most dynamic and prosperous regions, Flanders is experiencing a second Renaissance, is flaunting its heritage, and is intent on making its own mark on the world. But what about the rest of Belgium?

Most people cannot place Flanders on a map. For many, the name is inseparable from the trenches of World War I, so they think it is in France. Others have heard of Flemish painting, but see it as inseparable from Dutch art. This has been the fate of the Flemings for much of their history, and it is something they intend to put right. They already have their own flag – a black lion with red claws on a yellow background – their own national anthem (*The Flemish Lion*), and their own representative government. Could it become an independent country, as some Flemings ardently wish?

### Divide and rule

Flanders has never been an independent entity. Foreign rule began in AD843, when Charlemagne's kingdom was carved up *(see page 19)*. Flemings have tasted a degree of autonomy. Wealthy medieval cities won their own charters and liberties, which was a source of friction with the ruling French. However, the ruling classes, the *leliaerts* (after the French symbol of royalty, the *fleur-de-lys*) spoke French and always sided with the French. The rest of the populace, including merchants and guildsmen, were Dutch-speaking and known as the *clauwaerts* (after the claws of the Flemish lion).

Tensions came to a head at the start of the 14th century, when King Philip the Fair of France tried to regain Flanders. In 1302 the citizens of Bruges rebelled and massacred the *leliaerts*. Then the poorly armed Flemish took

on the mighty French and won the famous Battle of the Golden Spurs *(see page 20)*.

By 1327, France was back in control. Power passed to the Burgundians in 1384, and so began a Golden Age for Flanders, a period of prosperity and artistic triumph. Economically, however, Flanders was already on the slide when it was torn apart by religious strife in the 16th century. From 1793 to 1815 it was overrun by French revolutionary armies, who imposed French as the language of administration and education. When independence came in 1830, it was the French-speaking elite in Brussels that ruled. Leopold I, first king of the Belgians, married the French king's daughter.

**LEFT:** Ghent's Werregrate Street is the only street where graffiti is legal. **RIGHT:** ethnic diversity in Bruges.

## The Flemish Movement

There was a practical side to the dominance of French. Flemings spoke a variety of dialects, with no standardised form, so Flemish did not easily serve a centralised administration. But there was also a disdain that extended from language to culture. Flemings who wanted to get on in life had to learn French. Lawyers, administrators, the business community, the army, universities and the intellectual elite were dominated by French-speakers. Flemish, the language of the common people, was confined to domestic life.

The situation was aggravated by industrialisation. As Belgium became an industrial

nation in the mid-19th century, all the key resources – notably coal – were in Wallonia. Flanders remained a rural backwater, focusing on agriculture and cottage industries, such as lace-making. When Dutch-speaking people had to deal with the authorities, they had to enlist the help of someone who spoke French. Frequent examples of injustice included an episode in 1860 in which two innocent men were executed after a court case conducted in a language they did not understand.

Dissatisfaction gradually found a political expression. In 1838 Hendrik Conscience (1812–83) published *De Leeuw van Vlaanderen (The Lion of Flanders)*, a novel about

the lead-up to the Battle of the Golden Spurs. It was hugely popular, and rekindled the spark of Flemish national pride, making writing in Dutch respectable. Other writers pressed for recognition of the Flemish language, such as Jan Frans Willems (1793–1846), and the celebrated poet and priest, Guido Gezelle (1830–99). Father Adolf Daens (1839–1907) drew attention to the suffering of the Flemish working classes, and came into conflict with the church authorities; and Lodewijk de Raet (1870–1914) campaigned to have Dutch made the language of education at Ghent University. Initially this agitation, known as the Flemish Movement *(Vlaamse Beweging)*, focused primarily on language, but language plays an integral part in culture as a whole. In 1898, Dutch was officially given parity with French in Belgian administration, but the effects of this took decades to filter through.

## World War and disenchantment

World War I proved a turning point. About 75 percent of the frontline troops serving in the trenches behind the River IJzer were Dutch-speaking, and 75 percent of the officers could not speak Dutch. Thousands of men died because they could not understand the orders. Many others became politicised *flamigants* – advocates of Flemish emancipation. After the war, a cross-shaped memorial tower was raised at Diksmuide, near the IJzer, bearing the inscription AVV – VVK (Alles Voor Vlaanderen – Vlaanderen Voor Kristus; All For Flanders – Flanders For Christ). It became the object of an annual pilgrimage, the *IJzerbedevaart* (still held on the last Sunday of August).

The disenchantment of many Flemings towards the Belgian state led some to side with the German occupiers during World War I. After the war, they were vilified, even executed, and other Flemings were casually tarred with the same brush. The same happened in World War II: the Nazis actively exploited Flemish disenchantment and won the support of numerous collaborators. There were even Flemish regiments of the SS, who helped run a notorious prison camp at Breendonk, near Antwerp; many later perished on the Eastern Front. The Belgian Government's uncompromising treatment of such collaborators after the war remains a burning issue to this day.

## A reversal of fortunes

The linguistic imbalance moved slowly towards parity. In 1930, Ghent University dropped French as the language of education, and Flemish schools became Dutch-speaking. In the 1960s, the ancient university of Leuven went the same way after a protracted and sometimes ugly revolt. French-speaking students were rehoused in the new university of Louvain-la-Neuve to the south of Brussels.

The gradual progress towards a federal structure in Belgium since the 1970s has given greater autonomy to the regions (Flanders, Wallonia and Brussels). Flanders now has its own parliament and government, with powers over most domestic issues, although central government still controls areas of national interest – defence, justice and taxation.

But the real change is in the economy. Since the 1960s Flanders has prospered, with its port facilities and its light and high-tech industries, while the old heavy industries have collapsed. In 1955 the gross regional product per head in Flanders was 10 percent lower than in Wallonia; now it is 35 percent higher. A major issue today is "financial transfer". Many Flemings believe their prosperity is being siphoned off to prop up the inefficient economies of Brussels and Wallonia. Broadly speaking, Dutch-speakers want a free-market economy with minimal government intervention, while French-speakers put faith in government intervention to resuscitate their economy.

The Flemings are the majority in Belgium, representing 60 percent of the nation, but their point of view does not prevail because of the parity rules. Central government is divided equally between French- and Dutch-speakers, and any major legislation affecting institutions or social policy has to be passed by 50 percent of the French-speaking representatives. Effectively, this means that a minority is able to block the economic reforms the Flemings deem necessary. The financial transfers keep growing and the Flemings perceive this as undemocratic injustice, while French-speakers see themselves as the beleaguered minority and cling on to their constitutional rights.

**LEFT:** the Flemish flag floats proudly on Gravensteen castle in Ghent. **RIGHT:** cycling is a favoured family activity in the whole of Belgium.

## Bones of contention

Such imbalances, and the constant tussle between the regions and central government, have driven some Flemings to call for complete independence. The structure of the European Union helps to take the sting out of this issue. Under the EU umbrella, national borders have become less rigid, and the status of regions has been promoted. In clashes with the Belgian Government, Flanders can often appeal to the higher authority of the EU.

But there are plenty of Flemish activists and politicians who like to focus on tensions between communities, in the mixed-language municipalities along the linguistic borders, for

### FLEMISH AND DUTCH

The Flemish people speak a variety of dialects, and the dialects of one part of Flanders can't always be understood by people from elsewhere. Flemish *(vlaams)* is loosely called a language, but more strictly refers collectively to the dialects, which are variants of Dutch *(Nederlands)*, the *lingua franca* and official language. It varies slightly in pronunciation, sentence structure and the use of loan words from that spoken in the Netherlands, but the vocabulary differs by only about 2,000 words. The uniformity of Dutch in the Netherlands, Flanders and Surinam is monitored and regulated by the Dutch Language Union.

instance, where the language of administration and education is in contest. Belgium may have two languages, but it is far from bilingual. Flemings have to learn French at school; French-speakers can learn Dutch or English. Consequently, many of them never learn Dutch, to the frustration of Flemings, two-thirds of whom speak a second language other than Dutch. Recently they have taken to learning English, and turned their back on French.

Another bone of contention is Brussels. The city is now an administrative region in its own right, called the Brussels Capital Region. Flanders has claimed Brussels as its capital, and this is where its parliament and government

is located. This makes sense in that, historically, Brussels was a Dutch-speaking city, and it is surrounded by Flanders. But of a population of over a million, only a quarter is Dutch-speaking and the French speakers are worried that, if things go Flanders' way, they may become second-class citizens in a Flemish state.

## One nation

But most Flemings have little time for such friction, at least in their day-to-day lives. They muddle along happily enough with Belgian compatriots, and feel a sense of Belgian unity in any time of national crisis, such as during the paedophile scandals of the 1990s, or on the death of royalty. The majority appear to support the monarchy, symbol of Belgian unity (the Flemish were more in favour of retaining the monarchy in the critical referendum of 1950 than the Walloons). At ground-level they share many common interests: good beer, seafood, chips, pastries, home-grown vegetables, cut flowers, cycling and pigeon-racing. Like all Belgians, Flemings are solid citizens, placing strong emphasis on the family, and tend to respect authority. They also like creature comforts – new cars, efficient homes (two-thirds of Flemings are house-owners). They have inherited the practical virtues of their mercantile past, living in a densely populated and highly urbanised society.

In sport, Flemings will champion Flemish heroes, such as the tennis player Kim Clijsters (born 1983), and cyclist Eddy Merckx (born 1945). But they will happily support non-Flemish Belgians, and the national football

### PARTY POLITICS: SPLITTING AND SPLINTERING

Each Belgian region has its own political parties, and their support is distributed across the mainstream parties which are broadly divided into Christian Democrats, Socialists and Liberals – usually governing in coalition. When it comes to striking an attitude towards the Belgian state, the Flemish parties divide into three camps: Federalist (happy with the status quo, with some improvements), Confederalist (wanting greater autonomy), and Separatist (wanting independence).

The main voice of the Flemish Movement used to be Volksunie (People's Union), founded in 1954, which promoted greater recognition for Flemish language and

culture, and political autonomy. Volksunie split in 2000 to form the separatist Nieuw-Vlaamse Alliantie, which joined forces with the centre-right Christian Democrats; and Spirit, which joined forces with the Socialist Party. In 1977 a right-wing splinter group emerged, the Vlaams Blok (VB; Flemish Bloc). It campaigned for an independent Flemish republic, but demanded tough laws on immigration and a programme of repatriation – unpalatable policies that kept it permanently out of any coalition. The party was forced to disband in 2004 but reformed as Vlaams Belang (Flemish Interest) with a slightly modified programme *(see page 31)*.

team, the Red Devils. Their geographic backdrop of the polders and the North Sea coast may have subtly shaped the Flemish character differently to that of the Walloons, but in many ways Belgium is one nation divided by language.

## Folk culture

The Flemings have a fondness for pageants. Many of these parades have a religious base, such as the Procession of the Holy Blood in Bruges. This outward display of religious fervour is in keeping with the fact that 90 percent of Flemings are Catholics, and they gravitate towards the church for all the main rites of passage – but less than a fifth of them go to mass

thread in a constant round of socialising. This gift for socialising is also manifest in Flanders' lively bars and cafés and in Antwerp's nightclubs and trendy restaurants, often run by young, cosmopolitan professionals.

Like all Belgians, the Flemings are wary of pretension, their instincts finely tuned to detect sham. The result is an impressive agenda of good-quality concerts, operas, plays and films. The Festival of Flanders, held across the region, involves a programme of classical music of huge talent and ambition. The Flanders Opera (based in Ghent and Antwerp) stages productions of international stature. Flanders not only has an exceptional artistic heritage, but a highly

on a regular basis. Other festivals celebrate historical incidents (such as the Pageant of the Golden Tree in Bruges), or have older folkloric roots (the Cat Festival of Ieper). Giants (huge papier-mâché figures) play a prominent role in many folk processions, a tradition said to date back to the Counter-Reformation.

Such events are organised by guild-like clubs, many of ancient origin. They cover every kind of hobby, pastime, sport, intellectual pursuit, collecting passion, and social, work or military connection. They form a

active contemporary art scene. On the literary front, Bruges-born author and poet Hugo Claus (born 1929) is one of the most respected writers in the Dutch language, best known for *Het Verdriet van België* (*The Grief of Belgium*, 1983).

Through their cherished education system, the Flemings nurture talent in all fields. Antwerp has become a centre for fashion, producing a host of top designers *(see page 246)*. Even rock bands (such as dEUS, from Antwerp) are receiving international attention.

Flanders, which has always had to struggle against adversity, is proud of its achievements, especially those of recent decades, and is keen to show them off to the world.  ❑

**LEFT:** Moustache parade on the streets of Antwerp.
**ABOVE:** having fun during Ghent's Gentse Feesten.

# FLEMISH MASTERS

**Flemish art and architecture of the late-medieval period were the products of a wealthy, confident, sophisticated culture. There are parallels with those circumstances today and the result is a vigorous contemporary art scene**

For centuries, since Charlemagne established his court at Aachen in the 8th century, the artists of the Low Countries had been honing their skills in minute detail to produce illuminated manuscripts; the culmination of their art is the exquisite Book of Hours, the *Très Riches Heures du Duc de Berry* (*c*.1411), by friars from the Flemish province of Limburg. In the early 15th century these skills were transferred to a larger scale through the use of a new medium: oil paint. Oils allowed to paint on wooden panels with dazzling luminosity and precision. One of the earliest artists to adopt oil painting was Jan van Eyck (1390–1441) who, with his brother Hubert (1366–1426), painted the polyptych *The Adoration of the Mystic Lamb* (*see page 182*), now in Ghent's cathedral.

Other so-called Flemish Primitives emulated their skills. Rogier van der Weyden (*c*.1399–1464) brought a new emotional expressiveness to painting, as seen in *The Seven Sacraments* (1445). Dirk Bouts (1415–75), by contrast, conveyed pristine clarity, showing contemporary people behaving with eerie calm through times of gory crisis, as in his *Justice of Othon* (1471–73) and *Martyrdom of Erasmus*. But perhaps Jan van Eyck's only true rival for gem-like, spiritual beauty is the German-born Hans Memling (1435–94), who settled in Bruges and produced works for the Sint-Janshospitaal, where they can still be seen today (*see page 86*).

## The Italian link

Oil paintings, as opposed to murals, were portable and marketable, and cities like Bruges and Ghent had wealthy patrons to buy and commission them. A big shift in patronage took place in the 15th century: whereas previously the church had been the prime patron, now there was a secular demand, not only for private, devotional paintings on religious themes, but also for portraits, as seen in Jan van Eyck's famous *Arnolfini Marriage* (1434).

When, in the early 15th century, Bruges had become a major north European trading hub, it had a large international population, among whom were wealthy Italian bankers and mer-

**LEFT:** the *Arnolfini Marriage* (1434) by Jan van Eyck initiated a new chapter in art history.
**RIGHT:** *Madonna and Child with two Angels* (*c*.1480) detail, by Hans Memling.

chants, like Giovanni Arnolfini, a merchant from Lucca, who settled in Bruges in 1430. Well-to-do Italians bought Flemish paintings and took them home, where they were greatly admired. The *Portinari Triptych* (1476–78) by Hugo van der Goes (*c*.1435–82) was painted for Tommaso Portinari, the Medici family's agent in Bruges, and is now in the Uffizi Gallery in Florence. Flemish painters travelled to Italy, and oil painting was rapidly adopted by Italian artists, who made copies of Flemish paintings before setting out on their own paths to invention. Prior to this, Italian art had been largely devoted to fresco painting on walls, or panel painting using the tricky and labour-intensive

medium of egg-tempera. Antonello da Messina (*c*.1430–79) is thought to have been one of the first Italian oil painters; in 1475 he took his skills to Venice where they were seized on by artists such as Giovanni Bellini (*c*.1430–1516). Thus Flemish painting had a direct impact on the Italian Renaissance, and helped fuel the surge in Italian art and the breakthrough in representation later achieved by painters such as Leonardo da Vinci (1452–1519) and Titian (*c*.1485–1576).

It was not all one-way traffic. A new generation of Flemish painters such as Jan Gossaert of Maubeuge (1478–1532) travelled to Italy and came back with Renaissance-influenced ideas about the rules of perspective, the wonders of classical architecture and the potential of landscape. Others, such as Quentin Metsys (1466–1530), were strongly influenced by Renaissance trends brought to Flanders. As a result the work of these "Romanists" became more polished and sophisticated than that of the "Primitives", but it also lost some of its distinctive North European charm and vision.

### Brueghel

Pieter Brueghel the Elder (*c*.1525–69) travelled to Italy, but proved the exception by showing little of this experience in his painting. His images of Flemish village life – exuberant marriage celebrations in snow-bound winter scenes – are resolutely North European in tone. He even transfers biblical scenes (such as the *Massacre of the Innocents, c*.1565) to rural Flanders, to poignant effect. In his *Fall of Icarus* (1558), his ploughman tilling the field shows an almost comical nonchalance towards the tragedy taking place out at sea.

The charm of Brueghel's work, and that of his son Brueghel the Younger (1564–1638), lies in its almost naive directness. But other Flemish painters were acquiring considerable technical skills. Joachim Beuckelaer (1533–74), for instance, produced market scenes of astonishing complexity, with stalls piled high with fruit and vegetables.

By the 16th century the great cities of Flanders were in decline, through loss of trade and the turmoil of the religious strife that shook the Spanish Netherlands. Some relief came with the division of the United Provinces (the Netherlands) from the Spanish Netherlands, formalised by a series of treaties after 1609.

---

#### THE FLEMISH PRIMITIVES

A set of artists of the era of Jan van Eyck (15th century) are sometimes called the Flemish Primitives. It is a misleading term that sounds derogatory, but it relates rather to the original meaning of "primitive": belonging to the first stage of a new development. The new development in this case was the Renaissance, so the Primitives are seen as precursors. It is not a reference to a lack of sophistication – indeed the work of the Flemish Primitives is anything but unsophisticated. In addition to Van Eyck, the primitives include Robert Campin, the Master of Flémalle, Roger van der Weyden, Dirk Bouts, Hans Memling, Petrus Christus, Hugo van der Goes, and, the last in the line, Gerard David (c.1460–1523).

## The age of Rubens

This change in fortune coincided with a great rebirth of Flemish art, fuelled primarily by one man: Pieter Paul Rubens (1577–1640). Gifted and energetic, Rubens made Antwerp into a major city of the arts *(see page 47)*. His work inspired numerous Flemish artists, including portraitist Antoon van Dyck (1599–1641) and Jacob Jordaens (1593–1678), who is most readily associated with his rumbustious scenes of feasting. These prolific artists worked alongside printers, such as the Plantin-Moretus family in Antwerp, producing engravings for book illustrations as well as for sale in their own right. Once again, Flemish art was an international commodity; like Rubens, Van Dyck travelled to Italy and England, and painted flattering portraits of the aristocracy; he became court artist to Charles I, was rewarded with a knighthood, and was buried in St Paul's Cathedral in London.

Another line of Flemish art took the form of genre painting, depicting scenes from daily life – homes, inns, markets – on a small scale, often spiked with moral significance and mocking humour. Leaders in this field were David Teniers the Younger (1610–90), and Adriaen Brouwer (1605–38).

As the 17th century came to a close, so too did this second wave of great Flemish art, and for the next two centuries its products were largely derivative and unremarkable.

## Independence to fin de siècle

However, when Belgium became an independent nation in 1830, a search for national identity was reflected in the taste for public statues of historical figures, produced by sculptors such Paul de Vigne (1843–1901), responsible for the statue of the medieval heroes Pieter de Coninck and Jan Breydel in the Bruges Markt; and Jef Lambeaux (1852–1908), who produced Antwerp's Brabo fountain (1887). Meanwhile, the eyes of the art world were turned towards France as it went from the Realism of Gustave Courbet in the 1850s, through Impressionism in the 1870s to Post-Impressionism. Several

Belgian artists echoed these changes with considerable skill, such as Jan Stobbaerts (1839–1914) and Henri de Braekeleer (1840–88), who painted sombre and poignant Realist work; and Théo van Rysselberghe (1862–1926), who made an effective sortie into Pointillism. Emiel Claus (1849–1924) created a movement called Luminism, based on an Impressionist style that brings extraordinary, sparkling light to rural landscapes. Belgian artists also made a major contribution to Symbolism *(see pages 48–9)*, a movement closely associated with fin-de-siècle decadence. Certain artists can be clearly categorised as Symbolists, such as Fernand Khnopff and Leon Spilliaert, however

disparate their work. James Ensor (1860–1949), on the other hand, is virtually uncategorisable *(see box, page 44)*, but his style would later give rise to the Surrealism of René Magritte (1898–1971) and Paul Delvaux (1897–1994).

From the mid-19th century, Brussels became a hub of cutting-edge artistic taste; modern art and design was promoted by highly active groups such as Le Cercle des Vingt (Les XX; 1884–93) and La Libre Esthétique (1894–1914). A large number of Flemish artists trained at the Académie de Bruxelles. One notable name was Mechelen-born Rik Wouters (1882–1916), who produced Fauvist-style paintings of beguiling immediacy.

---

**LEFT:** *Peasant Wedding* (1568) detail, by Pieter Brueghel the Elder celebrates Flemish village life.

**RIGHT:** Adriaen Brouwer's *The Bitter Draught* (c. 1635), was innovative by depicting rowdy peasant "lowlife".

A determinedly Flemish group developed around the village of Sint-Martens-Latem, near Ghent. There were two schools: the first (1895–1901), included Valerius de Saedeleer and Gustaaf van de Woestijne, whose work is broadly reminiscent of the Symbolists. The Symbolist sculptor Georges Minne and Luminist Emiel Claus also formed part of the group. The second school (1905–10) was more Expressionist. First among them was Albert Servaes, but the best known is Constant Permeke, who painted distinctively bold socially engaged work in grungy earth colours. Another member, Gustave de Smet, settled permanently near Sint-Martens-Latem.

## Contemporary art

A number of Flemish artists made a mark in the 20th century. The semi-naive work of Edgard Tytgat (1879–1957) and Jan Brussel-mans (1884–1953), and the machinist abstraction of Victor Servranckx (1897–1965) is instantly recognisable. After World War II, Belgian art coasted along in the shadow of American movements, such as Abstract Expressionism. Nonetheless, in the 1960s, Flemish artists began to win international recognition. Marcel Broodthaers (1924–76) became famous for his iconic mixed-media sculpture *Casserole and Closed Mussels* (1964–65), an amusing take on Pop Art. The

### JAMES ENSOR

Born in Ostend to an English father and a Flemish mother, James Ensor (1860–1949) demonstrated early talent, painting landscapes, portraits and interiors in a confident, impressionistic style. But even in an early work such as *Woman Eating Oysters* (1882), there is a hint of caricature and darkness, a mood that burst to the forefront a few years later when Ensor began to produce the frenetic, weird, deeply personal paintings for which he is celebrated. Skeletons, puppets, masks, carnival characters and grotesque cartoon figures people his work, all captured with rapid brushstrokes of vivid colour. His painting style anticipated

Expressionism by about two decades; the only notable artist producing work in this vein during the 1890s was the Norwegian Edvard Munch.

However, Ensor was not a complete outsider. Although he lived most of his life in Ostend, he was also a founder-member of the leading Brussels art group Les XX; by the 1920s he had won national recognition, and was made a baron in 1930. His most celebrated painting, *Christ's Entry into Brussels in 1889* (1888), which caused a scandal when it was first shown, was bought by the J. Paul Getty Museum, California, in 1987 for the reported sum of US$15 million.

installation artist known as Panamarenko (b. 1940) produced huge, witty flying machines of PVC, paper, wood and metal. Luc Tuymans (b. 1958), celebrated for his flat-colour figurative painting, had a one-man show at Tate Modern in London in 2004; Wim Delvoye (b. 1965) is celebrated for his extraordinary installation *Cloaca* (2000), which reproduces the process of food digestion. Ghent's Stedelijk Museum voor Actuele Kunst (SMAK) and Antwerp's Museum voor Hedendaagse Kunst (MuHKA) have both earned international respect as cutting-edge galleries in tune with current trends. Once more, Flanders is at the forefront of international art.

## Architecture: medieval styles

Of all the buildings of medieval Flanders, the churches have proved the greatest survivors. Early examples have thick stone walls, heavy cylindrical columns, semi-circular arches and small windows. This style supposedly dated from Roman times, so is called Romanesque. By the 12th century, however, the church needed a more sophisticated expression.

Gothic architecture developed in France in the early 12th century. The pointed arch offered the potential for lighter, higher, more delicate structures, especially if supported by load-bearing buttresses on the exterior of the building. Belgium had its own take on Gothic, which, in church architecture, never reached quite the dainty, glass-filled perfection seen, for example, at Sainte-Chapelle in Paris, but was always more muscular and practical.

Scheldt Gothic – which developed in the early 13th century – is bold and solid, and often features double or triple lancet windows. Examples include Onze-Lieve-Vrouwekerk in Bruges and Sint-Niklaaskerk in Ghent (both 13th–15th century). Brabant Gothic emerged in the 14th century, and was used to build on a more ambitious scale, typically with high bell towers, triple naves supported by clustered columns, and multiple side-chapels; Antwerp Cathedral is a good example of this. The late 14th century saw the emergence of the aptly named Flamboyant Gothic, with delicate window tracery, spires, finials and sculpture. Unusually, Flamboyant Gothic was adopted for secular use, to splendid effect, notably in the great town halls, such as that in Bruges (1376–1420) and, especially, the exquisite Stadhuis in Leuven (1448–78).

## Renaissance and baroque

During the Renaissance in Italy the Classical architecture of ancient Rome was rediscovered and championed: classical columns, with fluted shafts and capitals, domes, rectangular windows and trabeate arches replaced the pointed arches of the preceding era. The Renaissance touched Flanders in many ways:

in learning and scholarship, and in painting, but in architecture, the pure classical forms of the Italian Renaissance had little impact. Rather, Flemish architects adapted the Renaissance style to their own practical needs and stylistic sensibilities. This is seen, for example, in the ornate Oude Griffie (1534–37) in Bruges. The supreme example is Antwerp's Stadhuis (1561–64); Renaissance influence is evident in the windows, the columns and pediment, the arches and niches, but the overall effect is incontrovertibly North European.

The religious strife of the 16th century caused profound disruption in Flanders. This was resolved in political settlements that saw

---

**LEFT:** the farcical and eerie *Death and the Masks* (1897), by James Ensor.
**RIGHT:** Antwerp's Renaissance Stadhuis.

Catholics remaining in Flanders. The new self-confidence of the Counter-Reformation found architectural expression in the baroque, a form of architecture richly embellished with ornament, such as garlands, swirls, barley-sugar twists, broken pediments, oval windows, and cherubs. Only a few churches in Flanders were built in pure baroque style, such as Sint-Walburgakerk (1619–41) in Bruges, and Sint-Carolus Borromeuskerk (1615–21) in Antwerp. But architects refurbished the ravished interiors of medieval churches in baroque style, as in Sint-Nicklaaskerk in Ghent; and added lavish pulpits by the likes of Artus Quellinus the Younger and Hendrik Verbruggen.

During the 18th century, neo-classicism, a more restrained form of classical architecture, spread through Europe, but its impact in Flanders was moderate, best seen in the Landhuis van het Brugse Vrij (1722–27) in Bruges.

### New styles

In Britain, a neo-Gothic movement had gathered pace, producing the new Houses of Parliament in 1834. This coincided with the Catholic revival. Many Catholics felt uneasy about neo-classicism, which they saw as aping the styles of ancient pagan cultures. This sentiment found fertile ground in Bruges, with its extensive population of expatriate Britons,

and strong church traditions. The result was a massive restoration project: much of Bruges is not so much medieval as neo-medieval. This includes the huge Povinciaal Hof (1881–1921) in the Markt. It was designed by Louis Delacenserie (1838–1909), a Bruges-born architect who restored much of the medieval fabric of the city, and demonstrated his versatility by designing Antwerp's magnificent neo-classical Centraal Station (1905).

As Belgium prospered in the late 19th century, the newly wealthy business class employed architects to build homes in any style they fancied – neo-Gothic, neo-Classical, neo-medieval. This style has been labelled Eclectic. A fine example of this is the late-19th century suburb of Antwerp, Cogels-Osylei. But some architects felt that they should stop looking backwards. Instead, they looked to the organic shapes of nature, and the result was "new art" – Art Nouveau. Belgian architect Victor Horta (1861–1947), maestro of Art Nouveau, designed the first-ever house in this style in Brussels (1893–95). Henry van de Velde (1863–1957), another leading designer, was appointed director in 1901 of the Arts and Crafts School in Weimar, Germany, which in 1919 became the Bauhaus. But while Art Nouveau spread rapidly through the Brussels suburbs, it had little impact in Flanders, seen only in scattered detail and isolated buildings.

### Contemporary architecture

Flanders had many problems to contend with in the 20th century: war, economic depression and aerial bombing. In one brief expression of optimism, Europe's highest skyscraper, the Boerentoeren, was built in Antwerp in 1932, but rose to a mere 87.5 metres (287 ft). Only in recent decades of economic and spiritual resurgence has new effort been put into architecture. This is seen in the imaginative restoration projects and new buildings that have revitalised Antwerp's waterfront, as well as a number of high-profile buildings, such as Bruges' Concertgebouw, built for the city's year as Cultural Capital of Europe in 2002. But city planners are deeply conscious that much of the prestige of Flanders lies in the glory days of its medieval past and the precious buildings that recall it. ❑

**LEFT:** the ornate pulpit inside Sint-Nicklaaskerk, Ghent.

# Pieter Paul Rubens

Pieter Paul Rubens (1577–1640) was one of the great geniuses of his age, a force of nature, a one-man industry. Born in Germany, the son of a Protestant lawyer from Antwerp who had fled persecution, he moved back to Antwerp with his mother after his father's death, and converted to Catholicism. He showed natural talent and began training as an artist aged 13. In 1600, aged 23, he went to Italy where he worked for the Duke of Mantua, and travelled widely, making copies of the works of the great masters for the duke's collection. Inspired by the light, and by the vigour and drama of paintings by Michelangelo, Titian and Caravaggio, he injected new dynamism into his own work.

Rubens returned to Antwerp in 1608 and the following year he was appointed court painter to Archduke Albert and the Infanta Isabella. He married Isabella Brant, the 17-year-old daughter of a leading Antwerp lawyer. His two triptychs painted for Antwerp Cathedral – the *Raising of the Cross* (1610–11) and the *Descent from the Cross* (1611–14) – caused a sensation. Commissions poured in, and by 1610 Rubens had enough money to buy a large house in Antwerp, which he turned into a comfortable home and a studio.

Rubens' supreme gift of draughtsmanship allowed him to create large, vigorous canvases. His style was in tune with his times: it had the grandeur and swagger of baroque architecture and the Counter-Reformation, and echoed the luxurious lifestyles of European aristocracy. Rubens produced at least 2,000 major paintings, but quite how much of the painting Rubens did is open to question: his studio employed a large number of pupils, assistants and specialist painters. Among his collaborators were Antoon van Dyck, Jacob Jordaens, Jan Brueghel, son of Pieter Brueghel the Elder, and an expert in flower paintings, Daniel Seghers, and Frans Snyders, all leading artists in their own right.

**RIGHT:** Rubens' *Descent from the Cross* (1612).

Demand came also from royal courts abroad: Rubens travelled to the court of Charles I of England in 1521; to Paris in 1522 to carry out major commissions for Marie de Medici, wife of Henri IV; and to the court of Philip IV of Spain in 1625. These journeys increasingly served as diplomatic missions on behalf of the Infanta Isabella, following the death of Archduke Albert in 1621; she put to good use Rubens' social skills and his knowledge of six languages (Dutch, Italian, Spanish, English, French and Latin). In 1626 Rubens' wife, the mother of his three children, died. In 1628 he went to Spain, were he met Velásquez (1599–1660),

and then to England on behalf of Philip IV of Spain to negotiate a peace settlement with Charles I, for which he received a knighthood. Charles also commissioned Rubens to paint the ceiling of the Banqueting House in Whitehall. In 1630, back in Antwerp, Rubens married Helena Fourment, the daughter of a wealthy silk merchant. He was 53, and she was 16; it was another happy marriage, and they had five children together. In 1635 he bought a grand country house near Mechelen, and spent much of his later life painting landscapes. He died at the age of 63, and was buried in Sint-Jacobskerk in Antwerp. ❑

# BELGIAN SYMBOLISM

**The paintings of the Belgian Symbolists made a vivid and fascinating contribution to the history of world art**

The flavour of much of the artistic production during the 19th century was Realism. Even Impressionism, although perceived as shockingly different, could be regarded as a kind of Realism, in its attempts to capture fleeting atmospheric moments of the "real" modern world, in rural villages as much as in urban settings such as railway stations and street scenes.

By the mid-1880s, writers and artists, and to some extent musicians, in both France and Belgium were beginning to search for something new, for a way of expressing the inner workings of the mind – the anti-rationalist world of imagination, emotion, myth and dreams. The term given to this movement was Symbolism. In effect, they were desperate to liberate their work from the constraints of reality.

A number of north Belgian artists took up the Symbolist theme, working in a broad range of styles. Leon Spilliaert (1881–1946) created moody, haunting scenes, often painted in black and white with a boldness reminiscent of poster art, depicting, for example, swimmers and the swirling sea, and forlorn architectural landscapes at dusk. He rarely used oils, preferring an immaterial substance to express the spiritual content of his work.

Fernand Khnopff (1858–1921) used a highly polished technique to paint images that are at once silent and outwardly calm, but are packed with suppressed emotion. Sometimes his work appears realistic, such as the women tennis-players in *Memories* (1889), and sometimes dreamlike, such as the cheetah with a human head in *Caresses/Art/ The Sphinx* (1896).

The sculptor Georges Minne (1866–1944) is best known for his small-scale statue *Fountain of Kneeling Youths* (1898), featuring five emaciated boys around a well, a bronze copy of which stands outside the Belfort in Ghent. James Ensor and Theo van Rysselberghe were both also associated with the Symbolist movement, as well as Jean Delville (1867–1953) and Léon Frédéric (1856–1940).

**ABOVE LEFT:** in *Who Shall Deliver me?* (1891), Khnopff interprets a poem by Christina Rossetti. **LEFT:** myth and legend were popular themes, as seen in *Vivien*, a plaster sculpture based on Tennyson's Arthurian poems called *The Idylls of the King*, also by Khnopff.

**ABOVE:** Khnopff's *Caresses/Art/ The Sphinx* (1896) is a classic work of Symbolism, prodding the subconscious with a heady mix of androgynous and hybrid beings, sensuality, exoticism and half-remembered myth.
**LEFT:** moody scenes are a theme of choice for Leon Spilliaert's work, like here in *Woman at the Edge of the Water* (1910).
**BELOW LEFT:** Khnopff continues with the enigmatic in *Memories* (1889), despite the more mundane subject matter.
**BELOW:** in his sculpture *The Fountain of Kneeling Youths* (1893), Georges Minne encapsulates the mood of spiritual unease and physical isolation present in much of the Symbolists' output.

# FOOD AND DRINK

Try North Sea shrimps or rich, thick stews, washed down
with the country's famous beer. Eat the world's best chips
from a roadside stall, or linger over the waffles and
hand-made chocolates. If you're on a diet, stay away

The Belgians love their food. You can see it in Brueghel's paintings of peasant feasts; and in the Michelin stars – the country has more Michelin-starred restaurants per capita than France. Not that they boast about it. Michelin stars are not their *raison d'être*, a good many chefs will tell you. A few even handed their stars back. "We didn't want people to think that we are too expensive", shrug the chefs. Don't you just love them?

Officially Belgium, with a population of just 10 million, is divided into five different regions, but gastronomically speaking there are just two main regions: Flanders and Wallonia. Put simply, the latter is rich in game and mushrooms; the former stuffed with fish, eels, chicken and vegetables. And there's Brussels in the centre, famous for its *stoemp* (mash with different kinds of vegetables), sausages, *moules frites*, and yes, the Brussels sprout.

The region of Flanders stretches from France to the Netherlands and has 67 km (40 miles) of wide, white, sandy beaches. The interior is made up of rich meadows where fat cows graze alongside canals thick with eels, the horizon broken by low, timber farm buildings and regimented rows of poplars, while medieval cities buzz with culinary life.

Flanders has hundreds of small restaurants producing some of Belgium's best bourgeois cuisine, plus celebrated chefs creating gastronomic magic. But what is Flemish cooking, exactly? Or Belgian cuisine, come to that?

---

**LEFT:** art on a plate: wonderful use of colours, textures and flavours. **RIGHT:** *stoemp*, a Flemish speciality.

They will tell you that their food is cooked with French finesse and served with German generosity. But the cuisine is deeply rooted in medieval cookery, a time when Flemish culture was riding high. The country has been invaded by most of Europe at one time or another, from the Romans to the Vikings, so they could not help but pick up a few cooking techniques and ingredients along the way. You can see it in their use of mustards, vinegars and dried fruits (there is a definite sweet and sour thing going on), and in the use of nuts, particularly almonds, plus spices such as cinnamon and peppercorns, harking back to the spice trade. Herbs are prominent, and beer rules – the Belgians drink more beer than wine and use it liberally in their cooking.

Traditional recipes vary from restaurant to restaurant, home to home. Take *waterzooi*, for example. This Flemish classic originally hails from Ghent, the capital of East Flanders, and is rumoured to have been Charles V's favourite dish. Half stew, half soup, it combines chicken with celery, carrot, onion and leeks, thyme, nutmeg, cloves and stock, then finished with cream. And everyone has their own way of doing it. Those on the Flemish coast make theirs with fish – whatever they have to hand. Sole, salmon and langoustines make regular bedfellows in a *waterzooï*.

for this dish. The ratio of shrimp to sauce is the key difference (woe betide anyone who uses a measly portion of shrimps, and eternal damnation awaits if they happen to be frozen). The sauce will vary, too – some use *gruyère*, others *Oud Brugge* (Old Bruges beer), some add a slug of Cognac, others a splash of whisky, some make the sauce thick enough to stand a spoon in, others make it runny. Cut through the crispy coating, and rivulets of shrimps should run onto your plate, combining with the deep-fried parsley that's always served alongside.

The best shrimps, say some, are those caught around Zeebrugge. Many of the country's top restaurants will specify Zeebrugge

## The mighty shrimp

The Belgians are among the biggest fish eaters in Europe and the country has developed a sophisticated seafood cuisine. But of all the produce plucked from the icy North Sea, the tiny sweet shrimps *(crevettes grises)* are the most fêted. They are nibbled, ready peeled, straight from the carton as you go about your daily shop – street food is endemic; or they spill out of a hollowed tomato, topped with a spoonful of home-made mayonnaise *(tomates aux crevettes grises)*; or combined with a béchamel sauce then coated with breadcrumbs and deep-fried *(croquettes aux crevettes)*. Restaurants pride themselves on their recipes

shrimps over all others. Ostend and Nieuwpoort further south also bring in shrimps: all are cooked in seawater on the boat.

When visiting the coast, you may catch a *peerdevisser* (shrimp fisherman) going about his ancient business. They don yellow oilskins and heavy boots and march into the surf on enormous horses, dragging nets as they go to catch the tiny shrimps, in a tradition dating back to the late 1400s. You will be thankful of their efforts, later, when you are sitting on a sunny terrace with a huge platter of shrimps before you, peeling each one reverently, savouring its sweetness, refreshing each mouthful with a glass of the local *wit* beer.

### Showing mussel

And what about *moules frites*? That is what most foreigners think of when they imagine Belgian cooking. Well, Belgium does not produce mussels any more (something to do with the heavy industry around the ports), they get them from the Netherlands, Spain, or France – although Dutch mussels are by far the best, they will tell you. They are served everywhere, in steaming cauldrons with a bowl of crunchy, twice-cooked chips, a mustardy mayonnaise, a hunk of bread to mop up the juices and a pint of beer to wash it down. Most agree that the Belgians make the world's best *frites*. It is the cooking twice that makes them so special.

Starchy, older potatoes are best. *Frites (frietjes)* are practically *the* national dish and the country has more than 6,000 chip shops, ranging from simple roadside huts and carts, to shops with all mod cons. Chips come generously salted with a line-up of sauces, from ketchup to garlic to ubiquitous mayonnaise, plus side orders of meatballs, beef stew and the like.

Oysters have gone the same way as the mussels. They are sold pretty much everywhere in Belgium, but are mostly brought in from

England and Holland, although Ostend has begun to revive the industry and chefs have started buying them again, albeit at a price. Flemish caviar, too, is having a renaissance, but quantities are small and prices rather steep.

### Keeping traditions alive

Fishing is still a family business in Flanders, and boats return stuffed with sparkling, squirming seafood – such as turbot, Dover sole, flounder, mackerel, crab, skate and cod. The latter is poached, served with boiled potatoes and Dijon mustard, while skate often comes with a *beurre noisette* and capers, or is set in aspic with pink peppercorns in an ancient Flemish recipe. Sole is served *à l'Ostendaise*, with lobster sauce, tomato, shrimps and fresh herbs. The countryside, too, provides another rich source of fish – eels. The land is crossed by rivers and broken up by peaceful lakes – a perfect breeding ground for this Flemish speciality.

One of the best ways to eat eel is in a green sauce *(paling in 't groen)*, popular for its subtle flavour and fresh green colour. Every chef has his own recipe, but the sauce invariably includes spinach, sorrel, chervil, parsley, tarragon and lemon balm. The skinned eel is sautéed for a couple of minutes, then white wine, shallots and herbs are added. Buy them, wriggling, at Bruges' medieval fish market.

**LEFT:** a shrimp classic: *tomates aux crevettes grises.*
**ABOVE:** seafood stall by the harbour in Ostend.
**RIGHT:** the ubiquitous *moules frites.*

## Hamming it up

Flanders also produces good ham. Ghent is famous for its own version of Parma ham. Called Ganda – the name Ghent is derived from the Celtic word Ganda, which means confluence – it is massaged with sea salt and left to mature for two months. Wash it down with a glass of local beer in the medieval Groot Vlees Huis (old meat market), with a light smear of eye-watering Tierenteyn mustard, another speciality. Belgium's voracious taste for mustard goes back to the Middle Ages when Ghent was in its spice-trading heyday. The tiny Tierenteyn mustard shop on the Groentenmarkt has been open since 1858 *(see page 154).*

*(see page 154).*

### ANTWERP'S JEWISH CUISINE

Some of Europe's best Jewish food can be found in Antwerp. Jews founded the city's famous diamond industry after settling here in the 13th century. The Jewish district is a short walk from the railway station, and has a population of around 18,000. Skills are handed down from parent to child. You can see it in the locally renowned Kleinblatt bakery, where they make stunning cheesecake, and at Hoffy's (52 Lange Kievit-straat) where Moishe Hoffman does a mean chicken soup with matzo balls. He will also do you a carp's head in aspic, if you ask him nicely. "It's a great old Jewish dish – the cheeks taste particularly good," he enthuses.

Flanders also claims to have invented the quiche. Called *flamiche*, the dish first appeared in Flanders in 1385. The original *flamiche* was made with leftover bread dough and fillings were cheese-based, though there were sweet versions, too. The region is also known for certain vegetables: the famous Brussels sprout is best sautéed in butter with bacon; and white asparagus, called white gold, is grown near Mechelen. Belgian endive (*witloof* in Flemish) is grown from a variety of chicory. It is prized mostly for its bitter, earthy flavour.

## Sweet things

Belgium makes some of the best chocolate in the world, and its *chocolatiers* are revered by Belgians and foreigners alike. The industry took off in the 1880s, helped by the acquisition of Congo, which opened up access to Africa's cocoa fields. Belgium's thing is praline – beautifully sculpted chocolate shells concealing gorgeous fillings.

Every Belgian has an opinion about whose chocolate is the best, and every town has at least one shop that sells them. In Bruges, head to Galler, just off the main square. In Ghent, try Luc van Hoorebeke, just behind the cathedral. Luc makes some of Flanders finest chocolates. You can watch him at work via a glass floor through to his kitchen. In Antwerp, stop for a few diamond-shaped pralines at Burie (Korte Gasthuisstraat). Lieven Burie's window displays are famous throughout the city and will often reflect local political spats.

Flanders has another claim to fame. The man who invented the ice-cream cone lived in Blankenberge. One day, in the 1920s, he was making a pancake when it curled up at the edges. So he rolled it up into a cone shape and filled it with ice cream. *Speculoos* are another classic – buttery biscuits with a sprinkling of cinnamon and cloves. And waffles have played a big part in the Belgian diet for centuries. There are hundreds of different recipes, varying from a rustic cake to delicate *gaufrettes* (tiny, wafer-thin waffle biscuits). They are eaten with butter, jam or honey, cream and fruit, but are at their best with vanilla ice cream, strawberries and cream. ❏

**LEFT:** two Flemish specialities in one: chocolate mussels at the Burie shop in Antwerp.

# Belgian Beer

**B**elgium is, of course, famous for its beer. No other country comes close to producing as many different types. There are around 120 breweries in the country, producing 500 beers, in a dozen major styles, with at least 50 sub-categories. And all cafés and restaurants in Belgium stock at least 10 different brews, so it is worth mugging up before you visit. Beer tourism is on the rise in Belgium. Once keen to keep people away, thinking that they would be put off when they saw how beers were actually made, and wanting to keep their ingredients a closely guarded secret, breweries are now throwing open their doors to visitors, and offering varying levels of facilities.

For some of them, it is a chance for a spot of positive public relations, for others, merely a way of shifting more beer. Some offer regular tours; others are open to tour groups only (ask the local tourist office for details). If you cannot get to see round a brewery, the next best thing is a visit to what is called the brewery tap, which could be a café, or a simple tasting room.

In Antwerp, head to the Brouwerij Duvel Moortgat (www.duvel.be), a large producer turning out consistently good beers, and still partly family-owned. Their top brew is Duvel (Dutch for devil), the first strong blond-style beer in Belgium, created in 1923. In Bruges, you will find De Halve Maan (www.halvemaan.be), makers of the Straffe Hendrik (Strong Henry) beer. They offer good guided tours around the modern brewery and the museum, and there are four dining rooms, where beer is an accompaniment to regional dishes. You also get great views of the city from the top of the building *(see page 85)*.

There are many more breweries to visit around the country. The swankiest, though, is Brouwerij Rodenbach in Roeselare, with the world's largest collection of beer ripening oak casks (www.rodenbach.be). And if

Belgium is the world's greatest producer of beer, then Leuven is Belgium's beer capital. The Flemish city is home to the brewing megalith Interbrew, the world's second-largest brewery. Yes, this is Stella Artois territory (and Hoegaarden and Leffe, plus all the other beers it brews), and its history is intertwined with the town.

Not only does no other country produce so many different styles of beer, but nowhere else produces brews that are so complex in character, from the spontaneously fermenting *lambics* to the beers brewed by Trappist monks. And no other country has beers that are quite so food-friendly – it

even has a strong tradition of cooking with beer. Belgium brewers have played around with herbs, spices, berries and fruits to flavour their beers since the Middle Ages, and the same imaginative approach is applied to cooking with the various brews, experimenting with the ways in which the subtle bitterness of beer adds to a dish.

An increasing number of the country's top chefs are developing this particular style of cooking in ever more sophisticated ways, which applies as much to the ingredients they are choosing to work with, as to the delicate art of pairing beer with food. Go and discover it for yourself. ❑

**RIGHT:** there is a strict protocol about serving beer in the correct glass.

# GENEVER, THE NATIONAL SPIRIT

**Genever is Belgian gin, the flavoured national spirit, and is traditionally accompanied by dried green herring**

At the beginning of the 19th century there was a brewery and a distillery in every Belgium town. Today however, there are only a handful of distilleries left in the country.

Genever was once derided as hooch for the working class, but Belgian distillers now produce genevers of exceptional quality. Its popularity among an older crowd has never diminished, and distilleries are now introducing lighter styles in a bid to tempt younger drinkers.

Genever was invented in the Low Countries around 1580, when a juniper-flavoured spirit was discovered by British troops fighting against the Spanish in the Dutch War of Independence. They knocked it back gratefully to give them what became known as "Dutch courage".

Rotterdam, which had an abundance of spices from the Dutch colonies in the East Indies, became the centre of genever distilling, while Belgium developed its own, similar style. Two world wars had a hard effect on production, with the occupying Germans stripping the distilleries of their copper stills to use for shell casings.

Genever is made by distilling an unfiltered and fermented mash of malted grains – mainly barley – and flavouring it with aromatics such as juniper berries, caraway seeds or fennel. It is the way distillers handle their flavouring ingredients that gives genever its distinctive style. The barley malt gives traditional genever more body and grain flavour than English-style gin, which uses neutral spirits and was developed after 17th-century Flemish distillers began trading in London.

There are three types of genever: Oude, the old, straw-coloured, pungently sweet style; Jonge, a newer style which tastes cleaner and more delicate; and Korenwijn, which is cask-aged with a high percentage of malted spirit.

**ABOVE AND BELOW:** these publicity posters, both designed in the 1920s, the top one for the Neefs distillery in Antwerp and the one below for the Bekaert distillery in Sint-Amandsberg, show that genever was enjoyed by both the working and the upper classes.

## HOW AND WHERE TO DRINK GENEVER

**How do you drink genever?** It is usually sold in a cylindrical stoneware crock and served straight up and chilled. To drink it, lean forward at the bar at a right angle and sip from that position. Once you have drunk the meniscus, you can pick up the glass and down the rest. The traditional accompaniment is dried green herring, although enthusiasts like Ronald Ferket *(see below)* have come up with a range of complementary dishes.

**TOP:** copper alembics to make genever at the Neefs distillery in Antwerp (early 20th century). **ABOVE:** female workers labelling genever bottles at the De Beukelaer in Antwerp in the early 20th century. **RIGHT:** how to drink genever, here in Ghent's 't Dreupelkot. **BELOW:** spoilt for choice: impressive genever display at De Vagant bar and restaurant in Antwerp.

**Where to try genever?** In Bruges, go to Het Dreupelhuisje (9 Kemelstraat, tel: 050-34 24 21), which has more than 100 types of genever on offer.

In Ghent, make a beeline for Pol Rysenaer's tiny bar at the end of an alley off the market square ('t Dreupelkot, 12 Groentenmarkt, tel: 09-244 21 20), which has been here for at least 20 years. Most of the town manages to stop by before the week is out and Pol knows what each of his regulars likes.

In Antwerp, head to the atmospheric De Vagant (25 Reyndersstraat, tel: 032-33 15 38), where the genever-expert owner Ronald Ferket has at least 200 different varieties. De Vagant even cooks with it and the first-floor restaurant offers genever-boosted Flemish staples and a genever-matching menu.

If you are really keen, visit the National Genever Museum in Hasselt, capital of Limburg province (19 Witte Nonnenstraat, tel: 011-23 98 60).

# BRUGES

A detailed guide to the city with the
principal sites clearly cross-referenced
by number to the maps

The medieval town of Bruges (Brugge to its inhabitants) is one of the most romantic destinations in Europe, a small jewel of misty canals, world-class art galleries, Gothic architecture and whitewashed almshouses. From the vertiginous belfry, viewed from the Roezenhoed-kaai, to the calm of Sint-Anna, it is a city of seduction and infinite surprises.

Bruges pulled itself out of the flood plains of Flanders to gain fame and fortune a millennia ago, driven by powerful cloth-trade corporations and guided by the ambitious counts of Flanders, who played a strategic game between the royal houses of England and France. A tidal wave in the 12th century widened the route to the sea, and Bruges became the most vibrant member of the Hanseatic League, a trading centre for amber, fur, oranges and wine. A fierce piety was inspired by the Relic of the Holy Blood, religious communities mushroomed and churches grew rich with the gifts of foreign merchants. The city's wealth reached its apex during the Burgundian rule, a golden age that started in 1369, attracting artists whose works launched a new era in painting, and putting on opulent festivities that are recreated in pageants and processions today.

When the estuary silted up and the dukes of Burgundy left, Bruges was beset by plague, poverty and famine, and eked out a living making lace. Then, in 1815, Britons returning from Waterloo chanced across the enchanting town preserved as if in aspic. A great regeneration effort was launched, Gothic buildings were repaired – which has led to the rather unfair jibe that Bruges is a "fake" medieval city – and the tourist era was launched.

Now the town centre is a pocket-sized museum piece, peopled by camera-wielding visitors. It is a clean, affluent place that seems innocent in comparison with the lively student centres of Ghent and Antwerp, but Bruges is not crippled by its past. The medieval street map may still be largely intact, with evocative names like Speelmansrei (Minstrels' Quay), Heilige Geeststraat (Holy Ghost Street) and Wijngaardplein (Vineyard Square), but with the inauguration of the striking new Concertgebouw, Bruges is back on the cultural map for a new generation. ❏

---

**PRECEDING PAGES:** the Bruges and Flemish flags floating high on the Markt square; daffodils carpet the grass at the Beguinage. **LEFT:** the picturesque Meebrug.

# THE CENTRE

Start your visit of Bruges in the busy, cobbled Markt then move on to the Burg, the second historic square. A tour of the centre takes in most of the famous landmarks, from the belfry to the town hall, from the Basilica of the Holy Blood to St Saviour's Cathedral

The energy of Bruges pulsates from its two central squares, the Markt and the Burg, the historic heart of the city's dual strengths: trade and the nobility.

The bustling **Markt ❶** has been the hub of daily life in Bruges for over 1,000 years, having served as a marketplace since 958. It is still the focal point of commercial activity, at the junction of many of Bruges' liveliest thoroughfares, and hosts markets, festivities and street entertainment. Its days as a car park have thankfully now ended, but buses and cyclists rattle across the cobbles, and horse-drawn carriage tours depart from here.

## The Belfry

Dominating the Markt, and the earshot of anyone within several blocks' distance, is the **Halletoren** or **Belfort ❷** (belfry; Tues–Sun 9.30am–5pm). The vertiginous 83-metre (272-ft) tower was built of bricks between 1280 and 1350 after its wooden predecessor had been destroyed by fire. The upper section, an octagonal lantern tower, was added in 1486, and leans very slightly to the south-east. A wooden spire that originally topped the tower was destroyed twice – once by lightning in the 15th century, then in the 18th century by fire.

Those who brave the 366-step climb are transported to a fantastic lookout post among the bells with an unobstructed view of the compact city, reduced to a toy town below. On the first level above the ticket office is the old treasury, a brick-vaulted room with deep alcoves shielded by intricate wrought-iron grilles, made to safeguard the city's irreplaceable documents: magistrates' papers, official seals and money. Each grille contains nine locks, for which the burgomaster

Map on page 67

**LEFT:** the red rooftops of Bruges viewed from the belfry.
**BELOW:** a horse-drawn tour of the Markt.

and the eight trade guilds' leaders held one key each, so the doors could only be opened with the agreement of them all. Laws and proclamations were read out from the balcony overlooking the Markt.

On the upper floors, as the stone steps give way to a wooden spiral with rope handrail, is the 6-tonne great bell, and at the top the marvellous 47-piece carillon (made in 1478 by Georges Dumery), which plays a different piece of music every quarter-hour. The bells are controlled either manually by the city bell-ringer, who sits in a room just below and gives regular concerts; or, more commonly, by a rotating metal drum in the room below.

The 360-degree view from the tower more than compensates for the climb. To the north, the wide canal marked by a string of modern wind turbines is the contemporary link to the sea and Zeebrugge, whose industrial outline is faintly visible on the horizon. The four wooden windmills on the former ramparts at the extremity of the Sint-Anna District are to the north-

**TIP**

The city tour bus departs from the Markt every hour. Tickets can be purchased on board the bus.

east. The most northerly of these is near the Dampoort, where cargoes entered Bruges in medieval times from Damme. To the southwest the red-brick Concertgebouw crouches crablike behind the imposing silhouette of Sint-Salvator's Cathedral. On a clear day you can see as far as Ostend, 22 km (13 miles) away, one of the towns whose names are engraved in the window ledges.

## Back at ground level

Forming a grand courtyard at the foot of the tower, the **Hallen** ❸ has been a commercial centre since the 13th century, and is now used for exhibitions and cultural events. The shops around the outside were added at a later date. In the summertime, benches are provided in the courtyard for audiences of the regular carillon concerts from the belfry.

Since 1896, traders have been permitted to run two stands on the Markt in front of the belfry selling Belgian chips. Business at these *fretkot* shows no signs of flagging, thanks to queues of hungry tourists. Mayonnnaise is the authentic topping for *frieten*, but there are plenty of other choices.

To the east of the Markt stands the **Provinciaal Hof** ❹, built in 1887–92 in extravagant neo-Gothic Burgundian style as the seat of the government of West Flanders. The red-brick end is the main post office, which occupies the site of the old Waterhalle or Lakenhalle, the vast medieval cloth hall which straddled the canal that passed beneath the building. Goods brought from ships docked in the city's outer ports would enter the building on flat-bottomed boats to be unloaded onto a covered quay.

The **statue** in the centre of the Markt commemorates Jan Breydel and Pieter De Coninck, two heroes of the Flemish rebellion against the French at the Battle of the Golden

**BELOW:** the neo-Gothic Provinciaal Hof.

Spurs in Kortrijk in 1302. Erected in 1887, it was inspired by the story of the battle in Hendrik Conscience's historical novel *The Lion of Flanders* (1838). Some believe the statue ignores a third important figure in the emancipation of Bruges: Jan Heem, the fuller or cloth improver, who became mayor of the city after the rebellion. Heem continued to fight alongside De Coninck, a weaver, in the violent social revolution lasting from 1323–28, which was suppressed at the Battle of Kassel. Breydel, a butcher who was renowned for his brutality, did not fight so consistently, and also profited from the troubles by selling food, horses and weapons to the Flemish fighters. History has honoured Breydel, but it was Heem, historians argue, who was the truly impassioned rebel.

The smaller gabled houses located on the north side of the square were occupied in the 17th century by trade corporations and fishmongers, whose market was held here until 1745 (notice the golden mermaid on one gable).

## Ancient houses

Two of the oldest houses in town stand on either corner of Sint-Amandsstraat on the Markt. On the left is the **Boechoute ❺**, dating from the late 15th century, with a weathervane from 1676. The **Craenenburg Café ❻** on the opposite corner, with its tiny turret on one corner and astrolabe on the other, is where the angry burghers of Bruges held Maximilian of Austria hostage in 1488, when he threatened to remove their privileges. Held behind a barred window in an upper room, he was forced to listen to the torture of his advisers, including Pieter Lanchals, his right-hand man and treasurer. Lanchals tried to mediate with the insurgents and was executed for his pains on the square below

*A heroic statue of Jan Breydel and Pieter De Coninck stands at the centre of the Markt.*

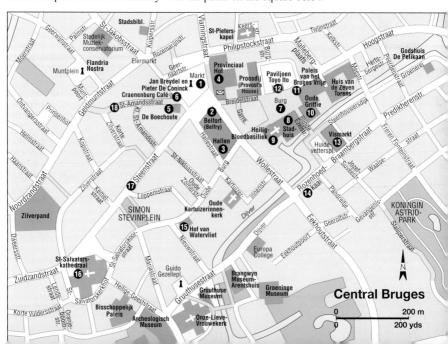

**Central Bruges**

Maximilian's window. The emperor never forgave the city for this cruel episode, and punished its population by shifting his attention to Antwerp, which contributed significantly to the decline of Bruges.

The upper floors of both these houses were popular with medieval visitors to Bruges, as they afforded good views of the jousting tournaments and processions that took place on the Markt. The square is tame by comparison today, but a café terrace makes an ideal vantage point to observe the endless activity – although you are advised not to eat here, as these places are (understandably) tourist-oriented and the food is mediocre.

### The Burg and the Stadhuis

Beside the post office runs the well-worn Breidelstraat (make sure not to trip over a busker), via which you reach the **Burg ❼**, the historic powerhouse of Bruges, which is mentioned in records dating as far back as the 9th century. Its name comes from the fortress that was built here in 865 by Baldwin Iron Arm, the first Count of Flanders, as a defence against Norman invasion.

On your left as you reach the square, topped with gold braziers and the figure of Justice holding her golden scales, is the former **Proosdij** (provost's residence; 1662). On the other side of its courtyard stands the residence of the governor, who represented the king in the province of West Flanders.

The Burg's centrepiece, though, is the **Stadhuis ❽** (town hall), a jewel of Gothic architecture begun in 1376 on the site of the former county prison and completed in 1421. It is the oldest civic building in Flanders and was widely copied – most notably in Brussels, Leuven and Oudenaarde. The counts of Flanders would appear on the balcony and pledge to respect the town's rights and privileges. Unlike today's tastefully scrubbed façade, the original would have been highly colourful, painted for protection against the elements. Beneath the windows are the coats of arms of towns that came under the jurisdiction of Bruges until 1795 – although

*Chips are a delicious Belgian invention.*

**BELOW:** tourists gather on the Burg.

their design was based on an inaccurate document, so they are not all correct. The 34 figures of saints, prophets and noblemen and women that decorate the niches are copies of the originals, which were removed by the Jacobins and their Flemish sympathisers, then destroyed on the Markt. They represent 34 important figures in the history of Flanders. Note the gold crowns atop the twisted chimney stacks. These were a gift from the king of France, who so approved of the wise aldermen of Bruges that he wanted to crown their breath as it left the chamber.

The building's highly decorated first-floor **Gothic Hall** (Tues–Sun 9.30am–5pm; admission charge), the only part of the building open to visitors, incorporates a fine rib-vaulted ceiling (renovated in the late 19th century), whose rib junctions are decorated with keystones depicting biblical scenes. The vaults rest on original stone consoles portraying the months of the year in scenes of rural life, and the four elements, a common Renaissance theme. The inscriptions beneath each of these

consoles was added at the same time as the murals, in the late 19th century, and contain errors in the old Flemish. The fireplace dates from the same period. In the adjoining **Maritime Chamber**, interesting old maps, engravings and paintings reveal the evolution of the region's geography and the city's layout.

## Basilica of the Holy Blood

The most visited monument on the square – and possibly in the whole of Bruges – is the **Heilig Bloed-basiliek ❾** (Basilica of the Holy Blood; summer daily 9.30am–noon, 2–6pm; winter 10am–noon, 2–4pm except Wed pm; free), which has been a place of pilgrimage for centuries, as it houses a relic that is said to be Christ's blood, brought from the Holy Land in the 12th century by Thierry of Alsace, Count of Flanders.

Tucked in the corner of the square, the highly decorative Renaissance façade conceals a much older edifice, composed of two chapels separated by a striking staircase. The lower chapel, dedicated to St Basil (1139) is a serene Romanesque place

Map on page 67

**TIP**

The old tourist office on the Burg is now closed. All information, reservations and ticketing is now at In & Uit at 34 't Zand, on the ground floor of the new Concertgebouw building.

**LEFT:** the superb vaulted oak ceiling of the Gothic Hall.
**BELOW:** the altar inside the Basilica of the Holy Blood.

**BELOW:** Procession of the Holy Blood. **RIGHT:** the ornate Oude Griffie.

of prayer with immense pillars and little ornament. A wooden virgin and child, venerated since the 14th century, is in the right nave, while the baptismal scene carved in Tournai stone on the tympanum dates from around 1150. The wooden trap door in the floor led to the tomb of 14th-century master stonemason Jan van Oudenaerde. The downstairs oratory was reserved for lowly worshippers, while the elite prayed in a chapel above, linked to the count's apartments in a palace called the Steen.

Nothing remains of the original upper chapel, as it was rebuilt in 1523, and again after the French Revolution, when its medieval stained-glass windows were sold (they are now in London's Victoria & Albert Museum). The second refit, carried out at Napoleon's request and taking nearly a century to complete, drew on the skills of master craftsmen and resulted in a harmonious neo-Gothic masterpiece, with an eye-catching, globe-shaped pulpit. The relic is presented for veneration on Friday in the right-hand nave, when a priest invites visitors to mount the dais, touch the ancient crystal cylinder containing the relic, say a prayer and make a donation.

The holy blood relic is the focus of an elaborate, costumed procession, the **Heilig Bloed Processie**, through the streets each Ascension Day. The highlight of the city's folkloric calendar, it is organised by the Noble Brotherhood of the Holy Blood, an order founded around 1400 to safeguard the relic and further its renovation (*see margin box*).

The single-roomed basilica **museum** (admission charge) contains items relating to the relic and the basilica, a number of which are worthy of attention, such as a precious reliquary (made by Jan Crabbe in 1617) in gold, silver and enamel, and a small silver reliquary (1612) which was a gift from Archduke Albert and Infanta Isabella. A Pieter Pourbus painting dated 1556 depicts the 31 members of the Noble Brotherhood of the Holy Blood, and a curious 15th-century manuscript called the *Book of Garments* shows the robes worn by the brotherhood, which is still a source of inspiration

for the annual procession. A tiny gold crown with precious stones belonging to Mary of Burgundy looks surprisingly crude in manufacture; and there's a ripped-open lead box in which the relic was hidden during the iconoclasm (in 1578, when for six years Bruges became a Protestant city and the basilica a public library) and again during the French Revolution (1797).

### Law and liberty

The building bridging Blinde Ezelstraat (Blind Donkey Street), to the left of the Stadhuis, is the old county records office, the **Oude Griffie** ❿ (occupied by law courts and not open to the public). Its 15th-century bas-relief depicts the ancient Persian legend of a king having a corrupt judge skinned alive, which features in a painting by Gerard David (in the Groeninge Museum), a popular cautionary tale in medieval times. The fussy-looking façade would have been even more colourful in the past, and is a prime example of 16th-century Flemish Renaissance.

At the east side of the Burg, the **Paleis van het Brugse Vrije** ⓫ (Liberty of Bruges Palace) was built in the 18th century on the site of a 1520s original, of which a small part has survived and is visible from the canal at the rear. Formerly the Palace of Justice, and now the town archive, it was the seat of an autonomous legal and administrative authority, the Brugse Vrije (created in 1121) which was within the County of Flanders, but did not include the city of Bruges.

The **Museum van het Brugse Vrije** (Tues–Sat 9.30am–12.30pm, 1.30–5pm; admission charge) within the palace, entered at the corner of the Burg, contains the assizes court and the fine **Renaissancezaal**. This aldermen's chamber is worth a visit for its ornate marble, oak and alabaster chimneypiece, made in 1528–31 in honour of Emperor

Charles V, who had finally freed Bruges from the yoke of feudal allegiance to France. The over-the-top oak carving depicts life-size figures of Charles and his heritage: Austrian-Burgundian grandparents on the left; Spanish on the right; with his parents featured in medallions. Below, the alabaster relief depicts four scenes from the story of Susanna and the Elders narrated in the Old Testament Book of Daniel, in which the young virgin is defamed by two lustful old judges – a cautionary tale to encourage aldermen to dispense justice equitably. Note the worked brass handles dangling from the fireplace; these were used by the regional delegates to the Brugse Vrije – rural nobles – who stood by the fire to dry their boots.

### Linking the centuries

The floating steel-and-glass covered walkway at the top of the Burg is the **Paviljoen Toyo Ito** ⓬, designed by the eponymous Japanese architect to celebrate Bruges' year as Capital of Culture in 2002. The modern construction connects the Burg of today

Map on page 67

*Emperor Charles V carved in oak in the Renaissancezaal of the Liberty of Bruges Palace.*

**BELOW:** the sleek Toyo Ito pavilion.

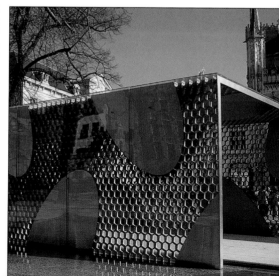

**TIP**

A boat tour of Bruges (10am–6pm daily in summer; weekends and holidays in winter, except Jan and Feb) offers the chance to get a swan's-eye view of the city. There are five embarkation jetties around the centre, and the tours are run in several languages. Longer boat trips are available to Damme, Beernem and Ostend.

**BELOW:** view from Rozenhoedkaai.

with its millennium-long history of fine architecture. Original visual snapshots of the Burg are possible from within the pavilion through the honeycomb forms of its structure.

It stands near the spot occupied by the city's former fortified cathedral, St Donatian's, until it was destroyed in 1799. It was here that Charles the Good was assassinated in 1127 by a group of conspirators who wanted to get their hands on the church treasures. They had to barricade themselves in the stronghold when a hungry mob came to join the plunder, but they eventually managed to escape with the treasures, which were never heard of again. Jan van Eyck was buried here in 1441 (his *Madonna van der Paele* hung in the church and was admired by Sir Joshua Reynolds on his visit in 1776). Philip the Good was laid to rest here, too, in 1467, while his great-grandson Philip the Handsome was baptised here in 1478.

St Donatian's was an important cultural institution in medieval times, with a great library, a music school and a scriptorium, where illuminated manuscripts were produced. Bookshops were clustered around the cathedral and attracted pioneers of the trade: William Caxton produced the first printed book in the English language in Bruges in 1474, a *Recuyell of the Histories of Troy*, ordered by Margaret of York, Duchess of Burgundy, before he left to introduce printing in England.

### Exploring city history

Just off the Burg in Hoogstraat (No. 6) was where Charles II of England held court when he was ejected by Cromwell (1656–58). Part of the house and its neighbour used to form the stupendous Huis van de Zeven Torens (Seven Towers House), named after the turrets that featured on a map of the city in 1562. Its façade retains elements of the original construction, *c.*1320, which should survive the ongoing conversion into loft apartments.

Continue down Hoogstraat, turning right after the Het Oud Huis de Peellaert hotel on Peerdenstraat. This leads to the Peerdenbrug, which gives a great view along the

canal to the tower of Sint-Salvators-kathedraal. This stretch of canal along Groenerei is one of the prettiest in Bruges and you can admire the back gardens of the lucky residents who live alongside it. Cross the bridge (notice the quaint De Pelikaan almshouses aligned just along Groenerei to the left before the bend in the canal, *see page 82*) then turn right to reach the semi-covered **Vismarkt** ⓭ (fish market), whose stone slabs were set up in 1822 and where each morning from Tuesday to Saturday the day's fresh catch from the North Sea is sold. Look back across the canal to admire the rear of the Stadhuis and the Brugse Vrije.

Alongside the canal beside a boat-tour jetty is the former Fishmongers' Corporation House, identifiable by the coat of arms with two gilded fish above its door. To the left, enter the attractive, semi-enclosed Tanners' Square: **Huidevettersplein**, with the Huidvettershuis (Tanners' House), dating from 1523. A right turn at the opposite end of the square brings you to **Rozenhoedkaai** ⓮ (Rosary

Quay), which offers the picture-postcard view of Bruges, with the belfry rising above the canal and the rooftops. This is where the maudlin protagonist of Georges Rodenbach's novel *Bruges-la-Morte* lived: "He would spend the whole day in his room, a vast retreat on the first floor whose windows looked out onto the Quai du Rosaire, along which the façade of his house stretched, mirrored in the canal." The location also inspired the 1906 poem *Quai du Rosaire* by Rainer Maria Rilke, a Rodenbach admirer.

Turn right across the canal into Wollestraat (belfry tower straight ahead), and then left into the L-shaped Kartuizerinnenstraat, where the half-buried cannon on the corner probably dates from the siege of Bruges by the Count of Nassau. It sits outside the Grote Mortier house (1634), which has a tiny detailed bas-relief above its windows. The street is named after the Carthusian convent whose occupants moved into the city for protection during the religious troubles of the Reformation in 1578. When the order was

*The fish market is one of the few notable structures bequeathed by the period of Dutch rule (1815–30).*

**LEFT:** the novelist Georges Rodenbach.

## Georges Rodenbach and *Bruges-la-Morte*

Georges Rodenbach (1855–98) never lived in Bruges but was to immortalise the city in his 1892 novel *Bruges-la-Morte*. It tells the story of widower Hugues Viane, who has retreated to Bruges to grieve for his young wife in a city chosen for its silence, monotony and melancholy. The town reflects his state of mind and recalls his loss in every canal reflection and curl of mist. In his foreword, Rodenbach described the town as an "essential character, associated with states of mind, counselling, dissuading, inducing the hero to act". One day, while out walking, Viane glimpses a young woman who appears the exact double of his wife, and embarks on a fateful attempt to bring her memory back to life. The book provoked a "cult of Bruges" among Symbolist artists and poets – Mallarmé, Rodin and Proust were fans – and inspired Rainer Maria Rilke, Thomas Mann *(Death in Venice)*, Korngold's opera *Die tote Stadt* (1920) and, it has been claimed, Hitchcock's *Vertigo*. But many people were furious at the negative depiction of their city and when Rodenbach died of appendicitis at the age of 43, Catholic forces blocked a request for a monument in his honour.

Map on page 67

*The marriage of Charles the Bold and Margaret of York in 1468 is re-enacted every five years in sumptuous style in the Gouden Boom Pageant, named after the prize awarded to the winner of the tournament at the wedding. The performance evokes the lives of the counts of Flanders and dukes of Burgundy, followed by a dance and a recreation of the reception.*

**BELOW:** inside
St Saviour's Cathedral.

dissolved in 1783 the Sisters of Charity from Ghent moved in. Part of the old abbey at the bend in the street is occupied by the social services, while the church (1716) serves as a military chapel – the façade bears plaques commemorating *Bruggelingen* who lost their lives in the two world wars.

## Along Oude Burg

The triumphal arch at the end of the street leads into Oude Burg, where the first two 16th-century houses on the left also belonged to the convent. Turn left and go to the second street on the right, a dead-end named Oude Zomerstraat with a lovely narrow Gothic façade at the end dating from around 1500. Further along Oude Burg, at No. 24, is a decorative façade dating from 1564 – note the detail in the upper-floor recesses. Just opposite is the **Hof van Watervliet ⑮**, the 15th-century residence of humanist Marcus Laurinus, whose prestigious guests included Spain's Juan Luis Vives and Erasmus of Rotterdam, who visited frequently between 1517 and

1521. Erasmus was so enthralled by the erudite company he met in Bruges that he called the city the Athens of the Low Countries. English statesman Sir Thomas More, who started on his political treatise *Utopia* (1515) while staying in Bruges on official business, was another frequent caller. Next door used to be the house of Pieter Lanchals, the unlucky advisor to Maximilan of Austria *(see pages 67–8)*.

Further along, at 33 Oude Burg, admire the exquisit Italian Renaissance façade just before you reach **Simon Stevinplein**, named after Simon Stevin (1548–1620), a physicist and mathematician who invented the sand-yacht. He is honoured by a statue in the centre of the square, which is flanked by café terraces and restaurants.

## Sint-Salvatorskathedraal

Continue past the square to the hulking flank of **Sint-Salvatorskathedraal ⑯** (St Saviour's Cathedral; Sun–Fri 2–5pm; free), whose tower is visible ahead. Turn right to enter the cathedral on Steenstraat. This is Bruges' oldest parish church (12th–15th century), although it only became the cathedral in 1834 after St Donatian's was destroyed. It is an unusual example of Scheldt Gothic architecture, although its 99-metre (325-ft) brick tower is Romanesque. It was begun in the 10th century but only gained its pinnacle nine centuries later.

It is richly decorated inside, with a wealth of painting and tapestries but not a lot of charm. Highlights including a baroque rood-screen topped by a monumental statue of God the Father by Artus Quellin the Younger, and late-Gothic choir stalls with impressive sculpted misericords (1430). Above these hang the coats of arms of the knights of the Golden Fleece, who assembled here for the order's 13th chapter in 1478

to elect a new leader. Their choice, Maximilian of Austria, conferred the title from the House of Burgundy to the Habsburgs. In the ambulatory, the first chapel clockwise contains the reliquary of Charles the Good, Count of Flanders who was killed in St Donatian's in 1127, as well as a macabre memento of his assassination: a floor tile allegedly soaked with his blood and said to provoke miracles when touched. A wooden effigy of the count can be seen in the nave.

The cathedral's **museum** (same hours as church; admission charge) in the right transept contains a number of valuable Flemish Primitives, including Dirk Bouts' 1475 *St Hippolytus Altarpiece* (with a panel by Hugo van der Goes), showing the saint's martyrdom, in which he was pulled limb from limb by four wild horses, plus works by Adriaen Ysenbrandt, Lancelot Blondeel and Pieter Pourbus. The treasury also holds a number of brass tomb plates, reliquaries and liturgical garments, including a piece of a tunic which allegedly belonged to St Bridget of Ireland (d. 523).

## Shops and restaurants

Alongside Sint-Salvators is **Steenstraat ⑰**. It has been a busy commercial artery for centuries and is now home to branches of the same stores that grace every high street in Europe, although some are lucky enough to occupy a building with a beautifully preserved façade. At the opposite end of Simon Stevinplein, across the road at 40 Steenstraat, is the oldest house on the street (dating from 1527) which used to be occupied by the shoemakers' corporation – you will see the stone boot on the façade and the white bear of Bruges at the top of the gable.

Next door was the Louis XIV-style Carpenters' Corporation (1764); while further along, at No. 25, is the Renaissance Masons' House (1621), with gilded ornamentation depicting the tools of sculptors, masons, stonecutters and architects.

Directly across the street from the latter is a tiny alley, the Kleine Sint-Amandsstraat. Turn down here to reach the restaurant hub of **Sint-Amandsplein**, with its 18th-century water pump. A former chapel honouring St Amandus stood here until 1817, and was allegedly founded by the saint in the 8th century when he brought Christianity to the region. **Sint-Amandsstraat ⑱** is an attractive pedestrianised street lined with modest restaurants and tea rooms, perfect for an end-of-day *pannekoek* or *witbier* while you mull over the sights of the neighbourhood. If you have any energy left, have a look at No. 26, where the pinions are decorated with allegories of the days of the week: the god of Mars for Tuesday, Venus for Friday and Saturn for Saturday.

You can rejoin the Markt at the east end of Sint-Amandsstraat, or just wait for the quarter-hour and follow the sound of the bells. ❑

Map on page 67

*Statue outside St-Saviour's Cathedral.*

**BELOW:** café life on Sint-Amandsstraat.

# RESTAURANTS, BARS & CAFÉS

## Restaurants

### Breydel – De Coninck
24 Breidelsstraat.
Tel: 050-33 97 46. Open
L & D Thur–Tues. €€
Unremarkable from
the outside, but those in
the know will tell you that
this comfortable dining
room is *the* place to
eat mussels in Bruges
(when in season; expect
quite a large portion)
and other fresh seafood
dishes, including lobster
and eels. Street-view
tables make it possible
to while away an after-
noon watching the
tourists being trotted
away in horse-drawn
carriages while indulging
in Belgians' preferred
pastime: gastronomic
indulgence.

### Chagall
40 Sint-Amandsstraat. Tel:
050-33 10 78. Open L & D
Mon–Sat, D only Sun. €
Whether you're out for a
few drinks or for a heart-
warming pot of mussels
in cream sauce, you may
have to fight for a table
on this popular bistro's
terrace, which is perfect
for people-watching
on the pedestrianised
Sint-Amandsstraat.
The cosy interior has
open hearth, wooden
beams and stained-
glass windows.

### Chez Olivier
9 Meestraat. Tel: 050-33 36
59. Open L & D Mon–Wed,
Fri–Sat. €€€€
Impeccable all-white
dining room overlooking
the most romantic
stretch of canal in
Bruges. A peaceful
and resolutely cool
upscale choice, set in a
beautiful 16th-century
building with meat-
focused, refined French-
Belgian flavours on
the menu.

### De Stove
4 Kleine Sint-Amandsstraat.
Tel: 050-33 78 35. Open
L & D Fri–Tues. €€€
Family-owned and
operated, De Stove
specialises in Flemish
cuisine with the stress
on salads, fish and
steaks. Mouthwatering
scallops on black pasta
with tomato tapenade,
and sea bream with
couscous, stuffed
aubergine and basil oil
are just some of the
pleasingly original menu
items in this unfussy,
intimate 20-seater set
in an old gabled house.
At the lower end of this
price bracket.

### De Visscherie
8 Vismarkt. Tel: 050-33 02
12. Open L & D Wed–Mon.
€€€€
The subtle flavours of
the sea are cooked to
absolute perfection in
this top-notch address
for fish and seafood,
situated right on the
fish market (Vismarkt).
A formal establishment
where the *maitre d'* will
attend to your every
whim, this is ideal for
a special occasion with
all the frills. A few meat
dishes are also available.

### Erasmus
35 Wollestraat. Tel: 050-33
57 81. Open L & D Fri–Wed.
€€
This simple yet comfort-
able restaurant set in
the eponymous hotel
is a tippler's dream, with
a great choice of beers
to accompany the likes
of crown of lamb with
parsley and mustard,
served with potato and
bacon gratin made with
Bush blond beer. With
a view over the canals,
it is definitely more
tourist-focused than
classy beer-cuisine
joint Den Dyver *(see
page 92),* but a fair bit
cheaper too. The menu
changes monthly.

### Kardinaalshof
14 Sint-Salvatorskerkhof.
Tel: 050-34 16 91. Open
L & D Fri–Tues, D only Thur.
€€€
At Kardinaalshof, the
accent is on comfort,
elegance and fine dining
with an emphasis on
seafood in this smart,
intimate town house
located just behind Sint-
Salvator's cathedral.
The bright upholstery
and fixed monthly menu
(with or without accom-
panying wines) lends an
atmosphere rather like
that of a private dining
room. This restaurant is
not a good choice for
small appetites: count
on five or six courses for
the evening meal, three
plus at lunchtime.

## Patrick Devos
### "De Zilveren Pauw"
41 Zilverstraat. Tel: 050-33
55 66. Open L & D Mon–Fri,
D only Sat. €€€€
Star chef and wine-taster
Devos gives his name
to this lavish temple of
gastronomy in the sump-
tuous "Silver Peacock",
former second residence
of the abbot of Ghent
cathedral. The ornate
13th-century gabled
frontage contrasts
sharply with the opulent
Art Nouveau interior,
the result of a late 19th-
century makeover.
The inventive and elabo-
rate menu using fresh
regional produce is
inspired, and further
enhanced by a selection
of top-class wines.

### 't Lammetje
3 Braambergstraat. Tel:
050-34 30 95. Open L & D
Tues–Sun. €€
Serving exactly what its
name – The Little Lamb –
implies, this snug eaterie
cooks lamb to perfection
and serves it in a cosy
dining room cluttered
with countrified bric-à-
brac; there is an open
hearth in winter. The
speciality is, unsurpris-
ingly, rack of lamb with
a choice of thyme and
honey, pepper or warm
herb-butter sauce, but
other Belgian favourites
such as chicory gratin,
Flemish beef stew,
mussels and steak get
equal billing.

## Bars & Cafés

### Het Brugs Beertje
(5 Kemelstraat) is as
small inside as its
reputation is large,
and has become a beer-
lovers mecca since it
was established some
20 years ago. The beer
menu is arranged
alphabetically to help
you locate your favourite
among the 250 on offer
or, if you cannot decide,
why not try the beer of
the month? A few light
meals are served and
there is a shop where
you can buy the T-shirt.
Open from 4pm.

### Staminee de Garre
(1 De Garre) is a place of
pilgrimage for beer fans,
many of whom struggle
to find the tiny alley it's
located in – more a door
in the wall off Breidel-
straat – or cannot get
a seat once inside (and
standing is not allowed).
Once in, the atmosphere
is friendly, not over
loud, and you will find
non-smoking seating
upstairs. The 130 beers
on offer are served with
cheese; the bar has
its own beer, the super-
strong 10.5 percent
Tripel de Garre.

### Craenenburg (16 Markt)
is probably the best-
known café in Bruges
as it was here that
Maximilian of Austria
was held hostage in
1488 when he tried to

impose heavy taxes in
Bruges, and where his
advisers were tortured.
Thankfully, the days of
fingernail-pulling are long
gone. This traditional
Flemish café, which
occupies a commanding
position on the Markt,
is an endless source
of entertainment.

### Sorbetière De Medici
(9 Geldmuntstraat)
upholds the Burgundian
traditions of fine feasting
in an ice-cream and
sorbet parlour that also
does some seriously
wicked cakes. Pretty
interior on two floors with
a terrace. Closes 7pm.

### Het Dagelijks Brood
(21 Philipstockstraat).
Local branch of the hit
Belgian bakery, which
serves breakfast, brunch
and teas around shared
scrubbed pine tables in
cities across the world.
Wholesome bread, tasty

chocolate spreads and
tarts, and a good variety
of open sandwiches.
Good for a quick bite;
not the best option
for big appetites.

### Kaffee L'aMaRaL (10
Kuipersstraat) is about
as close as Bruges gets
to club culture for a city
devoid of night life and
young people. The DJ
slots in the small venue
off the Eiermarkt bar
circuit are eclectic
enough to satisfy all
tastes in dance music
and draw a friendly crowd
of unpretentious young
things. Opens 9pm.

### PRICE CATEGORIES
Prices for three-course
dinner per person with a
half-bottle of house wine:
€ = under €25
€€ = €25–40
€€€ = €40–60
€€€€ = over €60

**LEFT:** the traditional Flemish brasserie Tom Pouce
occupies a row of gabled houses on the Burg.
**RIGHT:** drinking beer on the Markt.

# SOUTH AND WEST

The areas to the south and west of town contain
two of Bruges' greatest museums – the Groeninge and
the Gruuthuis – as well as the peaceful Begijnhof de
Wijngaard and the city's most famous brewery

**B**ruges is at its most languid and
seductive in the lush south of
the city. The town's wealth
may have been built on trade, but
the district concentrated south and
west of the Dijver feels far removed
from the outside world and its commercial imperatives, and the treasures
concentrated in its museums and
churches seem to stand aloof from the
wealth that brought them into being.

## The Dijver

Start at the Eekhoutbrug bridge on
Wollestraat at the top of the tree-
shaded **Dijver ❶**, with its imperious
statue (1767) of St John of Nepomucene, court priest of King Wenceslas
IV in Prague. John was thrown into
the River Moldau in 1393 after dis-
pleasing the king, and became patron
saint of the drowned. An over-priced
antiques and craft market along the
Dijver animates the waterside in high
season. Among the elegant buildings
on the left is the seat of the **Europa
College**, an influential school for
budding leaders of a united Europe.

## Groeninge Museum

Right next door to the college is the
**Groeninge Museum ❷** (Tues–Sun
9.30am–5pm; admission charge),
world-renowned for its collection of
Flemish Primitives and a treasure
trove of artistic riches. Its collection

spans the artistic development of the
Low Countries over six centuries,
including works by Hieronymous
Bosch, Jan van Eyck, Hans Mem-
ling, Gerard David, René Magritte,
Fernand Khnopff and Paul Delvaux.

Visitors who are limited for time
could restrict their visit to the first
four rooms, which are arranged
chronologically. The informative
audio guide is included in the ticket
price and is well worth following.
Built in 1929 on the site of a former
abbey, and restored in 2002–3, the

Map
on page
80

**LEFT:** the canal frontage
of St John's Hospital.
**BELOW:** the
Groeninge collection.

museum was originally opened to house the works formerly displayed in the Bruges Academy of Fine Arts. Many of the older works date from the Golden Age of Bruges, and were commissioned by the city's wealthy burghers, merchants and clerics, several of whom play support roles in the biblical scenes depicted.

One of the museum's most arresting paintings is Jan van Eyck's *Virgin and Child with Canon Joris van der Paele* (1436), a masterpiece of detail and depth. It is also among the most valuable, being the second-largest surviving work (after *The Adoration of the Mystic Lamb* altarpiece in Ghent's cathedral) by the artist who perfected the technique of oil painting: Van Eyck mixed powder colours, egg white, water and resin to invent a new paint formula that allowed for greater variety of colour and thinner application, a formula that was a fiercely guarded secret among Netherlandish artists. In this paint-

ing, the Virgin and Christ child appear to be welcoming the patron of the work, Canon van der Paele, along with his patron saint, George. The painting's predominant colours – blue, red, gold and white – echo the Bruges coat of arms. Their clarity is achieved through the application of several thin layers of paint.

The *Portrait of Margaretha van Eyck* (1439) shows the artist's wife. Margaretha seems composed and devoid of artifice, except for the fashionable horn style of her hair.

The magnificent *Last Judgement* (*c.* 1450–1516) by Hieronymus Bosch is a fantastical triptych of grotesque and bizarre creatures and scenes, with God delivering his judgement in the central, largest panel, and heaven and hell on either side. The work epitomises Bosch's moralism and satire on stupidity and evil, a pessimistic vision probably inspired by the economic malaise that marked the end of the Middle Ages.

*The Groeninge houses a superb collection of works by the so-called Flemish Primitives.*

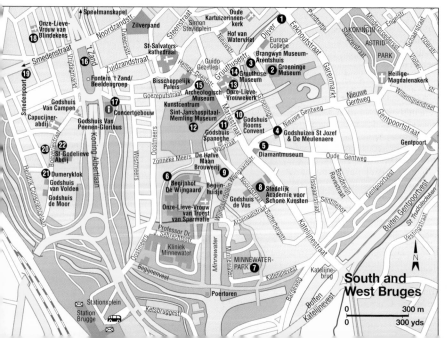

**South and West Bruges**

0          300 m

0          300 yds

*The Triptych of Willem Moreel* (1484) by Hans Memling was the first whole-family portrait in the Low Countries. The sitters are depicted on the side panels, kneeling piously with their children, all dressed in the high fashion of the day. Willem Moreel was a prominent local politician who commissioned the painting as an altarpiece for Sint-Jakobs church, where they wanted to be buried. The main panel shows St Christopher, the saint who protects against sudden death, transporting the Christ child across a river, flanked by saints whose names and legends echo the names of the donors.

Gerard David's *The Judgement of Cambyses* (1498) is a graphic and gruesome morality tale based on a Persian legend. It depicts, in large-scale close-up, the fate of the corrupt judge Sisamnes, as he is flayed alive. Painted to hang in Bruges Town Hall council chamber, it was intended to remind city aldermen – who also held a judicial role – of their duty of impartiality. David was the last of the great Flemish Primitives, and his work contains a number of Renaissance features, such as the putti.

The theme of corrupt judges reappears in *The Last Judgement* (1525) by Renaissance master Jan Provoost. Note in the bottom right corner the procession of damned individuals entering hell, most of whom are clergymen; the scene was over-painted in 1550 when Charles V issued a decree forbidding disreputable images of women and churchmen. The original was only revealed in 1965.

Although he inherited much from the Flemish Primitives, Pieter Pourbus (1524–84) was well imbued with the spirit of the Renaissance. His own *Last Judgement* (1551) is clearly influenced by similarly themed works by Jan Provoost and Michelangelo, who had completed the Sistine Chapel 10 years earlier.

Other unmissables include the beguiling Symbolist works of Fernand Khnopff (1858–1921), who grew up in Bruges, and those of his contemporary William Degouve de Nuncques (1867–1935), which are potent with psychological depth. A more down-to-earth style was chosen by the post-World War I Flemish Expressionists, Constant Permeke, Gustave De Smet, Jan Brusselmans and Gustave van de Woestyne, whose monumental *Last Supper* depicts the watchfulness of Christ. The Expressionists influenced Surrealist Paul Delvaux, whose *Serenity* was commissioned for the Groeninge in 1970.

On the first floor of the 18th-century **Arentshuis** at 16 Dijver is the **Brangwyn Museum ❸** (Tues–Sun 9.30am–5pm; admission charge), which is used as an additional exhibition space for the Groeninge. On display are works on industrial life, drawings, etchings and decorative objects made by Anglo-Belgian artist Frank Brangwyn (1867–1956). Best known as a book illustrator, Brangwyn was born in Bruges and donated most of his work to the city in 1936.

Map on page 80

*The term "Flemish Primitives" was coined in 1902 for an exhibition in Bruges of the school of 15th-century painting that flourished in the southern Netherlands, notably in Bruges, Ghent, Tournai, Brussels, Leuven and 's-Hertogenbosch. It was called "primitive" as it did not apply the principles of linear perspective.*

## Hans Memling

**H**ans Memling (c.1440–94) was born in Seligenstadt, near Frankfurt, and is thought to have arrived in Bruges at the age of 25, after working for a time in the Brussels studio of Roger van der Weyden. Inspired by his master, he developed a style of his own that was to be influential and enduring: it evokes the mystic, Christian spirit of the late Middle Ages and symbolises the prosperity of Bruges in the Burgundian era, which ended during his lifetime. Little is known of his origins, but an old story that he came to Bruges as a soldier wounded in the battle of Nancy, learned to paint while being tended in Sint-Jan's Hospital and donated paintings to his nurses, is widely agreed to be nonsense. Records show that within 15 years of living in Bruges, Memling, whose work found favour with the city's bourgeoisie, foreign elite and clergy, had become one of the city's richest men, owning several houses and employing a number of assistants. He died in the city in 1494 and is buried in Sint-Gillis Church, not far from Sint-Jorisstraat, where he lived with his wife and three daughters. Some of his greatest works have remained in Bruges: in the Memling Museum within the Sint-Janshospitaal chapel, and in the Groeninge Museum.

**TIP**

*Godshuizen* may be entered when the main gate is open; visitors are asked to enjoy the garden in silence.

## Godshuizen

Groeninge leads away from Dijver to peaceful and picturesque backstreets. Round two sharp corners at a crossroads, across from the end of Groeninge on Nieuwe Gentweg, are two pretty almshouses, 17th-century **Godshuizen St Jozef** and **De Meulenaere ❹**, built around a charming courtyard garden with a tiny chapel and water pump.

*Godshuizen* are typical Flemish almshouses, built from the 14th century onwards by wealthy families for the poor, sick or elderly, and by trade organisations for their retired members or widows. They comprised rows of tiny whitewashed houses, plus a chapel, shared privy and a garden, a patch of which was allotted to each house. They were frequently named after their benefactor. Bruges retains 46 *godshuizen*, most still used for their original purpose, and are allocated to the elderly by the town's social services department. The oldest is the 1330 "Rooms Convent" on Katelijnestraat *(see page 85)*. The prettiest, besides these in Nieuwe Gentweg, are the

Godshuizen Sint-Josse (Ezelstraat), De Vos (Noordstraat), De Pelikaan (Groenerei) and Zorghe, Paruitte and Schippers (Stijn Streuvelstraat), plus one between Kreupelenstraat and Kammakerstraat, which is reserved for the blind.

Follow Nieuwe Gentweg to the Katelijnestraat crossroads. To the left, a restored Gothic building is home to the **Diamantmuseum ❺** (daily 10.30am–5.30pm; admission charge), which recounts the story of diamond-cutting, displays antique jewels and evokes a glittering trade established in Bruges in the Burgundian era, but more commonly associated today with Antwerp.

Turn left down Katelijnestraat then right onto bustling Wijngaardstraat, where most facades conceal a tearoom, restaurant or souvenir shop. At the end of the street is a fountain where carriage drivers bring their nags for a hard-earned drink. The neo-Gothic building on the left was built in 1857 for the Sisters of Charity of St Vincent de Paul.

## Begijnhof de Wijngaard

**Wijngaarsplein**, opposite, was once a vineyard where grapes were grown for making vinegar. Turn right before the green to cross the arched Begijnhofbrug. Bunches of grapes on the bridge handrail and above the entrance recall the former setting of the **Begijnhof De Wijngaard ❻** (Vineyard Beguinage; daily 6.30am–6.30pm; free), one of Bruges' best-loved attractions. Founded in 1215 (the current doorway dates from 1776), the square of neat, whitewashed houses around a lawn was inhabited by Beguines – women who opted for a pious, contemplative life without taking holy vows *(see page 84)*. At its height, in the 17th century, the beguinage stretched as far as the station, numbering 200–300 houses, and was a self-governing community within the town, with a hospice,

**BELOW:** De Pelikaan almshouse entrance.

farm and brewery as well as the church. The word "sauvegarde" above the entrance attests to the royal protection granted by the Duke of Burgundy, assuring the beguinage's independent status. Many Beguines tended the sick, taught or had occupations in the cloth industry. Some were wealthy ladies who resided here for just a year, adopting a life of devotion and good works. The last Beguines left in 1927, when a Benedictine Order took over the site. Many of the houses are now occupied by lay people, but there is a guest house that forms part of the convent and accommodates individuals or groups for spiritual visits.

The beguinage is still infused with an atmosphere of serenity, and nuns can frequently be seen crossing the courtyard to the church. The square is at its best in spring, when daffodils carpet the grass, and the only sounds are the call of doves, the rustle of poplars and the church bell calling the nuns to prayer.

The sisters also staff the small **Begijnhuisje Museum** (daily 10–11.45am, 2–5pm; admission charge).

It is kitted out as a typical beguine's house, with red-tiled floor, traditional furniture and a small cloister garden with a well.

The begijnhof **church** dates from 1245 but was rebuilt in 1605 after a fire, then given a baroque makeover around 1700. The only object saved from the fire is a wooden (now gilded) statue of the Madonna (1300) on the side altar; an original Romanesque door is visible on the north façade. Liturgical celebrations include Gregorian sung offices.

## Minnewater Park

Leaving the beguinage at the far end brings you into **Minnewater Park** ❼ with its tree-fringed "Lake of Love". The name allegedly came from French novelist and poet Victor Hugo, who visited Bruges in 1837 and christened it the *Lac d'Amour*. It is assumed he was inspired by the word *minne*, medieval Dutch for "love". The local legend is that the *minne* was a watery ghost. It is said that a girl called Minna fled the house of her Saxon father rather than marry the suitor he had chosen

*The entrance door at the Beguinage dates back to 1776.*

**LEFT AND BELOW:** picturesque Minnewater, the "Lake of Love".

# The Belgian Beguinages

The begijnhof in Bruges is a beautifully preserved example of a beguinage, a housing community for pious women which were formed across the Netherlands from the 12th century onwards. Unlike nuns, Beguines did not take religious vows and they were financially self-supported. They committed themselves to a celibate life of devotion, but were not answerable to a superior and lived separately.

The name beguine is probably derived from the old Flemish word *beghen*, but with the word's secondary meaning of "to pray", not "to beg", for they were not mendicant orders. Other accounts attribute its origin to Lambert le Bègue, a Liège priest who died in 1180 after spending a fortune founding a cloister and church for the widows and orphans of Crusaders.

Initially, Beguines were solitary women who worked helping the poor and preaching. One of the earliest recorded was Mary d'Oignies (1177–1213), a contemporary of St Francis. She renounced her wealth, practised asceticism and convinced her husband to live with her in chastity. The two of them worked in a leper hospital.

Around the beginning of the 13th century, some Beguines grouped together, forming the first beguinage. In Belgium, they were founded in Mechelen in 1207, Brussels in 1245, Leuven in 1234 and Bruges in 1244. Some beguinages selected their members on the basis of social status, but others were open to all, and numbered their inhabitants in thousands. Many Beguines were relatively wealthy women, and had servants; a woman without means supported herself by manual labour or by teaching.

Their male counterparts, known as Begharads, were usually men of humble origin. They, too, were not bound by vows and did not follow a uniform rule of life, but they had no private property; they lived together in a cloister and ate at the same table.

Beguines have been described as the earliest women's movement in Christian history, a community of financially independent women who existed outside the church and the home, the two accepted spheres for women at the time. Their desire to live the life of Christ, ministering in the world and preaching holy scripture, did not find favour among the male religious orders, for whom the concept of a non-cloistered, unmarried religious woman, even if they were chaste, was quite disturbing.

Progressively, life in a beguinage started to resemble a monastic order: Beguines had to follow strict rules and were usually not allowed to leave without permission from their superior. They also became centres of mysticism, and indulged in flagellation and other practices that were considered heretical. In 1311, Pope Clement V accused the beguines of spreading heresy, and they were persecuted by the Catholic Church until the 15th century, when they were rehabilitated. Most of the beguinages were subsequently suppressed during the religious troubles of the 16th century and the few that survived were quashed during the French Revolution in the late 18th century. In Bruges, the last Beguines left in 1927. Today, the beguinage is administered by a community of Benedictine nuns, who staff the small museum and hold offices in the church. ❏

**LEFT:** a resident Benedictine nun.

for her. When her lover returned from battle against the Romans, he found her dead of cold and hunger by a stream in the woods. He built a dyke, buried Minna in the ground, then released the water to create a lake over her resting place. The romantic label has stuck and the park is a magnet for dreamy couples.

The lake serves a practical purpose, too: fed by the Ghent canal and the perimeter canal, water enters the city here, and the pink brick **lockhouse** (1519) regulates the level of the canals.

At the other end of the lake, beside the Minnewaterbrug, stands the **Poertoren** (gunpowder tower), a munitions store for the defence of the old fortified ramparts. Cross the bridge to follow the path through the park along the line of the ramparts that encircle the town centre. Passing the modern Bargebrug bridge across to the coach park, you soon come alongside the **Bargehuis**. This was the alighting point for Bruges' early tourists who arrived by luxury barge from Ghent, Nieuwpoort or Ostend. It is now a popular watering hole of a different variety. By the water, the Katelijnepoortbrug is an active swing bridge.

## Fine arts and beer

Return towards the centre of town up Katelijnestraat, which is of little interest until you reach the attractive **Stedelijk Academie voor Schone Kunsten** ❽ (City Fine Arts Academy). The academy occupies a 16th-century orphans' school run by the male equivalent of Beguines, Beghards. At the back of the academy, on Noordstraat, is the pretty almshouse, **Godshuizen de Vos**.

Straight ahead is the junction with Nieuwe Gentweg. Carry on, and take the first left, Walstraat, to the **Walplein**, a leafy square lined with restaurants and souvenir shops. Go round the square clockwise to

the brick-fronted **De Halve Maan Brouwerij** ❾ (tours Apr–Oct daily 11am–4pm; Nov–Mar 11am–3pm), maker of the Straffe Hendrik (Strong Henry) beer. Records note the existence of a brewery on Walplein as far back as 1564; this family-run business has been here since 1856. You can take a tour of the complex, which as well as its malt store, fermentation vats, barrel workshop and amazing rooftop view over the town, holds a collection of brewing artefacts acquired on the recent closure of the town's Den Gouden Boum brewery and museum.

Diagonally opposite, at the corner of Walplein, is Stoofstraat (Steamhouse Street), once the location of public baths with a dubious reputation. Slip down here to regain Mariastraat. Across the road, note the door to the city's oldest almshouse, **Godshuis Rooms Convent** ❿. Opposite, the **Godshuis Spanoghe** ⓫ is an L-shaped cluster of houses around a lawn in a tranquil spot near the canal. Turn left up Mariastraat and cross the bridge, which gives an excellent view of Sint-Janshospitaal.

Map on page 80

*The "Half-Moon" Brewery is now the only brewery still actively operating in the heart of the city.*

**BELOW:** the lockhouse in Minnewater Park.

## St John's Hospital

**Sint-Janshospitaalmuseum** ⑫ (St John's Hospital Museum; 38 Maria-straat; Tues–Sun 9.30am–5pm; admission charge) was previously known as the Memling Museum because of its exceptional collection of works by the artist. It is one of the oldest surviving medieval hospitals in Europe. Founded in the 12th century it functioned as a hospital until 1976. There is a fine Gothic doorway and, inside, the floor level is a metre below the road, which shows how the street level has been raised by centuries of repaving. The hospital section contains a wealth of objects evoking the history of medical care, but it is the art treasures in the 15th-century chapel that are most appealing.

Four of the six Memling paintings were especially commissioned for the chapel. The most famous of Memling's works is probably the *St Ursula Shrine* (*c.*1489), which is the centrepiece of the chapel. A diminutive panelled casket shaped like a miniature Gothic church painted in stunning detail, it recounts the story of Ursula's life and martyrdom.

*You'll be spoilt for choice for local beers in Bruges.*

**BELOW:** St John's Hospital's street entrance.

Rather larger, but just as great a masterpiece, is *The Mystical Marriage of St Catherine of Alexandria (Triptych of St John the Baptist and St John the Evangelist)*. Painted in 1479, it shows the infant Jesus on Mary's knee slipping a ring on St Catherine's finger as she kneels before them, while St Barbara reads a book on the other side. The beheading of John the Baptist is depicted on the left panel, and St John the Evangelist in Patmos on the right. It is claimed that the two women saints represent Mary of Burgundy (Catherine) and her stepmother, Margaret of York (Barbara).

The *Adoration of the Magi Triptych* was made for the private altar of its benefactor, Friar Jan Floreins. Its central panel shows a seated Virgin Mary in a ruined stable, a youthful King Balthazar by her side, and Floreins on his knees in the left foreground. The kneeling king on the right appears to be Charles the Bold, while the painter himself is peeping through a window. A larger version of the painting is displayed in the Prado Museum in Madrid.

The small *Lamentation* (Adriaan Reins Triptych, 1480), shows the donor on his knees on the right-hand inside leaf; while the *Portrait of a Young Woman* or *Sybil Sambetha*, shows its sitter's bewitching, translucent beauty. The *Virgin and Apple and Maarten Nieuwenhove* (1487) is a diptych that divides the divine and the secular. On the left the Virgin holds an apple, with the Christ child on her knee, while the second panel portrays Nieuwenhove, the donor.

The hospital **courtyard** is highly evocative of medieval Bruges, from the physic garden at ground level to the rooftop with a view of the church spire. It is enclosed by the hospital on one side and the 14th-century **pharmacy** on the other. It features medicine cabinets, pestles and mortars and old apothecary jars.

Beyond the courtyard, the extensive 19th-century hospital wards have been converted into the **Kunstcentrum Oud Sint Jan**, an exhibition space and congress centre with some peaceful canal-side cafés.

### Onze-Lieve-Vrouwekerk

Back across the street, on the corner of Mariastraat and the Dijver, is one of the beacons of Bruges, literally and symbolically: the **Onze-Lieve-Vrouwekerk** ⓭ (Church of Our Lady; Mon–Sat 9am–5pm, Sun 1.30–5pm; free). The church, with its 122-metre (400-ft) brick spire, is the city's tallest landmark, visible for miles. Built between 1290 and 1549, it is a mixture of styles – a baroque rood-screen truncates the nave and reduces the Gothic effect. But the church's most valuable treasures are its artworks. The most precious is Michelangelo's white marble *Madonna and Child* (1504), in a marble altar in the south nave. A beguiling work, it depicts the Virgin in a pose of contemplation, Jesus leaning against her thigh – this was the first work of art to represent the Christ child as an independent person. The statue is a rare Michelangelo work to have left Italy, and it did so by accident, sold to a Flemish merchant after the Italian family who commissioned it for Siena Cathedral failed to pay the artist. Walpole tried, unsuccessfully, to buy it for England in the 18th century; the French whisked it away to Paris during the Revolution; and the Germans swiped it in World War II.

Further artistic treasures are to be seen in the church's small **museum** (Tues–Fri 9.30am–12.30pm, 1.30–5pm, Sat till 4pm, Sun 1.30–5pm; admission charge), housed in the chancel, choir and ambulatory. Highlights are the 15th-century tombs of Mary of Burgundy and her father, Charles the Bold. The bronze figure of Mary is a delicate Gothic masterpiece, depicting the tragic, beautiful countess. Her father's mausoleum, in the same style, is far from its equal. Beneath the tombs are vaults with medieval frescoes uncovered in recent digs. Chapels around the ambulatory contain interesting paintings by Pieter Pourbus, Gerard David, Antoon van Dyck and others.

Map on page 80

**TIP**

A €15 museum pass gives access to any five of the 14 city-run museums, which include the Groeninge, Sint-Janshospitaal and the Halletoren (belfry).

**LEFT:** Michelangelo's exquisite *Madonna and Child* inside Onze-Lieve-Vrouwekerk.
**BELOW:** Onze-Lieve-Vrouwekerk spire.

### Gruuthuse Museum

The turreted Gothic mansion set around a courtyard next to the Onze-Lieve-Vrouwekerk is the former Palace of the Lords of Gruuthuse, now the **Gruuthuse Museum**  (Tues–Sun 9.30am–5pm; admission charge), a fascinating collection of decorative arts and everyday items that evoke the changing fortunes of Bruges from the 13th–19th century. Among the exhibits of particular interest are an upper-floor oratory, a 1520 bust of Charles V and a guillotine (which was used).

The palace's name is derived from *gruut*, a mixture of spices used to brew beer before being replaced by hops in the 14th century. The *gruut* would be stored in a warehouse *(gruuthuis)*, controlled by a designated individual. The Van den Aa family held the *gruut* concession in Bruges, and built their residence on the site of the razed warehouse in 1425. The oldest part of the building is alongside the canal, while the main wing was built in 1465–72 by Louis of Gruuthuse, one of Bruges' most influential citizens *(see box)*.

*Enjoying a drink on the terrace of the Gruuthuse café.*

The mansion's 23 rooms are well organised according to period and theme and packed with objects both curious and mundane. A four-piece tapestry series in the first room, dating from the early 17th century, is of considerable appeal. Tapestries were immensely precious pieces of work that only the richest individuals could afford. Made of wool and silk thread and inspired by great paintings, they often required months to make. The hangings recount in captivating detail the life of two shepherds – Gombaut and Macée. They were made at a time when the life of shepherds was associated with eroticism, and seem quite racy even by today's standards. A number of other unusual tapestries hang in the museum. Perhaps the most eye-catching is the baroque wall hanging depicting the seven liberal arts personified.

The second room contains the 1520 terracotta bust of Charles V, the young Holy Roman Emperor. He wears a wide-brimmed wooden hat and is recognisable by his narrow face and long chin – characteristic Habsburg features. Charles was born in Ghent and embodied the powerful houses of the Catholic emperor and the Burgundian Dynasty, thanks to the union of his parents Philip the Fair and Joanna of Castille. Opposite the bust is one of his son, Philip II of Spain. One of the oldest rooms is the large **kitchen** with an immense hearth, containing cooking utensils, food jars, water pots and a vast cauldron weighing 680kg (1,500lbs). Notice the iron moulds for making waffles, cakes and communion bread, and the ancient wine bottles. Beyond the kitchen is a small medical room, with graphic 18th-century drawings of deformed people, as well as waist-high mortars and pestles for mixing herbal preparations.

A first-floor room shows examples of rococo furniture and ornate silver tea, chocolate and coffee pots

### Louis of Gruuthuse

Louis of Gruuthuse was variously known as Louis of Bruges, Lord of Gruuthuse, Prince of Steenhuize and Count of Winchester. He played many roles during his eventful life. He served the dukes of Burgundy and was awarded the knights' chain of the Order of the Golden Fleece. As diplomat for Philip III, he helped finance Edward IV's campaign to regain the throne of England in 1461; he became provost for the Count of Flanders and general under Charles the Bold, on whose death he became the First Chamberlain of Duchess Mary of Burgundy and negotiated her marriage to Maximilian of Austria. A leading donor to his neighbouring church – where windows led to the oratory in the palace, enabling him to peer down into the church rather than attending mass with the rabble – Louis was also a generous patron of the arts and religious foundations. A charitable organisation he founded in 1464 required all the city's tailors to clothe the poor of Bruges every All Saints' Day. But all his honours and titles came to a sorry end in 1485, when Louis sided with the Flemish against the French, which provoked his fall from grace.

that reveal the new popularity of these drinks. A trade and currency room displays antique weights for measuring gold, 15th-century money boxes and a curious 1563 stone relief sculpture showing how coins were made. The trades guilds and corporations that were so powerful in Bruges are celebrated in a room containing a selection of medals and seals as well as ceremonial chains. More than 50 corporations in the city at one point helped regulate the rules of economic, social and professional life; while the guilds worked to further their members' spiritual and cultural values.

Upper rooms contain ceramics, furniture and religious artefacts, but it is the grisly arms room on the ground floor that attracts most attention: its guillotine was purchased by the city in 1796 and tested on a sheep before being used to carry out death sentences. At the time, the guillotine was considered an enlightened innovation, as it enabled swift and efficient execution. A slab of wood on three legs nearby was used for cutting off the hands and head of any-

body convicted of patricide. Charles II of England, who stayed in Bruges when he was ejected by Cromwell (1656–58l), is remembered in a black marble monument.

## Boniface bridge

On leaving the Gruuthuse, take the path between the museum and the church. You will cross the much-admired **Bonifaciusbrugje** (1910), which bridges a cool green stretch of canal flanked by vine-covered houses and a rare wooden façade. To the right, the statue of Juan Luis Vives (1492–1540) commemorates the Spanish humanist who lived in Bruges and was buried in Onze-Lieve-Vrouwekerk churchyard. Then double back round the other side of the church or cross the garden to the Arentshuis exit onto the Dijver.

Back at the junction of the Dijver and Mariastraat, along from the Sint-Janshospitaal, a discreet door in the brick façade is the entrance of Bruges' **Archeologisch Museum** ⓯ (Tues–Sun 9.30am–12.30pm, 1.30–5pm; admission charge). The collection, presented in a lively, edu-

Map on page 80

**BELOW:** the Gothic Gruuthuse Museum.

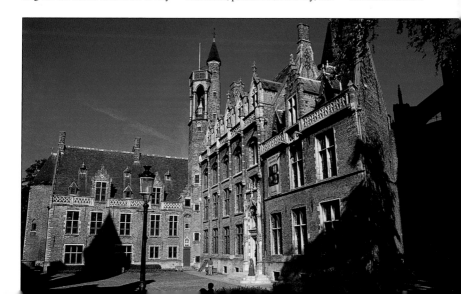

cational way, draws parallels and contrasts between daily life in the Stone Age, the Middle Ages and the present. Artefacts include painted medieval tombstones and vestiges of the St Donatian's Cathedral.

Outside the museum, turn left into the genteel Goetzeputstraat. Then cross over at the junction onto Hoogste van Brugge, at the end of which you turn left to reach the large open square of 't Zand.

### 't Zand

Major transformations on the **'t Zand** ⑯ in recent years have given a new burst of life to this once unappealing square, left vacant when the city's first railway station moved south. The ring road passes beneath the square, which is enlivened by funfairs and a Saturday market. Lined with cafés and brasseries to suit all tastes and budgets, the vista is dominated by the most remarkable new monument on the Bruges skyline: the **Concertgebouw** ⑰ (concert hall), created in 2002 to mark the city's year as European Capital of Culture *(see panel)*. At night, the

**RIGHT:** Bruges' new concert hall.

Concertgebouw takes on a lantern-like appearance, as lights from within sparkle onto the square.

The car park beneath 't Zand is topped by a playful **sculpture fountain** (1985–86) intended as an ode to Bruges past and present by artists Stefaan Depuydt and Livia Canestraro (who made the modern statues for the niches on the Stadhuis). The four groups of bronze sculptures represent bathing women, symbolising the cloth-industry towns of Bruges, Ghent, Antwerp and Kortrijk; cyclists; landscapes of Flanders; and fishermen, symbolising the city's never-ending battle with the sea and its maritime past.

The streets to the north and west of 't Zand are tranquil and typical residential neighbourhoods, ideal for a stroll. There are two routes available. You could take the canal leading north up Speelmansrei, to the **Speelmanskapel**, the former minstrels' guild chapel, dating from 1421, and now used as an exhibition space. This is the start of a lovely stretch of canal that you can wend your way along until you join the

## Concertgebouw

**T**he most striking recent addition to the Bruges skyline is the city's Concertgebouw (concert hall), a venue for music and performing arts that was opened to mark "Brugge 2002", when the city was European Capital of Culture. Until that date, cultural life had centred around the Stadsschouwburg, whose limited stage precluded the hosting of large-scale productions. Architects Paul Robbrecht and Hilde Daem set out to create a 21st-century concert hall that was open to the city: the cladding of 68,000 terracotta tiles was chosen for the warm glow that resonates with Bruges' historic red-brick houses; the pared-down interior is dominated by bare concrete and numerous windows and openings that provide snapshot views of the belfry and other Bruges landmarks. The concert hall hosts a number of top-flight musicians in residence, while the programme includes contemporary dance, rock music and video installations as well as the classical music repertoire. The city's tourist office, In & Uit (In & Out), has been relocated from the Burg to the wings of the concert hall, along with a trendy rebranding to match its hip new location.

merchants' quarter and northern district of Bruges *(see page 95).*

Alternatively, head west across the Markt to Smedenstraat, a smart shopping street. A short detour off the street, up Kreupelenstraat, leads to the almshouse and chapel for the blind, **Onze-Lieve-Vrouw van Blindekens ⑱** (Our Lady of the Blind). The buildings date from the 17th century, although their origins honour a promise made at the battle of Mons-en-Pévèle in 1304, against the French. The chapel is the departure point for the annual Feast of the Assumption procession held on 15 August. The alley beside the chapel leads through to the parallel Kammakersstraat.

Back onto Smedenstraat, head towards **Smedenpoort ⑲**, the fortified city gate at the end of the street that was built in 1367–68, although repeatedly transformed. The bronze skull serves as a reminder of the Ghent citizen who betrayed Bruges in 1688 by trying to open the gate for French invaders led by King Louis XIV. Follow the line of the old city ramparts through the park parallel to Hendrik Consciencelaan. Halfway along, the small brick house behind the trees is the **Waterhuis**, a pumping station dating from the 14th century; at the time, a horse-actioned pump was used to extract drinking water, which was then distributed to the various districts.

Turn left at the bottom of the park onto **Boeveriestraat ⑳**, which has more almshouses than any other street in Bruges. The oldest date from the 14th century, and an extensive renovation programme is under way to modernise the tiny homes for 21st-century occupants. Near the bottom, **Godshuis De Moor** was founded in 1480 for aged stonemasons, carpenters and coopers, while **Godshuis Van Volden** occupies the site of a medieval hospital for mentally ill children and foundlings.

Halfway up on the left is the **Dumeryklok ㉑**, a large bell from the city's belfry brought here to honour the 18th-century Dumery bell-foundry, which was located in this neighbourhood. The large **Sint-Godelieve Abdij ㉒** (1623) abbey and church on the opposite side of the street was built as a refuge for Benedictine nuns from Gistel, who remained in the city even when their own abbey was rehabilitated after the Reformation. The chapel and **Capucijnerabdij Monastery** on the left have a replica of the grotto of Lourdes just inside the gate.

Up at the top, on the right, the tiny 15th-century **Godshuizen Van Campen** and the 17th-century **Van Peenen-Gloribus** look too small to be inhabited by anyone but a hobbit, but are as endearing as they come. The godliest street comes to an end – and with it our journey into the other-worldly air of medieval Bruges – back at the futuristic-looking 't Zand. Two busy shopping streets, the Zuidzandstraat and the Noordzandstraat, run parallel to each other back in the direction of the Markt. ❑

Map on page 80

*The bronze bathing women sculpture on the 't Zand.*

**BELOW:** the 't Zand square is lined with lively cafés.

# RESTAURANTS, BARS & CAFÉS

## Restaurants

### Aneth
1 Marie van Bourgondiëlaan. Tel: 050-31 11 89. Open: L & D Tues–Fri, D only Sat. €€€€
Local foodies who like their fish adore Aneth and book ahead to celebrate special occasions. The roomy detached house overlooking a green square outside the ring road is worth the trip for top-class preparations of the day's catch fresh from the coast.

### De Bekoring
55 Arsenaalstraat. Tel: 050-34 41 57. Open L & D Wed–Sat, D only Sun. €€
Snug and romantic small bistro alongside the canal close to Minnewater Park, with low beams and a large old brick fireplace. Duck down and tuck in to Belgian staples such as snails in garlic butter, eels in green sauce or carbonade flamande (beef slow-cooked in beer).

### De Bron
82 Katelijnestraat. Tel: 050-33 45 26. Open L only Tues–Sat. €
Vegetarian restaurant alongside the Academy of Fine Arts and opposite a health-food store of the same name. Good options for vegans, too.

### De Lotteburg
43 Goezeputstraat. Tel: 050-33 75 35. Open L & D Wed–Sun, D only Sat. €€€
Elaborate fish creations such as shrimp cappuccino with coconut milk mousse, or tomato stuffed with aubergine, sautéed lobster and lemongrass, dominate the menu. This discreet side-street address between Onze-Lieve-Vrouwekerk and Sint-Salvators cathedral comes high in gourmets' ranking, and the clientele is known to include the odd Belgian celebrity. Lovely garden.

### Den Dyver
5 Dijver. Tel: 050-33 60 69. Open L & D Fri–Tues, D only Thur. €€€
Refined family-run house renowned for inventive beer cuisine that contrasts with the more typical Flemish cooking like carbonade flamande. All dishes – like duck breast with guinea fowl and mint mousse in a Chimay sauce with caramelised figs, and peach and chicory stew – come accompanied by selected Belgian brews; desserts are prepared with local genever. Not cheap, but unique.

### Den Gouden Harynck
25 Groeninge. Tel: 050-33 76 37. Open L & D Tues–Fri; D only Sat. €€€€
Formal haven of top-notch modern French gastronomy in a 17th-century former fishmonger's behind Groeninge Museum. Chef Philippe Serruys stamps his flair on sensuous creations such as smoked lobster with fig and date chutney, Muscovite potato and Sevruga caviar. Seriously luxurious experience.

### De Schaar
2 Hooistraat. Tel: 050-33 59 79. Open: L & D Fri–Wed. €€
Not many tourists venture out this way, but the food here is well worth a detour and the location – next to the lock on the Coupure – with a sunny canalside terrace, is both pleasant and authentic. The cosy, low-beamed bistro has an open fire on which its specialities are grilled. Great prices for the quality of food; locals reserve tables so it's wise to do the same.

### De Stoepa
124 Oostmeers. Tel: 050-33 04 54. Open L & D Tues–Sun. €
Sociable hangout near the station popular with a younger crowd for its informal atmosphere and cuisine with an Oriental twist. Vegetarian-friendly and as good for a nibble as a proper tuck-in. The walled terrace-garden is a fantastic sun trap on fine summer days.

### De Wijngaert
15 Wijngaardstraat. Tel 050-33 69 18. Open L & D, Thur–Tues (daily in July and August). €
No-frills, friendly service assured at this grill restaurant and tearoom along the well-worn tourist groove between the Beguinage and Onze-Lieve-Vrouwekerk. Well-prepared mussels, ribs and a lot more besides, but especially worth a stop for the house-speciality – sangría, made with red or white wine.

### Guillaume
20 Korte Lane. Tel: 050-34 46 05. Open D only Wed–Sun. €€€
Bijou, whitewashed cottage on a terraced street off the tourist circuit near the t' Zand. Houses a popular, high-quality bistro run by owner-chef Wim Vansteelant. The menu includes a small but tasty selection of starters and main courses with a distinct Franco-Belgian flavour, such as mackerel stuffed with Liège potatoes and mustard ham.

### Malesherbes
3-5 Stoofstraat. Tel: 050-33 69 24. Open L & D Wed–Sun. €
The all-female team is a winning combination in this simply decorated French deli and dining room in the so-called narrowest street in Bruges. With famously attentive service and a good atmosphere serving quality French produce, quiches and regional specialities.

## Marieke van Brugghe

17 Mariastraat. Tel: 050-34 33 66. Open L & D daily (except public holidays). €€
Recommended by locals despite being slap in the middle of tourist-ville, in the shadow of the Onze-Lieve-Vrouwekerk, this restaurant-brasserie-tearoom dishes up traditional Flemish fare: rabbit stew, *carbonade flamande* and a great fish soup. The terrace for people-watching is an added bonus, but service can be a little frosty.

## Salade Folle

13–14 Walplein. Tel: 050-34 94 43. Open L & D Thur–Tues (until 10pm). €
This bright, contemporary café and tearoom serves good soups, salads, quiches and pasta in generous portions. The setting is attractive, with rustic blond wood tables in lofty rooms stretched over two floors with a mezzanine. Good for lone diners.

## 't Botaniekske

26 Minderbroedersstraat. Tel: 050-33 27 90. Open: L & D Sun; D only Wed–Sat. €
Friendly neighbourhood restaurant run by an all-female team in a rustic old tavern with a large, cosy fireplace. House specialities include ribs and braised ham, but the menu caters for all tastes and includes fish, frogs legs and vegetarian options among its tapas, wok and pasta dishes. Rather out of the way but in a green location opposite the children's playground in Koningin Astridpark. The service is friendly and the locals love it, which is always good news.

## 't Putje

31 't Zand, Tel: 050-33 28 47. Daily L & D. €€
Facing the imposing new concert hall, the crisp tablecloths and smart wicker armchairs set this large, popular brasserie apart from the nearby run-of-the-mill pavement cafés on the 't Zand. Reasonably priced and good French and Belgian classics are served round the clock.

## 't Zwaantje

70 Gentpoortvest. Tel: 050-34 38 85. L & D Fri–Tues. €€€
If you've come to Bruges to indulge in romantic fantasies, this could be the icing on the cake, with its Tiffany-style lamps, mirrors, and candlelight. A local treasure that tourists have never really discovered, run by a welcoming family down near the Bargehuis off Katelijnestraat. Belgian-French cuisine is lovingly presented and served.

### Bars & Cafés

**De Halve Maan** (26 Walplein) is the only working brewery in Bruges, maker of Straffe Hendrik (Strong Henry) beer, this family-run business has been here since 1856. It serves a vast range of other brews too in its roomy and family-friendly tavern, which also caters for groups and offers a very reasonable dish-of-the-day. The sunny courtyard gets busy in fine weather. At **Carpe Diem – Detavernier** (8 Wijngaardstraat), wood-panelling, antiques and stained-glass doors make the perfect accompaniments to a truly olde-worlde tea experience in the Carpe Diem tearoom of the Detavernier patisserie and bakery. It's quiet and civilised, without being over-smart. Mouthwatering cakes and biscuits. **B-In** (38 Mariastraat) is a trendy lounge-bar and restaurant with regular DJ nights in a quiet spot behind Sint-Janshospitaal. By day, the tranquil terrace by the canal makes a good getaway from the overbearing crowds; by night, the bar draws a fashionable crowd, served by equally impeccable designer-dressed staff. For a more convivial atmosphere, head to **Lokkedize** (33 Korte Vulderstraat), a bar that hosts bands playing rhythm & blues, jazz, chanson or rock. Popular with a young crowd, who come for good home-cooked food until the early hours. Also lets flats and studio apartments in the rear.

### PRICE CATEGORIES

Prices for three-course dinner per person with a half-bottle of house wine:
€ = under €25
€€ = €25–40
€€€ = €40–60
€€€€ = over €60

**RIGHT:** traditional *moules frites* at La Moule Sacrée.

# NORTH AND EAST

The north and east of the city, from Jan van Eyckplein to Sint-Anna, is the merchants' and artists' quarters, with a lace-making centre and windmills, plus the fascinating Jeruzalemkerk, a haunted house and a chocolate museum

n medieval times the neighbourhoods to the north and east of the centre were closest to the city's gateway to the outside world, the canal route via Damme to the Zwin inlet. Merchants from all around Europe set up trading posts here, and their legacy is till present in street names like Spanjaardstraat (Spanish Street), Engelsestraat (English Street) and Oosterlingenplein (Orientals' Square). Most visitors today arrive in the south of town, at the coach park or railway station, and do not venture much north of the Markt. Their loss: beyond the grandiose Hanseatic quarter are the old artists' district of Sint-Gillis and the enchanting quaysides of Gouden Handrei and Pottenmakersstraat. To the east, the Sint-Anna district has the air of a country village, its streets disturbed only by the sounds of bicycle bells, windmill sails or the lick of a paintbrush as the area completes its renovation.

A tour of the area entails a considerable amount of walking, but can easily be covered in a good half-day: none of the museums or churches requires more than half an hour's attention and the other sights can be discovered at any time of day – early morning or sunset is perfect. Alternatively, break the walk in two to cover Hanseatic Bruges and Sint-

Gillis in one outing, and Sint-Anna up to Dampoort and the Potterie in another. The area also lends itself particularly well to a bicycle tour.

## Medieval traders' district

Set off north from the Markt up Vlamingstraat, once a busy trading thoroughfare, linking the commercial Markt with the economic district to the north. Halfway up on the left stands the **Koninklijke Stadsschouwburg ❶** (Royal Theatre), built in 1867 after a radical moment

Map on page 96

Map on page 96

**LEFT:** view along De Gouden Handrei. **BELOW:** Papageno from the *Magic Flute* in front of the Royal Theatre.

of urban planning, when the medieval street map was redrawn and an entire block razed. The neo-Renaissance theatre was designed by Brussels architect Gustave Saintenoy. The statue outside represents Papageno from Mozart's *The Magic Flute*; there is a copper-engraved score from the opera across the street.

Just ahead, the small Beursplein square, was the epicentre of trading Bruges, the meeting place for merchants and traders from the 13th–16th century. The Italian states were particularly well represented and set up illustrious lodgings and con-

*The Van der Beuse family shields fronting Ter Beurze Huis.*

sulates. One such house was the **Genuese loge ②** (Genoan Lodge) at 33 Vlamingstraat (1399). Its original crenellated curtain wall was replaced by a bell-shaped gable in 1720, when the building was taken over by serge traders from Hondschoote near Dunkirk, hence its subsequent name of **De Witte Saaihalle**. The Genoan coat of arms is still visible above the side door.

Behind Grauwwerkerstraat, the **Hof Bladelin** on Naaldenstraat was also home to wealthy Italians. The grand residence, with a decorative tower, was built *c*.1440 by Pieter

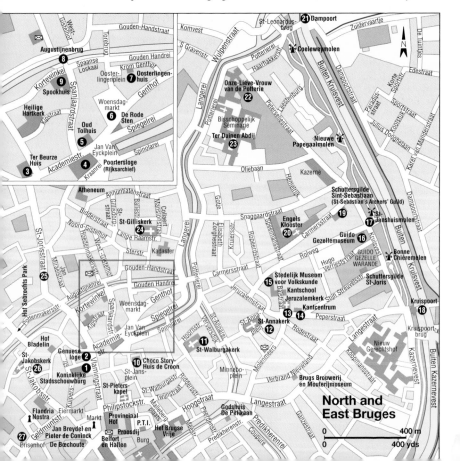

## North and East Bruges

| 0 | | 400 m |
| 0 | | 400 yds |

Bladelin, treasurer of the Order of the Golden Fleece. Later occupants are represented in stone medallions around the **courtyard** (10am–noon, 2–5pm, except Sun pm), the only section which is open to the public. They include Lorenzo di Medici, Tommaso Portinari (a Florentine who managed the Medici bank in Bruges), and the Count of Egmont, who was beheaded in Brussels by the Duke of Alba in 1568.

Those merchants who could not get bed space in their own consulate were often housed by local people such as the Van der Beuse family, whose **Ter Beurze Huis ❸** (1453) occupies the opposite corner of Grauwwerkerstraat on Vlaming-straat. Such families became mid-dlemen, introducing buyers and sellers, and acting as lenders, guar-antors and exchange agents until the deal was concluded under their roof. The Ter Beurze Huis became syn-onymous with this practice when the district was the cradle of Europe's trade system, and gave its name not only to the square outside but to places throughout Europe where merchants met to fix prices for the exchange of goods: *beurs* (in Dutch) and its equivalents in other lan-guages: *bourse, börse, bursa* and *bolsa*. Fittingly, the house is now occupied by a bank. Two other Ital-ian houses stood close by: the Venet-ian Consulate at 37 Vlamingstraat and the Florentine Lodge at 1 Acad-emiestraat – the latter is now the De Florentijnen restaurant.

## The Hanseatic heart

Academiestraat leads to **Jan van Eyckplein**, at the heart of Hanseatic Bruges. The two quays stretching ahead are where ships moored when they reached Bruges via Damme and Langerei. To house the mer-chants and courtiers representing the trading nations, great mansions were built between Spiegelrei and Genthof. Most had roomy, vaulted cellars for storing merchandise; many still exist and reveal traces of their past: a vast 14th-century mural was uncovered at No. 2 Spinolarei during renovations in the 1990s.

On the corner of Academiestraat and Jan van Eyckplein stands the slender-towered **Poortersloge ❹** (Burghers' Lodge), a 15th-century meeting place frequented by the city's wealthy patricians. Among them were members of the Witte Beer (White Bear) Association, a club whose emblem can be seen in a niche on the Academiestraat corner of the building *(see margin note)*. Now home to the city archives, the lodge became the Bruges Academy of Fine Arts during the 18th century, and housed the city's collection of Flemish Primitives.

The ornate Gothic building on the north side of the square is the **Oud Tolhuis ❺** (Customs House), whose façade was modified in 1477, al-though its history goes further back. At its core, behind the pointed gable, is a 13th-century merchant's house, with spacious rooms on the lower

*According to legend, the white bear is the oldest inhabitant of Bruges and caused terror in the region until confronted and nailed to a tree by Baldwin Iron Arm, the first Count of Flanders, in the 9th century. It figures, with the lion, on the city's coat of arms.*

**BELOW:** the Burghers' Lodge spire.

floors for storing goods, and living quarters upstairs. The small staircase extension and stone façade were added in the late 15th century, but the gable dates from two centuries later. The coat of arms above the door is that of Pierre of Luxembourg, Knight of the Golden Fleece, who benefited from the import taxes levied on goods entering the ports of Bruges. (The monarch, who levied the tax, often made a gift of the concession to a favoured individual.)

The adjoining sliver of a house also dates from the late 15th century and was occupied by *pijnders*, or porters, who are represented in stone carvings at the bottom of a pillar on the façade. Next door used to be the public weighing house. The combined buildings are now the seat of the provincial library, which holds 600 religious manuscripts and early printed books recovered from the Abbey of the Dunes in Koksijde.

Parts of the house called **De Rode Steen** (8 Jan van Eyckplein) date from the 13th century, but major changes were made in 1500 after a fire. The last major transformation

*Hans Memling's statue stands proudly on Woensdagmarkt.*

**BELOW:** Jan van Eyck-plein and the statue of the Flemish master.

dates from 1777. A century later, it was the first building to be awarded renovation funding, thus marking the start of preservation efforts to maintain the medieval character of Bruges. On the right of the steps leading to the door is a plaque honouring Georges Rodenbach, author of *Bruges-la-Morte* (1892), whose grandfather, Constantin Rodenbach, lived nearby *(see page 73)*.

### Traces of the 16th century

Go up Genthof to the left of the Rode Steen – do not miss the crenellated façade at No. 1 (*c*.1550) and the wooden cladding at No. 7, one of only two authentic 16th-century wooden façades remaining in the city. The **Woensdagmarkt ➏** was named after the vegetable market that used to take place here on Wednesdays, and boasts a statue of Hans Memling (1871) by Hendrik Pickery. Look over the roof at No. 10: the elegant turret behind the house, topped with a gilded ship, was originally part of a large edifice occupied by traders from Smyrna, and indicated on 16th-century maps.

### Potato Market

Until 1844, Jan van Eyckplein was called Academieplaats, and only took its current name when Hendrik Pickery's statue of van Eyck, the eminent 15th-century Flemish master, was inaugurated here in 1878. Even so, well into the 20th century it was still being referred to as Patattenmarkt (Potato Market), named after the potato sellers who were shifted here when the vegetable market on nearby Woensdagmarkt grew short of space. Potatoes continued to be sold in the square until just before World War I, and several older residents of Bruges are still familiar with the square's nickname.

Just beyond the Woensdagmarkt is **Oosterlingenplein** (Orientals' Square). It sounds as if it should evoke the spice-laden history of Bruges, but in fact refers simply to the German Hanseatic League (they were people from the east as far as the Flemish were concerned), which occupied a house at 1 Krom Genthof, the **Oosterlingenhuis** ❼, built in 1481. Something remains of the impressive building, which figured among the Seven Wonders of Bruges on a 16th-century map of the same name in the beguinage, but it retains little of its charm and is now occupied by offices.

## The Spanish quarter

Head up to the canal, where the lovely **Gouden Handrei** to the right introduces a tranquil branch of canal off Langerei, which traces a graceful arc round to the 't Zand in the west of the city. There can be few activities more guaranteed to lift one's spirits than to wander or cycle along its route, hazy and mysterious in the early morning and golden in the sunshine of early evening. Turn left and follow the canal along **Spaanse Loskaai**, the quay where Spanish ships unloaded their cargo, including Castillian wool to replace the increasingly rare English product. Triple-arched **Augustijnenbrug** ❽ (1294) was the first stone bridge in Bruges, built by monks of the former Augustinian friary (now a modern apartment building) on the opposite side, on Augustijnenrei.

Den Noodt Gods, the house on the corner of Spanjaardstraat, the next street on the left, was built in 1616 by Spanish merchant Francisco de Peralta, whose coat of arms decorates the Renaissance entrance. Since the 19th century, the building has been known as **Spookhuis** ❾, as it was said to be haunted by the ghost of an amorous Augustinian monk who had discovered a secret tunnel under the canal joining his friary to the convent in this building. He allegedly killed the object of his affections in a fit of passion and their two spirits continue to haunt the place. The building has changed hands frequently and been abandoned on more than one occasion.

Map on page 96

*Woensdagmarkt square features in the painting* La ville abandonnée *(1904) by Fernand Khnopff (in the Musées Royaux d'Art et d'Histoire, Brussels).*

**BELOW:** the three arches of the Augustijnenbrug.

**TIP**

Informative, three-hour guided bicycle tours of Bruges are provided daily from March to October by Quasi-Mundo, tel 050-33 07 75, www.quasimundo. com. Meet at 9.50am in front of the Toyo Ito pavilion on the Burg (no reservation required).

**BELOW:** Sint Walburgakerk's pristine white interior.

Across the street, a white stone façade is all that remains of the Torrehuis, a wealthy family abode from the early 16th century. On the corner with Kipstraat is De Hesp (The Ham), a 14th-century Gothic house fronted by a 17th-century gable. The house at 9 Spanjaardstraat (without a door) was where Ignatius of Loyola (1491–1556), founder of the Jesuit Order, stayed when in Bruges on holiday from his studies in Paris. It is now a tax office.

The end of the street returns to Jan van Eyckplein, which we cross to Biskajersplein, to the south. At No. 4 there used to stand De Groene Winkel, a humanist printing works owned by 16th-century printer and publisher Hubertus Goltzius, whose Officina Goltziana imprints are widely considered to be among the finest books of the time, and highly sought after by collectors today. Goltzius moved to Bruges in 1562 to undertake what was to be his life's work, in collaboration with wealthy humanist Marcus Laurinus: a history of the ancient world in nine volumes. Only four saw the light of

day. Disputes and financial problems prevented the completion of the project, and Goltzius died a lonely and ruined man.

A little further along, the elegant house sitting on the corner of Sint-Jansplein is the home of **Choco-Story ❿** (2 Wijnzakstraat; tel: 050-61 22 37; daily 10am–5pm), a privately owned museum that details the history of chocolate and caters for visitors in need of their daily fix.

## Sint Walburgakerk

Turn left after the museum down Sint-Jansstraat, then right and immediately left along Korte Riddersstraat which emerges directly before the charming baroque **Sint Walburgakerk ⓫** (1619–42; St Maartensplein; daily 10am–noon, 2–5pm; free). There is not much space in front of this fine oratory, commissioned by Brugean Jesuit Pieter Huyssens, to stand back and admire its orderly dimensions, but there are treasures aplenty within the cool interior, flooded with silvery light by two decks of pale grey stained-glass windows reflected in

the glistening black-and-white marble floor tiles. Probably the most remarkable feature is the carved Carrara marble communion rail that stretches across the width of the three marble altars.

The triptych on the right-hand wall, *Our Lady of the Dry Tree*, portrays the apparition of the Virgin to Philip the Good as he prayed before his victory against the French. It is the work of Pieter Claeissens the Younger, signed and dated 1620. The ornate wooden pulpit (1669) survived the French Revolution, when the church was transformed into a temple of law.

Follow Hoornstraat down the side of the church, where calm reigns until you emerge at the canal and are hit by the blast of tour-boat megaphones. Turn right and cross Sint-Annabrug to regain a sense of peace in the Sint-Anna district.

## Sint-Anna

The area around St Anna is cherished by local people as well as visitors fleeing the tour-guide crowds. Home in the 19th century to the poorest citizens, it was re-discovered by artists and, in their wake, young professionals, who have restored the rows of terraced houses. With few cars or shops, the neighbourhood appears calm and timeless, with a village atmosphere. The string of windmills along the river's grassy banks at the line of the city ramparts complete the picture.

Walk along Sint-Annakerkstraat until you reach the fine **Sint-Annakerk** ⓬ (Sint-Annaplein; Mon–Fri 10am–noon, 2–4pm, Sat 10am–noon; free). Enclosed by an elegant square, St Anna's mediocre outward aspect conceals a wealth of ornament within. Consecrated in 1624 on the site of a Gothic edifice, razed to the ground by fire in 1581, the church's baroque interior contains lashings of ornate woodwork,

marble and brass, an imposing *Last Judgement* (1685) mural by Henri Herregoudts, and other evidence that this has long been a busy and well-loved parish church. The pink marble spiral columns are high kitsch and their form is picked up in details throughout the church. In former times, the counter on the left as you enter was where the poor would sign their name (or make their mark) in registers each time they attended mass, so they could receive tokens to exchange for food and clothing on feast days.

## The Jeruzalemkerk

When leaving Sint-Annaplein, turn immediately right onto Jeruzalemstraat, where a strikingly unusual church, the fruit of a wealthy family's piety, is located. The **Jeruzalemkerk** ⓭ (Mon–Fri 10am–noon, 2–6pm, Sat till 5pm; combined admission ticket with the Lace Centre) was built between 1428 and 1465 and is a most curious combination of Byzantine and Gothic styles. A private commission by a wealthy family of Genoese merchants, the

Map on page 96

*Lifelike figurines displayed inside Sint-Annakerk.*

**BELOW:** the Adornes family shields grace the brick walls of the Jeruzalemkerk.

*A fine antique example of lacework at the Lace Centre.*

Adornes, it is still owned by their descendants. Spared pillage or destruction throughout the centuries thanks to its private chapel status, it is remarkably well preserved.

Opiccino Adornes arrived from Genoa in 1307 to look after his city's trading relations in Bruges. Two of his brothers brought the plans of the Holy Sepulchre Church in Jerusalem back from a pilgrimage to the Holy Land and, in a papal bull from Martin V dated 12 May 1427, gained the right to build a church, based on these plans, next to their house. The Gothic interior is dominated by the mausoleum of Anselm Adornes, and his wife, Marguerite van der Banck. Other family members are buried beneath the church, and their shields adorn the mausoleum. Anselm (born 1424) was burgomaster of Bruges, but was murdered in Scotland in 1483 while on a consular mission. Although buried in Linlithgow, his heart was brought back to Bruges in a leaden box to be laid beside his wife.

The lofty interior is rich with symbols of mourning and penitence. The number of relics – such as that of the original crucifix contained in a silver cross behind a wrought-iron grill – show how the church escaped the scourges of iconoclasts. Beneath the choir is a crypt containing a Calvary, and a door leads to a replica of the Holy Sepulchre, with a copy of the tomb of Christ, the slab broken in two places, just like the one in Jerusalem. The stained-glass windows show members of the Adornes family, backed by heraldic arms.

Atop the tower outside sit the Jerusalem cross, and the wheel and palm of St Catherine, to symbolise the journey of Anselm and his son to Jerusalem and Mount Sinai in 1470.

Next door to the church, the **Kantcentrum** ⑭ (lace centre; same times and ticket as Jeruzalemkerk) occupies the former Adornes residence, with a 15th-century Gothic façade but devoid of original features inside. The centre is a non-profit-making foundation that aims to continue the work of the Sisters Apostle, who started teaching lace-making in Bruges in 1717. Each afternoon, demonstrations of the craft of bobbin lace are held.

## Lace-making in Bruges

It's not unusual in Bruges to see an elderly lady taking the afternoon sunshine in her doorway, twiddling dozens of tiny wooden bobbins on a thick cushion on her lap. It looks like the most time-consuming activity imaginable, yet lace-making began as a time- and money-saving drive to keep up with fashion: unlike embroidery, lace decorations could be removed from one garment and stitched onto another. The Bruges technique of bobbin lace took off in the course of the 15th century and employed huge numbers of citizens during centuries of hardship. Poor women and children would make lace in their homes, for a price fixed by the seller, who supplied them with linen thread. The lace makers had no corporation to defend their interests, and won no recognition for their work, even when it graced Europe's courts. Mechanisation put an end to the trade and the women that still practise the craft today do so only as a hobby. The lace in the shops may look authentic to an untrained eye, but it is likely to have been made by underpaid workers in East Asia, where Flemish missionary nuns taught the craft at the turn of the 20th century.

A **museum** displaying lace varieties is set in six almshouses behind the church, but the presentation is uninspiring, with no labelling and poor lighting. Round the corner in Balstraat is a **Kantschool**, which runs lace-making classes.

## Folklore and poetry

Further up Balstraat on the left, in a row of whitewashed *godshuizen* intended for retired shoemakers, is the **Stedelijk Museum voor Volkskunde** ⓕ (43 Balstraat, tel: 050-44 87 11; Tues–Sun 9.30am–5pm; admission charge), the city museum of folklore. Modest yet appealing, it offers a fascinating peek into what people did in Bruges before they all started working in tourism. The reconstructed interiors include a schoolroom, living room and a number of workshops representing the trades of cobbler, clogmaker, tailor, hatter, cooper, pharmacist and confectioner (sweet-making demonstrations are held on Thursdays). You can end your visit with a refreshing drink in the museum's quaint tavern, De Zwarte Kat.

Turn right at the end of Balstraat onto the pretty Rolweg, where you can visit the **Guido Gezellemuseum** ⓖ (Tues–Sun 9.30am–12.30pm, 1.30–5pm; admission charge), which celebrates the work of the Flemish poet-priest Guido Gezelle (1830–99) in the house where he was born. The residence and lovely walled garden is entirely devoted to the story of his life and work, from his childhood and seminary teaching to his political writings and poetry. Gezelle was at one point abbot of Sint-Anna and his poetry has been translated into no less than 17 languages. He also became heavily involved in the Flemish Movement and endeavoured to develop an independent language, distinct from Dutch and including elements of the West Flanders dialect, in which he wrote his poems.

## Windmills and the city gate

The top of Rolweg is separated from the canal by a park along the line of the former city ramparts and by a hillock topped with one of the city's four surviving windmills,

Map on page 96

**TIP**

The curious assembly of artefacts in the Folklore Museum includes the extensive pipe collection of Belgium's first prime minister, Achille van Acker, who was born in Bruges.

**BELOW:** the schoolroom display at the Museum of Folklore.

**Sint-Janshuismolen** ⑰ (May–Sept Tues–Sat 9.30am–12.30pm, 1.30–5pm; admission charge). Sint-Janshuis and the Coelewey Mills *(see below)* are satellites of the Folklore Museum and hold demonstrations of the miller's craft. They hail from the 19th century when the ramparts were dotted with 29 such mills, mainly milling grain. Although the mound appears on records as early as 1297, the original windmills were all destroyed; those still standing come from elsewhere.

The other three mills, the **Bonne Chieremolen**, **Nieuwe Papegaaimolen** and **Coeleweymolen** are within sight and walking distance, a few hundred metres either way.

Along the ramparts south of the windmills is the freshly restored **Kruispoort** ⑱ city gate (early 15th century, but repeatedly rebuilt), a vestige of the second town wall of 1297. The gate has a wholly different aspect depending on your approach. An attacker coming from outside would have been faced with two squat, cylindrical towers linked by a machicolated battlement – whose floor contained holes through which defenders could drop stones or molten lead on the enemy. The town's citizens, in contrast, would have seen the gate's more elegant profile, with slender octagonal turrets, dripstone moulding and other medieval details.

## Archers and Augustinians

Follow the canal up towards Dampoort, pausing at the top of Carmersstraat. There are two old archery clubs along the town's perimeter here: **Schuttersgilde Sint Joris** and, at 178 Carmersstraat, the ancient, exclusive **Schuttersgilde Sint-Sebastiaan** ⑲ (St Sebastian's Archers' Guild; May–Sept Tues–Thur 10am–noon, Sat 2–5pm; Oct–Apr Tues–Thur and Sat 2–5pm; admission charge), in a curious brick building with a skinny hexagonal tower. This guild has been based here since the 16th century and it is still an active and prestigious longbow club. The guild's reputation began during the Crusades, and it soon became an elite archery club. Charles II of England gave the place cachet when he came here in exile in 1651. He formed a royal regiment of guards in 1656, which accompanied him back to London when the monarchy was restored in 1660. All British monarchs since have been honorary members of the guild, as is the Belgian royal family.

The entrance gate is decorated with the shield of Jerusalem brought back from the Holy Land. Inside, visitors can see its precious possessions, archives and mementos left by illustrious members, some of whom still come here for target practice, either in the garden or in a long, covered shooting gallery.

A little further down the same street at No. 85 is Our Lady of Nazareth **Engels Klooster** ⑳ (English Convent; daily 2–4pm and 4.30–5.30pm except first Sun of the month and August). This community

*The regiment formed by Charles II later became known as the First or Grenadier Regiment of Foot Guards and returned to Belgium to fight in both world wars.*

**BELOW:** Sint-Janshuismolen is the only authentic surviving Bruges windmill.

of Augustinian sisters was established when many religious orders were banished from England in the 17th century. One of the Englishwomen sent here to complete her education was Anne Mary Edmonstone, who came to convert to Catholicism in order to marry pioneering English naturalist Charles Waterton (1782–1865), founder of the world's first nature reserve. The convent has an historically important library of English books and runs a guesthouse.

Up past the most northerly windmill you arrive at the **Dampoort ㉑**, site of a former city gate and access to the sea via the port of Damme. The Damsevaart canal begins on the other side of the road junction, and its towpath is a popular cycle route. The junction is now dominated by a busy lock basin where two road bridges are frequently raised. Turning left into Potterierei, the road follows the watery route into town taken by shiploads of luxury items brought for exchange in medieval Bruges: Castillian oranges and lemons, Oriental spices, Mediterranean velvet and brocade, Baltic fur and amber.

### Potterierei

On the left side of the canal, a little way down, at No. 79, the ancient **Onze-Lieve-Vrouw van de Potterie ㉒** (Our Lady of the Pottery; Tues–Sun 9am–12.30pm, 1.30–5pm) is named after the potters who lived in the neighbourhood and worshipped in the local chapel. The church started life as a hospice founded in 1276 by Augustinian nuns, and became a retirement home in the 15th century (a large part of the complex retains this role today). The church and the **Potterie-museum**, part of the former hospital, contain some fine art objects and artefacts. The museum includes a rare collection of lepers' rattles (16th-century) and a wealth of ancient furniture. There are a number of interesting devotional panels and medieval sculptures, a Pieter Pourbus triptych, Delftware, and a surprisingly rich treasury with a good collection of silver, several 15th–16th-century *Books of Hours* and a rare 16th-century *Book of Miracles*. The oldest part of the **church** is the left-hand nave, dating from 1359. Its two side altars are adorned with

*The George's Archers guildhouse at No. 59 Stijn Streuvelsstraat contains a fine collection of crossbows.*

**BELOW:** reflections along the Potterierei.

**BELOW:** the imposing Sint-Jacobskerk.

embroidered antependia made of gold and silver thread (*c.* 1565). The choir altarpiece is an *Adoration of the Shepherds* by 17th-century local artist Jacob van Oost the Elder. In the right nave stands what is said to be the oldest Netherlandish miracle statue, the wooden Our Lady of Mons-en-Pévèle, from the early 14th century, named after the eponymous 1305 battle. The Miracle Tapestries (1550–1600) in the main nave on the left depict miracles associated with the Virgin Mary in a lively style resonant of 16th-century daily life.

Follow the canal beneath the plane trees to the massive, baroque Groot Seminarie (Episcopal Seminary), established in 1834 in the former **Ter Duinen Abdij ㉓** (Abbey of the Dunes) dating from 1627. The abbey gained its name because the original foundation was in Koksijde, beside the sea. The monks were forced to create a new priory in Bruges when their home was threatened by the encroaching sands.

The abbey was closed in 1796 and subsequently became a school, a museum and a library until the seminary took over. It still retains many artistic treasures from the old abbey, but is not open to the public. Behind the façade is a classical Cistercian abbey, cloister, gardens and a surprisingly large meadow. To the left is the 18th-century church, an elegant edifice disguising an interior in a poor state of repair.

## St Gillis

Cross the wooden bridge opposite the seminary and continue down Langerei, turning right at the quaint Kleine Nieuwstraat to enter the peaceful artists' quarter of **Sint Gillis** (St Giles). The low rows of terraced houses feel humble beneath the wide Flemish sky. The modest workers' cottages are now desirable residences and are being renovated by a new generation of arty young professionals, centuries after the district was occupied by the greatest names in Flemish painting.

A left turn into Baliestraat takes you past the rustic *estaminet* Het oud Handbogenhof to the parish church of **Sint-Gilliskerk ㉔**, a neo-Gothic hall-church of agreeably

stout proportions. Only the chunky stone pillars inside date from the original 1250 construction, the rest having been rebuilt in the 19th century, including a brick tower similar to that of Sint-Salvator's Cathedral. The artist Hans Memling was buried here in 1494 and is remembered by a plaque beside the entrance (his tombstone was removed).

A number of interesting paintings in the church include a polyptych by Pieter Pourbus (1564) and three works by Jan Garemijn in a series of six recounting the retrieval of white slaves from Algeria by the Trinitarians. The church organ is reputedly one of the best in the city.

### St Joris

Wander through the quiet backstreets towards **Sint-Jorisstraat** ㉓. This street, and the parallel Jan Miraeelstraat, were sought-after addresses for artists in the 15th century. Pieter Pourbus (1523–83) lived on the east side of Jan Miraelstraat, while Gerard David and Antoon Claeissens lived on Sint-Jorisstraat, Memling owned two houses here and Lancelot Blondeel lived a couple of doors away. Jan van Eyck received illustrious guests in his home and studio south of Sint-Gilliskerk on the corner of the Torenbrug and Gouden Handstraat.

Later, the neighbourhood became something of an English colony. An orphanage on Sint-Jorisstraat was run by an English family until World War I; engravings collector John Steinmetz stayed here en route to Venice in 1819; and an English seminary was located on Gouden Handstraat. The house on the corner of Sint-Jorisstraat and Clarastraat was owned by English art historian James Weale (1832–1917) who, in partnership with poet Guido Gezelle, launched a magazine and is credited with re-discovering and identifying the works of Memling and many other Flemish Primitives.

Turn left down Sint-Jorisstraat back towards the Vlamingbrug. On the corner of Sint-Jorisstraat and Poitevinstraat a **tiled mural** depicts the ravages of the plague in the 17th century. The disease re-occurred with devastating frequency over the centuries, severely depleting the population. The mural, made in 1910 to replace the original, has distinguishable Art Nouveau features.

### Sint-Jakobsstraat

**Sint-Jakobsstraat** was the heart of princely Bruges in the Burgundian era. The street was the location for scenes in Harry Kümel's 1971 horror mystery *Malpertuis*, starring Orson Welles. In the film, Cassavius (Welles) holds his nephew and niece prisoner, along with figures from Greek mythology, in a labyrinthine house from which they cannot escape even after his death.

There is nothing horrific about nearby **Sint-Jakobskerk** ㉖ (Tues–Sat 10am–noon, 2–5pm; Sun–Mon 2–5pm; free). Due to its strategic location between the merchants' quarter and the Duke of Burgundy's

Map on page 96

*Sint-Jacobskerk looks down on Sint-Jacobsstraat.*

**BELOW:** peaceful canal life.

Map on page 96

*The Order of the Golden Fleece was founded in 1430 by Philip the Good to honour his marriage to Isabella. Membership was restricted to 24 knights, then 30 and later 51 and was denied to non-Catholics. When the House of Burgundy was absorbed into the Habsburg empire, control of the order passed on to the king of Spain.*

**BELOW:** the Prinsenhof.

Prinsenhof residence, it gained generous endowments in the 15th century, although many treasures were removed or destroyed by pillaging iconoclasts in 1580.

Originally built in 1220 in cruciform style, Sint-Jakobskerk was quickly enlarged into a three-naved Gothic hall-church. The 18 altars belonged to trade guilds and corporations. Subsequent renovations in baroque and neo-Gothic style first removed and then restored its medieval aspect. A number of Flemish Primitive masterpieces were painted for this church, including works by Hans Memling, Hugo van der Goes and Roger van der Weyden.

These have been removed, but some exceptional works remain, including the *St Lucy Legend* (1480) by an anonymous contemporary of Memling, dubbed the Master of the Legend of St Lucy. Located in St Anthony's Chapel, it tells the story of Lucy, a wealthy virgin of Syracuse who, in gratitude for the recovery of her sick mother after her pilgrimage to St Agatha's tomb, gave all her goods to the poor. This did not please the man to whom she was betrothed and he had her condemned to death.

Note Lancelot Blondeel's 1523 altarpiece, made for the surgeons' and barbers' corporation; and two triptychs by Pieter Pourbus. The mausoleum of Ferry de Gros (1544), treasurer of the Golden Fleece, features among the finest examples of Flemish Renaissance sculpture.

## Prinsenhof

The location of a palace built for the dukes of Burgundy in the 15th century can be reached via Moerstraat, turning left at Ontvangersstraat to reach a small square on the left, once the palace courtyard of the **Prinsenhof ㉗**. The present building is a neo-Gothic copy of the former palace. It is due to be renovated and turned into a hotel, but at the time of writing it appears abandoned and dilapidated. The original Prinsenhof, the main residence of the dukes of Burgundy, hosted many sumptuous festivities. Philip the Good married Isabella of Portugal here in 1430, and held a banquet in a hall decorated with tapestries made of gold thread specially for the occasion. Every dish was delivered on a gold platter, to the sound of trumpets, while jousting entertained the guests outside.

But sorrow began to shroud the palace after the violent death of Philip's son, Charles the Bold, in 1477. Then, in 1482, came the untimely passing of Mary, Duchess of Burgundy, aged 25. Her death led to widespread mourning, and the building never recovered its former glory.

By then, Bruges was in decline. The Zwin was silting up and Flemish clothmakers could no longer compete with their English peers. Mary's widower, Maximilian of Austria, tired of the town's constant rebellion, shifting his favours to Antwerp. The Prinsenhof was sold and later destroyed. By the early 16th century, the Golden Age of Bruges was over. ❏

# RESTAURANTS, BARS & CAFÉS

## Restaurants

### Brasserie Forestière
15 Academiestraat. Tel: 050-34 20 02. Open L Mon–Tues & Thur, L & D Fri–Sat. €
Very reasonably priced, popular and laid-back diner in an elegant town house with marble fireplaces and bare wooden tables. Caters for vegetarians with friendly service. Open till 6pm on lunch-only days.

### Curiosa
22 Vlamingstraat. Tel: 050-34 23 34. Open L & D Tues–Sun. €€
Cellar tavern with a vaulted ceiling and brick walls. Surprisingly tourist-free despite its proximity to the Markt, it serves a broad range of dishes, from salads and steaks to seafood specialities. Groups welcome.

### De Florentijnen
1 Academiestraat. Tel: 050-67 75 33. Open L & D Tues–Sat. €€€
Stylish eaterie set in a modern retake of a medieval interior. It has a lively buzz and dishes up superb Italian-French food.

### De Karmeliet
19 Langestraat. Tel: 050-33 82 59. Open L & D Tues–Sat. €€€€
The sumptuous surroundings behind a discreet façade complement the jaw-dropping culinary creations here. This renowned establishment occupies a gastronomic class of its own and is a legend beyond Belgium's borders, thanks to the true genius of its indefatigable owner-chef Geert Van Hecke.

### In Den Wittenkop
14 St-Jakobsstraat. Tel: 050-33 20 59. Open L & D, Tues–Sat. €€
Mellow café-bistro lined with impressive retro enamel advertising panels. Classic Belgian dishes include traditional *waterzooï* made with langoustines rather than white fish or chicken. Lush terrace to the rear.

### Koto
15 Potterierei. Tel: 050-44 31 31. Open L & D Thur–Sun; D only Tues–Wed. €€€
Japanese restaurant with authentic decor, in the Hotel Medici. The speciality is *teppan yaki* grilled meat and fish, but it also serves traditional favourites including sushi and tempura.

### Lotus
5 Wapenmakersstraat. Tel: 050-33 10 78. Open L Mon–Sat. €
Popular and long-established mainly vegetarian restaurant. Very good value for the carefully prepared dishes. The daily meat option is lamb moussaka or lamb stew, both with organic meat.

### Rock-fort
15 Langestraat. Tel: 050-33 41 13. Open L & D Tues–Sat. €€€
Fashionable new bistro with a simple formula: good food, generous portions and stylish decor.

### Tom's Diner
23 West Gistelhof. Tel: 050-33 33 82. Open D only, Wed–Mon. €€
Convivial gem highly popular with the locals which can be hard to find, as it doesn't look open. The focus is on tasty food in a candlelit setting with exposed brick walls.

### Zen
117 Beenhouwersstraat. Tel: 050-33 67 02. Open L only Mon–Sat. €
A wholesome and varied dish-of-the-day is all that's on the menu besides soup in this vegan-friendly café.

## Bars & Cafés

### Patisserie Servaas van Mullem
(56 Vlamingstraat) is a superb bakery and pastry shop with a stunning range of fruit tarts and rich cakes. There is a small teak-tabled terrace alongside the shop. **Kant** (6 Kraanplein) is a lounge bar with club sounds and ultra-design focus. Mediterranean-inspired food is served from 6pm in great style but do expect small portions. **Vlissinghe** (2 Blekersstraat), founded in 1515, is the oldest café in Bruges, with wood-panelled walls and long oak tables. It serves simple bar food and has a good-sized garden. **De Versteende Nacht** (11 Langestraat) is the best jazz bar in town; small and intimate, it holds regular jam sessions and live performances. **De Verloren Hoek** (178 Carmersstraat) has a delightful location overlooking the Sint-Janshuismolen windmill. Its laid-back terrace and simple bar food make it a popular venue. **De Republiek** (36 Sint-Jakobsstraat) is the café of the Cultuurhuis de Republiek that includes the Lumière art-house cinema next door. Popular with a young, alternative crowd, it serves cocktails and exotic light food. **Du Phare** (2 Sasplein) is a music bar-brasserie with a lively atmosphere, varied food (Creole, Thai, steaks) and live blues and jazz. A large green terrace beside the canal is a draw. **Vino Vino** (15 Grauwwerkerstraat) is a wine, tapas and blues bar with a friendly owner and faithful following.

### PRICE CATEGORIES

Prices for three-course dinner per person with a half-bottle of house wine:

€ = under €25
€€ = €25–40
€€€ = €40–60
€€€€ = over €60

# THE BRIDGES OF BRUGES

"The dark memory came to haunt him, emerging from under the bridges, where faces weep tears from invisible springs"

Georges Rodenbach's *Bruges-la-Morte* depicts the dying Bruges, abandoned after its Golden Age, where the sadness of its grey buildings, shroud of mist and tolling bells is deepened by the melancholy canals that reflect the narrator's grief (*see also page 73*). Thankfully, there is no such mournful parallel for today's visitors, who are likely to find the bridges of Bruges inspire awe rather than tears, their low granite arches hunched close to the water like punctuation marks along the serene stretches of canals, or *reien*.

The canals were begun in the early Middle Ages. Large sea-going vessels docked in the outer port of Damme, where goods were transferred onto smaller boats to enter Bruges. Here, a network of canals encircled the city and crossed north to south via the Markt, where the vast Lakenhalle provided a covered unloading area. Imported goods like silks and silverware, leather, spices and diamonds were offloaded in the merchants' quarter along Spiegelrei and Spaanseloskaai. Boats docked in the Minnewater basin before sailing onward into Flanders and to Ghent. These days, private boats are banned on the *reien*, which look mirror smooth on the quiet stretches and in low season, when the tour boats cease plying the waters.

**ABOVE:** the attractive Duinenburg is a wooden drawbridge supported by two stone arches; it crosses the Langerei, a canal in the Potterierei district, in north-eastern Bruges.
**ABOVE LEFT:** picturesque bridge over the tranquil Potterierei.
**BELOW:** the Meebrug stone bridge appears on many a postcard of Bruges, and painters also find inspiration from its graceful span.
**RIGHT:** linking the old with the new, the Conzett Brug was built to celebrate Bruges' year as European Capital of Culture in 2002.
**BELOW RIGHT:** Sint-Jan Nepomucenus-brug honours the patron saint of the drowned.

## THE HIGHLIGHTS

**MEEBRUG AND PEERDENBRUG.** The grey stone of these two bridges along picturesque Groenerei is softened by a covering of lichen and creepers. The single arch of each bridge is reflected in the canal, framing a shimmering image of quayside houses.

**BONIFACIUSBRUG.** A majestic example of the Gothic revival in Bruges, this scenic footbridge across the canal behind the Arentshuis and the Gruuthuse Museum was built in 1910 but could have been here for centuries from the patina of its stone.

**AUGUSTIJNENBRUG.** The first stone bridge in Bruges, built in 1294 by monks from the former Augustinian friary on the north side of the canal.

**VLAMINGBRUG.** Built in 1331 as a continuation of the busy thoroughfare leading to the artists' district to the north, this two-arched bridge leads to the pretty Pottenmakersstraat.

**DUINENBRUG.** This small wooden bridge, supported on two stone arches across the Langerei, makes this part of the Potterierei seem distinctly less urban.

**CARMERSBRUG.** Look down to the wall by the water where a modern stone statue of a Carmelite monk holds a staff to measure the water's depth.

**SINT-JAN NEPOMUCENUSBRUG.** This busy bridge is crowned by the imposing statue of St John of Nepomucene, patron saint of the drowned, who was thrown in the Moldau in Prague in 1393 by King Wenceslas IV.

**CONZETT BRUG.** Great scrolls of rusted metal span the canal above the walkway of weather-washed wood on this modern bridge, designed by architect Jürg Conzett and commissioned to mark Bruges' year as European Capital of Culture in 2002.

**ABOVE:** another gem of a bridge, the Peerdenbrug, one of the oldest stone bridges in Bruges.

# AROUND BRUGES

Excursions from Bruges take you to Damme, a village
founded as a medieval port; De Haan, a 19th-century
beach resort; the modern container-port of Zeebrugge;
the polder village of Lissewege; the belle-époque
resort of Ostend; and the Ypres war memorials

**A**fter a visit to Bruges, you may
wish to escape from the crowds
and head for the more peaceful surrounding villages and towns.

## Damme

Only 7 km (4 miles) from Bruges,
**Damme ❶** is perfect for a bicycle
trip along the canal. It came to prominence as the city's principal outer
port in the Middle Ages, when cargo
ships from the Baltic and Mediterranean would dock here and unload
their wares onto smaller vessels for
transit into the city. Long after the
decline of Bruges, Damme remained
a strategic stronghold. Now it has
reinvented itself as the Flemish book
village, modelled on Britain's Hay-
on-Wye. Its well-preserved monuments, windmills and olde-worlde
charm make it a popular destination
for a Sunday lunch jaunt, and so it
boasts plenty of good, but not cheap,
restaurants. To get there, cycle up the
Damse Vaart or take the 43 bus from
Bruges (journey time: 20 minutes).

In 1134 the low-lying region
around Damme was struck by dis-
aster in the form of a great storm and
tidal wave. But this was to bring good
fortune to the tiny settlement as the
wave enlarged the Zwin inlet (now
a nature reserve east of Knokke), and
opened a sea route as far as Damme.
The village developed into a major

port, and a canal was built to link
it with the thriving cloth town of
Bruges. In 1180, Count Philip of
Alsace granted Damme privileges
and toll exemptions, including the
valuable monopoly on claret and
Swedish herring. Trade flourished
and a construction boom took off.

During the 12th–16th century, the
village expanded and enjoyed great
affluence and patronage. Everyone
who travelled to Bruges passed
through Damme and it became a key
post. When the French captured the

**Map
on page
114**

**LEFT:** a river barge
arriving in Damme.
**BELOW:** windmill in the
Damme countryside.

town in 1213, their 1,700-strong fleet could be contained in the harbour. The town was soon regained by the Flemish and the first fortifications were built. A second city wall was built in the early 15th century.

Damme's good fortune declined swiftly when access to its harbour silted up and trade shifted to ports nearer the coast. The town gained a new role as a military fortress when it was on the frontline in wars between the Spanish and the Dutch in the 16th and 17th centuries. The seven-point star-shaped Spanish fortifications are well preserved. Despite the ramparts, the town was captured by the Duke of Marlborough in 1706. The main canal running through Damme today is the Damse Vaart, built by Napoleon to link Bruges with the Schelde. Belgian independence in 1830 put paid to this project, and the canal only goes as far as Sluis, but its construction ripped through the centre of town, destroying buildings and waterways.

Damme once had a large number of medieval buildings, of which a few remain. The pretty **Stadhuis** (town hall; July–Aug 10am–noon, 2–6pm) on the Markt, is an intricately worked piece, built in 1241, then rebuilt in 1464. The current building has remained largely intact ever since, and contains some fine Gothic features in the upper-floor hall of justice and magistrates' room. The bell tower contains 25 bells, a sundial and a clock (1459). The oldest bells in Flanders – the Bells of Trade and the Bells of Victory (1392 and 1398 respectively) are in the building, but they ceased to be used in the tower in the 1970s.

On the square outside is a statue of Flanders' literary father, poet **Jacob van Maerlant** (1235–93), who was the first to write in Diets, the dialect of the region, and translated many encyclopaedic works from Latin into the vernacular for the education of local people.

*Charles Delporte sculpture outside Onze-Lieve-Vrouwe-kerk in Damme.*

**BELOW:** lovely Damme rooftop.

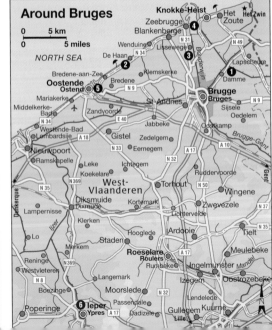

The **Onze-Lieve-Vrouwekerk** (Kerkstraat; Easter and May–Sept 10.30am–noon, 2.30–5.30pm; admission charge) is Damme's best-known landmark. Its high, flat-topped tower is typical of churches in the polders. Part of the old church lies in ruins. The 43-metre (142-ft) **tower** (separate admission charge) is worth the climb for the far-reaching view.

Like Bruges, Damme has a **Sint-Janshospitaal** (33 Kerkstraat; Easter–end Sept daily 2–6pm; admission charge), founded in 1249 and paid for by the tax on wine. Augustinian friars and nuns cared for the sick and elderly, while pilgrims could spend the night here. Its original chapel and infirmary now house a museum.

Damme is the birthplace of legendary hero **Thyl Uilenspiegel**, and the **Huyse De Grote Sterre** (3 Jacob van Maerlantstraat) museum details his life and many incarnations. The rebel was immortalised in an 1867 epic novel by Charles de Coster, in which he led the resistance against the Spanish occupiers. The many owl references around town refer to his name: *Uilenspiegel* means "owl-mirror".

## De Haan

More than a century ago, King Leopold II (1835–1909) oversaw the construction of the bathing resort of **De Haan** ❷. Since then, careful town planning paid off and it is the only Belgian resort that has resisted high-rise development, and retained a genteel, and slightly prim, charm. De Haan is ideal for a brief seaside escape in the height of summer or for bracing walks along the sand in cooler weather, followed by a hot chocolate topped with Chantilly. The **coastal tram** that brought the first tourists to De Haan in 1886 is the best means of reaching the town, even if it is no longer powered by steam. The **De Haan aan Zee tram stop** is an attraction in itself, an Art Nouveau building dating from 1900 in the cottage style characteristic of the town. From Bruges, the quickest route is to take a train to Ostend (of which there are two or three an hour) and then the coastal tram towards Knokke. Alternatively, the 31 bus from Bruges station goes direct to De Haan and the journey time is 40–50 minutes.

Map on page 114

*The coastal tram follows the line from De Panne to Knokke, making no less than 70 stops along the way.*

**BELOW:** the De Haan aan Zee tram stop.

## A Muddy Place

Interestingly, Damme's original name: "Hondsdamme", came from the old Flemish word *honte*, which means "muddy place at the mouth of a stream". And the early inhabitants of the low-lying lands saw a lot of mud indeed. They had to contend with the perpetual problem of flooding, and erected dykes to create agricultural land (polders) and protect themselves against the onslaught of the sea. The image of a running dog on Damme's coat of arms is due to a misinterpretation of the old name, *hond* meaning dog in Dutch. But who knows, maybe it was an early attempt at rebranding an image?

The area that is now De Haan was once the site of two of the oldest polder villages, Klemskerke (1003) and Vlissegem (988), whose inhabitants made their living mainly from shrimp fishing. Fast forward to the early 19th century, and the region was fighting a losing battle against the effects of wind erosion. Considerable effort went into planting trees and grasses adapted to survive the hostile conditions. Rabbits, too, were a constant nuisance, nibbling at the protective vegetation and destabilising the dunes with their burrows. A solution was found: a hinterland of woodland was created between Ostend and Blankenberge, which would hold back the dunes and at the same time provide pleasure for visitors to these two resorts.

In 1888, the **De Haan Hotel** (The Rooster Hotel), which gave the town its name, opened for business and became a popular holiday destination. Shortly afterwards, the king granted two architects a 90-year concession on a large piece of land with the instruction to build a beach town. The result was a harmonious collection of villas in belle-époque style, each surrounded by gardens and hedges. Strict rules determined the planting of green areas and the height of buildings. The rules still apply and the district, known as the **Concession**, lends De Haan its character and style.

The town was patronised by the Belgian royals – King Leopold II had the country's first golf course established here, among the dunes to the west of the town. He opened the **Royal Golf Club**, still a delightful small course, on 1 July 1903. Probably the most famous visitor was Albert Einstein, who spent six months here with his wife in 1933. They had taken refuge in Belgium after a voyage from the United States, during which they learned their property in Germany had been confiscated. The Einsteins stayed in the **Villa Savoyarde**, which still stands on Shakespearelaan. Einstein maintained his close friendship with Belgium's Queen Elisabeth, to whom he continued to write until his death in 1955. He received many visitors, including James Ensor, with whom he dined at the Cœur-Volant restaurant – a famously publicised dinner that led many restaurants in the area to offer "Einstein menus".

The scientist liked to take tea at the **Belle-Vue Hotel** (Koninklijk Plein) where, some 20 years earlier, Austrian author Stefan Zweig had stayed. But Einstein was on a Nazi wanted list, and although he wandered freely around the promenade and dunes, to the consternation of his bodyguards, the couple were forced to move on, first to England and then to the United States as the threat to Jewish intellectuals grew.

Today, the well-heeled resort is popular with middle-class families, and a horde of Dutch and German tourists. Most come for the long sandy beach, which stretches for several kilometres in either direction

*In 1889, playwright Maurice Maeterlinck, winner of the Nobel Prize for Literature in 1911, was one of the illustrious guests of the De Haan Hotel.*

**BELOW:** the Belle-Vue Hotel has seen many prestigious guests.

before you hit the next town. Even on the most crowded of days it is still possible to walk from the centre and find a quiet patch of sand. De Haan is proud of its active sailing and windsurfing club, **Watersportclub De Windhaan** (on the eastern beach), which rents out catamarans and teaches kite-surfing.

To enjoy a romantic view at sunset, wander east along the beach to the **Spioenkop** at Wenduine. The pretty little red-roofed pavilion is on the site of a guardpost shown on an 18th-century military map of the Austrian Netherlands.

An alternative to the beach is the dense dune wood, covering 63 hectares (157 acres), that surrounds De Haan. Thick gorse and briar roses can make the going tough off the paths, but there are well-trodden tracks, and bridle paths for riders (there are three riding stables in De Haan). Three **nature reserves** protect the vegetation: De Kijkuit cares for the rough and prickly plants that fight to survive in the sand behind the dunes; De Zandpanne is centred around a pond in the woods, where you might spot a sparrowhawk; and D'Heye exemplifies the sandy heathland further inland.

## Lissewege

The historic polder village of **Lissewege ❸**, situated between the city and the coast, is resolutely steeped in the past, with its 13th-century church and nearby Gothic abbey farm. Trains going from Bruges to Zeebrugge-Strand (beach) stop in Lissewege.

Linked to Bruges by the tranquil Lisseweegs Vaartje canal, Lissewege is a picturesque idyll. Pretty whitewashed houses cluster all around the early Gothic church, **Onze-Lieve-Vrouwekerk**, which has a typical Scheldt-Gothic brick tower that originally served as a lighthouse. A small village **museum** (15 June–15 Sept Sun–Fri 2–5.30pm; 16 Sept–14 June Fri, Sun and school holidays; admission charge) details the 1,000 year-long history of "the white village", a history that was largely influenced by **Ter Doest**, the massive Cistercian abbey just outside, which organised the cultivation

*Typical villa in the beautifully preserved district of Concession, in De Haan.*

**BELOW:** enjoying the fine weather on De Haan's beach.

of land within the polders, and got the inhabitants involved in larger-scale agriculture. The abbey farm estate is worth a visit for its 60-metre (195-ft) **13th-century barn** (free), a rare surviving example of what was then a lowly edifice, but which has stood the test of time extraordinarily well. The estate is popular among *Bruggelingen* who flock here to dine in the Hof ter Doest restaurant.

## Zeebrugge

It was Belgium's unstintingly ambitious King Leopold II who breathed life into **Zeebrugge ❹**. Desperate to restore to Bruges its reputation as an international trading hub, Leopold approved the construction of a vast sea-port between Knokke and Blankenberge, and of an industrial inland port north of Bruges. Thirty years later, in 1907, Leopold saw his dream realised, and cut the ribbon of the new port of Zeebrugge (literally, Sea-Bruges), linked to its medieval neighbour by the broad Boudewijn canal. Astonishingly, plans for the 12-km (7-mile) waterway had existed since 1446.

During World War I the Germans occupied the port and used it as a U-boat base, and it was destroyed by British bombers in April 1918. But Zeebrugge rose again, and established its reputation as the country's largest fishing port, which it remains. The fresh catch passes through an ultra-modern wholesale fish market in the port but there are numerous fishmongers in town as well. The old fish market has been converted into a maritime theme park, **Seafront Zeebrugge** (7 Vismijnstraat), whose prize exhibit is a 100-metre (328-ft) Soviet Foxtrot submarine B143, which can be explored. The rest of the museum brings to life the history of the North Sea coast and Bruges, the development of the fishing industry and the origins of the immense sea-port.

The transformation of Zeebrugge to a major container and ferry port (which runs passenger services to Hull, England and Rosyth, Scotland) has not been painless for the people of the polders. The industrial zones have absorbed acres of farmland and, with them, ancient water channels

*The St George memorial on Zeebrugge's dam commemorates the British Royal Navy's contribution to the Battle of Zeebrugge in 1918.*

**BELOW:** fishing boat in Zeebrugge harbour.

and irrigation systems. Meanwhile, factories, warehouses and roads continue to encroach on havens of calm such as Lissewege and Dudzele.

Recent years have seen strenuous efforts to reinvent the town as an attractive visitor destination. There is a broad sandy beach, a lively marina and a promenade stretching far out along the western dam. On a cultural note, an annual sand sculpture festival draws dozens of sculptors from all over the world.

## Ostend

**Ostend ❺** (Oostende), Belgium's largest seaside resort was discovered by Belgium's bourgeoisie in the 1880s, when they flocked here to benefit from the newly found health benefits of seawater. They arrived by the train-load in the elegant steel and glass **railway station** that appears somewhat outsized (although it is served by a daily high-speed service to Paris). The coastal tram, which shuttled tourists the length of the Belgian coast, from De Panne on the French border to Knokke in the north, was electrified in Ostend in 1897. There are now two or three direct trains an hour from Bruges and the journey takes just under 15 minutes.

With its theatre, casino, racecourse and charming belle-époque hotels, Ostend aimed to rival the French resorts of Deauville and Biarritz, models of elegance and sophistication. Its wealthy guests lodged in stunning villas and showy town houses. In 1873 King Leopold II had a residence built, which his descendants continued to frequent until the 1970s; it was finally put on the market in 2005. Visitors included Russian tsars, the Shah of Persia, the Emperor of Germany and Britain's Queen Victoria, who attended the English church. The English adored Ostend, where they would arrive by ferry from Dover to play lawn tennis, golf and beach croquet. In the 1860s there were around 2,000 British residents out of a total population of 16,000.

World War II bombing and postwar austerity took their toll. The Brussels–Ostend motorway, built in the 1950s, encouraged weekend trippers, which in turn led to the construction of concrete apartment blocks. Ostend lost its grandeur but not its appeal: on fine weekends the whole population seems to decamp to the coast, packing trains and clogging the E40 motorway.

In its early years, the **Casino Kursaal** (Monacoplein) recreated the luxury of an ocean liner, complete with gaming and billiard rooms, ballrooms, smoking salons, lounges, restaurants and a concert hall. Destroyed by the Nazis, it was rebuilt in 1953 in maritime style and recently underwent a major renovation as a convention and concert venue. Spruced-up facilities include the **Ostend Queen** fish brasserie, opened in collaboration with Brussels chef Pierre Wynants of the three-starred Comme Chez Soi.

*Going surfing in the North Sea.*

**BELOW:** Ostend's railway station.

*One of Ostend's most unexpected residents was soul legend Marvin Gaye, who lived here for two years in the early 1980s. While here, Gaye wrote his hit* Sexual Healing, *in self-imposed exile from a life of drug and alcohol abuse. Shortly afterwards, he returned to Los Angeles where he was shot dead by his father at the age of 44.*

**BELOW:** seafood stall by the harbour, Ostend.

At the opposite end of the promenade is the luxurious **Thermae Palace Hotel**, a 1930s spa. It stands above the elegant 400-metre/yard **royal arcades**, a colonnaded walkway built in 1905 to link the royal villa to the racecourse.

Ostend's most illustrious son is painter James Ensor (1860–1949), whose canvases opened the way for Surrealism and Expressionism. Ensor mocked the bourgeoisie in canvases peopled by haunting carnivalesque masks and skeletons, in a spirit much reminiscent of Bosch. He was one of the founders of the **Dead Rat Ball**, a glamorous masked and costumed party, named after a Montmartre café, that still takes place each year. The house in which he lived and worked from 1917 until his death has been converted into a museum, the **James Ensorhuis** (27 Vlaanderenstraat; Christmas holiday weekends, Easter, June–Sept 10am–noon, 2–5pm; admission charge), on the upper floors of a souvenir shop once owned by his aunt and uncle. It contains the interesting yet bizarre bric-à-brac of

his home and studio as well as reproductions of his work, but no originals. These can be admired in the city's **Museum voor Schone Kunsten** (Fine Arts Museum; Wed–Mon 10am–noon, 2–5pm; admission charge) located on Wapenplein, along with the work of several of his contemporaries.

Ostend also boasts a good modern art museum, the **Provinciaal Museum voor Moderne Kunst** (PMMK; 11 Romestraat; Tues–Sun 10am–6pm; admission charge). As well as a large permanent collection of modern and contemporary Belgian art, with works by eminent artists such as René Magritte, Constant Permeke, Leon Spilliaert, Pierre Alechinsky and Panamarenko, which are shown in rotation, the museum regularly organises temporary exhibitions.

**Visserskaai** is lined with fish stalls and restaurants serving a fare of sea snail soup, Ostend sole, oysters and mussels. Early each working day fishing boats draw up and sell their catch to restaurateurs from across the country. Beside the quay, at the **Noordzeeaquarium** (Apr–Sept daily 10am–12.30pm, 2–6pm; Oct–Mar Sat–Sun only), you will learn more about the flora and fauna of the North Sea. The highlight of the marina just round the corner is the three-masted former Belgian Navy training yacht, the **Mercator** (July–Aug 10am–5.30pm, Easter–June, Sept closed 12.30–2pm; Oct–Mar Sat–Sun only), which gives a taste of the life of a sea cadet.

If you still haven't had your fill of the natural elements, then plan a visit to the new attraction created on the instigation of Belgian astronaut Dirk Frimout, **Earth Explorer** (128b Fortstraat, near Fort Napoleon; daily 10am–6pm; admission charge), a scientific theme park that explores the power of the elements and the cause of natural disasters.

## Ypres

In 1260, at the height of its success as a cloth-trading centre, **Ypres ❻** (Ieper) was one of the largest cities in Europe with a population of 40,000. Things began to fall apart when it sided with England, on which it depended for wool supplies, during the Hundred Years' War. As the victim of French reprisals, power struggles and outbreaks of plague, Ypres' star waned as Bruges' ascended.

The town next gained prominence during World War I. In 1914, when the Belgian Army flooded the polders to the north in an attempt to stop the German advance, the British Army attacked from there. The town was half encircled by German forces, but the British hung on. The Ypres Salient, as this section of the Western Front came to be known, was the focus of repeated offensives over the next four years. The fierce battles claimed hundreds of thousands of lives, but the lines barely shifted. Ypres became inextricably linked to accounts of trench life amid mud, rats, poison gas and shell craters, a byword for the horrors of war.

A visit to Ypres can constitute one of the most moving experiences of a visit to Belgium. Hourly trains connect Bruges to Ypres (change at Kortrijk). The journey takes approximately 1¾ hours.

The town's buildings have been reconstructed in medieval splendour after being razed to the ground. Start your visit on the vast **Grote Markt**, the hub of political and commercial life. The immense **Lakenhallen** (Cloth Hall) bears witness to Ypres' role in the international cloth trade of the Middle Ages, when it was a staunch rival of both Bruges and Ghent. Larger than a cathedral (132 metres/432 ft) long, with 48 doors to the street) it was built alongside the Ieperlee River (now vaulted); boats could even sail into the building to unload their cargos. Atop the Lakenhallen sits the 70-metre (230-ft) **Belfort** (belfry), with 49 bells. The Gothic-Renaissance **Nieuwerck** next door is the town hall.

The Lakenhallen is home to the **tourist office** and the town's most interesting museum. **In Flanders Fields** (Apr–Sept daily 10am–6pm;

Map on page 114

**TIP**

Ypres tourist office is open Mon–Sat 9am–6pm (till 5pm in winter) and Sun 10am–5pm (tel: 057-23 92 20).

**LEFT:** Hill 62, the scene of bitter trench fighting by Canadian troops in 1916.
**BELOW:** fallen for their country: fields of crosses in the French Cemetery.

*Commemorating the Great War heroes on Armistice Day.*

**BELOW:** the Menin Gate War Memorial.

Oct–Mar Tues–Sun 10am–5pm; admission charge) is named after the poem by Canadian physician and poet John McCrae (1872–1918) who died on active service. The museum, which opened in 1998, brings to harrowing life the history of a terrible conflict that claimed 550,000 lives on the Flemish front. Its fascinating and moving collection of memorabilia, pictures and sound archives recalls the daily routine of a soldier.

The war is remembered in haunting fashion each evening at 8pm sharp at the **Menenpoort** (Menin Gate), where buglers have played the *Last Post* every night for nearly 80 years in tribute to all those who died. The arch, built by the British in 1928, is engraved with the names of 54,896 of the 100,000 Commonwealth soldiers who have no known grave. Those who perished after July 1917 are commemorated in the memorial at Tyne Cot *(see below)*.

Other sites of interest include the **Sint-Jan Godshuis** (31 Ieperleestraat; 10am–12.30pm, 2–6pm; admission charge), which houses the city museum. The almshouse

dates from 1270, but was rebuilt in 1555. It was one of the few buildings left standing in 1918. Ypres' poignant history is illustrated here in maps and pictures.

Gothic **Sint-Maartenskathedraal** contains the tomb of Bishop Jansenius, founder of the Jansenist doctrine. In the side altar a retable depicts the siege of the town in 1383. The towering spire (100 metres/328 ft) is visible from miles around. Next door are the remains of a cloister and episcopal palace.

**St George's Memorial Church** (Elverdingsestraat) was erected in memory of the British and Commonwealth soldiers who lost their life in the Great War; it was inaugurated in 1929. It is now part of the Church of England's Diocese in Europe. Its local congregation is swelled by many people who come to visit the battlefields.

Ten km (6 miles) northeast of Ypres, the **Tyne Cot Military Cemetery** is the most visited of the 170 graveyards in the area, and the largest Commonwealth cemetery in the world. It was the site of the Third Battle of Ypres, at the village of Passendale (Passchendaele).

## Cat-throwing festival

One of Flanders' more bizarre folkloric festivals, the **Kattenworp** (cat throwing), takes place in the Grote Markt on the second Sunday in May when a jester flings toy cats from the top of the belfry. Rather than a disdain for fluffy toys, it recalls an ancient tradition involving live cats and the casting out of evil spirits – a practice maintained until 1817 (it was revived between the two World Wars). A much larger festival, the **Kattenstoet** is held every three years on the second Sunday in May, when there is a full costumed and choreographed procession with 2,000 participants, horses and decorated floats. ❑

# RESTAURANTS

## Restaurants

### Damme

**Bij Lamme Goedzak**
13 Markt. Tel: 050-35 20 03.
Open L & D Fri–Wed. €€
Regional dishes a
speciality in this ancient
house opposite the town
hall. Fixed-priced menus,
eel and lobster menus.
Large rear terrace.

**De Damsche Poort**
29 Kerkstraat. Tel: 050-35
32 75. Open L & D Tues–Sat,
L only Sun. €€€
Flemish staples include
shrimp-stuffed tomatoes,
Zeeland oysters and
baby sole. Smart old
farmhouse, elegant dining
room and lovely garden.

**Napoléon**
4 Damse Vaart Zuid. Tel:
050-35 32 99. Open L & D
Thur–Mon, L only Tues. €€
Classic spot by the canal,
favoured by an older clientele. Sweetbreads in port,
eels in tartare sauce,
steak and fish dishes.

### De Haan

**Rabelais**
2 Van Eycklaan. Tel: 059-53
33 99. Open L & D Wed–Sun,
D only Tues (no D Tues Sept–
Apr). €€€€
Fine dining in sumptuous
setting. Specialities
include wild duck with
mushrooms, cashew nuts
and goose liver glaze.

**Strand Hotel**
19 Zeedijk. Tel: 059-23 34
25. Open L & D daily. €€
Comfortable hotel-
restaurant with a prime

position on the prome-
nade. Weekly fixed menu
and staples like sole,
mussels and frogs' legs.

**'t Zuid**
5 Grotestraat. Tel: 059-51 21
90. Open L & D Wed–Sun.
€€€
Seasonal produce and
fresh fish with creamy
sauces served in an
attractive villa with an
Art Deco interior.

### Lissewege

**Hof Ter Doest**
4 Ter Doeststraat, Lissewege.
Tel: 050-54 40 82. Open L & D
daily. €€
This old abbey farm
houses a family-run
restaurant attracting
hordes of Bruggelingen
for weekend lunches.
Good portions of Belgian
fare, served without fuss.

### Zeebrugge

**Mon Manège à Toi**
44 Vismijnstraat. Tel: 050-55
05 60. Open L & D daily. €€
North Sea dishes pre-
pared by much-awarded
chef Yvo Degraeve. On
the charmless street of
the Seafront Zeebrugge
visitor attraction, it has
an appealing dining room
with a long refectory
table and a grill.

**'t Molentje**
211 Baron de Maerelaan.
Tel: 050 54 61 64. Open L & D
Thur–Sat, Mon–Tues. €€€€
Unprepossessing house
near Bruges–Zeebrugge
road, renowned through-
out Flanders. Chef Danny

Horseele knocks up cre-
ative wonders with foie
gras, oysters and eels.

### Ostend

**Beluga**
33 Kemmelbergstraat. Tel:
059-51 15 88. Open L & D
daily. €€
Stylish bar-restaurant
specialising in seafood.
Warm and welcoming.

**David Dewaele**
39 Visserskaai. Tel: 059-70
42 26. Open L & D Tues–Sun.
€€€
Chef David Dewaele has
built a fine reputation for
his original fish dishes.
A treat for the senses.

**Le Grillon**
31 Visserskaai. Tel: 059-70 60
63. Open L & D Fri–Wed. €€
Long established res-
taurant. Classic Belgian-
French fish cuisine and
steaks. Friendly service.

**Ostend Queen**
Kursaal Westhelling. Tel:
059-29 50 55. Open L & D
daily. €€€–€€€€
Fish brasserie on the
top floor of the reno-
vated Kursaal, under the
patronage of Pierre
Wynants, chef of Comme
Chez Soi in Brussels.
Specialises in sole, fish
soup, seafood platters;
reasonably priced week-
day lunch menu and a
smart dress code in the
evening. Pleasant views
over the sea.

**Petit Nice**
62b Albert I Promenade. Tel:
059-80 39 28. Open L & D
Thur–Tues. €€

Unpretentious 1920s-
style restaurant on the
promenade. Wide choice
of fish dishes, good value
fixed-price menus and an
excellent chef.

### Ypres

**De Ruyffelaer**
9 Gustave de Stuersstraat.
Tel: 057-36 60 06. Open D
Wed–Fri, L Sat–Sun. €
This friendly restaurant
near Grote Markt is
proud of its olde-worlde
image. The traditional
menu includes ox tongue
in tomato sauce and
chicken in cherry beer.

**De Waterpoort**
43 Brugseweg. Tel: 057-20
54 52. Open L & D Thur–Fri,
Sun–Tues, D only Sat. €€
Excellent grill restaurant,
stylish but informal, 10
minutes' walk from the
main square. Salads and
vegetarian options.

**Old Tom**
8 Grote Markt. Tel: 057-20 15
41. Open L & D daily. €–€€
Authentic hotel-restaurant
on the main square.
Mussels, steaks, eels
and other staples are
excellent. Service can be
slow when the terrace
gets busy on sunny days.

### PRICE CATEGORIES

Prices for three-course
dinner per person with a
half-bottle of house wine:

€ = under €25
€€ = €25–40
€€€ = €40–60
€€€€ = over €60

## BRUGES TRANSPORT

# GETTING THERE
# AND GETTING AROUND

## GETTING THERE

### By Air

Most international airlines fly into Brussels National Airport (tel: 0900-70 000; www.brusselsairport.be) at Zaventem, just outside Brussels. The airport is linked to an underground railway station, with direct trains to Brussels and Ghent. The journey to Bruges involves one change at Ghent and takes 1 hour 30 minutes.

Taken together, British Airways, BMI, Virgin Express and SN Brussels Airlines operate virtually an hourly day service between Brussels and London – less frequently from other cities around Britain. Aer Lingus and SN Brussels Airlines fly between Dublin and Brussels. Ryanair flies from many cities in Britain and Ireland to Charleroi (or Brussels Charleroi, as the airline calls it), about an hour by bus from Brussels. The best way to get to Bruges from Charleroi is to take the Ryanair shuttle bus to Bruxelles Midi station and board a train to Bruges. The total journey time is about two hours.

There are direct daily flights to Brussels from many cities in North America and Canada, among them New York, Washington, Chicago, Atlanta and Toronto.

### By Car

Bruges is located on the E40 motorway linking London with Istanbul. Drivers coming from Britain can travel through the Channel Tunnel on a Eurotunnel Shuttle from Folkestone. Although you can just turn up and buy a ticket, it is worth booking ahead at busy times of the year to avoid a long wait. From the E40, follow signs to Brugge Centrum for addresses in the centre of town. Parking in the old town can be a problem, and navigation is difficult because of the network of one-way streets. Ask your hotel, when booking, if they can provide a map with the route indicated. Most hotels do not have parking spaces, so after dropping off your luggage, you will have to take your car to the car park next to the railway station. You can claim a free public transport ticket for each person in the car by presenting your car park ticket at the office of De Lijn, the Flanders public transport operator, located outside the railway station, and telling them how many people are travelling in the car.

### By Train

Bruges lies on the main railway line connecting Brussels with Ghent and the Belgian coast. Trains from Brussels to Bruges

### PHONE NUMBERS

The local phone numbers given in this guide include the Bruges local area code (050). When dialling from abroad, omit the first 0 of the code.

take about one hour. For train times see the Belgian railway website (www.b-rail.be). You can travel from London or Ashford to Brussels by Eurostar (www.eurostar.com), and your ticket will enable you to travel free on Belgian railways to and from Bruges (within 24 hours of the time stamped on the Eurostar ticket). Fast intercity trains (IC) to Bruges are modern and comfortable, but often crowded at weekends in the summer. The main station lies just outside the old city. It takes about 10 minutes to walk into town, but there are frequent shuttle buses from the station to the Markt square.

### By Sea

Superfast Ferries (www.superfast.com) operates a luxurious fast ferry service nightly between Rosyth in Scotland and Zeebrugge, 15 km (9 miles) from Bruges. The crossing takes around 17 hours. There are also sailings every night from Hull to Zeebrugge operated by P&O Ferries (www.poferries.com), taking around 12 hours. Ferry services between Dover and Ostend were axed some years ago because of competition from the Channel Tunnel, but there are frequent crossings from Dover to Calais, about one hour's drive from Bruges, and from Ramsgate to Dunkirk, just 40 minutes away.

## By Coach

The cheapest way to get to Bruges is by coach. Eurolines runs a daily service from Victoria Coach Station in London. The journey takes about six hours. In the UK, tel: 08705 143219; www.eurolines.com.

## GETTING AROUND

### Buses

Most places in Bruges are easily reached on foot, although you may want to take a bus from the station to the town centre. The city is served by a network of small buses operated by De Lijn. A single ticket bought on the bus costs €1. Cheaper options include a day pass (€3), or a 10-journey pass, which can be used on public transport throughout Flanders (€7.50). Tickets have to be inserted in the orange scanner near the doors every time you board a bus.

### Car Parks

Parking within the old town is almost impossible, and most tourists are advised by their

### WHERE TO HIRE A BIKE

**E Kar**: 44–48 Vlamingstraat, tel: 050-33 00 34.
**Eric Popelier**: 14 Hallenstraat, tel: 050-34 32 62.
**QuasiMundo**: 5 Nieuwe Gentweg, tel: 050-33 07 75; www.quasimundo.com.
**'t Koffieboontje**: 4 Hallenstraat, tel: 050-33 80 27.

hotels to leave their vehicles at the large car park next to the station, which has space for 2,000 cars, or in one of four other car parks in the old town. The charge for parking next to the station is reasonable, and includes free travel on the city buses *(see page 124)*. Hotel guests are allowed to drive into town to drop off baggage and to collect it when they leave.

## On Foot

The compact scale of Bruges and the quasi absence of cars make it an ideal city for strolling around. It takes approximately 20 minutes to walk from the railway station to the main square. The tourist office has mapped out four walks within the city, covering themes such as "Europeans in Bruges", and "The Unknown City". The walks are described in English on the website www.brugge.be.

## Cycling

It's clear as soon as you arrive that Bruges is a city of cyclists. Although everywhere is within walking distance, you might want to rent a bike to cycle around the ramparts or take a trip out of town. The most popular trip is along the tree-lined Daamsevaart canal to the charming little town of Damme, where you can admire the town hall before diving into one of the local restaurants for a hearty Flemish lunch.

Several shops hire bikes by the hour, day or week. The main outlets are in the narrow Hallenstraat, next to the belfry, but the cheapest and most convenient option for those coming by train is to rent a bike directly at the station, as you can book the bike when you buy a ticket to Bruges and it will be ready when you arrive. QuasiModo organises a series of guided bike tours in Bruges and the surrounding countryside, daily from March to October.

## ORIENTATION

Bruges is a compact town with all the main sights, hotels and restaurants located within the medieval ramparts. When looking for an address, it is helpful to know that a *reie* is a canal, a *plaats* is a square and a *straat* is a street. If you are navigating without a map, the easiest way to get to the centre is to look for the octagonal top of the belfry. Elsewhere in town, church spires provide useful landmarks.

## Day Trips

Bruges is a good base for day trips to other cities in Flanders. The railway station is easy to reach and well-served by fast trains. There are direct trains to the four large beach resorts of Ostend, Zeebrugge, Blankenberge and Knokke. Ostend is a bustling resort with excellent museums and typical Belgian restaurants, while Zeebrugge is a smaller town with a good maritime museum and several fish restaurants on the old harbour. Blankenberge has a more popular apppeal, while Knokke is one of the most elegant resorts on the North Sea coast.

Many tourists make a day trip to the historical town of Ypres, which is surrounded by World War I cemeteries. While it is possible to reach Ypres by train, it is easier to book a minibus tour organised by Quasimodo (tel: 050-37 04 70; www.quasimodo.be). The tour takes in cemeteries, war bunkers and museums; it lasts 7h30.

## Information

The city recently opened a new centre for tourist information and ticket reservations, called **In & Uit Brugge**. It is located on the ground floor of the new imposing Concertgebouw, 34 't Zand, tel: 050-44 86 86; www.brugge.be (daily 10am–6pm, Thur 10am–8pm).

BRUGES

GHENT

ANTWERP

# BRUGES ACCOMMODATION

## SOME THINGS TO CONSIDER BEFORE YOU BOOK A ROOM

### Choosing a Hotel

Bruges has very few grand old hotels. Older establishments, most of which are clustered around the 't Zand, tend to be somewhat gloomy; it was only in the 1970s, when the city began to clean up its polluted waterways, that new hotels began to appear along the canals, often in tastefully restored houses. Numerous stylish hotels have now opened, which make for the perfect choice for a romantic weekend. They attract a great number of British guests, and the decor tends to be English country house rather than hip and modern.

With a bit of searching, you should be able to track down an idyllic hotel room, either with a view of a canal, or tucked under the eaves of an old merchant's house, or looking out on a neat Renaissance garden.

Almost all of the 100 or so hotels are located in the old town, making it very easy to get around on foot.

### Timing

Bruges is at its best in the spring, when daffodils cover the begijnhof lawns. In summer, the light can be as sharp as a Van Eyck painting. The busiest times are Easter and July to mid-September. While the centre gets crowded, the outer fringes remain blissfully calm. The city is quieter in the autumn, although be warned that the weather can be blustery. The number of visitors drops off dramatically in winter, although December has become busy, thanks to the introduction of a Christmas market. The low season runs from January to February; during that time of year many hotels and restaurants close, but the city can be particularly atmospheric, especially if there is snow.

### Reservations

Hotels can be booked by phone – receptionists invariably speak good English – but this means you will pay the full price. You can often get a substantial reduction by booking online, although this may take several days to process. It is still best to phone a hotel if you need something extra, such as a child's cot.

The Bruges Tourist Office offers a free booking service which proves extremely useful for last-minute reservations. You can check out availability and make a booking via their website (www.brugge.be) or by phone (from abroad, tel: 050-44 86 21). The association of hoteliers' website (www.hotels-brugge.org) also provides an instant online booking service and is more user-friendly.

Resotel (tel: 027-79 39 39, fax: 027-79 39 00, www.belgium hospitality.com; open Mon–Fri 8.30am–6pm) is another free accommodation booking service for the whole of Belgium which offers competitive hotel rates.

### Cost and Quality

All hotels in Belgium are graded from one to five stars, according to their facilities (or lack of them). As a general rule, the price is determined by the number of stars, which provides a certain guarantee of quality but takes no account of factors such as the friendliness of staff or character of the building. You may find an atmospheric one-star hotel for a fraction of the price of an uninspired four-star establishment.

The quality of accommodation is generally high and hotels that fail to meet standards are quickly downgraded by the Flanders Tourist Office. Most hotels occupy old buildings in quiet locations, although several international chains have recently been allowed to build modern hotels in the heart of the town. Rates normally include a buffet breakfast.

The tourist office may offer special deals, which usually include a room, a meal, and a few extras such as free museum entry or a guided tour.

# THE CENTRE

Hotels in the centre of Bruges are conveniently close to the main squares and museums, although rooms can sometimes be noisy if they overlook a busy street, and canal traffic can be loud as well.

Northern Bruges is quieter, with most hotels located on residential streets. The southern quarters are quiet, too, with restaurants and cafés geared towards a younger clientele. Hotels are situated close to the station and the beguinage.

## Expensive

### De Orangerie
10 Karthuizerinnenstraat
Tel: 050-34 16 49
Fax: 050-33 30 16
www.hotelorangerie.com
A firm favourite with visiting celebrities, De Orangerie occupies a charming 15th-century convent with water lapping the walls. Located in a narrow street close to the belfry, it couldn't be more central. A recent stylish makeover has transformed it into a chic boutique hotel furnished with fine antiques. There's a lakeside terrace and a romantic orangerie. You'll be charged extra for breakfast.

### De Tuilerieen
7 Dijver
Tel: 050-34 36 91
Fax: 050-34 04 00
www.hoteltuilerieen.com

A luxurious 45-room hotel in a pale pink mansion facing the main canal. With courteous staff and antique-stuffed rooms, this is a hotel that is hard to resist. Some rooms have views of the canal, while others face the garden. There is also a bright swimming pool and sauna. Breakfast is expensive, and you may prefer to order coffee and croissants from a nearby patisserie.

### Die Swaene
1 Steenhouwersdijk
Tel: 050-34 27 98
Fax: 050-33 66 74
www.dieswaene-hotel.com
Most people fall in love with this lovely brick-built hotel on a quiet, tree-lined canal situated close to the centre. It's an irresistible building, with old wooden staircases and heavy oak furniture. The 22 rooms come in different sizes and styles, some of them with elegant four-poster beds. A candlelit restaurant, pool and sauna add to the allure. There is a Romeo and Juliet package aimed at honeymooners.

## Moderate

### Jan Brito
1 Freren Fonteinstraat
Tel: 050-33 06 01
Fax: 050-33 06 52
A small gem in the heart of Bruges, this 23-room hotel occupies

a 16th-century merchant's house with a secluded Renaissance garden. Tastefully decorated, with marble fireplaces, thick carpets and an oak staircase.

### Oud Huis De Peellaert
20 Hoogstraat
Tel: 050-33 78 89
Fax: 050-33 08 16
www.depeellaert.com
A stylish hotel set in a 19th-century mansion in the heart of the old town. Inside, you'll find an artistic blend of antiques and modern details such as Alessi cutlery. The beds are comfortable and the buffet breakfast is one of the best in Bruges.

### Relais Bourgondisch Cruyce
41–47 Wollestraat
Tel : 050-33 79 26
Fax : 050-34 19 68
www.relaisbourgondischcruyce.be
A gorgeous small hotel in two gabled houses with timbered façades backing onto a canal. Decorated in sumptous 17th-century Flemish style with carved furniture, stone floors and large fireplaces. The 16 bedrooms are individually designed, combining traditional decor with a hint of modern design. Ask for a room with a canal view; those at the front overlook a restaurant-filled square.

### Romantik Pandhotel
16 Pandreitje
Tel: 050-34 06 66
Fax: 050-34 05 56
www.pandhotel.com

A comfortable, family-run, 23-room hotel in a secluded corner of Bruges close to the centre. Set in a converted 18th-century carriage house, this boutique hotel is brimming with cachet and bedrooms are appealing, if on the small side. The breakfast room is furnished in country-house-kitchen style.

## Inexpensive

### Ensor
10 Speelmansrei
Tel: 050-34 25 89
Fax: 050-34 20 18
www.ensorhotel.be
This friendly 12-room hotel occupies a brick building on a quiet canal close to the 't Zand. The rooms are plainly furnished, but well-maintained, and all have en-suite bathrooms, making this one of the best budget hotels in the city.

## PRICE CATEGORIES

Price categories are for a double room with breakfast:
**Expensive**: €200–300
**Moderate**: €100–200
**Inexpensive**: under €100

BRUGES

GHENT

ANTWERP

# SOUTH AND WEST

## Moderate

### De Barge
15 Bargeweg
Tel: 050-38 51 50
Fax: 050-38 21 25
www.debargehotel.com
Wake up to the sound of ducks outside the window in this unusual hotel located in a converted Flemish canal barge. The rooms may be small, but they have an appealing nautical flavour, with white wood, blue paint and bright red lifejackets laid out on the beds. The hotel has a bar, terrace, restaurant and car park. Located just outside the old town, a brisk 10-minute walk from the centre.

### Egmond
15 Minnewater
Tel: 050-34 14 45
Fax: 050-34 29 40
www.egmond.be
This attractive, small hotel is located in a gabled Flemish mansion next to the romantic Minnewater lake. The interior is furnished in an appealing Flemish traditional style, complete with tiled floors, oak chests and 18th-century fireplaces. The eight bedrooms look out on a rambling garden, making for peaceful nights. There is a car park for guests, and the station is just a 10-minute walk away. No credit cards.

## Inexpensive

### Botaniek
23 Waalsestraat
Tel: 050-34 14 24
Fax: 050-34 59 39
www.botaniek.be
A stylish little hotel located in a quiet street close to the Astridpark. The nine-room establishment occupies an 18th-century town house furnished in an elegant Louis XV style. Rooms on the top floor have wonderful views of gabled houses and ancient spires.

### 't Keizershof
126 Oostmeers
Tel: 050-33 87 28
The perfect place for anyone travelling on

a tight budget, this compact, seven-room establishment is located in a pretty little street close to the railway station. The rooms are as cheap as they come, yet they are clean and comfortable. A notice at the entrance sums up the owner's outlook. "When you are sleeping, we look just like one of those big fancy hotels."

# NORTH AND EAST

## Expensive

### Relais Oud-Huis Amsterdam
3 Spiegelrei
Tel: 050-34 18 10
Fax: 050-33 88 91
www.oha.be
Overlooking a quiet canal in the heart of the old merchants' quarter and near the Markt, this romantic 22-room hotel set in a 17th-century trading house has a wooden staircase, chandeliers, beams and stunning antique furniture. There is also a pretty interior courtyard. Skip the hotel breakfast, which costs extra, and walk five minutes to Het Dagelijks Brood (21 Philipstockstraat) to enjoy coffee and delicious croissants in a typical French farmhouse interior.

## Moderate

### Adornes
26 St Annarei
Tel: 050-34 13 36
Fax: 050-34 20 85
www.adornes.be
Overlooking a quiet canal, this pretty little 20-room hotel occupies a row of traditional brick houses in the charming St Anna quarter. The rooms are comfortable and bright, some with oak beams. Breakfast is included in the price of the room. There are free bikes for guests' use as well as a limited number of underground parking spaces. All Adornes guests receive an advantage card to enjoy special entrance prices to museums and boat trips.

### Aragon
22 Naaldenstraat
Tel: 050-33 35 33
Fax: 050-34 28 05
www.aragon.be
This well-run hotel is located in the heart of the old merchant's quarter, opposite a palace once owned by the Italian Medici family. The 42 rooms were recently renovated in a comfortable English-country-house style.

### Bryghia
4 Oosterlingenplein
Tel: 050-33 80 59
Fax: 050-34 14 30
www.bryghiahotel.be

This friendly, family-run hotel is situated in one of Bruges' most peaceful neighbourhoods, as it is rarely visited by tourists. The 18-room hotel occupies a 15th-century building that once belonged to the Hanseatic merchants. The interior is quite cosy and tastefully furnished with comfortable sofas and exposed wood beams. Some rooms enjoy a view of a sleepy canal.

## Inexpensive

### Asiris
9 Lange Raamstraat
Tel: 050-34 17 24
Fax: 050-34 74 58
www.hotelasiris.be

A small, family-run hotel in a quiet quarter close to the lovely Sint-Gilliskerk. The 11 bedrooms are furnished in a plain, modern style aimed at travellers on a budget and families. The rooms under the eaves are a tight squeeze. Breakfast is included in the price, making this one of the best inexpensive hotels in town. Special rates are offered out of season.

### Karel De Stoute
23 Moerstraat
Tel: 050-34 33 17
Fax: 050-34 44 72
www.hotelkareldestoute.be

Named after one of the 15th-century dukes of Burgundy, this intimate hotel occupies a building that once formed part of the Prinsenhof ducal residence. Run by a friendly couple, the nine-room hotel offers a relaxed atmosphere right in the heart of the old town. The rooms are spacious and attractive. Some have oak beams, while two have bathrooms located in a 15th century circular staircase tower. The bar is in an ancient cellar with a vaulted brick ceiling. There is also free internet access.

### Ter Reien
1 Langestraat
Tel : 050-34 91 00
Fax : 050-34 40 48
www.hotelterreien.be

As its name suggests, the "hotel on the canal" is a small hotel located along one of the most beautiful canals in the city. Notably, it occupies the house where the Symbolist painter Fernand Khnopff spent his childhood. The rooms are bright and comfortable. There is a breakfast courtyard.

## BED & BREAKFAST

There are a growing number of bed and breakfasts *(gasthuizen)* in Bruges. These are located in private homes, and offer an inexpensive alternative to hotels. By law, Belgian B&Bs cannot have more than three rooms, so the atmosphere is intimate. Many are owned by local artists, architects and designers, and some have stunning interiors and gardens. The owners are nearly always ready to provide you with insider advice on the best restaurants and cafés in the area. These places are ideal for single travellers or couples, although bear in mind that they don't provide the services of a hotel. To locate a B&B, visit the Bruges Guild of Guest Houses website, which lists 44 approved addresses (www.brugge-bedandbreakfast.com). Bookings can normally be made online, although most owners do not accept credit cards.

### Absoluut Verhulst
1 Verbrand Nieuwland
Tel: 050-33 45 15
www.b-verhulst.com.

A stylish B&B in a striking, red 17th-century house. Three bright rooms include a large loft and a funky duplex.

### Baert
28 Westmeers
Tel: 050-33 45 15
www.bedandbreakfastbrugge.be.

Friendly B&B in a former stable building near the new Concert-gebouw. There are two small rooms with private canal-side terraces that catch the afternoon sun. Parking is in the owner's garage.

### Dieltiens
40 Waalsestraat
Tel: 050-33 42 94
Fax: 050-33 52 30
www.bedandbreakfastbruges.be.

Run by a musical family in a grand 18th-century mansion close to the heart of Bruges. The three rooms are tastefully decorated.

### Lut & Bruno Setola
12 Sint-Walburgastraat
Tel: 050-33 49 77
Fax: 050-33 25 51
www.bedandbreakfast-bruges.com.

Situated in an interesting area, off the tourist trail. The three rooms are located under the eaves of a 17th-century house, with wonderful views across the old rooftops.

### Number 11
11 Peerdenstraat
Tel: 050-33 06 75
Fax: 050-33 06 75
www.number11.be.

Not the cheapest B&B in town, but worth every euro. The owners have turned a 17th-century gable house into one of the most alluring retreats in the city, offering three large rooms, and a wood-panelled lounge with a blazing fire.

## HOSTELS

There are several youth hostels in the historic quarters of Bruges that offer basic accomoda-tion for backpackers.

### Bauhaus
135–137 Langestraat
Tel: 050-34 10 93,
Fax: 050-33 41 80
www.bauhaus.be.

Large hostel in the alternative quarter with 80 rooms, sleeping from two to eight people. There is bike rental, a cybercafé and a bar.

### Snuffel Sleep-In
47–49 Ezelstraat
Tel: 050-33 31 33
Fax: 050-33 32 50
www.snuffel.be.

A more austere hostel with rooms sleeping 4 to 12 people.

## SELF-CATERING

For longer stays, you might consider booking a flat or house. This is often much cheaper than a hotel, especially as you can eat at home. The minimum stay is usually two days. The tourist office recommends 50 owners of rental properties on their website. Most properties can be booked online through their own websites.

### PRICE CATEGORIES

Price categories are for a double room with breakfast:
**Expensive**: €200–300
**Moderate**: €100–200
**Inexpensive**: under €100

BRUGES

GHENT

ANTWERP

## BRUGES ACTIVITIES

# THE ARTS, FESTIVALS, NIGHTLIFE, SHOPPING AND SIGHTSEEING

### THE ARTS

Bruges has a reputation for being quiet in the evening, but visitors should be able to track down an interesting classical concert or organ recital, or even a local rock band playing in a medieval cellar. To find out what's happening locally in Bruges, pick up the free culture listings *Exit*, usually found lying around in the tourist office, in cafés, and in theatre foyers. Ask at the tourist office if you have trouble finding a copy.

#### Concerts and Opera

Bruges has a strong musical tradition that goes back to the Middle Ages. As well as concerts in churches, visitors can listen to music on the town carillon as they wander along the canals.

The modern **Concertgebouw**, which opened in 2002, is the main cultural venue in Bruges (34 't Zand; ticket agency: tel: 070-22 33 02; www.concertgebouw.be; for other information tel: 050-47 69 99). The concert hall seating 1,300 people is used for large orchestral performances, contemporary dance and opera. A smaller, 300-seat hall is the venue for experimental music, jazz recitals and literary events.

For something with more of an edge, head to the new Muziekcentrum **Cactus** in the St Andries district (27 Magdalenastraat, tel: 050-33 20 14; www.cactusmusic.be), where the programme juggles an adventurous mix of rock, folk, blues, country, jazz and disco.

#### Carillon Concerts

The city's 17th-century carillon hangs in the tower of the Cloth Hall on the Markt. The carillon is programmed to play a different tune, ranging from Mozart to Jacques Brel, every 15 minutes. But it is worth stopping to listen to one of the 45-minute concerts given by the town carillonneur, which begin at 2.15pm on Wednesday, Saturday and Sunday. The best place to stand is in the courtyard of the Cloth Hall.

#### Cinema

Bruges has many small cinemas that screen a wide range of films. Most are shown in the original language, but children's films are usually dubbed into Dutch. **Cinema Lumière** (Sint Jacobsstraat, tel: 050-34 34 65; www.lumiere.be) is a small art-house cinema that shows independent contemporary films and the occasional black-and-white classic. The cinema listing site www.cinebel.be has a full list of films in Bruges.

### Dance and Theatre

Performances of modern dance, often featuring innovative Flemish companies, are regularly staged in the modern Concertgebouw. The **Stadsschouwburg** (29 Vlamingstraat, tel: 050-44 30 60; www.cultuurcentrumbrugge.be) is a 19th-century theatre with an exciting programme of theatre, poetry, dance and contemporary music. If you're after more alternative vibes, check out **De Werf** (108 Werfstraat, tel: 050-33 05 29; www.dewerf.be), a hip theatre with contemporary drama from Flanders and the Netherlands, jazz concerts and kids' theatre on Saturdays and Sundays.

### FESTIVALS AND EVENTS

#### May

**Meifoor** Sprawling funfair complete with stalls and rides on 't Zand, Simon Stevinplein and Koning Albertpark.
**Holy Blood Procession** (Ascension Day, which always falls on the last Thursday in May) A most spectacular historical procession that has its roots in the early Middle Ages. Dating from 1291, this deeply religious ceremony venerates a holy relic believed

## TICKETS

Tickets for concerts and plays are sold at the In & Uit box office, located on the ground floor of the Concertgebouw, 34 't Zand. It is open daily 10am–6pm (Thurs 10am–8pm). For online information and bookings, visit the website www.tinck.be.
For phone bookings, tel: 070-22 50 05.

### Museum Passes

You can save money on museum entry charges by buying a Combiticket (€15), which allows you to visit any five museums. There is also a Fietscombiticket (€15), which provides a hired bike for a day, entry to three museums, and a free drink in an historic Flemish inn attached to the Folklore Museum. The tickets are sold in the In & Uit bureau.

to contain some drops of Christ's blood. Lasting several hours, the impressive procession has a cast of thousands, including musicians, dancers, soldiers and even a flock of sheep.
**Beach Labyrinth** (Zeebrugge) Lose yourself in the extensive sand maze on the beach at Zeebrugge, just a short train ride from Bruges. This event lasts from May to July.

### July

**Cactus Festival** A summer festival that brings acclaimed bands to a beautiful waterfront location in the Minnewater Park.
**Festival of Flanders** A major festival of classical music with performances taking place throughout Flanders. The venues in Bruges range from traditional churches and concert halls to historic houses and castles.

### September

**Open Monument Day** Historic buildings usually inaccessible are open to the public one day only.

### December

**Kerstmarkt** Bruges hosts an atmospheric Christmas market on Simon Stevinplein, with an artificially chilled ice-skating rink on the Markt under the medieval belfry (daily from 10am–10pm).
**Snow and Ice Sculpture Festival** A magical exhibition featuring beautiful ice sculptures created by teams of professional carvers from the world's coldest zones.

## NIGHTLIFE

Bruges might seem a little quiet after dark, but it is more lively than it looks. Much of the action happens inside small bars and cafés, away from the tourist traps. You won't find noisy groups wandering the streets, or crowded squares where everyone meets, but you will discover dark Flemish bars where you can drink an exquisite Belgian beer while listening to some good jazz.

Visitors who come to Bruges in the summer might be happy enough sitting out on a pavement terrace. There are dozens of cafés with terraces on squares like the Markt and 't Zand, but it is worth hunting out some of the more intimate outdoor spots, like the café terraces facing the Astridpark or the sublime terrace shaded by trees at the end of the Groenerei.

Live music in Bruges tends to begin earlier than in Antwerp or Brussels. Start with a visit to **De Republiek** (36 Sint-Jacobsstraat, tel: 050-34 02 29), a candlelit brown café attached to a theatre complex. This is a good place to check out fly posters, and pick up word-of-mouth tips on jazz and folk concerts. Look out for the programme in **Cactus** (see Concerts, page 130), which regularly organises dance events and concerts by young bands in the Magdalenazaal in the St Andries suburb.

Eiermarkt, a small square north of the Markt, has a cluster of lively cafés that blast out music into the night. Some of the cafés along Langestraat offer sophisticated music, such as **De Versteende Nacht** (11 Langestraat, tel: 050-34 32 93), a jazz café filled with comic-book ephemera.

A tour of the specialised beer bars of Bruges might begin in De Garre, a tiny Flemish tavern hidden down a narrow alley off Breydelstraat, where you can select one of the 130 beers on offer. You can then head across town to **De Brugs Beertje** (5 Kemelstraat), a brown café run by Jan de Bruyne and his wife, Daisy, that sells more than 300 ales. For a quiet bar to end the evening, head to **'t Estaminet** (5 Park), overlooking the romantic Astridpark. Order a glass of the heavenly Poperings Hommelbier, and listen to some of the best jazz in Bruges.

**The Top** (5 Sint-Salvatorskerkhof), is a lively bar in the shadow of the cathedral, where local young people mix with tourists looking for decent dance sounds in the early hours. But the last place to close is likely to be **Joey's Café**, located in the elegant Zilversteeg shopping centre where the noise doesn't bother anyone. Run by a friendly local musician, this is a relaxed place to enjoy good music long after most of Bruges has gone to bed.

## SHOPPING

### What and Where to Buy

Bruges has a reputation for twee boutiques selling chocolate and lace, and there is no shortage of these, but there are some surprisingly stylish shops in this small town. Unfortunately, the lace on sale is mainly mass produced in the Far East, although a few shops remain faithful to the local handmade product. There is no shortage of good chocolate shops, many selling unique handmade chocolates manufactured in a tiny room at the back of the shop.

All too aware of the dowdy souvenirs sold in many shops, the city recently launched a competition to encourage designers to produce tasteful contemporary souvenirs. The results have still to reach the shops, but there are already a few unusual souvenirs on offer, such as local beers, reproduction 16th-century maps or reproductions of some of the paintings you can see in the Groeninge Museum.

The main international shops, including an Inno department store, are found along the **Steenstraat**, which runs from the Markt to 't Zand. But if you're after the more fashionable boutiques, these are located in the parallel streets of **Geldmunt** and **Noordzandstraat**, and in the **Zilverzand** shopping centre. The lace and chocolate shops can be found everywhere, but most are concentrated along Wollestraat and Katelijnestraat.

## Beer

**The Bottle Shop** (13 Wollestraat, tel: 050-34 99 80) might look like a tourist trap, but it is a serious beer shop with more than 850 ales on offer, including Trappist beers and rare Flemish labels. It also sells Belgian genever in stoneware jars and an astonishing selection of bottled water.

## Books

Founded in 1888, **De Reyghere** (12 Markt, tel: 050-33 34 03) sells books, international newspapers and magazines. It has a small selection of English fiction and guide books to Bruges. The travel bookshop next door sells international guide books and maps.

## Calligraphy

**De Patience** (2 Spinolarei, tel: 050-34 21 89; www.bnart.be) is a small canal-side gallery and shop run by the American calligrapher Brody Neuenschwander –

who worked with Peter Greenaway on the film *Prospero's Books*. The shop stocks original calligraphy, notepaper and postcards.

## Cartoon Books

The **Tintin Shop** (3 Steenstraat, tel: 050-33 42 92; www.tintinshop-brugge.be) sells T-shirts, books, cards, scale models and jigsaw puzzles featuring the eponymous Belgian comic book hero.

## Chocolates

Few people would dream of leaving Bruges without at least a small box of chocolates. There are branches of Leonidas, Neuhaus and Godiva all over town, but it is worth calling at one of the local chocolate shops for a selection of hand-made goodies. The tiny **Dumon** near the main square (6 Eiermarkt, tel: 050-34 62 82) has friendly staff and divine chocolates. The more spacious **Sukerbuyc** (5 Katelijnestraat, tel: 050-33 08 87) is a family business that produces some of the richest chocolates ever made. For a little more chocolate extravagance, head to The Chocolate Line (19 Simon Stevinplein, tel: 050-34 10 90, www.thechocolateline.be). You'll be tempted just marvelling at their wonderful novelty window displays. This chocoholic's paradise specialises in odd combinations, from chocolate and chilli to the more daring chocolate and wasabi creation.

## Design

Who says Bruges is old-fashioned? A quick look inside the **o-nivo** design centre at 25 Wollestraat proves that there's more to Bruges than lace and chocolate. Look inside **Callebert** (tel: 050-33 50 61; www.callebert.be) for a striking selection of glassware, cutlery and furniture by some of Europe's best designers. The shop next door, called simply **B** (tel: 050-49 09 32) was founded by Katrien van Hulle to sell contemporary design by innovative young Belgians.

**BELOW:** an original palette of chocolate flavours.

## Fashion

The Brussels designer **Olivier Strelli** has established a loyal following in Bruges, with a large shop selling womenswear at 3 Eiermarkt, tel: 050-34 38 37; and a smaller branch for menswear nearby at 19 Geldmuntstraat, tel: 050-33 26 75. For classic Spanish clothes, **Joaquim Jofre** (7 Vlaamingstraat, tel: 050-33 39 60) sells crisply tailored women's clothes and a range of accessories in a sumptuous interior imported from Spain. **L'Héroine** (32 Nordzandstraat, tel 050-33 56 57), is a striking boutique with clothes by some of the most exciting Flemish designers. The downstairs area is devoted to menswear by Dries van Noten and womenswear by Martin Margiela, while the upper floor has dresses by Kaat Tilley, Ann Huybens and Mieke Cosyn.

## Lace

Sadly, the overwhelming majority of the lace sold in Bruges is now mass produced in factories in the Far East. A pleasant exception is **'t Apostelientje** (11 Balstraat, tel: 050-33 78 60), whose owners insist on the real thing. Hand-made by local women, the delicate lace is sold in a boutique close to the Lace Museum.

## Museum Miscellany

Located in a former stable building, the **Groeninge Museum** shop at 16 Dijver offers an inspired selection of art books, jewellery, games, postcards, posters and children's art books. Closed on Monday.

## Music

**Rombaux** (13 Mallebergplaats, tel: 050-33 25 75) is a beautiful music shop that has been run by the same Bruges family for three generations. The 19th-century interior is crammed with everything from classical music to new-wave Flemish folk, and the staff can track down almost any performer you can name.

## OTHER ACTIVITIES

### Guided Tours

Walking tours of Bruges are organised every day in July and August, and on Saturday and Sunday in June and September. They begin at 2.30pm outside the tourist office. Reservations are essential. An unusual culinary walking tour of Bruges called Amuse Gueule is organised on Sunday from 11.30am–3.30pm by the Ghent-based **Vizit** (tel: 078-15 01 49; www.vizit.be). The walking tour calls at four restaurants along the way to sample a dish and drink a glass of wine.

## SIGHTS AND ATTRACTIONS

### Children's Activities

Children generally enjoy boat tours on the Bruges canals, and, if you can afford it, a trip through the streets on a horse-drawn carriage. They might also enjoy climbing the belfry for a view of the city. The **Groeninge Museum** is fun to tour with children, especially the modern art section, and the **Museum voor Volkskunde** has a series of reconstructed interiors, including a school, a shop and a cobbler's workshop. Little ones also usually enjoy exploring the Sint-Janshuismolen, a working windmill situated on the town ramparts.

The **Boudewijnpark** is a large theme park on the outskirts of Bruges with plenty to keep children entertained for a whole day, including a large dolphinarium.

If your children feel the need to dig a hole in the sand, the long sandy beaches at **Ostend** and **Zeebrugge** are just a short train ride away.

For a more active experience, try one of the excellent bike tours organised by **QuasiMundo** (www.quasimundo.com), daily from

**ABOVE:** fun on the Markt.

March to October. They have a huge stock of bikes in all sizes, along with safety helmets and children's seats. Children under the age of eight go free.

## SPORTS

**Cycling** is the main sport in Bruges, practised by everyone, young and old. The best routes for cycling are north of the city in the flat polderland between the city and the coast.

Bruges has three **swimming pools**, all located outside the old town. The most convenient for visitors is the Zwembad Jan Guilini (41 Keizer Karelstraat), just to the east of the old town, a 10-minute walk from the centre.

For those who prefer to watch sport rather than participate, there is always **football**. Club Brugge (or FC Bruges) is one of Belgium's top football teams. It plays in a modern stadium in Olympiabaan, in the city's western suburbs.

One of the country's best **golf courses** is near Bruges at Knokke (Royal Zoute Golf Club, 14 Caddiespad, Knokke-Zoute, tel: 050-60 12 27).

Other popular Flemish sports are pigeon racing, tennis, archery and the faintly ridiculous pastime of finch-singing contests.

BRUGRS

GHENT

ANTWERP

# GHENT

A detailed guide to Ghent with the principal sites
clearly cross-referenced by number to the maps

Ghent may not have the unspoiled, harmonious medieval appearance of Bruges, but it has its own well-preserved historic centre, threaded by winding canals and cobbled streets and speckled with stalwart old buildings. This is complemented by a spirited social life, a significant cultural scene and an authentic urban temperament that save the city from being just another living museum.

As a city of rivers and canals, Ghent has been likened to Venice (but not as often as Bruges has). One of the first of many visitors to do so was the English diarist John Evelyn. In 1641 he wrote: "The Ley and the Scheld meeting in this vast Citty divide it into 26 Ilands which are united together by many bridges somewhat resembling Venice."

Called *Gent* in Dutch and *Gand* in French, the prosperous capital of Belgium's Oost-Vlaanderen (East Flanders) province has a population of around 250,000 and is located at the confluence of the Schelde (Scheldt) and Leie rivers. This geographical asset helped its development as an important trading town in the medieval period, and there is still a distinct old mercantile feel to modern Ghent. Today, it has the country's third-largest port, after Antwerp and Zeebrugge, an inland harbour connected to the sea by a canal that goes north 32 km (20 miles) through Dutch Zeeuws-Vlaanderen (Zeeland-Flanders) to the Westerschelde (Western Scheldt) estuary at Terneuzen.

Perhaps even more to the city's satisfaction, Ghent is widely considered by Flemings to be their cultural heartland – though not without some objections from Bruges and Antwerp. Ghent owes its historical importance primarily to the cloth trade and to having been a seat of the medieval counts of Flanders and their successors, the dukes of Burgundy. It flourished during the Middle Ages, and for a period around the start of the 15th century it was the second-largest city north of the Alps after Paris. Today, its vibrant economy revolves around the port and the chemical, steel and automobile industries, as well as publishing, banking, tourism and other service sectors. It also lies at the heart of a fertile agricultural region. ❏

**PRECEDING PAGES:** personalised bike on Grasburg; the Graslei, Ghent's magnificent promenade. **LEFT:** Het Gravensteen is Ghent's medieval legacy.

# EAST OF THE LEIE

Within the curve of the river as it loops through the old part of town are many of Ghent's stellar attractions. Few museums are among them, but there is no shortage of impressive churches, venerable buildings and the beguiling sights and sounds of the bustling city centre

If you arrive by train at **Gent-Sint-Pieters**, on Koningin Maria Hendrikaplein, take a moment to wander around the station, which was designed by architect Louis Cloquet (1849–1920), and opened in time for the Ghent World Fair in 1913. Cloquet used Belgian materials as far as possible and had the interior decorated with sgraffito-work depicting the principal towers of Ghent, Bruges, Kortrijk, Ypres, Oudenaarde, Mechelen, Ostend, Antwerp, Tournai, Mons, Namur and Liège. The station restaurant is so notable that it is almost worth missing your train to eat there.

To get to the centre, take the No.1 tram from under the bridge to your left, and get off at Korenmarkt.

## Korenmarkt

**Korenmarkt ❶**, as the name indicates, is where the city's corn market was held in times past. The corn was unloaded from the barges at the adjacent Graslei quays before being brought here to be traded. Korenmarkt is now a bustling square speckled with pavement cafés, although its modern role as a busy public transport hub rather spoils it. Some of the surviving 15th-century buildings still have a corn loft. The 13th-century patrician house, **Het Borluutsteen** at Nos 6–7 is particularly noteworthy.

The city's former **Postgebouw ❷** (post office) is an extravagant pile of sand-coloured stone and spires, with a prominent clock tower, in the southwest corner of the square. It is an inventive pastiche of neo-Gothic and neo-Renaissance styles dating from 1898–1909, designed (like the station) by Louis Cloquet. Since 2000 it has been transformed into a bijou shopping mall. The sculpted busts gracing the façade are those of 23 20th-century heads of state. The artist Prosper Cornelis (1864–1922)

Map on page 142

**LEFT:** fire-eater performing in front of Graslei.
**BELOW:** Ghent is a great place to buy antique toys.

**TIP**

During the summer, a walk around Ghent at night can be a magical experience as many of the buildings are floodlit. For the rest of the year they are illuminated only on Friday and Saturday evening.

was commissioned to work on the interior murals. Behind the old post office rises the **Sint-Michielsbrug** (St Michael's Bridge), which spans the Leie *(see page 167)*.

Dominating the east side of Korenmarkt, **Sint-Niklaaskerk** ❸ (St Nicholas's Church; Tues–Sun 10am–5pm, Mon 2.30–5pm; free; entrance on Cataloniëstraat) is one of Ghent's great churches. Built between the 13th and 15th centuries on the site of a Romanesque predecessor, this relatively plain Scheldt variation on the French Gothic theme has been restored over the past 40-

odd years to something approaching its original lines. Some baroque interior additions were the main victims of this restoration, having been excised, although the striking baroque high altar with its theme of *The Last Judgement* survived. Destruction of a more drastic nature had taken place in the mid-16th century, when the church was one of many victims of the militant Protestant *Beeldenstorm* (Iconoclastic Fury) which was rife in the Low Countries. The city's merchants and guilds and a local rhetorical society called *De Fonteyne* (The Fountain)

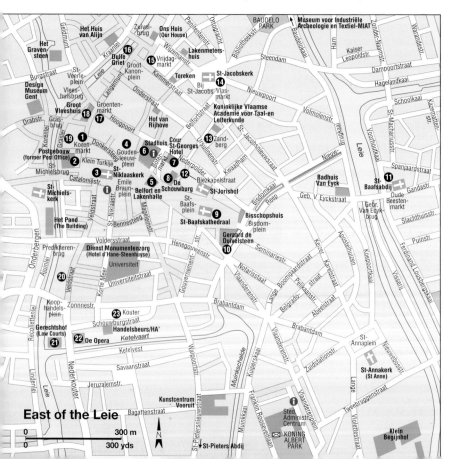

**East of the Leie**

0 ___ 300 m
0 ___ 300 yds

built chapels for themselves inside. Of the "three towers of Ghent" that have become a signature image of the city, St Nicholas's spire was the first to be built – the others are the belfry and the tower of St Michael's Church. Its crossing tower is flanked by four corner towers.

On Cataloniëstraat (Catalonia Street), which grazes the south flank of St Nicholas's, is the **Gildenhuis van de Metselaars** (Masons' Guildhouse), dating from 1527. Somehow it got misplaced over the centuries and was rediscovered in the 1970s hiding behind the façade of a building that was scheduled for demolition. Although spared from the wreckers, it had to pay a price: six modern bronze sculptures of dancers and an equally modern glass structure were tacked on for some wacky reason. It now houses the **tourist office** for East Flanders province (entrance round the corner at 2 Sint-Niklaasstraat; tel: 09-269 26 00). Note that a later copy of the building stands on Graslei.

Stroll along the atmospheric side street Klein Turkije (Little Turkey) north of the church. The medieval buildings lining the street house a raft of fast-paced dance cafés. Pause for a look at the gloomy limestone facade of the 13th-century building at No. 4, **Den Rooden Hoed** (The Red Hat), a reference to the traditional fez worn by Turks. This was formerly the Spice Merchants' Guildhall, whose members sourced many of their wares from Ottoman Turkey. It is now a smoky tavern called Winners Sports Bar.

An alternative route exits from Korenmarkt a block further north. In medieval times, crooked and atmospheric Donkersteeg must have fully justified its name: "Dark Alley". Today it is notable for restaurants, cafés and shops, among them the renowned Georges seafood restaurant at Nos 23–27, in business since 1924; the old-fashioned Flemish butcher's, Zwanenpoel, famed for its lamb and other meats, at No. 33; and the congenial coffee salon, Mokabon at No. 35.

## Goudenleeuwplein

Either route brings you out onto aristocratic **Goudenleeuwplein** ❹ (Golden Lion Square). To your left, at No. 7, is the distinctive Renaissance façade (*c.*1580), of Amadeus II *(see page 164)*, a sister restaurant to the original Amadeus rib house in the Patershol. Even if you don't eat here, be sure to sneek a peek at its restored Art Nouveau interior.

Along its southern edge, Goudenleeuwplein melds with Emile Braunplein, in which a large bell stands anchored to the ground on a plinth. This is *De Triomfante*, cast in 1660, using the brass from an earlier bell called *Roeland* that was said to "send a storm throughout the country" whenever it tolled from the tower to call the citizens to arms in defence of their greatly valued freedoms. It did so once too often, in the tax revolt of 1539, and the Habsburg

Map on page 142

*Quirky bronze dancers on top of the Masons' Guildhouse.*

**BELOW:** the Kornmarkt with the Post Office spire behind.

Ghent-born Emperor Charles V ordered it destroyed. The re-cast bell was dropped (figuratively speaking) from the belfry carillon in 1950, having hung mute in the tower ever since it cracked in 1914.

Next to the bell is a fountain surrounded by a sculpture-group of five naked, kneeling boys. The striking ensemble, created in 1892 by Symbolist Georges Minne (1866–1941), is called *De Bron der Geknielde Jongelingen (The Fountain of Kneeling Youths, see page 49)*. Gentenaars have invented an altogether earthier name for it – *De Pietjesbak*, which roughly translates as *The Willie Tray*.

### Belfort and Lakenhalle

Straight ahead is an unmissable complex of medieval buildings, the **Belfort en Lakenhalle ❺** (belfry and Cloth Hall; mid-Mar–mid-Nov daily 10am–12.30pm and 2–6pm; guided tours to carillon Easter and May–Sept at 2.10pm, 3.10pm and 4.10pm; admission charge), which soars 91 metres (298 ft) high and is crowned by a portly gilded copper dragon. It is made of three segments:

a lower tier of Tournai limestone; an upper tier of harder-wearing freestone; and the ornate central spire and four corner turrets, which were added as recently as 1913. When it was built (1313–80) the belfry was a lofty symbol of the city's civic pride and freedom, and the power of its guilds, and it is today a UNESCO World Heritage Site. Ghent's jealously guarded charters and privileges were held in the ground-floor *Secreet*, in a sturdy wooden chest behind multiple locks and doors.

The viewing platform, 66 metres (216 ft) above ground level, is an ideal place to get a feel for the city's layout from on high. Should your legs not be up to the climb, there's an elevator to whisk you up there and back down again. The carillon is served by a *carillonneur* who takes this route up to the special keyboard and performs a full-scale concert every Friday and Sunday (11.30am–12.30pm), and regularly throughout the week-long *Gentse Feesten (see page 155)*. A mechanical substitute handles the routine jingles that chime every 15 minutes.

*The ill-fated De Triomfante tolls no more and is anchored to the ground.*

**BELOW:** the Belfort rising out of the great Lakenhalle.

### Hemeny's Bells

The famed Dutch bell founder Pieter Hemony cast 37 bells for the belfry carillon in 1659, followed by three subsequent bells, called *De Triomfante*, in 1660. A complex dispute followed over whether the bells were in tune and Hemony (who had virtually invented the technique of tuning bells in the first place) never did get paid for his work, which provoked him to castigate the aldermen of Ghent for being "shameless", "ungodly" and "fraudulent". The carillon, now with 54 bells, restored during the 1970s and reinstalled in 1980, still includes 24 of the original Hemony bells (which sound just fine).

The belfry rises out of the great Lakenhalle, where wool and Flemish cloth were once stored and traded, and which housed the inspection commission for the weavers who created most of Ghent's wealth. Work on the Cloth Hall began in 1425 in the full flush of the city's prosperity and had more or less come to a stop by 1441; not until 1903 was it finally completed. In a second-floor hall is the museum of the Koninklijke en Ridderlijke Hoofdgilde van Sint-Michiel (Royal and Chivalric High Guild of St Michael), an order of swordsmen.

Part of the building, including an extension in Louis XV style on Goudenleeuwplein (1741), was used as a prison until 1902. This section now houses the office of the city *Ombudsvrouw* (ombudswoman). In the council cellar is Ghent Tourism's Information Office *(see margin tip)*.

## Botermarkt

Across the **Botermarkt** (Butter Market) from the Cloth Hall stands the city's **Stadhuis ❻** (town hall; guided tours only, from the tourist office at the Cloth Hall, Tues–Sun 9.30am–5pm; admission charge). It was built in two main styles and tweaked during several additional stages. The lavish, late-Gothic north façade on Hoogpoort somewhat resembles Bruges' town hall.

Around the corner on the Botermarkt, you jump forward to the Renaissance period with the Schepenhuis van Ghedeele (1595–1618). There is a less-impressive Renaissance segment near the bottom end of the Hoogpoort face (1580–82), while the 18th century saw the addition of a dab of baroque and a touch of rococo, on the Stadhuissteeg and Poeljemarkt sides respectively. The construction wasn't finally wound up until 19th-century neo-Gothic devotees added the last few details, like the niche statuary – although

most of the niches still remain empty. During the 20th century, various renovations and repairs were carried out, and in 2000, on the quincentenary of Charles V's birth, his statue and one of his aunt, Margaret of Austria, were added.

On the guided tours you visit the magnificent **Pacificatiezaal** (Pacification Hall), formerly the Hall of Justice. In 1576 the Pacification of Ghent was signed here, a treaty that provided for freedom of religion and (for a time) ended the religious conflict between Catholics and Protestants so that both sides could combine their fire against the occupying Spanish. The walls are emblazoned with the arms of the counts of Flanders; the black-and-white tiled floor takes the pattern of a maze symbolising the uncertain search for justice. A rectangular Gothic spiral staircase occupies the corner between the armoury/banquet hall and the throne room, dating from 1781, where Habsburg Emperor Joseph II was received.

On the other side of the Botermarkt, just at its intersection with

**TIP**

For tourist information, visit Toerisme Gent's Infokantoor located in the Lakenhalle cellar, at 17a Botermarkt (tel: 09-266 52 32; open Apr–Oct daily 9.30am–6.30pm; Nov–Mar daily 9.30am–4.30pm).

**BELOW:** the arms of the count of Flanders on the walls of the Pacification Hall.

Nederpolder, rises the step-gabled, Romanesque **Cour St-Georges Hotel** ❼, its sandstone façade decorated with coats of arms from Flanders, Burgundy and the Habsburg Empire. An original building here dated from 1228, and was rebuilt in the 15th century, during the reign of Duchess Mary of Burgundy, as the guildhall of Ghent's Guild of Crossbowmen. During the Middle Ages, the guild, whose patron saint was St George, had its practice ranges here. It functioned in Mary's time as the local seat and residence of the Flemish *Staten Generaal* (estates general, or parliament). In 1477 it hosted the banquet for the successful negotiations between Mary and the ambassadors of Emperor Frederick II of Austria for her marriage to his son, the heir to the Habsburg throne, Archduke Maximilian. Earlier that year, her rebellious Flemish subjects had forced Mary to sign here a charter, the *Keurrecht* (Great Privilege), confirming the civic freedoms of the Flemish towns.

At the time of writing, the old building was closed for essential

*"I can hardly endure to call a place so dignified by such a name," complained the 19th-century English diarist, Dorothy Wordsworth, after visiting Botermarkt square. The butter market itself used to be held in the town hall's cellar.*

**BELOW:** Sint-Baafskathedraal façade detail.

structural repairs and renovation of its graceful manorial interior, and the hotel was confined to an annexe at Nos 75–77 on the other side of Hoogpoort, in two 18th-century town houses, De Groote Scaec, with a neo-Classical gable, and the rococo Huis Serlippens, which are both notable enough in their own right but inevitably lack the antique character of their centuries-older cousin.

Botermarkt hosts a number of fine restaurants and watering holes. Among the latter is Ghent's oldest bar, Den Turk (No. 3) in a building dating from at least 1340 (and perhaps as far back as 1228); it inevitably attracts many tourists.

## Sint-Baafsplein

Occupying the open space between the Cloth Hall complex and the cathedral is **Sint-Baafsplein** (St Bavo's Square). This central district has been dubbed *Het Kuip van Gent* (The Barrel of Ghent), the area where historically the city's movers and shakers had their homes.

On the square's north face stands **De Schouwburg** ❽ (theatre), built in neo-Renaissance style and dating from 1899. The colourful mosaic on a bow-shaped panel on the gable depicts *Apollo and the Muses*. While the resident NTGent repertory group has a solid reputation, many visitors, whose ability to follow a play in Dutch is usually quite limited, consider the theatre's leading lure to be its lively foyer café, and the chance to eat, drink and look cool on its balcony terrace overlooking Sint-Baafsplein when the weather is fine.

A modern, rectangular water pool and fountain out front boasts at its centre a memorial to the Flemish cultural activist and man of letters Jan Frans Willems (1793–1846). The sculpture at the fountain's centre portrays the Maid of Flanders backed up by a warrior.

## Sint-Baafskathedraal

You have now arrived in front of **Sint-Baafskathedraal** ❾ (St Bavo's Cathedral; Apr–Oct Mon–Sat 8.30am–6pm, Sun 1–6pm; Nov–Mar till 5pm; cathedral free, admission charge for *The Adoration of the Mystic Lamb* chapel), one of the world's great Gothic cathedrals. Originally plain Sint-Janskerk (St John's Church), dedicated to John the Baptist, who was then the city's patron saint, it was promoted (when a bishopric was established in Ghent in 1561) to a cathedral dedicated to St Bavo, a 7th-century saint from the Haspengouw district east of Brussels. Built between the 14th and 16th centuries in a combination of sober Scheldt Gothic and more flamboyant Brabant Gothic styles, the cathedral bears witness to the wealth of Ghent in its heyday. It stands atop the crypt of a 12th-century Romanesque church, which replaced a 10th-century edifice, the oldest parish church in Ghent. Despite lacking a spire, the tower is 82 metres (269 ft) high.

The cathedral's cavernous, echoing space contains a wealth of historical treasures. In several of the ambulatory chapels are important works of art, among them *St Bavo's Entry into the Monastery of Ghent* (1624), an altarpiece by Pieter Paul Rubens (the artist portrayed himself as the kneeling supplicant taking holy orders, wearing a red-cloak); and Frans Pourbus the Elder's altarpiece *Jesus Among the Scribes* (1571), in which Jesus, though still a child, amazes the elders of the temple with his erudition; the onlookers include Emperor Charles V, King Philip II of Spain, and the artist Pieter Brueghel the Elder; other panels depict *Christ's Circumcision* and *Christ's Baptism*.

In the vast crypt is Justus van Gent's notable yet derivative altarpiece *Calvary Triptych* (1466), in which Moses appears in various guises. Among sculptural highlights are the baroque high altar (1719) by Hendrik Frans Verbruggen; the Flemish rococo pulpit in white marble and oak (1745) by Laurent Delvaux; statues and tomb sculptures of a number of bishops of Ghent; and two sets of armorials of

Map on page 142

*After visiting the local sights, why not try the local beers?*

**LEFT AND BELOW:** the cathedral's vast interior is home to several masterpieces, notably Rubens' *St Bavo's Entry into the Monastery of Ghent.*

*The Ghent altarpiece
was stolen by
Napoleon, who had it
removed to Paris. The
Nazis looted it again
during World War II.
Each time it found its
way back to the city.
But one of the panels
– the one depicting
the wise judges – is
a modern copy of an
original stolen by
thieves in 1934 and
never recovered.*

**BELOW:** alfresco
on Sint-Baafsplein.

the medieval chivalric order the Knights of the Golden Fleece, who twice held chapter meetings here. The baroque organ from 1653, the biggest in the Low Countries, has no fewer than 7,000 pipes and three keyboards. Among other valuable relics in the crypt are faded 15th–16th-century murals; and gold and silver religious vessels, among them the graceful silver *Reliquary of St Macharius* (1615), by Hugo de la Vigne, presented by the citizens of Mons in gratitude for being delivered from the plague.

What most visitors come to see, though, is Jan van Eyck's polyptych altarpiece, the first among the so-called "Seven Wonders of Belgium", *The Adoration of the Mystic Lamb* (*c*.1420–32), also known as the Ghent Altarpiece *(see page 182)*. A masterpiece of early Flemish art, it is exhibited in the former baptismal chapel, on the left as you enter the cathedral. If the entrance fee to view the altarpiece seems a bit steep, you can see a copy free in the Vijd Chapel behind the high altar – but it's not quite the same thing.

## To Sint-Baafsabdij

Southeast of the cathedral, on Limburgstraat, is a bronze sculpture group (1913) of brothers Jan and Hubert van Eyck. A medallion on the building opposite is dedicated to Gheeraert Vilain (*c*.1210–70), known as "de Duivel" (the Devil), whose nickname may be due to his cruel character or his swarthy skin – take your pick. A little further on you will find **Geraard de Duivelsteen** ⑩, a fortified Romanesque mansion, dating from 1245 (with a chunk of 19th-century neo-Gothic), flanking a blocked-off arm of the Schelde. This has been an armoury, a monastery, a school, an asylum, a prison, an orphanage and a fire station. It currently houses the East Flanders office of the national archives.

From here it's a short stroll along waterside Bisdomkaai to Bisdomplein and Ghent's graceful **Bisschopshuis** (Bishop's Residence; 1841–45). Neo-Classical but with some of the first ever neo-Gothic elements in Belgian architecture, it is connected to St Bavo's Cathedral by way of a landscaped garden.

Although it is a fair stretch east from here, if you are in walking mode this would be the time to strike out for the Romanesque and Gothic ruins of **Sint-Baafsabdij** ⑪ (St Bavo's Abbey; currently closed for restoration; no re-opening date announced), on the east side of the Leie, after the river has made a long, curving loop through the north of the old town and streamed south along its eastern flank. You go by way of Oude Beestenmarkt (Old Animal Market), where pets are sold at a Sunday market, then on Gebroeders Van Eyckstraat to a pair of connected bridges, the Van Eyckbrug and the Slachthuisbrug, spanning the river between the not very attractive yachting quays. Off to the left, on Veermansplein, is Belgium's first-ever indoor swimming pool,

the **Badhuis Van Eyck,** which opened its doors in 1886. An alternative route to the abbey that's easier on the shoe leather is to board bus Nos 17 or 18 from Vlasmarkt *(see below).* Both stop near the abbey's entrance at 7 Gandastraat.

Founded around 630 by St Amand, a French Benedictine monk, the abbey grew in power and wealth – allowing a century or so for recuperation after a Viking devastation in 851. It takes its name from Amand's contemporary, Belgium's own St Bavo, who entered the monastery after leading a life of dissolution and died there around 650. John of Gaunt (Ghent), son of the English king, Edward III, was born here in 1341. It was Habsburg Emperor Charles V who brought about the abbey's demise, as part of his punishment of Ghent for its revolt in 1539. He expelled the monks and began construction of a fortress on the grounds, the Spanjardenkasteel (Spanish Citadel), garrisoned by Spanish troops, whose mission was to ensure that Ghent toed the imperial line and paid its taxes promptly. This military base was demolished in the 19th century.

The ruins of the remaining abbey buildings are overgrown with ivy and other creepers, moss and hanging plants. Among the surviving edifices are the 12th-century, domed octagonal *lavatorium* (bathhouse); the *kapittelzaal* (chapter house) and the *refter* (refectory), both dating from the 13th century; and the 15th-century *kloosterpand* (cloister). Their mouldering walls combine with the restful grounds, teeming with 150 different species of wild flowers and plants, to create an atmospheric, spiritual experience.

Installed in the grounds and the cellars, the **Museum voor Stenen Voorwerpen** (Museum of Monumental Carvings) is a rather eclectic collection of religious statuary, gargoyles, columns and capitals, mosaics, tombstones and funerary sculptures (including the supposed tombstone of Hubert van Eyck, the lesser-known artist brother of Jan). These have been recovered from various Ghent churches and buildings, some no longer extant.

Map on page 142

**TIP**

In the compact city centre most of the interesting sights and historic treasures are within easy walking distance. Beyond this central zone, it makes sense to use De Lijn public transport, in particular the four tram lines (Nos 1, 4, 21, 22) and, when the suspended service is resumed in 2006, the one trolley-bus line (No. 3).

**BELOW:** sculpture honouring Jan and Hubert van Eyck.

### Van der Sickelen mansions

Back in the city centre at St Bavo's Cathedral, look out for adjacent **Biezekapelstraat** , a narrow lane that has on occasion been used as a film set, which leads north from the corner of Sint-Baafsplein. There is a fine 19th-century neo-Renaissance house at the start on the left. Across the street is the vast **Bisschoppelijk Seminarie** (Episcopal Seminary), built in various phases from 1623 to the end of the 19th century; the most notable section is due to Ghent architect David 't Kindt (*c*.1750).

Further along, on the corner where the lane dog-legs to the right – at a spot dubbed *Het Vrijershoekske* (Lovers' Corner) – you will find the rear entrance to the city's music college, the **Koninklijk Conservatorium**. This is in the **Achtersikkel** (Rear Sickle) house, part of a turreted patrician residence built in a medley of Gothic and Renaissance styles that belonged to the wealthy and influential Van der Sickelen family, whose family crest was three sickles. In the arcaded courtyard, whose various architectural elements span

a period from the 14th–16th century, note a bas-relief of Orpheus serenading wild beasts with his lyre. At the next dog-leg is a shrine containing a *Madonna and Child*; local lore has it that during the religious wars a Protestant trooper discharged his firelock at the statue and the ball rebounded, killing the soldier.

At the end of Biezekapelstraat, look back to admire a fine view of St Bavo's tower. The opposite end of the lane is itself framed by Van der Sickelen mansions: the fortress-like, Romanesque **Kleine Sikkel** (Small Sickle) at 2 Nederpolder, which has been restored and houses municipal offices; and the more refined 15th-century Gothic **Grote Sikkel** (Great Sickle), with a double step-gable, across the lane at 64 Hoogpoort. The three sickles of the family emblem are visible on the Tournai limestone front façade of both houses. Grote Sikkel's neighbour, the **Zwarte Moor** (Black Moor) has been transformed inside as part of the Royal Conservatory; the house next door is the **Grote Moor** (Great Moor).

*Notice the three sickles of the Van der Sickelen family emblem on the Tournai limestone façade of the Kleine Sikkel building.*

**BELOW:** reflected houses along Onderstraat.

Map on page 142

## Zandberg Square

Cross over Nederpolder to Zandberg, passing on the corner an over-restored mansion, the **Hotel Vanden Meersche**. This started out as a 14th-century inn called De Pelicaan (The Pelican), was converted during the 16th century to the Flemish Renaissance style, bought in 1736 by the Lord of Berlare and Bareldonck, rebuilt in several phases, then restored more or less to its 16th-century appearance in the 20th century. Until September 2005, this was a convent of the Zusters der Kindsheid Jesu (Sisters of the Child Jesus), but it is now occupied by departments of the city administration.

**Zandberg ⑬** is a small square surrounded by several handsome 18th-century town houses and marked by a water pump attached to a plain stone **obelisk** with a perfunctory imperial eagle on top. This was erected by the French occupation authorities who wished to commemorate Napoleon's visit in 1810. It is rather hard to imagine that the little emperor with the outsize ego would have been greatly impressed by the monument. Take note of the fine and invariably bustling seafood and vegetarian restaurant **De Warempel** at No. 8.

Something of a diversion west from Zandberg, the **Hof van Rijhove** at 20–22 Onderstraat is another of those venerable old Ghent buildings that have been altered constantly throughout the centuries and today have a public function. Traces of the earliest construction date back to the 12th century, before the property came into the hands of Simon de Rijke, a wealthy cloth merchant, who built it up as a suitably patrician residence. It changed hands in the 16th century to a wealthy political family who up-scaled the edifice into something more akin to a palace. It now houses various city government departments.

## Royal Academy

Koningstraat goes north from Zandberg. Near the end, on the right at No. 18, stands the **Koninklijke Vlaamse Academie voor Taal- en Letterkunde** (Royal Flemish Academy of Language and Literature), in a magnificent rococo mansion, the Hotel Van Oombergen. Built of honey-hued sandstone and sporting a mansard roof, it was designed by Ghent architect David 't Kindt and completed in 1746. The academy, founded in 1886, was installed in these elegant premises in 1892. Ironically, in view of the foundation's mission to promote Flemish culture, as a counterweight to what partisans saw as the overweening Francophone fashion, the mansion, both inside and out, is a masterpiece of the French Louis XV style. Alas, it is rarely open to the public.

By way of **Vlasmarkt**, a neat little square that supports a cluster of dedicated drinkers' cafés that stay open into the wee hours, you come to a larger square called **Bij Sint-Jacobs**. Although it is known for its antiques shops and weekend Pron-

*Those with a passion for antiques will want to spend some time on Bij Sint-Jacobs.*

**BELOW:** trendy Gentenaars love their lifestyle shops.

delmarkt flea market – and for the Trefpunt café at No. 18 – most of the square is taken up by the twin Romanesque towers, central spire and great, melancholy-looking pile of stone that is one of Ghent's oldest churches. Various elements of **Sint-Jacobskerk** ⓮ (St James' Church; Apr–Oct Fri–Sat 9.30am–12.30pm; free) date back to 1093, although the bulk of it is 13th–15th century Scheldt Gothic. Like many Catholic churches in Flanders, its interior ornementation underwent the depredations of the Protestant *Beeldenstorm* (Iconoclasm) in the 16th century, and therefore much of what remains is baroque and later. St James's is not really a part of Ghent's tourist circuit, and you will find it is not always open.

### Vrijdagmarkt

Even if you didn't get inside the church, it is a convenient marker en route to **Vrijdagmarkt** ⓯. This vast, bustling square is bordered by trees and surrounded by magnificent old guildhouses and mansions – many of which house busy cafés

*Vrijdagmarkt is home to the Bird Market on Sundays.*

**RIGHT:** Jacob van Artevelde on bike.

and restaurants that spread tables onto the square in fine weather. It hosts the busy Friday market that its name represents, which has been going steady since the 13th century, along with markets on Saturday and Sunday (the Bird Market), and generally performs the role of *Grote Markt* (Great Square) that Ghent, unlike most Flemish towns, does not have – or not in name, at any rate.

Throughout the centuries, Vrijdagmarkt has been the scene of popular entertainments, such as public executions (the last one happened in 1863), jousting tournaments, parades, and the Joyous Entry (presentation) of assorted rulers, ranging from low-grade blue-bloods, through to the counts of Flanders and the dukes of Burgundy, up to the Habsburg emperors. The birth of Emperor Charles V in Ghent in 1500 was celebrated in style: it was deep winter and the authorities flooded Vrijdagmarkt so that children could ice-skate on it.

On the square's northern corner is **Ons Huis** (Our House), the imposing 1902 headquarters of the Ghent

## Insurgence in the Square

During centuries of conflict with powerful overlords, the people of Ghent, who are called the Gentenaars, have risen up more often than most in Flanders. At such times, Vrijdagmarkt has often provided the stage for gatherings of the insurgent burghers. Sometimes they went head to head with each other, as happened on Evil Monday in 1345 when rival weavers and wool-makers engaged in a deadly clash about politics that left the square littered with corpses. In the centre stands a bronze sculpture (1863) of the wealthy textiles merchant and brewer Jacob van Artevelde (c.1290–1345), its base adorned with the insignia of the city's medieval guilds. In 1338, during the Hundred Years' War between the English and the French, Van Artevelde brewed up a storm by raising the Ghent merchants and guilds in rebellion against the Count of Flanders on the side of England's King Edward III. He was assassinated during the weavers' and wool-makers' riot after suggesting that Edward the Black Prince, the son of Edward III, should be made Count of Flanders.

Socialist Workers' Society, *Vooruit* (Forward). Just glimpsing the gigantic gold letters on the façade of this oddly proportioned, vaguely Art Nouveau edifice, proclaiming *Werklieden Aller Landen Vereenigt U* (Workers of the World Unite), must have been enough to give any passing capitalist an aneurysm.

Among the guildhouses, the most notable is the step-gabled **Gildenhuis van de Huidevetters** (Tanners' Guildhouse), at Nos 33–36, dating from 1450–83 but containing elements going back to 1422. The cloth weavers' quality commission used to meet in the building's round tower, the **Toreken** (Little Tower), on the corner of Kammerstraat. In order to shame workers who produced material that was not up to scratch, the bolt of linen or cloth was displayed to the public from the large metal ring that you see below the tower railings. The weathervane at the top has the form of a shapely mermaid, which is the good-luck charm of the tanners' guild. It now houses the Poëziecentrum (Poetry Centre).

Across the square, at No. 25, the **Lakenmetershuis** (Cloth Measurers' House), dates back from 1770; it is now the headquarters of the Willemsfonds. Behind the baroque 17th-century façade, the **Keizershof** restaurant at No. 47 is a trendy place to eat. Nearby at No. 50, **Dulle Griet**, also known as the **Bieracademie**, is a fine Old Flemish tavern with 250 beers on offer, among them the potent Kwak *(see margin note)* and Ghent's own beers Stropken, Gentse Tripel and Augustijnerbier.

Just off Vrijdagmarkt, by way of Meerseniersstraat, is Groot Kanonplein (Big Cannon Square). The square is so called because of the massive, Burgundian-epoch, cast-iron artillery piece known as **Dulle Griet 16** (Mad Meg) that occupies it. Weighing in at 16,400kg (16 tons) and measuring more than 5 metres

(16ft) from breech to muzzle, the red-painted behemoth looks like it has been deliberately emplaced to slam its cannonballs into any group of militant socialists who happen to come charging around the corner from their workers' palace on Vrijdagmarkt. But the great cannon was a dismal failure. Having been brought to Ghent during the religious wars of the 16th century to help defend its Protestant status against a rampaging Spanish Catholic army, it cracked the very first time it was test-fired (although it may have done some cannonading at the siege of Oudenaarde a century earlier). Mad Meg has its back to the Leie, which is crossed at this point by the Zuivelbrug to the west bank *(see next chapter, page 167)*.

## North of Vrijdagmarkt

A diversion northwards along the gentle curve of handsome Baudelostraat leads to the Leie. At 2 Ottogracht, just off the main street, is the sole surviving edifice of 17th-century **Baudelo Abbey**: the abbatial chapel. Most of the abbey's

*At Dulle Griet tavern you have to deposit a shoe before they let you have a Kwak beer; otherwise the special 1.2-litre glasses, with rounded bases and wooden frames that allow them to stand upright, have a tendency to walk.*

**BELOW:** Van Artevelde turns his back on the impressive Ons Huis on Vrijdagmarkt.

properties bit the dust in 1795 due to the depredations of anti-clerical revolutionary French troops and their local supporters, and the monks themselves were forcibly expelled by the invaders. Tucked within the bend of the river nearby, what is now **Baudelo Park** was formerly the abbey gardens.

*The mustard sold in Tierenteyn-Verlent is still prepared according to a secret family recipe dating back to 1790.*

A little way upstream, at 9 Minnemeers, the **Museum voor Industriële Archeologie en Textiel/MIAT** (Museum of Industrial Archaeology and Textiles; Tues–Sun 10am–6pm; admission charge) occupies the several floors of a former cotton mill. It tracks Ghent's industrial history and the story of its labourers in the modern era. Some of the museum's Industrial Revolution-era machinery is still in clattery working order. Among the exhibits is one of the first mechanical looms, which the mayor of Ghent smuggled out of England (breaking the strict export laws) at the end of the 18th century. With this loom, and others modelled upon it, a new era of economic prosperity dawned in Ghent, releasing it from a long period of decline.

**BELOW:** step back in time at the Tierenteyn-Verlent grocery shop.

### Groentenmarkt to Graslei

In the opposite direction from Baudelostraat, the busy shopping street Langemunt runs down to a junction with Hoogpoort. To the right, heading towards Het Gravensteen *(see page 173)*, the **Vleeshuisbrug** spans the Leie. To the left, **Hoogpoort** mixes shops, cafés, restaurants and old houses on its way to the Stadhuis. Directly ahead is a busy square called **Groentenmarkt** ⑰ (Vegetable Market). Despite its name, the market square originally hosted a fish market, supplied from canal barges that tied up alongside; now it is best known for the adjacent meat market building. It also hosted the medieval pillory – what with scraps of fish, meat and vegetables from the various markets that had gone past their sell-by date, there must have been plenty of disgusting stuff to hurl at the pillory's unfortunate occupants.

At No. 3, traditional Ghent mustard, made to a secret recipe by the olde-worlde shop **Tierenteyn-Verlent**, makes a good souvenir. Before getting caught up in the shops, however, you might want to take some time out for three of Ghent's most notable taverns. At the end of the Groot Vleeshuis tiny **'t Galgenhuisje**, at No. 5, dates from 1783. Beside the Leie, **'t Dreupelkot**, at No. 12, stocks around 100 different varieties of Belgian genever, many of them artisanal favourites, and all of them lethal. A few doors along at No. 9, right next to the Leie and with a waterside terrace, **Het Waterhuis aan de Bierkant** serves over 100 Belgian beers, including Ghent's own Stropken, Gentse Tripel and Augustijnerbier.

The restored Gothic **Groot Vleeshuis** ⑱ (Great Meat Hall; Tues–Sun 10am–6pm; free) occupies the west side of the square. This long, covered meat market, built of grey sandstone blocks in the castel-

lated form of a fortified stronghold, has little step gables, dormer windows and a wooden interior roof in the shape of an inverted ship's hull. Dating from 1404–10, it was the central processing, store and sales hall for the city's butchery trade, and included the butchers' guildhouse and chapel. Only the best-quality meat was sold here, to those who could afford it. The poor gathered at the 1542 **Penshuizekens** (Offal Houses) just outside on Pensmarkt, where scraps of discarded meat were handed out, and which are now fast-food stands and *frietekotten* (Chips stands) and small shops. There hasn't been a meat market here since the 19th century. Today, the Groot Vleeshuis hosts a promotional outlet and restaurant where you can sample and buy regional food and drink products from the Oost-Vlaanderen (East Flanders) province.

**Grasbrug** (Herb Bridge) is the final landmark before Graslei. Standing in the middle of this bridge over the Leie, looking first north to the point where the Lieve canal angles away towards Het Gravensteen, and then south to take in the inspiring view along Graslei and Korenlei, is one of Ghent's minor marvels. You might be hard put to avoid popping down to one of the tour-boat docks along the quays *(see margin note)*.

## Graslei

Along the east bank of the Leie, **Graslei** ⑲ (Herb Quay) forms one half of the quays of the old Tusschen Brugghen (Tussen Bruggen in modern Dutch, meaning Between the Bridges) that lie between Grasbrug and Sint-Michielsbrug. Together with its west-bank neighbour **Korenlei** *(see page 169)*, this port area formed the busy commercial heart of the city from the 11th–18th century. The most important product was grain, shipped here from northern France for the whole of Flanders and stored before being transported the short distance to Korenmarkt *(see pages 141–2)*. Another important product was stone – Tournai limestone and harder-wearing Balegem sandstone. With their splendid Gothic and baroque façades, richly ornamented with stepped or curving gables, false

Map on page 142

**TIP**

Tour boats afford wonderful views of Ghent as they nose along rivers and canals. Boats, both open-air and glass-roofed, depart regularly from the quays on Graslei and Korenlei among other places.

**LEFT:**
festival fun on Graslei.

## Gentse Feesten

If you're in town during the 10 days of the annual Gentse Feesten (Ghent Festivities), around mid-July, you are likely to think you've arrived in a madhouse. In 2005, the independent festivals website, www.localfestivities.com, listed the Gentse Feesten as the third-finest European street festival, after Valencia's Las Fallas and the Oktoberfest in Munich. The entire city spills out onto the streets for the fun. There's a wide range of street music and theatre, puppet shows, a panoply of cultural events – and an awesome amount of alcohol consumption. The focus of the serious partying is the square Bij Sint-Jacobs and neighbouring Vlasmarkt, around Sint-Jacobskerk (St James's Church), but other city squares are also used as open-air venues, as are Korenlei and Graslei. An important part of the proceedings is the Stroppendragers (Noose Bearers) Procession, recalling Emperor Charles V's humiliation of the rebellious citizenry in 1540 *(see page 25)*.

In 2006, the dates for the Gentse Feesten are 15–24 July; in 2007, 14–23 July. For further information, contact Dienst Feestelijkheeden (tel: 09-269 46 00; www.gentsefeesten.be).

fronts and lavishly decorated cornices, many of the houses along both quays were warehouses or the headquarters of powerful local guilds. These have been restored and rebuilt frequently over the centuries, so not everything here is as it once was – especially not the café and restaurant terraces that now grace several of them. But the overall effect is magnificent and the scene is now a favoured subject for photographers, particularly in the golden glow of late afternoon. After dark, the illuminated façades glow like jewels, and are reflected on the shimmering surface of the Leie.

Starting from the point closest to Grasbrug, the initial sequence of buildings on Graslei, Nos 1 to 7, are 19th- and 20th-century re-inventions of the original buildings. These transformations might not always be architecturally rigorous or historically accurate, yet their effect, when set against the more authentic buildings on this much-reworked waterfront street, is not too shabby. It is a scene that is set right from the start by the pair of red-brick, step-gabled houses, **Nos 1–3**, at right angles to the quay. They look too good to be true and are indeed restorations, done in time for the 1913 Ghent World Fair, on far earlier buildings of uncertain provenance.

The bright red-and-white paintwork of the brick building at **No. 4** almost dazzles by Graslei standards, and the 18th-century aspect of its rebuilt exterior is attested by the date 1725 on the side gable along Hoeiaard. Across a narrow alley called Schuddeveestraatje, the perfunctory baroque pediment of **De Beerie**, at No. 5, fixes the date of this rebuilt structure at 1726. **De Witte Leeuw** (The White Lion) at No. 6 was given a 16th-century look in 1913, completing a saga of changes through the centuries to a house that dates from 1349. **No. 7** looks quite the 16th-century part, with its worn brickwork, step gable and red-and-white wooden shutters, and the inconvenient fact that it's a 1913 reworking of an existing building seems somehow secondary.

Pretty much the same can be said about the Brabant Gothic **Gildenhuis van de Metselaars** (Stonemasons' Guildhouse) at No. 8, also known as Den Enghel (The Angel). Seemingly dating from 1527, but actually from 1912, it is based on the plans for a building that never actually stood on Graslei. The original was discovered in the 1970s behind a later façade in Cataloniëstraat *(see page 143)*. Like its older cousin, this one has slender pinnacles and is decorated with a central emblem of an angel and with reliefs of four Roman martyrs (the *Quatuor Coronati*) who were the guild's patrons.

At No. 9 is the first **Gildehuis van de Korenmeters** (Corn Measurers' Guildhouse), dating from 1435, where officials weighed grain and assessed its quality. By 1540, the guild had moved to roomier accommodation further up Graslei.

*(see page 143)*.

*The English author William Makepeace Thackeray wrote disparagingly in 1844 of the city's "dirty canals and old houses", while noting that it possessed "more beershops than any city I ever saw". Visitors nowadays might be interested to note that Thackeray's comments retain some validity, though no longer to quite the same extent.*

**BELOW:** Graslei is the hub of Ghent's café life.

**Het Spijker** (or Het Korenstapel-huis), at No. 10, is the Romanesque Corn Stockpile House (*c.*1200). The front of its solid Tournai limestone façade leans outward by a centimetre for every metre of height, up to the top of what is Belgium's oldest step gable, in order to make the task of raising sacks of grain easier. For more than 500 years, until 1734, this was the city's storehouse for corn paid as customs dues. Now it hosts the fancy Belga Queen restaurant (*see page 164*).

Squeezed into a tiny space next door is the Flemish Renaissance **Tolhuisje** (Little Customs House; 1682), at No. 11. Now an intimate little café, this was originally the office of the corn staple's revenue officer. The **Korenmetershuis** (or Cooremetershuys), at Nos 12–13, is the second House of the Corn Measurers. This red brick and white stone building is basically Gothic and dates from 1540, but has a late-baroque step gable, cartouches and other decorative elements (1698).

At No. 14, quite close to the Sint-Michielsbrug and next to the rear of

the old post office, stands the ornate **Gildenhuis van de Vrije Schippers** (Guildhouse of the Free Boatmen). These boatmen had the right to transport cargoes on the rivers Leie and Schelde, including the waters within the city limits, and they trans-shipped cargoes from the tied boat-men, who did not. Built on an existing structure (1355), it has a façade dating from 1531 that is mostly in Brabant Gothic, with a few touches of the emerging Flem-ish Renaissance style. A relief of a caravel is situated above the door-way on the sandstone façade, restored in 1904, and reliefs of boatmen, and of the arms of Emperor Charles V, Burgundy, the Habsburgs, Castile and Leon, Flanders and Ghent are on the gable.

From here, you can climb the steps to the Sint-Michielsbrug and cross over the picturesque bridge to reach the west bank of the Leie (*see pages 167–79*). Taking Pakhuisstraat instead, along the side of the old post office, brings you to the Koren-markt, from where you can go south to explore the Opera district.

Map on page 142

*Due to its university, Ghent is a youthful town; in fine weather students take their books, or ice-creams, to the Graslei steps.*

**LEFT:** Corn Measurers' House.
**BELOW:** Guildhouse of the Free Boatmen façade detail.

## Veldstraat

Leading south from the Korenmarkt, **Veldstraat ⑳** is a long, invariably bustling, pedestrianised shopping street (but watch out, because a tram line runs through it). In 1814, the baroque mansion **Hotel Schamp** (1717–21), at Nos 45–47, hosted the US delegation to the negotiations between Britain and America aimed at ending the war of 1812 (the delegation was led by John Quincy Adams, who later became president of the United States). The Treaty of Ghent was signed on Christmas Eve. A plaque on the wall of what is now a fashion store commemorates the city's hospitality to the American peace commissioners. Next door, the tobacconist, **Caron**, is noted for its cigar selection; it also sells fountain pens and accessories.

Across the street, at No. 60, the old-fashioned *pâtisserie alsacienne* **Bloch**, in business since 1898, is something of a fixture on the local café scene for its rustic looks and elegant service. A gentle stroll west along Hoornstraat leads you to a fine view up and down the Leie

**BELOW:** shopping on Veldstraat.

from **Predhikerenbrug** (Preachers' Bridge). In the other direction, at 9 Volderstraat – a much more exclusive shopping street than Veldstraat – stands the neo-Classical **Aula Academica** (1826) of the University of Ghent. Founded in 1817 at the behest of King William I of the Netherlands (to which Belgium was then attached), the university was constructed on the site of a Jesuit College and has a massive peristyle portal of eight stone columns with Corinthian capitals, architrave and triangular pediment.

One of the finest and most imposing of the city's mansions, the **Hotel d'Hane-Steenhuyse**, at 55 Veldstraat, was a long time in the making. The front façade is primarily baroque, the rear façade facing the garden is neo-Classical, and elements of the interior, including the grand staircase, are rococo. But bits and pieces of other styles are in there too, dating from 1761 up to the 20th century, all on the frame of a medieval fortified house. It had its 15 minutes – or hundred days – of fame in 1815 after the French king,

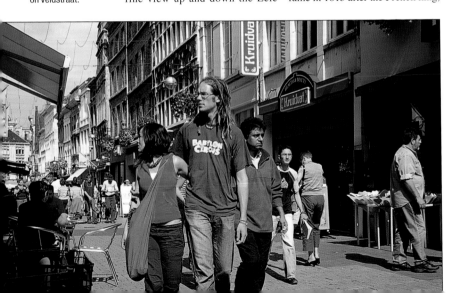

Louis XVIII, hightailed it out of Paris one step ahead of a resurgent Napoleon and took up residence here in the safety of Ghent until the emperor had fought and lost the Battle of Waterloo. The mansion, which has a splendid ballroom, now houses the city's Dienst Monument-enzorg (Monument Care Service), which looks after Ghent's listed historical monuments, of which this is an eminent example.

Napoleon's nemesis, Britain's Duke of Wellington, occupied at about the same time the beautifully restored **Hotel Arnold Vander Haeghen** (known as the Hotel Clemmens at the time), an equally impressive mansion dating from 1746 across the street at No. 82. Among its fine salons is one with Chinese silk wall hangings. Ghent City Council's Cultural Affairs Department and Arts Service are now commodiously installed here.

A duo of monumental buildings, as imposing as anything that has gone before on Veldstraat, brackets the southern end of the street, just before it comes to an end at the canal bridge over Ketelvaart, which connects the Leie with the Muink-schelde, an arm of the River Schelde. On the west side, on Koophandelsplein next to the Leie, stands the impressive neo-Classical **Gerechtshof** ㉑ (Law Courts; 1846). The pediment atop the Corinthian colonnade standing at the front sports a suitably complex, legalistic image of the Justice flanked by lawyers, accused persons and convicted felons. A monastery of the *Recolleten* (Recollect) friars, a branch of the Franciscan Order, once occupied the site.

Across the way in Schouwburg-straat is the equally neo-Classical, L-shaped **De Opera** ㉒ (Opera House; 1840), the Ghent base of the highly regarded Vlaamse Opera (Flemish Opera). It was designed by the same municipal architect, Louis Roelandt, who was also responsible for the Gerechtshof. Roelandt contrived a design for what was at first called the Grand Théâtre, and presented a solid and dignified face to the outside world. Inside, a pair of flighty but brilliant Paris designers, Humanité-René Philastre and Charles-Antoine Cambon, allowed their imaginations to run amok, with draperies, chandeliers, carved wood, paintings, sculpture and *trompe l'oeil* images, making it resemble a transplanted piece of Versailles. This happy mix was retained in a restoration and modernisation that ended in 2002. The in-house Café Théâtre restaurant in the foyer has become a byword locally for modish design and culinary good taste.

## Kouter

The square called **Kouter** ㉓ (or *Keiter,* as you will sometimes hear it pronounced) is quite different from others in the city. While Vrijdagmarkt *(see page 152)* is a living memento of Old Flanders, Kouter dates from a period when Ghent was

Map on page 142

*Although it pales in comparison to fashion mecca Antwerp, Ghent is host to many trendy boutiques.*

**BELOW:** the Opera House is Ghent's leading venue for theatre and classical music.

steeped in Francophone culture and is today surrounded by the sober façades of banks. On Sunday the square is filled with colour, as plants and flowers change hands during the Grote Bloemenmarkt (Big Flower Market). Also on Sunday, the graceful wrought-iron bandstand (1878) is a popular podium for band music. A modern sculpture of a leaf on the square is matched by other leaves engraved on the stones (each of which can be seen in the central panel of Van Eyck's *The Adoration of the Mystic Lamb; see page 182*).

At 172 Kouter, the **Hotel Falligan** (1755) is an ochre-toned mansion in rococo style, with the kind of opulent interior salons that only a seriously wealthy patrician family could have afforded. Placed in 1884 above the Corinthian columns fronting the central façade are two somewhat baffling and contrary sculptures: Apollo, the Greek god of poetry, holds a bow; and Diana, the Greek goddess of the hunt, holds a harp. The mansion now houses a *letterkundige kring* (literary society), the Club des Nobles.

Bringing an additional touch of culture to the square is the restored, rococo **Handelsbeurs** (Exchange) concert hall on the square's south face (No. 29). Graced now with the trendy name **HA'**, it puts on all kinds of music (world, folk, jazz, classic and rock), and has the oh-so-cool café-restaurant Ha' inside. The Handelsbeurs became the commercial exchange at the start of the 20th century, having started out as the Guard House (1739). Designed by architect David 't Kindt, it quartered a unit of the Imperial Guard during the period of Austrian rule. The building's former warlike character is confirmed by the image of the Maid of Ghent surrounded by militaria on the bow-shaped pediment in front of the domed mansard roof. It is quite appropriate because the land

*A happy stallholder at the Sunday Grote Bloemenmarkt.*

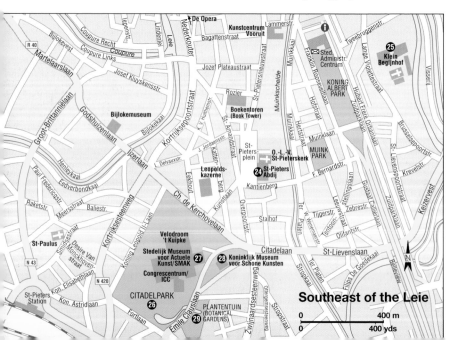

**Southeast of the Leie**

0 ———— 400 m
0 ———— 400 yds

on which Kouter stands was once used as a practice range for archers, and as a parade ground.

## South of Ketelvaart

East of Kouter, Walpoortbrug crosses Ketelvaart. Going a little way south along Walpoortstraat brings you to the twin-turreted **Kunstcentrum Vooruit** (Vooruit Arts Centre), at 23 Sint-Pietersnieuwstraat. This occupies the restored Feestlokaal (Festival Centre) built in 1914 for the *Vooruit* (Forward) cooperative society as a "palace of socialist culture". It's in a fantastical style that draws on Art Nouveau but goes off in its own multiple directions, from daintily decorative to severely minimalist. Inside, among a maze of halls and function rooms, is the superb Majolicazaal (Majolica Hall), decorated with faience tiles. In its new role as a performing arts centre – music, theatre, dance – Vooruit attempts to live up to its avant-garde patrimony. The large café is a big draw with cultured youth, who can be tolerably reflective most of the time, but who on DJ nights mix cultural affairs with copious amounts of beer and hard liquor. **Het Licht** (The Light), a "futuristic" 1930s building standing at No. 128 that was Vooruit's former editorial offices and printworks, has also been reinvented. As **Backstage**, it is now a venue for small-scale theatre, and also boasts a fine café.

Further down, just off Sint-Pietersnieuwstraat on Rozier, the **Boekentoren** (Book Tower; 1940), designed by Belgian architect Henry van de Velde (one of the founders of Art Nouveau), rises out of a complex of University of Ghent buildings as a highly visible symbol of learning. The university library is 64 metres (210 ft) high, has 24 storeys flooded with natural light and contains more than 2 million books.

Centred on the city's dowdy but lively student quarter around Sint-Petersplein, atop a hill called Blandijnberg, stands the monumental **Sint-Pieters Abdij ㉔** (St Peter's Abbey). The former Benedictine abbey traces its history back to St Amand in the 7th century and has known periods of power and wealth

**TIP**

If you have enjoyed getting around town on Ghent's four tram lines (Nos 1, 4, 21 and 22), you might want to sample Belgium's only trolley-bus line (No. 3), which hums out from central Korenmarkt to suburban Mariakerke in the northwest, and in the southeast crosses over the Schelde on the Gentbrugge bridge.

**LEFT:** time out at the Vooruit café.
**BELOW:** the twin towers of the Vooruit Centre.

and periods of total collapse. After its spoliation by Protestant iconoclasts in the 1566 *Beeldenstorm*, the abbey was slowly rebuilt during the Catholic resurgence, and much of it is 17th-century. The domed abbatial church, **Onze-Lieve-Vrouw Sint-Pieterskerk** (Our Lady's at St Peter's; 1722), complete with a fine baroque interior and a small Treasury, took St Peter's in the Vatican for its model. A section of the abbey complex is occupied by the **Kunsthal Sint-Pietersabdij** (St Peter's Abbey Art Gallery; Tues–Sun 10am–6pm; admission charge), which mounts a changing programme of art exhibitions. You will also see an imaginative recreation of a monk's daily life, and a marvellous café, De Kleine Comptoir.

Installed in the abbey infirmary, **De Wereld van Kina** (Kina World; Mon–Fri 9am–5pm, Sun 2–5.30pm; admission charge) is a natural history museum aimed primarily at school-age children. Display cases are laden with minerals, fossils, shells and insects, and dioramas with stuffed birds and other wildlife.

*If the Floraliapaleis seems to bear more than a passing resemblance to a railway station, that's because it was intended to be one. The building was supposed to be dismantled after the 1913 World Exhibition and shipped out to the Belgian Congo for service with the railways there, but World War I got in the way and this never happened.*

**BELOW:** Citadelpark is an oasis of tranquillity.

A departure from all this is the remarkable scale-model of Ghent as it looked during the reign of Habsburg Emperor Charles V, who was born in the city in 1500 (*see page 24*). This is accompanied by a sound-and-light show that tells the story of Ghent in those days.

East of the abbey, on the far side of the Muinkschelde, the green tentacles of **Koning Albertpark** (King Albert Park) spread through a rectangular space once occupied by Ghent's main railway station. Between the park's eastern border and the Leie, along Lange Violettenstraat, you'll find the tranquil **Klein Begijnhof** ㉕ (Small Begijnhof), also known as the **Begijnhof Onze-Lieve-Vrouw Ter Hoye** (Our Lady of Hoye). It looks like a walled 17th-century town in miniature, and is one of the finest surviving examples of these foundations in the Low Countries. Like other Flemish beguinages it is a UNESCO World Heritage Site. Established in 1234 as a home for pious women, it had its original wooden houses replaced by the present ochre-painted brick ones from about 1600. The begijnhof church (1658) was extended by a baroque front gable in 1720, and several chapels and a former infirmary are dotted around the complex. The entire site has been undergoing extensive restoration since 1994, expected to end by 2010.

Just north of the Klein Begijnhof is **Sint-Annakerk** (St Anne's Church; 1862), a mix of 19th-century variations on Romanesque, Gothic and Byzantine.

### Citadelpark

At 22 hectares (54 acres), leafy **Citadelpark** ㉖, just north of Sint-Pietersstation, and Ghent's largest park, was laid out as a badly needed green lung for the city between 1870 and 1910 on the site of a demolished fort. At the park's heart stands a com-

plex of halls and pavilions. Among these are the iron-and-glass **Floraliapaleis** (Floral Palace), which is currently being refurbished; the **casino**, which has housed the city's modern art museum since 1999 *(see below)*; the **Velodroom 't Kuipke** bicycle-racing track; and the large **ICC** congress centre. In the southeast corner is a pond with grottoes and waterfalls. Concerts take place in summer at a handsome cast-iron **bandstand** (1885). A section of the park around the site of the old open-air Groentheater (Green Theatre) is used at night by the city's gay folk.

The **Stedelijk Museum voor Actuele Kunst/SMAK ㉗** (Municipal Museum for Contemporary Art; Tues–Sun 10am–6pm; admission charge) has been a leading-edge cultural force in Belgium. You enter the museum by way of a row of square columns into a series of white-painted halls through which natural light pours from glass-domed ceilings. The fine collection counts more than 2,000 works dating from 1945 to the present day and covers movements such as Cobra, pop art, minimalism, conceptual art and *arte povera*. Belgian artists Marcel Broodthaers, Jan Vercruysse, Panamarenko and Wim Delvoye, are among those represented here, along with well-known international artists such as Francis Bacon, Asger Jorn and Andy Warhol. Other avant-garde figures featured include Joseph Beuys, Vito Acconci and Marina Abramovic.

At the park's edge, the century-old **Koninklijk Museum voor Schone Kunsten ㉘** (Royal Fine Arts Museum; www.mskgent.be) is closed until late 2006 for rebuilding and renovation. Like the premier art museums in Brussels, Bruges and Antwerp, Ghent's is a storehouse of great Belgian painting, from the Flemish Old Masters Van Eyck and Rubens, to Magritte and Ensor,

along with works by Dutch and other European painters. Temporary closure of the brightest star in the city's cultural firmament is a real blow to visiting culture vultures – and would be worse still except that the collection's most important elements are on display at other venues around town. For instance, St Bavo's Cathedral has Hieronymous Bosch's wonderfully grotesque *The Bearing of the Cross* (*c.*1500). Other spaces have been found at Design Museum Gent, MIAT and SMAK, as well as at the Leopoldskazerne (Leopold Barracks), situated on nearby Charles de Kerchovelaan.

Just outside Citadelpark, the **Plantentuin ㉙** (Botanical Garden; Mon–Fri 9am–4.30pm, Sat–Sun 9am–noon; free) of Ghent University has occupied this site on Ledeganckstraat since 1903. On a pleasant stroll through its 2.75 hectares (7 acres) of glasshouses and exterior beds set around a pond, you can see 8,000 species of trees, plants and flowers from all over the world, creating a changing palette of colour throughout the year.  ❏

**Map on page 160**

*The SMAK Museum opened in its current location in late 1998; the new refurbished premises used to be a casino.*

**BELOW:** colourful exhibit at SMAK.

# RESTAURANTS, BARS & CAFÉS

### Restaurants

#### Amadeus II
7 Goudenleeuwplein.
Tel: 09-233 37 75. Open D
daily. €€
A distinctive Art Nouveau-style interior, in symbiosis with the restored 1600s Flemish Renaissance exterior, means there's plenty to look at here, not least the view on the atmospheric Gouden-leeuwplein. The menu features ribs and grilled meat and seafood alter-natives, just like at the Amadeus in Patershol *(see page 180).*

#### Belga Queen
10 Graslei. Tel: 09-280 01 00.
Open L & D daily (tearoom daily 3–7pm). €€€
This eight-centuries-old Romanesque grain store-house ("Het Spijker")

has been fitted out as a temple of swish design and modish cuisine, featuring a restaurant, a tearoom, a lounge bar and even a cigar lounge. The food ranges from patisserie-style snacks to brasserie fare that emphasises Belgian recipes and ingredients. All of the wines featuring on the list originate from Belgian winegrowers around the world; and through its collaboration with Palm Breweries, a large range of high-quality Belgian beers is also available.

#### Brasserie HA'
29 Kouter. Tel: 09-265 91 81.
Open L & D Tues–Sat, L Sun
€€–€€€
Elegant yet cool, the Handelsbeurs Theatre's café-restaurant serves

refined but not too high-brow French and Belgian cuisine – light and breezy for lunch, candle-lit romantic for dinner – to foodies and theatregoers alike. A fantastical multicolored modern chandelier graces the main dining room, and in the summer you can enjoy your meal seated on the lovely outside terrace overlooking the Ketelvaart canal.

#### Brasserie Pakhuis
4 Schuurkenstraat.
Tel: 09-223 55 55. Open
Mon–Thur 11.30–1am,
Fri–Sat 11.30–2am. €€
Perhaps a little too conscious of its trendi-ness, this French-Italian brasserie occupying a restored industrial warehouse, replete with cast-iron pillars, wrought-iron balustrades, and oak and marble tables delivers on the plate. The oyster and seafood platters are especially noteworthy. Snacks are served outside of regular mealtimes.

#### Café Théâtre
5–7 Schouwburgstraat. Tel:
09-265 05 50. Open L & D
Sun–Fri, D Sat. €€–€€€
Ghent's neo-Classical Opera House foyer restaurant has taken on a life of its own as a place of exquisite taste. Opera lovers and just plain foodies fill the two levels to sample Belgian and world cuisine in

ultra-chic surroundings, complete with subdued lighting and wood floors. Its sucess is such that a new lounge bar has opened next door. The staff is both friendly and experienced.

#### De Warempel
8 Zandberg. Tel: 09-224 30
62. Open L Mon–Fri. €–€€
The busy yet convivial atmosphere at this seafood and vegetarian diner goes with the cus-tomers' need to grab a quick, healthy lunchtime bite, but the interior bustle is tempered by a restful view of tranquil Zandberg. The food – world cuisine items such as couscous with grilled aubergines – is cooked by capable hands.

#### Georges
23–27 Donkersteeg. Tel:
09-225 19 18. Open L & D
Wed–Sun. €€–€€€€
Old-fashioned virtues show up in the decor, cooking, price and ser-vice of this restaurant which is in its third generation of family owners since 1924, and still tickling the palettes of seafood lovers. The wide-ranging menu features Zeeland mus-sels, fresh from the in-house seawater tanks.

#### Keizershof
47 Vrijdagmarkt. Tel: 09-223
44 46. Open L & D Tues–Sat.
€€
Overwhelming in its vastness, this three-floor

restaurant is set in a 17th-century building on Ghent's main central square. It has been run by the same owners for the past 25 years. Both decor and service are cool and breezy; the food is a mix of modern continental – with a selection of tasty salads, steaks and pasta dishes – and more traditional Belgian fare.

**Le Grand Bleu**

15 Snepkaai. Tel: 09-220 50 25. Open L & D Tues–Fri, D Sat. €€–€€€€

Set in a small Provençal-style house with a lovely terrace by the Leie, west of Sint-Pietersstation, this seafood specialist is well worth going out of your way for. Its Mediterranean-influenced fish dishes are highly prized and the wide range of lobster variations quite simply legendary. A few succulent meat dishes are also available.

**Theatercafé De Foyer**

17 Sint-Baafsplein. Tel: 09-225 32 75. Open L & D Wed–Mon. €–€€

So polished a performance does the brasserie of Ghent's acclaimed Schouwburg Theatre put on for its continental meals and snacks that the actual play's not necessarily what people are drawn here for in the first place – and if your Dutch is

sparse, you might be tempted to give that a miss altogether. The menu features typical Flemish starters like *asperges à la flamande* and the ubiquitous *croquettes de crevettes* and the mains range from delicious local fish to juicy steaks. There's also an ever-so-desirable balcony terrace overlooking Sint-Baafsplein; it's advisable to book a table in advance as the terrace gets filled up pretty quickly in fine weather.

### Bars & Cafés

This part of Ghent, which takes in the very-much-alive centre of town, is filled with great cafés, in styles ranging from the utmost traditional to the most ultra-modern. You might want to try the genever specialist **'t Dreupelkot** (12 Groentenmarkt), where this traditional Belgian tipple is given due care and attention *(see pages 66–7)*. If genever isn't your thing, but beer is, toddle the short distance instead to **Het Waterhuis aan de Bierkant** (9 Groentenmarkt), a justifiably popular bar set in a great location right beside the Leie; try Ghent's own beers Stropken, Gentse Tripel and Augustijnerbier here. Across the

way, on the end of the Groot Vleeshuis, you will find **'t Galgenhuisje** (5 Groentenmarkt), a tiny café dating from 1783, where it's easy to meet local people. Romantic Graslei can easily look like one long café terrace filled with tippling tourists, and **De Witte Leeuw** (6 Graslei), with more than 300 different kinds of beer on sale in a 17th-century alehouse, gets at least its fair share. A few doors along, the little **Het Tolhuisje** (10 Graslei), is a more traditional Ghent café, in the harbour's former Toll House. No one could accuse Vrijdagmarkt of suffering from a shortage of cafés. Among the square's highlights is the Old Flemish-style **Dulle Griet** (50 Vrijdagmarkt), with its 250 different beers, including the renowned

Kwak, and Ghent's own brews – Stropken, Gentse Tripel and Augustijnerbier. South of the Ketelvaart canal that defines the southern boundary of the city centre, the restored Kunstcentrum Vooruit is a remarkable vision of a working-class culture palace dating from 1912. Its vast **Kafee Vooruit** (23 Sint-Pietersnieuwstraat), is now a popular hangout for students in particular and trendy folks in general, and serves drinks, coffee and snacks.

### PRICE CATEGORIES

Prices for three-course dinner per person with a half-bottle of house wine:

€ = under €25
€€ = €25–40
€€€ = €40–60
€€€€ = over €60

**LEFT:** Ghent's genever specialist for the last 20 years is 't Dreupelkot, a tiny bar at the end of an alley.
**RIGHT:** Dulle Griet is a Ghent institution; just don't forget to ask for your shoe back if you've ordered a Kwak.

# WEST OF THE LEIE

The left bank, west of the Leie, has an atmospheric 17th-century district, the Patershol, dotted with restaurants, cafés, and interesting little boutiques. And the imposing castle, Het Gravensteen, is one of the city's most notable sights

The left bank of the Leie doesn't have quite the same cachet as that of the Seine in Paris, but it still has a great deal to offer.

From the Korenmarkt, take the road to **Sint-Michielsbrug ❶** (St Michael's Bridge), which spans the Leie. This neo-Gothic arched bridge (1910) affords an outstanding vantage point from which to admire the beauty of the city centre, yet it looks somehow discordant in the space it occupies. Eastwards, you get a photogenic view of the "three towers of Ghent": those of Sint-Niklaaskerk, the belfry and Sint-Baafskathedraal. The outlook northwards extends past the Romanesque, Gothic and baroque façades of the warehouses and guildhouses on Graslei and Korenlei, beyond the tour-boat docks below Grasbrug, and on to the towers of Het Gravensteen. Southwards, the Leie slides past the apse of Sint-Michielskerk and the old Dominican cloister known as Het Pand, on the west (left) bank of the river.

## St Michael's and Het Pand

Just off the far end of the bridge, on the left, the most obvious identifying feature of the Brabant Gothic **Sint-Michielskerk ❷** (St Michael's Church; open only during services; free) is its truncated and unfinished tower. Standing on the site of a 12th-

century chapel, this is one of Ghent's trio of great medieval churches. Begun in 1440 as the church of the wealthy brewers' guild, it was abandoned for almost 60 years after the Protestant Iconoclasts of 1566 went to work with hammers and torches on all things Catholic throughout the Low Countries. It was only finished more than 200 years later, with various bits and pieces of baroque being bolted on up to 1650. As for the spire, it was intended to go even higher than Antwerp Cathedral's

Map on page 168

**LEFT:** Patershol rooftop.
**BELOW:** the neo-Gothic Sint-Michielsbrug.

123 metres (404 ft), but both money and enthusiasm ran out, and the brewers are said to have finessed their failure by claiming that the soft riverside ground could not support its weight. The many chapels off the side aisles and chancel make the interior seem immense. Among the religious paintings and sculptures it contains is Antoon van Dyck's *Christ on the Cross* (1630).

Adjoining the church to the south, occupying a stretch of the west bank of the Leie along Onderbergen as far as the Predikherenbrug (Preacher's Bridge), **Het Pand** ❸ (The Build-

ing; open office hours; free) is a former Dominican abbey founded in 1228 and built around a small hospital dating from 1201. The abbey expanded over the centuries, and contained one of the finest libraries in the Low Countries, established in the 15th century with a grant from Margaret of York, Duchess of Burgundy. Protestant "reformers" of 1566 tore up the books, many of them rare works and priceless illuminated volumes, and tossed the pages into the nearby river.

Abandoned as a religious foundation in 1823, Het Pand has been

*So many fragments of paper and parchment were thrown from Het Pand's monastery library into the Leie in 1566 that a chronicler noted that it was possible to cross the river without getting one's feet wet.*

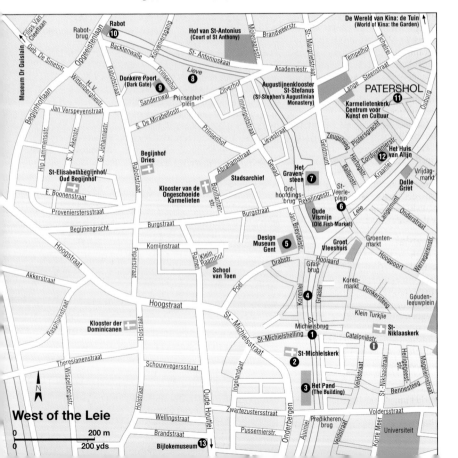

**West of the Leie**

0 ___ 200 m
0 ___ 200 yds

restored and converted (1971–91) by Ghent University to house university offices, a congress centre, a restaurant and museums. The ornamental courtyard garden is worth a visit in its own right. Small specialist university museums are housed here and can be visited only by prior arrangement. Due to move to a permanent location – provided that one can be found or built – the archaeological collection has prehistoric, Egyptian, Etruscan and Roman pieces. The ethnographic collection covers items from Africa, South America, Asia and Polynesia. The Museum for the History of Medicine includes surgical instruments dating from the Gallo-Roman period. A collection of full-size photographs of paintings by Hieronymous Bosch goes by the name Imaginair Museum Dierick.

Directly across Sint-Michielsbrug from the Sint-Michielskerk stands the atmospheric **Graaf van Egmond** restaurant *(see page 180)*. In the 16th century, the building in which it was housed belonged to Count (Graaf) Lamoraal van Egmond, who, along with Count van Hoorn, was beheaded on the Grand-Place in Brussels for opposing the Catholic Inquisition, led in the Low Countries by the brutal Spanish Duke of Alba.

## Korenlei

A flight of steps leads down from the bridge to **Korenlei** ❹, across the water from the equally distinctive Graslei *(see page 155)*, and like its neighbour a part of the old Tussen Bruggen (Between the Bridges) harbour district between Sint-Michielsbrug and Grasbrug. During the 18th and 19th centuries most of Korenlei's port-related buildings lost their original purpose. Many were renovated in time for the 1913 Ghent World Fair, although the restorations were unfortunately not always done with great care for historical accuracy. Korenlei's buildings suffer a bit by comparison with Graslei's, but some are equally fine.

Below the Graaf van Egmond, the two step-gabled, red-brick houses **De Lintworm** (The Tapeworm), at No. 24, which now house the Crypte restaurant *(see page 180)*, and the adjoining corner house at No. 23, were restored to approximately their 16th-century character, when it was the Brewers' Guildhouse, although the restorers could just as well have gone as far back as the Romanesque originals (*c.*1200).

Across a narrow alley, **No. 22** was given a mansard roof and a triangular pediment in 1731, above an elegant, pastel-toned neo-Classical façade decked out with pilasters. This adjoins the rather sober neo-Classical **Hof Van Fiennes** (Van Fiennes Mansion), at No. 21, which housed the city's Mercantile Chamber and Stock Exchange from 1730, before being rebuilt in 1833 and modernised since then. It has now been divided into luxury apartments.

Backing onto the open cobblestoned square next to the Hof Van

Map on page 168

*King Philip II of Spain was once a guest at Count Lamoraal van Egmond's home (now the Graaf van Egmond restaurant). Philip may not have been a welcome guest, considering the ocean of blood he caused to be spilled as he strove to reassert Catholic dominance in the Low Countries.*

**BELOW:** window display in a lace shop in Korenlei.

Fiennes, **No. 20** dates from 1914 and is a somewhat perfunctory architectural doodle on neo-Classical design, with medallions and small Ionic columns. Right next door, at Nos 17–19, the **Hotel de Ghellinck**, a neo-Classical mansion built in 1849 for the wealthy de Ghellinck family, is notable for its fine scrollwork and pilasters with Corinthian capitals. Its neighbour, at Nos 12–16, is the even more impressive neo-Classical mansion **Hotel Dons de Marnicx**, built in 1853 and of particular interest for its four massive pilasters.

Next come **De Roode Meulen**, at No. 11, dating from 1823; **De Stadt Doornick** (The City of Tournai), a 1955 reconstruction of a late 16th-century house, at No. 10; and **De Swaene** (The Swans) at No. 9, restored in 1949 to the approximate look of an earlier step-gabled building, the offices of the De Swaene brewery that was built in 1608–9, and later became a bordello. Note the two carved swan medallions high up on the façade. Behind their preserved façades, this whole section was in the process of being trans-

formed into a Marriott Hotel at the time of writing.

At No. 7, the **Gildehuis van de Onvrije Schippers** (Guildhouse of the Tied Boatmen) dates from 1739 and was the headquarters of the rivals to the Free Boatmen, whose *pied à terre* was on Graslei (*see page 157*). The tied boatmen gained a measure of freedom around this time and savoured the moment by commissioning this extravagant piece of pale-pink-and-white, Flemish baroque architecture, dubbed *Den Ancker* (The Anchor). It must have been conceived at least in part as a poke in the eye for their rivals. Restored in 1974, it stands next to a tour-boat dock. Among its ornamental elements feature carved dolphins and lions, as well as a swirling bell-gable crowned by a gilded caravel weather vane. The magnificent interior hosts the fine Allegro Moderato restaurant, a bar, called De Onvrije Schipper, and a terrace out on the picturesque riverbank cobblestones.

**De Vijf Helmen**, at Nos 4–5, recalls a brewery of that name that once stood here. The splendid neo-Classical affair that replaced it in 1765 was designed by the renowned Ghent architect David 't Kindt. Before leaving Korenlei you might want to bear in mind that Drabstraat, which leads off it to the left at this point, has a great trendy French restaurant called **Het Blauwe Huis** (The Blue House), at No. 17; you cannot easily miss it since the façade is painted, you guessed it, blue.

## Design and delectables

Take some time out to stroll onto adjacent Grasbrug to enjoy a memorable view from this bridge up and down the Leie and along the Lieve canal (going all the way over the bridge takes you to Graslei), before returning to stroll into Jan Breydelstraat.

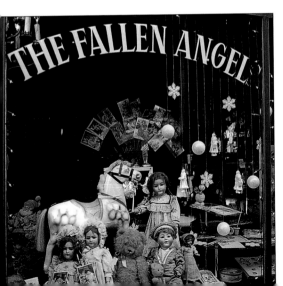

At No. 5, occupying the Hotel de Coninck, a restored baroque mansion designed by David 't Kindt, built around a courtyard and dating from 1755, is the **Design Museum Gent ❺** (Tues–Sun 10am–6pm; admission charge). The museum covers two main areas: there is a succession of 18th- and 19th-century period rooms, with tapestries and other applied arts and crafts; and occasionally bizarre furnishings, applied art, craft and interior design from the 20th century to the present day. The emphasis is put on Art Nouveau and Art Deco including the work of Belgian Art Nouveau masters Henry van de Velde, Victor Horta and Paul Hankar. The original wing at the front houses the former collection, and a modern wing at the rear holds the latter. Among the highlights is the period dining room and its collection of Chinese porcelain. Some items belonged to Louis XVIII, who fled to Ghent in 1815 to escape from a briefly resurgent Napoleon, before the Battle of Waterloo.

Jan Breydelstraat is an all-round interesting short street. You can buy both flowers and flower-based ice cream – including jasmine, iris and wild rose flavours – in **Boeketten Papaver** at No. 6. Next door, at No. 8, **Brooderie** is a fine bakers with a café that serves vegetarian snacks, and also manages to be a neat little Bed & Breakfast. On the other side of Appelbrugparkje, a small garden overlooking the confluence of the River Leie and the Lieve canal, is the exquisit French restaurant **Jan Breydel**, at No. 10, and in summer you can dine on its outdoor terrace. Further along on the other side of the street, at No. 35, is the notable **Hotel Gravensteen**, set in a mansion built in 1865 for a local textiles tycoon, at the end of the old carriageway. Great shops are found here; have a browse at **Uit Steppe & Oase**, at No. 21, with Islamic decorative arts and crafts pieces; **The Fallen Angels**, at Nos 29–31, which specialises in quality bric-à-brac – toys, for instance – that does not quite fall into the antiques category; and **Raj**, at No. 40, with its authentic Indian and Oriental furnishings, jewellery, curios and other items.

Map on page 168

*A merry-go-round using Alessi kitchen utensils at Design Museum Gent.*

**LEFT AND BELOW:** Design Museum Gent's 20th-century wing; colourful furniture by designer Alessandro Mendini.

Directly ahead on the far side of Burgstraat, standing at No. 4, is a Flemish Renaissance house, known as **Het Huis Met De Gekroonde Hoofden** (House With the Crowned Heads), for its constellation of 14 medallion portraits of counts of Flanders and dukes of Burgundy, Habsburg emperors and kings of Spain. Among them are Count Louis of Male, dukes Philip the Good and Charles the Bold, emperors Maximilian of Austria and Charles V, and King Philip II of Spain. It is now a restaurant called, unsurprisingly, De Gekroonde Hoofden.

### Grisly tales

The bridge across the Lieve canal from Burgstraat into Rekelingestraat is called the **Hoofdbrug** (Head Bridge), also known as Onthoofdingsbrug (Beheading Bridge). It seems that heads may have been removed here, in the shadow of the Castle of the Counts. A no-doubt legendary tale from the 14th century tells of a rebel who was sentenced to behead his equally seditious father on the bridge, but the blade flew from the son's sword hilt as he was wielding it for the fatal stroke and both men were acquitted.

Rekelingestraat runs into **Sint-Veerleplein ⑥**, named after an 8th-century female martyr. The square's old gabled houses belie a gruesome past. Prior to the late 18th century, it contained a wheel of torture and a gallows. Murderers and thieves, magicians and witches, forgers and heretics, vagabonds and robbers were strangled, beheaded, hanged, and flayed on the wheel or bound and thrown into vats of boiling oil or water. A punishment post in the middle, surmounted by a lion of Flanders, was placed here in 1913.

Leading back from the square, at No. 5, and occupying the upper angle of the Y created by the junction of the Leie and Lieve waterways, is the monumental baroque entrance to the **Oude Vismijn** (Old Fish Market). Dating from 1690 and restored in 1872, after the old market had been destroyed by fire and rebuilt in neo-Gothic style, the entrance is guarded by a trident-flourishing Neptune standing on a seashell drawn by two

*Neptune guards the entrance of the Old Fish Market.*

**BELOW:** the head-turning Hoofdbrug.

winged horses, accompanied by some dolphins, and flanked on a lower level by the reclining figures of a woman with a catch of fish and a man holding a sail, representing the rivers Leie and Schelde respectively. The fish market is no longer held here and the building is currently in a state of suspended animation, waiting for something useful to be done with it.

## Het Gravensteen

Between Sint-Veerleplein and the Lieve stands the forbidding fortification built of Tournai limestone, **Het Gravensteen** ❼ (Castle of the Counts; Apr–Sept daily 9am–6pm; Oct–Mar daily 9am–5pm; admission charge). Its brooding presence seems laden with medieval menace even today, although much of it is a 19th-century reconstruction.

Inside, you can visit the dungeons and torture chamber whose mere existence played an important part in the counts of Flanders' efforts to win hearts and minds – and when that proved unattainable, to rip out hearts and destroy minds.

Het Gravensteen was modelled on the ponderous castles constructed by the Crusaders in the heart of hostile territory in Syria and the Holy Land, and admired by Count of Flanders Philip of Alsace, who campaigned there in the late 12th century. Realising the usefulness of having one in the heart of hostile territory on his own doorstep he completed this smaller version in 1180. At first, it served as a residence and a fortress. After the 14th century, the counts tired of the damp, gloomy place and decamped across town to more comfortable new quarters at the Prinsenhof *(see page 175)*. The castle became a prison, its inner courtyard used as a place of execution and the crypt as a torture chamber. A mint, courts of justice as well as a cotton mill were at various times installed on the premises.

Beyond the twin-turreted, fortified gateway, a covered passageway leads to the central bailey (courtyard), in which stand the crenellated battlements of the keep, and the residence of the counts. Here in the Great Hall, in 1445, Duke Philip the

Map on page 168

*Torture and execution were not confined to within the castle's walls. Medieval Ghent was full of institutions which were empowered to "interrogate painfully" and execute suspects.*

**BELOW:** the ominous Castle of the Counts.

# Charles V, Son of Ghent

The future ruler of the Habsburg lands in the Low Countries, France, Austria and Italy; Holy Roman Emperor of the German Nation; King of Spain and the Spanish lands in the Americas; and claimant to the crowns of Hungary and Bohemia – the list runs to more than 70 titles – first drew breath at the Prinsenhof in Ghent on 24 February 1500. Charles's birth was celebrated in style: it was deep winter and the city authorities even went to the trouble of flooding Vrijdagmarkt so that children could skate on it when the water froze. Robert Browning's poem *How They Brought the Good News from Ghent to Aix* tells of the excitement aroused by the royal birth. Although Charles was baptised in St Bavo's Cathedral, the future emperor, who had a sickly constitution, was soon removed to Mechelen, to be brought up there by his aunt, Margaret of Austria.

Aside from the involuntary act of being born there, Charles's main contribution to Ghent was obliging several hundred of its leading citizens to parade before him barefoot and in their nightshirts, their necks adorned with hangman's nooses. Ghent ruefully recalls this humiliation every year in the six-hour Stroppendragers (Noose Bearers') Procession. To assure his control, Charles had imposed political centralisation on his far-flung realms, an act that went down badly in Ghent, which saw itself as an independent city-state on the lines of Florence. Wealthy and dynamic, it was one of the biggest cities north of the Alps at the time, and resented being kept within a straitjacket. Despite Charles's local-boy-made-good origins, Ghent rose against him in 1539 over the touchy subject of taxes levied to finance his wars.

If the burghers of Ghent were relying on a sentimental attachment to his birthplace to save them from his wrath, Charles soon disabused them of this notion. In addition to the scary episode with the nooses, the incensed emperor further curtailed the city's freedoms; depleted its coffers so seriously that work on the dazzling new Stadhuis (town hall) had to be deferred for more than a generation; ordered its grand tocsin "Roeland" to be lowered from the belfry; and ensured there would be no repetition of the rebellion by sending the monks of Sint-Baafsabdij packing and installing a Spanish garrison in a fortress on the abbey grounds.

Physical traces of the great emperor's presence are few and far between today. All that survives of the Prinsenhof is a single gateway, the Donkere Poort, although there is a statue of Charles on the Prinsenhof square. Then there is the Sint-Jorishof Hotel, where he stayed for a time when it was a guild residence. And his is one of the heads portrayed on the Huis Met De Gekroonde Hoofden (House With the Crowned Heads). In the museum De Wereld van Kina (Kina World) you can peruse a scale-model of Ghent as it looked during his reign.

Charles might not have endeared himself to the people of Ghent in most respects but they clearly appreciated this proud bon mot he once delivered about the city of his birth: *Je pourrais mettre Paris dans mon Gand* (I could put Paris in my Ghent). In translation it sounds bizarre, until you realise that the French words for glove (*gant*) and Ghent (*Gand*) are pronounced identically. ❏

**LEFT:** the mighty emperor Charles V ruled over an empire on which the sun never set.

Good feasted in lavish Burgundian style with his Knights of the Golden Fleece. The counts' quarters now house a museum documenting the medieval system of criminal justice, a gruesome collection of tools and tales of torture, either to force a confession or to kill the condemned in the grisliest possible manner; and a museum of antique weapons and armour. The top level of the main tower affords a superb view.

## The Prinsenhof district

Het Gravensteen stands right beside the narrow **Lieve canal** ❽, which curves north and northwest from the point where it branches off from the River Leie. The first canal linking Ghent to the sea was dug over a period of 18 years beginning in 1251 and was used primarily by textile and corn traders. It used to stretch as far as Damme, the outer harbour of Bruges, but it now reaches no further than the northwest edge of Ghent city centre before being cut off – making it in effect a canal to nowhere. In this area are a number of places of interest worth taking in *en passant,* but not going too much out of your way to see.

A short leisurely stroll from Het Gravensteen will take you to the **Berg van Barmhartigheid** (literally the Mountain of Mercy). This fine example of early baroque and Flemish Renaissance architecture, erected at 13 Abrahamstraat was founded as a credit institution in 1622 during the regency of Archduke Albert and Archduchess Isabella of Austria. For 300 years, the citizens of Ghent were able to borrow money here, albeit at an exorbitant rate of interest. Since 1930 it has housed the city archives.

On the south bank of the Lieve once stood the **Prinsenhof**, the vast palace dating from 1353 that the counts of Flanders, and later the dukes of Burgundy and the Habs-

burg emperors, used as their local *pied à terre* after moving out of gloomy Het Gravensteen. Unfortunately, not much in the way of ancestral ruins remains. The Prinsenhof, where Habsburg Emperor Charles V was born in 1500, is a case-study in *Sic transit gloria mundi.* It had ornamental gardens, fountains and no fewer than 300 rooms, but all that remains after centuries of demolition and fire is an entrance gateway, the **Donkere Poort** ❾ (Dark Gate) and a mere scrap of the exterior wall on Bachtenwalle. On the tranquil square called Prinsenhof stands a statue of Charles, donated in 1966 by the city of Toledo in southern Spain, and a model of the palace.

Just west of the Donkere Poort the **Rabot** ❿ marks the end point of the Lieve. Built in 1489–91 to provide better protection for a weak link in the city's walls – the point where the canal crossed the moat – this fortified water gate, flanked by two towers, is the sole surviving city gate and one of the few remnants of the medieval fortifications.

Map on page 168

*The Berg van Barmhartigheid was based on models from Italy where this kind of institution was called in Latin Mons Pietatis.*

**BELOW:** the Rabot is a rare vestige of medieval Ghent.

*In some Patershol restaurants (and in others around the city), you can eat two Ghent specialities: waterzooï (chicken or fish stew, simmered in its own stock, with cream, white wine and vegetables) and Gentse stoverij (beef and beer stew, ideally accompanied by Ghent's own piquant Tierenteyn mustard).*

Northwest from the Rabot, on the far bank of the Verbindingskanaal (an east–west canal that connects Ghent harbour to the new Bruges canal, the Brugse Vaart), is the oddly fascinating **Museum Dr Guislain** (43 Jozef Guislainstraat; Tues–Fri 9am–5pm, Sat–Sun 1–5pm; admission charge). This is a museum of psychiatry – or at least of what passed as treatment for the mentally ill in times past – housed in a rambling 19th-century former mental asylum. It gets inside the mind of its subject through photography, art and other exhibits.

## Beguinage and almshouses

Back on the Lieve's west bank, beyond the end of Burgstraat, is another faded remnant of the city's glorious past: the **Sint-Elisabeth-begijnhof** (St Elizabeth Beguinage). Also known as the Oud Begijnhof (Old Beguinage), it was founded in 1242 by the Countess of Flanders, Joan of Constantinople, as a home for *Begijnen* (Beguines) – religious women who were similar to nuns, but took no vows *(see page 84)*. One of the largest such institutions in Europe, it occupied an area of marshy ground just outside the walls and was ringed by a wall and a moat, with its own church, dating from 1641. The church still stands, between Proveniersterstraat and Begijnhofdries. Most of the begijnhof's small houses and cottages date from the 16th and 17th centuries, but this tranquil refuge continued to function into the 19th century. Later the remaining Beguines removed to the Sint-Amandsberg Begijnhof *(see page 185)*. The beguinage is far enough from the centre to make it worth taking a tram (lines 1 and 4).

On the way back to Het Gravensteen, the 17th-century **Klooster van de Ongeschoeide Karmelieten** (Cloister of the Discalced Carmelites – "discalced" means barefoot), at 46 Burgstraat, has a church dating from 1712. Between Burgstraat and Hoogstraat, the **School van Toen** (School From Back Then; schooldays 9am–noon, 2–4pm; Wed am only; free), at 8 Klein Ramhof, has a period classroom and other school set ups dating from 1901.

East of the Lieve on Sint-Antoniuskaai, among the canalside quays, the baroque **Hof van Sint-Antonius** (Court of St Anthony; 1645) was originally the guildhouse of the Ghent arquebusiers, before being taken over as a *godshuis* (almshouse) for elderly men. It incorporates a small park. Closer to the centre, the 17th-century **Augustijnenklooster Sint-Stefanus** (St Stephen's Augustinian Monastery) at 1 Academiestraat houses an important archive and library of antique books.

## Patershol

The restored and trendy district of **Patershol** ⓫ behind Het Gravensteen is a maze of 17th-century streets, lanes and alleys (most of them now pedestrian-only) lined by small brick houses. Ironically,

**BELOW:** the red-bricked St Elizabeth Beguinage.

Map on page 168

this was once the least-desirable part of town. In early medieval times it was the tanners' quarter, a period recalled in the name Corduwaniers-straat (Cordwainers Street) – cord-wainers were leather workers. It later became home to other manual workers and even a number of fine patrician families who settled here in the area of Het Gravensteen. With industrialisation, this part of town developed into a weavers' quarter, until the textiles factories that sup-ported them closed or moved out. It later became a low-life slum and red-light district, and was only just saved from demolition, being given over to gentrification instead. Res-toration during the 1980s brought out the underlying bijou nature of many of the properties. Restaura-teurs, boutique owners, antiques dealers and artisans have moved in, but it is still at heart a residential dis-trict and the number of incoming businesses is controlled – not until one closes is another allowed to take its place, to preserve the residential character. Around 100 Patershol buildings are protected monuments.

Entering Patershol by way of Kraanlei (Crane Quay), alongside the Leie, Nos 1–14 date from the 14th and 15th centuries. At No. 17 is the restaurant 't Buikske Vol *(see page 180),* which has a sculpted bronze image of a *Manneken-Pis* above the doorway. It resembles the famous symbol of Brussels, a foun-tain in the shape of a piddling little boy, but unlike the one in Brussels, Ghent's doesn't piddle. It's actually thought to be a statue of a youthful Bacchus, the Roman god of wine.

Further along Kraanlei, at No. 65, is the restored **Huis van Alijn** ⓬ (Alijn House; Tues–Sun 11am–5pm; admission charge), the city's fasci-nating folklore museum, housed in scores of tiny rooms ranged around a courtyard garden; notably, it was once a children's home/hospital, the Kinderen Alijnsgodshuis. The origins of the almshouse goes back to a feud between two rival Ghent guild families, the Rijms and the Alijns. This conflict came to a head in 1354 over the hand of a girl called Godelieve. When she elected to marry Hendrik Alijn, instead of her

*Huis van Alijn façade detail dating from when the house was a children's hospital.*

**BELOW:** the Huis van Alijn courtyard.

*An annexe to the Huis van Alijn is a late-Gothic chapel called the Drongenhofkapel, at 15 Drongenhof, off riverside Oudburg and backing onto Plotersgracht. Now an exhibition space, it is open to the public during exhibitions.*

**BELOW:** room of the Governors of the Chamber of the Poor at the Bijloke Museum.

intended, Simoen Rijm, the jilted man killed his rival and his brother – shades of *Romeo and Juliet's* squabbling Montegu and Capulet families. The verdict of the law was that the Rijm family homes should be demolished, and Simoen was ordered to build an almshouse or hospice on land donated by the Alijns. The original was replaced in 1519 by the present one, consisting of 18 small Flemish Renaissance houses with red-painted doors and shutters and dormer roofs. To this was added in 1540 the late-Gothic **Sint-Catharinakapel** (St Catherine's Chapel), which features an elegant wooden altar.

In this superb setting, the folklore museum conveys a picture of life in Ghent and Flanders in general from around 1900 through an inventive recreation of workshops, shops, and domestic living and dining rooms. These include a clogmaker's workshop, a barber's shop and a chemist's laboratory. Themes from everyday life and popular entertainment are also covered. Even though performances are in Dutch, the **Puppet**

**Theatre** should hold plenty of fascination for children; and grown-ups have their own kind of entertainment in the museum's traditional tavern, **'t Cafeetse**.

Still further along this riverside quay, you can admire a number of highly decorated old houses that each have a moral to tell. No. 75, a 17th-century step-gabled house called **De Klok** (The Clock), is decorated with allegorical bas-reliefs representing love, faith and justice, and the cardinal virtues: caution, moderation, justice and strength. At No. 79, the **Huis van de Werken van Barmhartigheid** (House of the Works of Mercy), from 1643, depicts on its façade of red brick and sandstone the seven works of charity, though only six – feeding the hungry; giving drink to the thirsty; clothing the naked; sheltering the stranger; freeing the imprisoned; and visiting the sick – are portrayed directly. The seventh, burying the dead, seems to have been judged too depressing and is suggested only symbolically. Traditional Ghent gingerbread, candies and biscuits

are now sold within, at the twee Temmerman *confiserie*: be sure to try some. No. 81, dating from 1637, has on its façade female images of the five senses, plus those of a flute player and a winged deer, hence its dual names: **De Fluitspeler** (Flute-Player's House) and **Den Vliegenden Hert** (The Flying Deer). High up on the baroque gable are representations of the three virtues: faith, hope and love.

At the junction of Lange Steenstraat and Vrouwebroersstraat stands the **Karmelietenkerk** and **Caermersklooster** (Carmelite Church and Monastery). The Carmelites – founded at Mt Carmel in the Holy Land – came to Ghent in 1287 and added to their foundation over the next six centuries. The name Patershol (Monk's Hole) originated with these friars, and seemingly refers to a water source on the premises. Much of their once-extensive property is now public housing; the 14th–16th-century church is owned by East Flanders province and is an exhibition space, the Provinciaal Centrum voor Kunst en Cultuur (Tues–Sat 10am–5pm when an exhibition is running; free).

North of Patershol, a breath of scented air awaits at **De Wereld van Kina: de Tuin** (Kina World: the Garden; Mon–Fri 9am–5pm, Sun 2–5.30pm; free), at 55 Berouw. The botanical garden of the city's natural history museum *(see page 162)* is the oldest botanical garden in Flanders, and is an entertaining place for children as well as adults. On a stroll through its varied biotopes and landscapes, you will see ponds, an arboretum, greenhouses, bee hives, an orchard, and trees, as well as around 1,500 different species of flowers and plants. There's all kinds of hands-on stuff for children to do in the museum area, on themes like the honeybee, botany, and the spider.

## Bijloke Museum

Still on the west bank of the Leie, but far to the south (and south of the Coupure canal), is the 14th–17th-century Cistercian nunnery, the Bijlokeabdij (Bijloke Abbey) at 2 Godshuizenlaan. It now hosts the **Bijlokemuseum** ⓭ (Thur 10am–1pm, 2–6pm, Sun 2–6pm; admission charge) with medieval paraphernalia: weapons, clothing, tapestries, musical instruments, Carolingian silver coins, porcelain and glassware, primarily from Ghent and East Flanders.

A highlight is the fascinating painting *Panoramic View of Ghent* (1534) by an anonymous master. These are accompanied by a fine collection of Chinese art. In the Guild Hall are historical mementos of Ghent's guilds, and for some reason a model sailing ship. Apart from all this, a chance to view the former abbey – in particular the frescoed, 14th-century refectory with a barrel-vaulted ceiling – and its grounds justifies a visit. The entrance gateway came from the Sint-Elisabethbegijnhof *(see page 176).* ❑

*Cuberdons, these "red noses" filled with raspberry jam, are a Ghent speciality.*

**BELOW:** the Bijloke Museum stands on lovely grounds.

# RESTAURANTS, BARS & CAFÉS

## Restaurants

### Amadeus

8–10 Plotersgracht. Tel: 09-225 13 85. Open D daily. **€€**

You're likely to get ribbed for dining here. Ribs are virtually the only things on the menu, aside from a few dishes for those who get dragged along by ribs fans. They are served *à volonté* (all you can eat) so make sure you're hungry! Ribs are evidently popular in Ghent, especially when served in a warm atmosphere in the Patershol district. You drink your wine from the bottle that is on your table. At the end of your meal a simple "measure-procedure" determines the cost of the wine you consumed.

### Bij den Wijzen en den Zot

42 Hertogstraat. Tel: 09-223 42 30. Open L & D Tues–Sat. **€€€**

Don't let the country-bumpkin name ("At the Wise and the Fool") fool you. The Patershol's oldest restaurant is perfectly cosmopolitan on the plate. In its trio of rustic, 16th-century rooms it serves up memorable Flemish fare, including *waterzooï op Gentse wijze*, with fish as the main ingredient (in some versions of this popular dish the main ingredient is chicken).

### Cœur d'Artichaut

6 Onderbergen. Tel: 09-225 33 18. Open L & D Tues–Fri, D Sat. **€€€**

Salads – some of them sporting the artichoke hearts of the restaurant's name – are among the special concoctions at this cool spot housed in an 1826 town house with a patio terrace, located a block south of Sint-Michielskerk. The cooked dishes – on a menu that meanders across Belgium, southern Europe and Asia – are inventive, too. The fixed menu changes on a monthly basis.

### Crypte

24 Korenlei. Tel: 09-223 61 91 95. Open L & D Tues–Sun. **€€–€€€**

Atmosphere takes you a long way when you dine amid arched, bare stone walls and columns in a cellar that dates from around 1100; this place has been converted to a bistro-grill house underneath the Graaf van Egmond restaurant *(see below)*. And the Flemish food – featuring steak, fish and goose dishes – is pretty memorable too. From the terrace, there is a great view of the three towers of Ghent and the Leie.

### De Blauwe Zalm

2 Vrouwebroersstraat. Tel: 09-224 08 25. Open L & D Tues–Fri, D Mon & Sat **€€€–€€€€**

"Seafood for foodies" is the motto here – and it's as true now as when it was first formulated. The handwritten menu's various marine delights are first-class quality, and the elegant modern interior, stretching through several small adjoining Patershol houses, is easy on the eye. There's also a nice garden terrace.

### Eethuis Avalon

32 Geldmunt. Tel: 09-224 37 24. Open 8am–6pm Mon–Sat **€**

Across the street from the Gravensteen, Avalon is a far cheerier medieval reference. Among its informal bio-vegetarian concoctions, homemade soup served with home-baked bread, followed by a slice of savoury quiche seems like lordly fare. The antique-tiled main room is a protected monument and there's also a charming small garden terrace.

### Graaf van Egmond

21 Sint-Michielsplein. Tel: 09-225 07 27. Open L & D daily. **€€–€€€**

A perch above Korenlei affords a view of the three towers of Ghent from the manorial interior of a cavernous building that dates back to around 1200, but was rebuilt in Flemish Renaissance style in the 1660s. A wide range of traditional Flemish dishes is headed by Ghent's very own *waterzooï* and *stoverij*.

### Jan Breydel

10 Jan Breydelstraat. Tel: 09-225 62 87. Open D Mon, L & D Tues–Sat. **€€€–€€€€**

Overlooking the scenic confluence of the Lieve canal and the River Leie, and with a waterside terrace next to little Appelbrug Parkje, this fine restaurant serves a carefully considered range of French haute cuisine, in an elegant setting that matches the attention to detail of the menu and the service.

**LEFT:** Tintin fun on a Ghent café terrace.
**RIGHT:** all the ingredients you need to make a *waterzooï*, one of Ghent's culinary specialities.

### Raj

45 Kraanlei. Tel: 09-234 34
59. Open D Mon–Fri,
noon–midnight Sat–Sun
€€–€€€

In a setting of refined
Indian style, this restau-
rant-cum-teahouse has
a sophisticated take
on sub-continental and
world cuisine. The
smoke-free air inside
adds a fragrant touch all
by itself. The superb garden terrace at the back is
ideal for summer dining.

### 't Buikske Vol

17 Kraanlei. Tel: 09-225 18
80. Open L & D Mon–Tues,
Thur–Fri; D Sat. €€–€€€

The "Full Little Stomach"
is the homely name for a
cosmopolitan Patershol
restaurant on the Leie
waterfront. It reflects a
successful combination
of seeming opposites:
smart yet relaxing decor,
professional but affable
service, and from the
open kitchen quality

Flemish and continental
cuisine with a touch of
invention and fun.

### Valentijn

1 Rodekoningstraat.
Tel: 09-225 04 29.
Open L & D Mon–Wed,
D Fr–Sat, L Sun. €€€

A broad range of refined
French cuisine is served
in this smallish restaurant
spread out on two warmly
coloured, flower-bedecked
floors of an old house
in the Patershol district.
Extremely popular among
the Ghent locals, this
is also a great place to
experience a romantic
tête-à-tête by candlelight
– and not just because
of the name.

### Vier Tafels

6 Plotersgracht. Tel: 09-225
05 25. Open D Mon, L & D
Tues–Sun. €€

Located in the heart of
the medieval Patershol
district, not too far from
the Castle of the Counts,
this plant-bedecked

restaurant serves up
Flemish tradition, in
dishes like *waterzooï*,
but goes far beyond this
with an intriguing range
of world cuisine that
includes such prime
ingredients as reindeer,
kangaroo and crocodile.

## Bars & Cafés

The west bank of the Leie
has plenty of neighbour-
hood bars but not so
many places that really
stand out as you will find
on the east bank. One
that does though is
**De Onvrije Schipper** (7
Korenlei), the cellar bar,
with a waterside terrace,
of the elegant Guildhouse
of the Tied Boatmen.
Wine and cheese go
together like peaches and
cream at medieval-style
**De Tap en De Tepel** (7
Gewad), across the water
from Het Gravensteen,
where they are accompa-

nied by folk, medieval
and Renaissance music.
The café of a folklore
museum might seem
likely to be strained and
artificial, but that is not
true in the colourful
**Cafeetse** (65 Kraanlei),
the traditional tavern of
the Huis van Alijn. For
great Italian ice cream,
served in determinedly
untrendy surroundings,
visit the family-owned
parlour **Veneziana**
(6 Geldmunt), located
across from Het Graven-
steen, which has been
doing the business to
great local satisfaction
for generations.

### PRICE CATEGORIES

Prices for three-course
dinner per person with a
half-bottle of house wine:

€ = under €25
€€ = €25–40
€€€ = €40–60
€€€€ = over €60

# GHENT'S MASTERPIECE

**The awe-inspiring polyptych in Ghent's cathedral is a marvel of colour, naturalism and religious symbolism**

Jan van Eyck (*c*. 1390–1441), born at Maeseyck (Maaseik) in Limburg, was the court painter to the Duke of Burgundy, Philip the Good. Although he was traditionally credited with inventing oil painting, this was not so. His use of oils, however, was revolutionary; he brought to instant perfection what was still a new medium, infusing his subjects with an inner glow and surrounding them with symbolic meaning. A key work by Van Eyck, and one of the world's art masterpieces, is *The Adoration of the Mystic Lamb* (1432), a 20-panel polyptych altarpiece in Ghent's Sint-Baafs-kathedraal (St Bavo's Cathedral; *see page 147*).

It tells the story of the Christian mysteries, from the Fall to the Redemption, and in particular that of the Eucharist. Its dazzling use of colour and naturalistic rendering of people and scenery sounded the death knell for the formal, religious art of the Middle Ages. One minor item that may have upset the burghers of Ghent was the inclusion in the central panel of a view of the Onze-Lieve-Vrouwekerk (Church of Our Lady) in Bruges, Van Eyck's adopted home town.

Not everyone appreciated naturalism in the service of religious art. In the late 18th century, Emperor Joseph II of Austria took exception to the nakedness of Adam and Eve, and the panels depicting them were replaced by two clothed figures. Today, the original Adam and Eve, which had been hidden away, have been restored to their rightful place. However, the bottom left panel, featuring the just judges, is a copy; the original was stolen in 1934 and never recovered. The work was originally hung in the cathedral nave but has now been moved to a side chapel.

**ABOVE:** in its time the altarpiece has been stolen by Napoleon and looted by the Nazis, but it always found its way back to Ghent – except for the panel depicting the wise judges, which is a copy of an original stolen in 1934.

**BELOW:** main panel showing the Adoration of the Mystic Lamb. The lamb's blood flows into a chalice, symbolising the Eucharist.

## CONTROVERSIAL COMPOSITION

Some controversy surrounds this extraordinary work. Did Jan van Eyck paint it alone, or did he collaborate with his older brother Hubert van Eyck (*c.* 1370–1426)? The latter is not mentioned in any documents but is cited in an enigmatic inscription to be found on the frame of the altarpiece. This describes Hubert as the greatest painter who ever lived and says that he started the work, which was completed by Jan – who was almost Hubert's equal as a painter.

Hubert was living in Ghent in 1424, and it is known that Jan moved from a position in The Hague to one in Bruges in 1425, the year work on the altarpiece began. The inference is that Hubert began the work alone then called for his brother to assist him, before dying the following year. Despite this inscription, many art historians believe the altarpiece to be the work of Jan alone. Almost nothing is known about Hubert's life and work – a surprising state of affairs for "the greatest artist of all time". Nowadays, of course, that accolade is more often applied to Jan.

This is not the only enigma associated with the altarpiece. There is also the question of how such a revolutionary work of art, so complex in its detail, and so rich in religious and metaphysical allusions, came to be created in the first place. Who and what provided the motive force? We know that it was commissioned by local patrician Joos Vijd and his wife Isabella Borluut for their chapel behind the cathedral high altar (where it was displayed until 1986).

Art historians through the centuries have ascribed the grasp of detail to the tradition of painting miniatures, and the inspiration to a flowering of creativity in Flanders as the Burgundian era progressed.

**LEFT:** detail of the Singing Angels from the left wing of the altarpiece. In the right wing the angels are depicted playing musical instruments.

# AROUND GHENT

For a change of pace, take an excursion out of
town to find historical castles turned into country
manors, to explore a nature reserve and a water
recreation area, or make a leisurely tour along
the pastoral banks of the rivers Schelde and Leie

**S**outh and east of Ghent are the
directions in which to head for
outdoor activities, sleepy villages with an artistic heritage, and
Flanders' blooming flower district.

## Sint-Amandsberg

In the eastern Ghent suburb of **Sint-Amandsberg**, on the north bank of
the Schelde, is the **Groot Begijnhof
❶** (Large Beguinage; 1874). It stands
just beyond the Dampoort railway
station, along Engelbert Van Arenbergstraat. Built in a gloomy neo-Gothic style, its walled complex of
80 cottages, convents, infirmary and
church makes for an interesting comparison with the older beguinages in
Ghent itself. It only came into existence because the Sint-Elisabeth-begijnhof area *(see page 176)* was
under increasing development pressure, and it was decided to build
anew on a greenfield site. The Groot
Begijnhof is now being redeveloped.
Part of it houses a small **Begijnhof
Museum** (Wed–Thur and Sat–Sun
9–11am, 2–5pm; admission charge)
covering the history of the Beguines.

Nearby, in **Het Illuseum** (123
Victor Braeckmanlaan; Sun 2–6pm;
admission charge), the museum of
optical illusions, everything is far
from being what it seems. More
than 100 optical illusions challenge
your eye-brain capabilities.

The **Campo Santo** cemetery, in
which many noted figures from
Ghent's worlds of art, science and
culture are laid to rest, stands on Sint-Amandsheuvel hill. Focal points
are Sint-Amanduskapel (Chapel of
St Amand) and Sint-Amanduskerk
(Church of St Amand).

## East of Ghent

The **Kasteel van Laarne ❷** (Laarne
Castle; Tues–Sun 10am–noon, 2–6pm; admission charge) was commissioned in 1157 by Thierry of

**Map
on page
186**

**LEFT:** the moated and
turreted Laarne Castle.
**BELOW:** horses in the
Ghent countryside.

Alsace, Count of Flanders. Built in hard-wearing grey Balegem sandstone it is surrounded by a moat, on land enclosed by a bend in the River Schelde, 8 km (5 miles) east of Ghent, and west of Laarne village. One of the best-preserved medieval castles in Belgium, it has none of Het Gravensteen's dark air of menace. Among the surviving elements of the original edifice, and additions in the 13th and 14th centuries, is the solid main tower, flanked by two corner towers. A triple arched bridge crosses the moat to the central keep. In the 17th century some walls were removed and replaced with comfortable Flemish Renaissance living quarters, with mullioned windows, and a loggia was added over the entrance.

Purchased by the state in 1962 for a symbolic 1 Belgian franc, the castle is now a protected monument. Inside, there are 16th-century Brussels tapestries, including a pair depicting hunting scenes, *The Hunts of Maxi-*

*milian*, and a series showing scenes from the life of a nobleman. There is also 17th- and 18th-century furniture from Antwerp and France, and a fine collection of silverware from the 15th–18th century. A fine French restaurant fills a nearby annexe.

Ghent stands at the heart of the East Flanders *Bloemenstreek* (Flower district), which plays an important role in the economy of the province in general, and of Ghent in particular as its distribution hub. Some 10 km (6 miles) further out along the Antwerp road from Sint-Amandsberg, **Lochristi ❸** is one of the centres of this flower industry. From the end of July till October, the village is perfumed by begonias carpeting the vast, colourful surrounding fields. The district is also famed for its azaleas, roses and orchids.

Southwards, where the Schelde winds its way towards Dendermonde, **Donkmeer ❹** lake, 17 km (11 miles) east of Ghent, is set in a horseshoe-

**BELOW:** river cruise on the Schelde.

shaped remnant of a former bend of the river, left high and eventually dry when the waterway cut a new course through the East Flanders plain some 10,000 years ago. Turf cutters took over where nature left off, scooping out an extensive hollow now filled with water again. The shallow lake, which covers 86 hectares (213 acres), has developed as a recreation centre and the surrounding wetlands as a nature reserve. You can hire small boats, and there are cafés and restaurants dotted around the shore.

About 30 km (19 miles) southeast of Ghent, near Zottegem, **Kasteel Leeuwergem** ❺ is a 17th-century country manor. It is the private residence of Baron Baudouin della Faylle d'Huysse and not open to the public, but you can stroll through its grounds, laid out in the style of Le Nôtre, the 18th-century French landscape designer, and contain an unusual theatre.

### The Schelde Valley

The **River Schelde** ❻ flows southwest to northeast from its source in northwest France and across the Belgian border into Wallonia to Tournai, then into Flanders, through Oudenaarde and on to Ghent. Taking the opposite direction – upstream from Ghent, you can join the river at **Merelbeke**, for a tour by car or bike. On the way through this scenic valley, you can go past the polder-like fields of the river's floodplain, dotted with the red roofs of farmhouses and views of an occasional passing river barge. Or take the road higher up the slope that passes through sleepy little villages like Melsen, Vurste and Semmerzake, whose most notable features are likely to be a venerable church or a stately home or two.

Somewhat larger and with a modern shopping district, **Gavere** is of some local historical importance. Here, on 23 July 1453, took place the decisive Battle of Gavere between the armies of the Ghent citizens and guilds, and the Duke of Burgundy, Philip the Good. Victory went to Philip in a hard-fought contest, ending Ghent's five-year rebellion to defend its privileges. In front of the Town Hall is a statue of the Ghent warrior Valeir; he has a beer named after him in honour of his courage.

Map on page 186

*In France and Wallonia (French-speaking Belgium) what the English call the River Scheldt is called the Escaut. In Flanders, it changes its name to Schelde. The River Leie is known in France as the Lys.*

**BELOW:** nautical fun; fishing and kayaking on the River Schelde.

*Sint-Martens-Latem was known as an artist's colony before World War II; it still presents itself as an artists' village and has many galleries.*

**BELOW:** the fairytale-looking Kasteel Ooidonk occupies a scenic spot on the River Leie.

## The Leiestreek

Following an almost parallel course to the Schelde, but a little further west, the River Leie, which also has its source in northwest France, also flows southwest to northeast through Flanders, and debouches into the Schelde at Ghent. Heading upstream along the Leie from Ghent to Deinze takes you through the **Leiestreek** (Leie district), a tranquil region that had a strong influence on modern Belgian art. You can make this tour by car, bike and boat.

The Leiestreek begins opposite the village of **Drongen ❼**, at the **Stedelijk Natuurreservaat Bourgoyen-Ossemeersen**. This municipal nature reserve has an importance that belies its mere 220-hectare (534-acre) surface area. Squeezed up against the southwestern edge of the ever-expanding city, its landscape of intermittently flooded grasslands criss-crossed by small canals and streams is a sanctuary for birds and other wildlife. A series of nature trails provides denizens of Ghent with a breath of fresh air and a place of escape. In Drongen itself

is the modernised and rebuilt **Oude Abdij** (Old Abbey), which can trace its roots back to an early 7th-century foundation, and is now run by the Jesuits as a retreat and educational centre. A little way upstream, the pretty village of **Afsnee ❽** has a 12th-century Romanesque church, Sint-Jan-de-Doper (St John the Baptist), and a tiny passenger-and-bike ferry across the Leie.

At the neighbouring village of **Sint-Martens-Latem ❾**, the whitewashed houses, bright flower gardens, a 15th-century windmill, and the picturesque wooded river banks all provided inspiration for the Symbolist artists of the early 20th-century First Latem School, and the slightly later Flemish Expressionists of the Second Latem School. Among the eminent artists who worked and lived here or in nearby Deurle were the sculptor Georges Minne and the painters Gustave De Smet, Leon De Smet and Constant Permeke. Nowadays, although Sint-Martens-Latem retains much of its charm, it is more a wealthy dormitory suburb of Ghent than a genuine village. There are several private galleries here, and the **Museum Gevaert-Minne** (45 Kapitteldreef; currently closed for renovation), which houses a collection of sculptures by Minne.

A little further upstream, around a bend in the Leie, is **Deurle ❿**. Here you can visit the **Museum Gust De Smet** (Easter–Sept Wed–Sun 2–6pm; Oct–Easter till 5pm; admission charge), on Gustaaf De Smetlaan, which contains some of the artist's paintings and sketches. On Museumstraat there are two further museums: the **Museum Leon De Smet** (Easter–Oct Sat–Sun 2–6pm; Nov–Easter till 5pm; free), which likewise has works by the artist; and the **Museum Dhondt-Daenens** (Tues–Sat 1–5pm, Sun 11am–5pm; admission charge), which takes the work of both schools as its theme.

## Kasteel Ooidonk

Around 11 km (7 miles) southwest of Ghent, between Bachte-Maria-Leerne and the west bank of the Leie is **Kasteel Ooidonk**  (Apr–June and first 2 weeks Sept Sun and hols 2–5.30pm; July–Aug Sat–Sun and hols 2–5.30pm; grounds: daily all year; admission charge). Surrounded by a moat, this is one of the most enchanting castles in Flanders. Some of its foundations date from the 14th century, when it was built as a defensive outpost for Ghent. It was destroyed many times during the wars of the 16th century and rebuilt towards the end of that century, more along the lines of a country mansion at a time when Flanders had been brought back under Spanish control. It retains this look and character today.

At the front, the arched portico is surmounted by a loggia with 10 windows, and above that step gables, a steeply pitched slate roof, and distinctive onion-domed turrets and chimneys above circular balconies. Each corner of the moat has a round tower.

The castle is the residence of Baron Van Nevele and most of it is closed to the public, but at the times listed above you can visit a splendid suite of apartments furnished largely in 19th-century style. For nearly 200 years Ooidonk belonged to the wealthy Montmorency family. Philip II of Montmorency, who spent his youth here, became famous as Count Van Hoorn who, together with Count Lamoraal van Egmond, was beheaded in 1568 on the Grand-Place in Brussels for treason (*see pages 25–6*). Portraits of the two ill-starred patricians can be seen in the apartments, along with fine paintings, tapestries, porcelain and silverware. You can visit the extensive woodland grounds all year round and quaff a Belgian beer in the castle's tavern, Koetshuis Ooidonk, just outside the gate.

North from Ghent, the dreary industrial landscape along both sides of the Gent-Terneuzen canal is a route best avoided. The picture brightens considerably, though, once you cross the border into Dutch Zeeuws-Vlaanderen (Zeeland Flanders). Westwards, there is not much of overarching appeal until you reach the environs of Bruges. ❏

*"Cold and loveless, Cold and loveless, Blows the wind from Bruges to Ghent"* wrote Belgian songwriter Jacques Brel (1930–79). If you travel west from Ghent on a winter's day you will understand what he meant.

---

# RESTAURANTS

### Deurle

**Brasserie Vinois**
31 Ph. De Denterghemlaan. Tel: 09-282 70 18. Open L & D Wed–Fri and Sun, D Sat. €€–€€€
In a renovated 1930s villa, Vinois adds a bold touch in its modern decor and its preparation of French-Belgian dishes. Garden terrace.

**Orangerie**
Auberge du Pêcheur, 41 Pontstraat. Tel: 09-282 31 44. Open L & D Tues–Fri, D Sat, L Sun €€€€
One of Belgium's outstanding restaurants, part of an equally fine hotel beside the Leie. Noted for its gastronomic weekend packages. The refined French cuisine is served in a formal dining room or, in summer, in the garden. There's also a less pricy brasserie.

### Lochristi

**Leys**
89 Dorp West. Tel: 09-355 86 20. Open L & D Tues and Thur–Sat, L Sun–Mon €€€
A loyal local clientele enjoys this old-fashioned restaurant. The service is both friendly and impeccable. The fine French cuisine is served in an elegant belle-époque dining room. The garden terrace is an added bonus in the summer.

### Sint-Martens-Latem

**De Klokkeput**
8 Dorp. Tel: 09-282 47 75. Open L & D daily 11–1am €€–€€€
Occupying a handsome house in the heart of this artistic village, this chic brasserie has modern art on the walls and a garden terrace that is heated when the weather turns cold. The seasonally changing continental menu includes a good-value menu of the month. Outside of mealtimes, the tearoom serves pancakes, charcuterie and other mouthwatering snacks.

● ● ● ● ● ● ● ● ● ● ● ●
*Prices for three-course dinner per person with a half-bottle of house wine. € under €25, €€ €25–40, €€€ €40–60, €€€€ over €60.*

# GHENT TRANSPORT

## GETTING THERE AND GETTING AROUND

Although still relatively new to tourism, the historical city of Ghent is located at the heart of a dense network of roads and railways, making it easily accessible from many other European cities such as London, Paris and Cologne. The city is approximately a 30-minute journey either by car or by train from both Brussels and Bruges and about a 40-minute one from Antwerp and Lille, in the north of France. The nearest airport to Ghent is Brussels Zaventem, 11 km (7 miles) from the city centre.

### GETTING THERE

#### By Air

Most international airlines fly into Brussels Zaventem airport, near Brussels *(see page 124)*. The airport has its own railway station with frequent direct trains to Ghent. The journey takes about one hour. For cheaper flights, Ryanair touches down at Charleroi Airport (Brussels South). To reach Ghent, take the Ryanair

shuttle bus to Bruxelles Midi station and change onto a train to Ghent. Expect a total journey time of well over one hour.

#### By Car

Ghent is at the intersection of two international motorways, running from Lisbon to Stockholm (E17) and from London to Istanbul (E40). Drivers from Britain can put their car on a Eurotunnel Shuttle train through the Channel Tunnel, from Folkestone to Calais in France – the journey through the tunnel only takes about 35 minutes. From Calais, get on the E40 motorway. When approaching Ghent, drivers on the E40 should follow signs to the E17 motorway and then turn onto B401 to Ghent Centrum for addresses in the town centre (the motorway intersection has no exit number). Parking can be a problem, since a large area of the city centre is car-free, but there are nine car parks on the edge of the traffic-free zone *(see Car Parks)*.

#### By Train

Ghent lies on the main railway line connecting Brussels with Bruges and the Belgian coast. Trains from Brussels take about 30 minutes to reach Ghent. You can travel from London or Ashford to Brussels by Eurostar

**BELOW:** all trams have destination signs and numbers at the front.

## PHONE NUMBERS

The local phone numbers given in this guide include the Ghent local area code (09). When dialling from abroad, omit the first 0 of the code.

(www.eurostar.com), and your ticket will enable you to travel free on Belgian railways to and from Ghent (within 24 hours of the time stamped on the Eurostar ticket). The main station is Gent Sint Pieters, about 2 km (1 mile) from the town centre but within walking distance of the main art museums. Trams run regularly from the station to the city centre.

### By Coach

The cheapest way to get to Ghent from the UK is by coach. Euro-lines runs a daily service from Victoria Coach Station in London, and the journey takes about 6 hours. In the UK, tel: 08705 143219; www.eurolines.com.

## GETTING AROUND

### Trams and Buses

Many tourist attractions in Ghent can be reached on foot, although it is possibly worth taking a tram from the station to the centre. A single ticket bought on the bus costs €1. Cheaper options include a day pass, also valid for Bruges, which costs €3, and a 10-journey pass, which can be used on public transport throughout Flanders (€7.50). Tickets have to be inserted in the orange scanner every time you board a bus. A network of night buses has recently been put in place.

### Car Parks

Ghent has created a harmonious urban centre by turning a large area of the historic city into a car-free zone. As part of this ambitious plan, new signs have been put up for drivers, showing the best route to follow (the Parkeerroute or P-route) to reach one of the nine car parks on the edge of the car-free zone. The signs also flash the number of free parking spaces. When booking a hotel, it is recommended to ask for advice on driving into town; the receptionist should be accustomed to giving out directions.

### Bike Hire

The main sights in Ghent can be reached on foot, but it is worth hiring a bicycle to explore the outlying district such as Sint-Amandsberg and the River Leie. Bikes can be rented for half a day or a day at **Biker**, 16 Steendam, tel: 09-224 29 03.

### Boat Tours

Boat tours of the Ghent canals begin from a landing stage on the Korenlei. The 40-minute tours cover a small but interesting stretch of the city's extensive waterways, passing the Graven-steen, the old fish market and the Rabot city gate. For information, tel: 09-223 88 53.

## ORIENTATION

Ghent is a much larger city than Bruges, and therefore there are places that cannot be conveniently reached on foot. The main historic quarter is reasonably compact, with the cathedral, the main museums and most hotels located close together. But the main railway station and several art museums are in southern Ghent, close to the Citadelpark, which require the use of public transport.

When looking for an address in Ghent, it is helpful to know that a *kaai* is a quay, a *plein* is a square and a *straat* is a street. If you are navigating without a map, the easiest way to find your way to the centre is to look for the distinctive row of three spires.

### Day Trips

Ghent is a good base for day trips to other cities in Flanders. The railway station is well served by fast trains to Bruges and the Flemish coast, with direct trains to Ostend, Zeebrugge, Blanken-berge and Knokke, as well as to the historical town of Ypres.

**BELOW:** Ghent is very flat, which makes it a perfect city for cycling.

## **GHENT** ACCOMMODATION

# SOME THINGS TO CONSIDER BEFORE YOU BOOK A ROOM

### Choosing a Hotel

Ghent has only recently developed as a tourist destination and, while several new hotels have opened in Ghent in recent years, the choice of accommodation is still fairly limited compared to Bruges or Brussels. Many travellers therefore stay in Bruges, and visit Ghent as a day trip. While this can easily be done (the train journey is a simple 30-minute hop), it is more interesting to hunt out a good hotel in Ghent, if only to wander along the atmospheric ancient canals after dark.

Despite some new establishments opening in Ghent, there are still no grand luxury hotels at the top end of the market. Most tourists tend to settle for one of the modern places close to the cathedral, such as the Sofitel, Novitel or Ibis, which are well-located but low on atmosphere. For those looking for something more original, the best bet may be the often-stylish Bed & Breakfasts.

### *Timing and Booking*

Ghent can be enjoyed at any time of year, although it can be bleak in January and February. The busiest times are Easter and from July to mid-September, when it can be difficult to find a room at short notice. Unless you are a 24-hour party person, it is best to avoid the annual 10-day Gentse Feesten in mid-July, when the town centre is impossibly crowded and no one gets a wink of sleep.

The tourist office offers a free booking service, useful for last-minute reservations. You can check out availability and make a booking via their website (www.visitgent.be) or by phone (from abroad, tel: +32 9-225 36 41). They organise special deals, which usually offer a hotel room, a meal, and extras such as free museum entry or a guided tour. Rooms can also be booked in person at 17A Botermarkt. You are required to pay a €5 deposit which is deducted from your hotel bill. It is worth consulting Internet hotel booking sites for special rates, although online bookings often take several days to process. Resotel (tel: 02-779 39 39, fax: 02-779 39 00, www.belgiumhospitality.com) is a free accommodation booking service for the whole of Belgium which offers competitive hotel rates.

Several years ago, the city launched a bold plan to keep traffic out of the city centre. While this means Ghent is a wonderful city for strolling, it makes life slightly awkward for anyone with a car. Ask, when you book, about reaching the hotel and parking. Some hotels have a limited number of parking spaces, while others have special rates in nearby underground car parks for their guests.

### *Cost and Quality*

There are several large French chain hotels clustered around the cathedral, but these have little to recommend them apart from their location. However, the situation may well improve when a new 149-room Marriott Hotel opens in mid-2006 (www.marriott.com) on the Graslei waterfront, concealed behind the façades of five 15th-century guildhouses.

Hotels are graded from one to five stars, according to the facilities they offer. While this provides a useful indication of standards, the system doesn't take account of the character of a building or helpfulness of staff. The international chain hotels often have a high star rating, but a two-star hotel or a B&B can sometimes be far more appealing.

It takes some searching to find an idyllic hotel room in Ghent, but you should be able to find something interesting eventually, whether it is a room in an old house furnished with curious antiques, or one with a view of the city skyline. Room rates normally include a buffet breakfast.

# EAST OF THE LEIE

### Expensive

**Sofitel Gent Belfort**
63 Hoogpoort
Tel: 09-233 33 31
Fax: 09-233 11 02
www.sofitel.com
Located right in the centre of Ghent, beside the cathedral and town hall, this hotel offers an architecture influenced by the Art Nouveau style. There is a wide choice of spacious rooms – if a little too corporate – a fitness centre and a sauna.

### Moderate

**Boatel**
44 Voorhoutkaai
Tel: 09-267 10 30
Fax: 09-267 10 39
www.theboatel.com
Ghent's first floating hotel caused a stir when it opened a few years ago. Located in the Portus Ganda, a new city marina, this former 1951 canal barge has been converted into an unusual small hotel. It contains five small rooms with porthole windows located in the former cargo hold and two more roomy suites on the upper deck. A 10-minute walk gets you into town.

**Chambre Plus**
31 Hoogpoort
Tel: 09-225 37 75
www.chambreplus.be
Mia Ackaert has created three sublime rooms in a massive 18th-century mansion in the centre of Ghent.

Ask for the Sultan Room for a wildly romantic decor inspired by the Middle East, or pick the Congo Room to sleep amid jungle-print fabrics. But the best (and most expensive) choice is the Côté Sud, a separate apartment decorated in Mediterranean style, with a lounge, an open fire and a jacuzzi where you can take a bath under the night sky. A delicious breakfast is included in the price.

**Cour St Georges**
2 Botermarkt
Tel: 09-224 24 24
Fax: 09-224 26 40
www.courstgeorges.be
Considered by some as the oldest hotel in Europe, the Cour St Georges dates back to 1228. It originally served as a meeting place for the Guild of Archers and was the setting for several historical events in the Middle Ages. But its heyday is long past, and it now offers visitors a convenient location in the city centre, soberly furnished rooms and a romantic Old Flemish restaurant.

**Ghent River Hotel**
5 Waaistraat
Tel: 09-266 10 10
Fax: 09-266 10 15
www.ghent-river-hotel.be
This stylish waterfront hotel opened in 2004 near the Vrijdagmarkt. Some rooms occupy a restored 19th-century sugar factory, while

others are located in a 16th-century town house. When booking, ask for one of the rooms in the former factory, as these have oak beams, brick walls and odd industrial implements used for decoration. The rooms in the modern extension are plainer. The hotel has a rooftop breakfast room with striking views of the old city, a jetty and a fitness room.

**Novotel Gent Centrum**
5 Goudenleeuwplein
Tel: 09-224 22 30
Fax: 09-224 32 95
www.novotel.com
A modern hotel on a cobbled square in the heart of the old town, close to the cathedral, museums and restaurants. The rooms are spacious and well-equipped, although the style is slightly corporate. This is a good choice for those travelling with children, as two children can share their parents' room free of charge. Some children may be tempted to leap in the outdoor pool, but it tends to be quite chilly most of the year.

### Inexpensive

**Flandria**
3 Barrestraat
Tel: 09-223 06 26
Fax: 09-233 77 89
www.flandria-centrum.be
This appealing budget hotel is located in a quiet street behind the cathedral. The 23 bed-

rooms (17 with bathrooms) are bright and comfortable, some with views of the cathedral. The owners provide a warm welcome, and allow children to stay in their parents' room for free.

**Ibis Gent Centrum Kathedraal**
2 Limburgstraat
Tel: 09-233 00 00
Fax: 09-233 10 00
www.ibis.com
Not the most imaginative of choices, but this 120-room Ibis hotel is perfectly located in the centre of Ghent. With the cathedral right outside the door, those who stay here get to look at the famous Van Eyck altarpiece before the crowds arrive. The rooms are modern and functional, and the staff are friendly. A second, slightly cheaper Ibis hotel is located nearby (the Ibis Gent Centrum Opera), but this is an older and less-appealing building.

### PRICE CATEGORIES

Price categories are for a double room with breakfast:
**Expensive**: €200–300
**Moderate**: €100–200
**Inexpensive**: under €100

BRUGES

GHENT

ANTWERP

# WEST OF THE LEIE

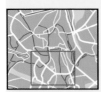

## Inexpensive

**Adoma**
19 St Denijslaan
Tel: 09-222 65 50
Fax: 09-245 09 37
www.hotel-adoma.be
A friendly, family-run hotel close to the railway station, a 10-minute tram ride from the centre. The 15 rooms are decorated in a comfortable, modern style. The only disadvantage is the proximity of the railway line, so not really the best place for anyone who has trouble sleeping. Free car park.

**Astoria**
39 Achilles Musschestraat
Tel: 09-222 84 13
Fax: 09-220 47 87
www.astoria.be
An attractive 17-room hotel close to the railway station. The rooms are clean and comfortable, and the owners welcoming. The location is good for those arriving by train, but a long hike or 10-minute tram ride from the centre.

**Erasmus**
25 Poel
Tel: 09-224 21 95
Fax: 09-233 42 41

A friendly hotel located in a 17th-century house close to the centre of Ghent. The interior is furnished with odd antiques and paintings, including a suit of armour in the breakfast room. The 11 bedrooms come in various sizes, each with its own quirky charm. The rooms at the back look out on a seductive Renaissance courtyard garden.

**Gravensteen**
35 Jan Breydelstraat
Tel: 09-225 11 50
Fax: 09-225 18 50
www.gravensteen.be
An elegant hotel in a 19th-century building facing the Gravensteen castle. The marble hall is decorated in imposing French Second Empire style, while the elegant bedrooms are bright and comfortable. Private car park.

## BED & BREAKFAST

There are more than 60 bed and breakfasts in Ghent, often located in beautiful old houses that have been recently renovated. Although not particularly cheap, they often offer extras like the use of a bicycle, a kitchen or a garden. Most are run by friendly locals who can recommend the best restaurants and interesting events. The easiest way to book is through the website of the Ghent Guild of Guest Houses, which lists 67 approved addresses (www.bedandbreakfast-gent.be).

**Atlas B&B**
40 Rabotstraat
Tel: 09-233 49 91
www.atlasbenb.be
A seductive B&B in a 19th-century mansion near the city centre. Run by two Flemish globetrotters, Atlas is filled with globes, maps, odd antiques and exotic relics. Each of the three rooms is decorated in the style of a different continent, while the sitting room is warmed by a blazing fire.

**Cuberdon**
76 Wolterslaan
Tel: 09-324 49 78
Fax: 09-324 49 78
www.cuberdon.be
Jurgen and Kurt have turned a plain 1930s town house on a quiet tree-lined street into a sublime B&B. Of the three rooms, one has an en-suite bathroom, and the other two a shared bathroom. Everything is just right, from the welcome chocolate on arrival, to the free internet access. One small drawback though: the house is a 30-minute walk from the centre of town.

**Engelen Aan de Waterkant**
11 Ter Platen
Tel: 09-223 08 83
www.engelenaandewaterkant.be
A slightly mystical two-room B&B located in a 19th-century town house in the student quarter. The interior is decorated in a sublime designer style, with wooden floors, massive mirrors and luxurious beds. Breakfast is brought to the room on a large tray.

**La Maison de Claudine**
20 Passemierstraat
Tel: 09-225 75 08
Fax: 09-225 75 08
For pure bohemian charm, this is hard to resist: a 17th-century former convent with a choice of two luxury suites and one smaller room (all en-suite). The largest suite is a vast penthouse under the oak eaves, with views over the spires. The other suite spreads onto two floors in a former coach house, which looks out on a neat Italianate garden. Breakfast is served in a large living room with a blazing fire, or out in the garden in summer.

## YOUTH HOSTELS

**De Draecke**
11 Sint-Widostraat
Tel: 09-233 70 50
www.ghent-hostel.com
De Draecke, located in a quiet cobbled lane in the heart of the old town, is the only youth hostel in Ghent. The rooms are modern, with a choice of doubles, triples or dormitories. There is a bar, a library and internet access.

## SELF-CATERING

You can rent an apartment in the centre of Ghent for a weekend or longer. **Belex** (www.belex-belgium.be) has a range of apartments for two people, in Belfortstraat, behind the town hall.

# GHENT ACTIVITIES

# THE ARTS, FESTIVALS, NIGHTLIFE, SHOPPING AND SIGHTSEEING

## THE ARTS

To find out what's happening in Ghent, pick up one of the free listings magazines, *Zone09* or *Week-Up*. Both are in Dutch, but you should be able to make out what's on and where. Get a copy at the tourist office, in cafés and theatre foyers. Some listings information is also available online at www.weekup.be/gent. For information in English, *The Bulletin* lists a selection of events.

### Concerts and Opera

The **Vlaamse Opera** (Flemish Opera, 3 Schouwburgstraat) stages exciting operatic performances and classical concerts of baroque and contemporary music in a sumptuous 19th-century building near the law courts, the main classical-music venue in Ghent. The Vlaamse Opera also programmes other performances in a splendid opera house in Antwerp *(see page 258)*.

### Cinema

Film history was made in Ghent when Joseph Plateau, a professor at Ghent University, demonstrated an early version of cartoon animation using an invention named the phenakistoscope. As well as hosting an annual film festival, Ghent has several art-house cinemas screening a mix of film classics and off-beat 16-mm productions. Large crowds gather inside **Kinepolis**, a sleek multiplex that hosts the annual film festival (12 Ter Platen, tel: 09-265 06 00; www.kinepolis.be). Movie buffs prefer the more intimate mood of the film houses clustered around Sint-Annaplein. **Studio Skoop** (63 Sint-Annaplein, tel: 09-225 08 45) is the main art-house venue, while **Sphinx** (3 Sint-Michielshelling, tel: 09-225 60 86) has a more edgy feel. Film students crowd into **Film-Plateau** (3 Paddenhoek, tel: 09-264 38 72), where screenings are introduced with a short lecture, while other young fans settle down to watch low-budget experimental films at **Art Cinema Off Off** (Begijnhof ter Hoye, 237 Lange Violettestraat, tel: 09-217 02 19; www.offoff.be). The site www.cinebel.be lists all films in Ghent cinemas.

### Dance and Theatre

**Vooruit** is the main venue for experimental dance and theatre in Ghent (www.vooruit.be). Located in the heart of the student quarter, Vooruit was built in 1912 by the Ghent socialist movement as a festival hall for working-class people. It is a vast complex, with a concert hall, cinema, theatre, workshop spaces and a large café. This is the place to catch a contemporary Flemish dance performance by Wim Vandekeybus or new Flemish drama by Jan Fabre. It also stages jazz, rock, techno and hip hop, as well as literary events and exhibitions.

## FESTIVALS AND EVENTS

### June

**City Parade** A wild, free, street party featuring dance music, floats and parties (www.cityparade.be).

### July

**Festival of Flanders** A major festival of classical music with performances in various venues, from concert halls to old abbeys. **De Gentse Feesten** One of the most appealing festivals in Europe, the 10-day Gentse Feesten draws a crowd of over a million to Ghent. Begun in the 19th century as a workers' festival, it was relaunched by a local folk singer in the 1970s. Events now range from a glitzy ball to a bohemian street-theatre festival. There are also parades, open-air cinema, free entry to museums, rock concerts, a blues festival and jazz performances.

TICKETS

The Gent Museumpas is a three-day pass valid for 15 city museums and monuments. It also includes admission to special exhibitions.

**Ten Days Off** Formerly known as Ten Days of Techno, this major festival of club music features some top DJs in two venues. Runs at the same time as the Gentse Feesten (www.10daysoff.be).

## September

**Open Monument Day** Historic buildings that are not usually accessible are open to the public.

## October

**Flanders International Film Festival** Not the most celebrity-studded of events, but the annual festival offers an eclectic sampling of movies from all over the world, including the occasional quirky Flemish film.

## November

**I Love Techno** Launched in 1995, this has grown into one of the biggest techno raves in Europe. Held on the edge of the city in the Flanders Expo exhibition hall, it draws great DJs (www.ilovetechno.be).

## NIGHTLIFE

Nights out in Ghent are fun, with crowds of cheerful revellers out on the streets, and small bars often staying open until sunrise. The old quarters are especially magical after dark, with footsteps echoing in the traffic-free streets and soft spotlights picking out architectural details. When the rain holds off, crowds gather on the cobbled Graslei quayside to catch the last of the sun, then head to one of the 270 bars.

Local young people gather in the early evening on the Korenmarkt, diving into places like **Damberd** (19 Korenmarkt), a

historic tavern dating from the 15th century that reinvented itself in 1978 as a bohemian jazz café with live jazz on Tuesday evenings.

A 10-minute stroll from the centre, the **Hotsy Totsy Club** (1 Hoogstraat) has been a Ghent nightlife hotspot for decades. Famous for its jam sessions, the club draws a mixed crowd.

The student quarter in southern Ghent has no end of cool bars and music clubs, many of the liveliest strung out along the narrow Overpoortstraat. But weekends can be quiet, as the main night for student partying is Thursday.

The restored **Patershol** district is another good area for bars, some of them located in beautiful historic buildings. These places tend to be more upmarket, catering to a quiet, intellectual crowd.

The **Vrijdagmarkt** offers another cluster of cafés and bars, including the legendary **Dulle Griet** (50 Vrijdagmarkt), where customers who order a Kwak beer are forced to deposit one of their shoes in a basket (to stop them running off with the glass).

## SHOPPING

### What and Where to Buy

Ghent is a quietly stylish city with a compact shopping district south of the cathedral. The main chain stores are on **Veldstraat**, including a branch of **Inno** (Ghent's only department store), while upscale fashion boutiques are located in a beguiling pedestrianised quarter bounded by **Bennesteeg, Magaleinstraat, Voldersstraat** and **Sint - Niklaasstraat**. For off-beat collectables and specialised boutiques, go north to the warren of crooked streets around the Gravensteen, such as **Jan Breydelstraat**.

### Beer

The **Craenkindershuys** (2 Kraanlei, tel: 09-224 33 09) boasts a large selection of Belgian beers and beer glasses.

### Chocolates

For sublime hand-made chocolates, take a look inside **Temmerman** (79 Kraanlei, tel: 09-224 00 41), located in an historic waterfront building. The speciality is *cuberdon*, a sweet cone filled with sticky raspberry.

### Collectables

Ghent has several upmarket antiques shops, but the real fun is in rummaging through a dusty collection of old objects that no one else wants. The best place to begin is **N'Importe Quoi** (11 Burgstraat, tel: 09-223 06 17), a cluttered shop filled with china, posters, sofas and paintings. **The Fallen Angels** (29–31 Jan Breydelstraat; tel: 09-223 94 15) is a rambling antiques shop crammed with tin toys, boxes of old postcards, china dolls, nostalgic advertising signs and quirky circus posters.

### Fashion

**Bennesteeg** is the first stop for women looking for stylish, upmarket clothes. **Oona** (12 Bennesteeg, tel: 09-224 21 13) sells sleek clothes in a minimalist interior with bare concrete walls. **Lena Lena** (19 Bennesteeg, tel: 09-233 79 47) sells stylish clothes in larger sizes by Belgian designer Miet Crabbé. Elsewhere in Ghent, **Het Oorcussen** (7 Vrijdagmarkt, tel: 09-233 07 65) is a striking boutique set in a 16th-century house where top Antwerp designers such as Dries van Noten and Ann Demeulemeester are displayed. Men looking for similar cool chic should check out **Hot Couture** (34 Gouvernementstraat, tel: 09-223 74 07), with clothes by Van Noten and other designers. **Movies** (Sint-Pietersnieuwstraat, tel : 09-223 59 19) is in the thick of Ghent's edgy student quarter.

The neo-Gothic **Postgebouw** (post office) of 1910 has been converted into an upmarket shopping centre, **Post Plaza** (16 Korenmarkt) with designer boutiques for men and women.

## Food

Foodies take note: for a taste of the food of Flanders, take a look inside the **Groot Vleeshuis** (7 Groentenmarkt, tel: 09-267 86 07; www.grootvleeshuis.be). This massive stone market hall was built in 1419 for the butchers of Ghent. Long abandoned and neglected, the building has now been converted into a huge food hall, where whole Ghent hams hang from ropes tied to wooden beams. The hall is now occupied by outlets selling some of the best food from the East Flanders province, including ham, cheese, chocolate, truffles, mustard and beer. In its restaurant, everything on the menu comes from East Flanders, so don't even think of asking for a Coke.

## Jewellery

**Christa Reniers** (1A Bennesteeg, tel: 09-224 33 52) is a cutting-edge Brussels jewellery designer who produces original rings and necklaces inspired by natural forms. This is her only outlet outside Brussels.

## Lace

Ghent is mercifully free of cheap lace shops, but you will find the genuine hand-made article sold at **Kloskanthuis** (3 Kraanlei).

## Markets

For odd curiosities salvaged from Ghent attics, take a look at the flea market held in the square **Bij Sint Jacobs**, just north of the town centre, every Friday, Saturday and Sunday morning. An attractive flower market is held on the **Kouter** every Sunday morning.

## Music

This small city has a surprising number of dedicated music shops where you can track down every type of sound ever committed to vinyl or CD, from local lad Helmut Lotti to darkest Goth sounds. Although Ghent's branch of French megastore **FNAC** (88 Veldstraat, tel: 09-223 40 80) is smaller than most, it's a useful place to

pick up mainstream pop and classical music. The fun really starts when you devote some time to dawdling around the quirky music shops in the student quarter, each with its odd obsessions and even odder opening hours.

A firm feature of the alternative scene since 1969, **Music Mania** (197 Bagattenstraat, tel: 09-225 68 15) has three floors filled with every type of music, including jungle, jazz and reggae. **Pyrrhus** (145 Nederkouter, tel: 09-234 16 74) is a specialised hardcore music shop with its own label; while **City Beatz** (4a Lammerstraat, tel: 09-234 34 29) puts the emphasis on hip hop, ragga, funk and jazz. But music shops don't come much more quirky than **Dune** (17 Geldmunt, tel: 09-223 38 37). In a relaxed atmosphere, the owner offers a strange mix of music, from Irish folk to soundtracks of long-forgotten films.

## Mustard

The mustard sold in **Tierenteyn** (3 Groentenmarkt, tel: 09-225 83 36) is still prepared according to a secret family recipe invented in 1790. It's worth glancing inside the sumptuous shop interior, which retains its original furnishings from 1858. The mustard is scooped out of a large vat and sold in tiny ceramic pots.

## OTHER ACTIVITIES

### Guided Tours

For a distinctly different view of Ghent, book a river cruise and pub crawl led by the feisty town crier. Held on most days of the year at unpredictable times, the price includes tots of Flemish gin in two different cafés along the route. Book at least a month in advance through **Gent Watertoerist** (7 Graslei, tel: 09-266 05 22, www.gent-watertoerist.be). The crier also offers a Sunday morning tour of five markets, from April to September (www.towncriers.be).

**Vizit** (tel: 09-233 76 89; www.vizit.be) offers a series of unusual walking tours of the city. The four-hour culinary walking tour (Saturday 6–10pm) calls at four different restaurants to sample a single dish and drink a glass of wine. "Nibbling Through Ghent" is a two-hour tour every Saturday, starting at 4pm, that visits several shops to sample specialities such as cheese, chocolates and ham.

## SIGHTS AND ATTRACTIONS

### Children's Activities

A boat trip on the **Ghent canals** is likely to wow smaller children, especially when the guide points out Dulle Griet, the world's least-successful cannon. Follow this up with a visit to the **Gravensteen**, an impressive castle with a grim collection of torture instruments. Older children may enjoy the excellent **Museum of Industrial Archaeology and Textiles**, 10 minutes from the centre. The old industrial building is crammed with impressive machinery, a textile workshop and a reconstructed World War I trench. Round off the day with a visit to the ice-cream shop opposite the Gravensteen.

## SPORTS

Ghent offers a generous range of sports facilities for a small town, although most venues are out in the suburbs. The city has four good **swimming pools**, the most convenient being the Zwembad Van Eyck (1 Veermanplein), a 10-minute walk from the centre. The oldest in Belgium, this is a pool with lanes for serious swimmers, plus a children's pool.

The main sports centre is the **Blaarmeersen Recreation Park** (5 Zuiderlaan), which has tennis courts, basketball pitches, an artificial ski slope and an outdoor pool open in summer.

# ANTWERP

A detailed guide to the city with the
principal sites clearly cross-referenced
by number to the maps

**A**ntwerp can rightly claim to be not just the most exciting city in Belgium, but one of the most inviting destinations in Europe. What makes it stand out is a variety of attractions that draw in equally varied groups of visitors. Quite simply, it is a city that has something for everyone. For some, Antwerp is first and foremost the home of Pieter-Paul Rubens, where a whole trip can be planned around a visit to his elegant home, the Rubenshuis; a tour of the city's excellent Fine Arts Museum, which devotes an extensive section to the great master; and tracking down his religious paintings in the opulent churches for which he painted them.

Other visitors are attracted by the fact that Antwerp is one of the fashion capitals of Europe. What began a few years ago, when a handful of hip local designers (later to become known as the Antwerp Six) took the international fashion world by storm, has now transformed the whole city into a cutting-edge symbol of style. This vibrant creativity is visible not only in the dozens of couture showrooms, but also in a host of chic restaurants where the decor is as innovative as the cuisine, and in a funky bar and nightlife scene that begins with cool lounges featuring in-house DJs and ends with high-voltage techno parties.

In between these two extremes, Antwerp is also a hub for avant-garde photography and contemporary art museums, 16th-century mansions, tempting antiques boutiques and colourful flea markets. There is a definite frisson to be felt when walking through the world's most important diamond district where millions of pounds change hands every day; or discovering the challenging modern architecture that is converting the area of the abandoned docklands, Het Eilandje, into what will be a vibrant city of the future. More than anything, Antwerp is an absolutely fantastic place for eating and drinking, whether you favour a traditional steaming plate of mussels, accompanied by a heaped portion of crispy chips, or a fusion recipe of locally caught sole simmered in a Thai green curry; a foaming glass of Antwerp's favourite De Koninck beer in a smoky traditional bar, or a pina colada in a laid-back cocktail lounge. ❑

---

**PRECEDING PAGES:** Antwerp's skyline is a harmonious mix of old and modern; Antwerp's bustling main square, the Grote Markt. **LEFT:** taking it easy on the docks of Antwerp.

# THE OLD CENTRE

Start your tour in the sumptuous Grote Markt
square and end in the newly redeveloped docklands,
visiting en route some excellent museums and
secret corners of the city, and checking out Rubens'
masterpieces in the Cathedral of Our Lady

he starting point for any visit to Antwerp has to be the **Grote Markt ❶**, a sumptuous square in the heart of the old city centre, marked by the towering Stadhuis, its 16th-century town hall and by grand guildhouses fronted by opulent façades and golden statues symbolising the ancient trades.

## Grote Markt highlights

Right in the middle of all this architectural grandeur is an eye-stopping blue statue representing an athletic figure poised atop a bubbling fountain. This is the **Brabo Fountain**, named after the mythical hero, Silvius Brabo, a Roman warrior who is credited with liberating residents from an evil giant and giving the city the name "Hantwerpen", which became the modern Antwerpen. Legend has it that the giant Antigoon demanded tolls from each ship passing the bend of the city on the River Schelde (Scheldt) and summarily chopped off the hand of those who refused to pay. Brabo fought and slew the giant, cut off his hand and threw it into the river, symbolising a free waterway, the key to Antwerp's future prosperity. Look closely at the statue and you will observe that Brabo is holding a severed hand; the ghoulish meaning of the word *Hantwerpen* is "to throw a hand".

Towering up behind the Brabo Fountain is the monumental **Stadhuis ❷**, the city's landmark building. Unlike the Gothic architecture of the Stadhuis in Brussels, Antwerp's town hall is the first example of Flemish-Italian Renaissance, constructed in 1565 by a group of Flemish and foreign architects who reflected the cosmopolitan society present in the city. While the building is immensely impressive from the outside, the interiors are also worth seeing, as the plush salons,

Map
on page
206

**LEFT:** the athletic
Brabo Fountain on the
Grote Markt.
**BELOW:** Antwerp lives
up to its avant-garde
reputation.

*The Grote Markt is lined with impressive guildhouses topped with the golden figures of the guilds.*

decorated in the 19th century with magnificent paintings and frescoes by artists such as Leys and Verhaert, are as splendid as the flamboyant exterior. There used to be daily organised tours of the Stadhuis, but the ever-present problem of security concerns has led to them being suspended. Check at the tourist office, though: during special events the tours may operate again. At other times it is always worth asking at the entrance, as the guards often let tourists have a peek inside. Although the guildhouses all around the Grote Markt illustrate the immense wealth and culture of Antwerp's Golden Age, in the 16th and 17th centuries, many are actually reproductions, built some 150 years ago based on paintings of the originals. The ones to look out for are the White Angel that sits above house No. 3; a statue of St Michael, patron saint of barrel makers, at No. 5; and St Sebastian, who looks after the guild of archers,

at No. 9. The Grote Markt is very much a vibrant, living square, packed with people at all times of the day and night. It is a favourite place of local people and visitors alike, to gather round the Brabo Fountain and watch the world go by, or sit on a pavement terrace at one of the dozen cafés, bars and brasseries dotted around the square. Some of these are tourist traps where you are likely to be overcharged for the privilege of sipping a coffee or a beer at an outdoor table. The most popular spot is the venerable Den Engel, a traditional *estaminet,* which is easy to spot because of the line of top-hatted coachmen outside waiting to take tourists on a scenic city tour in their horse-drawn carriages.

### Two museums

The bustling Grote Markt offers a slice of contemporary Antwerp life, but the **Volkskundemuseum** ❸ (Tues–Sun 10am–5pm; admission

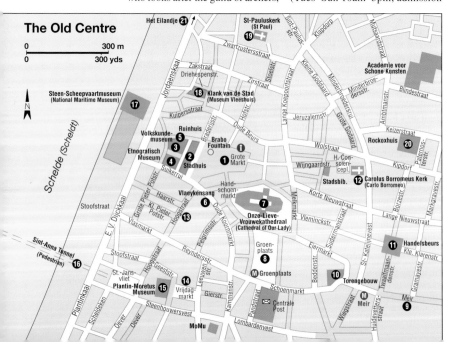

charge), on an adjacent side street, provides a more leisurely look at the way people lived in the 18th and 19th centuries. The Belgians are very good at these kinds of museums – most major cities have their own – which are aimed as much at residents, especially schoolchildren, as at visitors, to ensure that old traditions and folklore don't just disappear. This particular museum began 100 years ago as the private collection of a local poet, Max Elskamp, and now stretches over several historical guildhouses where just a small selection of its 180,000 items are exhibited. Every aspect of daily life is on show, among which are a recreation of an ancient pharmacy, an alchemist's laboratory, and the traditional Flemish *Poesje* puppet theatre. This is an amusing, irreverent museum, where a penny-farthing bike sits alongside a nobleman's carriage and a grand fairground organ stands next to an early jukebox.

While the Volkskundemuseum details regional Flemish ethnology, the **Etnografisch Museum** ❹ (Tues–Sun 10am–5pm; admission charge) nearby transports you to more distant lands, making a bold attempt to illustrate art, culture and artisan crafts from Africa, Asia, South America and Oceania. Belgium once had an extensive colonial empire, but the background to this outstanding, eclectic collection is based more on Antwerp itself, and the worldwide links forged by its thriving port. There is a lot more here than the primitive masks, wooden sculptures and exotic deities you'd expect to find in this kind of museum, including an interesting section devoted to colourful textiles from around the world.

Both these museums are often missed by visitors too busy concentrating on Rubens, but if time permits, their outstanding collections are well worth a visit.

## Subterranean Antwerp

Right next door to the entrance of the Volkskundemuseum is a brand new attraction, the **Ruinhuis** ❺. The *ruin* refers to Antwerp's medieval underground water system, a maze of subterranean canals now open to the public. It is possible to do a mini-visit and just go down to where the canals begin, but to really discover the secrets of subterranean Antwerp join a guided tour. Although the visit begins with a short journey in a small boat, you soon have to get out and continue on foot on a 1.5-km (1-mile) walk that lasts over an hour. You have to don Wellington boots and protective clothing, and carry a torch. At the end of the tour, when steps finally lead up into daylight, you will find you are right over on the other side of the city. There is a café for a refreshing drink, and then the return part of the visit is above ground, back to the Grote Markt.

## Secret corners

Running off on all sides of the Grote Markt is a maze of narrow streets and alleyways heading into different

Map on page 206

**TIP**

All Belgian cities are bicycle-friendly and Antwerp is no exception. Children can cycle safely, and the tourist office (Grote Markt 13, tel: 03-232 01 03) can advise on where to rent bikes or how to join a guided tour.

**BELOW:** trotting through Antwerp.

parts of the city. It is very easy to get lost, as even the best maps can seem impossible to follow. But that is half the fun of discovering the historical centre – roaming around with no particular plan in mind. Wandering down a dark passageway you may come upon a smoky tavern packed with noisy afternoon beer drinkers avidly watching a cycling race, Belgium's favourite sport, on television; finding a cool bar filled with arty students sipping red wine and listening to funky jazz; or a tiny bistro serving a delicious *carbonade de bœuf*, the traditional Flemish casserole of beef braised in beer.

The most secret spot is the **Vlaey-kensang ❻**, a picturesque maze of 16th-century alleys hidden behind an anonymous gate at No. 16 Oude Koornmarkt, a busy street lined with colourful restaurants and bars. This was once inhabited by shoemakers, but fell into ruin and was about to be demolished in the 1960s when a young entrepreneur bought the whole place. He renovated the houses and turned them into antiques shops, although they have now been converted into cafés and restaurants. Today, a tiny sign hangs above the entrance to Vlaeykensang making it easier to spot. This is now a favourite spot for music lovers to come and listen to the carillon concerts of the cathedral, far from the throng of crowds just outside in the Grote Markt and Groenplaats.

## The Cathedral of Our Lady

The Grote Markt is divided from Antwerp's other massive square, Groenplaats, by the **Onze-Lieve-Vrouwekathedraal ❼** (Cathedral of Our Lady; Mon–Fri 10am–5pm, Sat 10am–3pm, Sun 1–4pm; admission charge), a towering white Gothic masterpiece. Just by the entrance, in Handschoenmarkt, by the tableau of ancient statues, there is usually a street artist who disguises himself as one of the figures and succeeds in giving both children and adults a fright whenever he moves a fraction. Work started on the cathedral in 1352, replacing a small Romanesque parish church. It took 169 years to complete the construction, but when everything was

**BELOW:** Vlaeykensang is a hidden gem right in the city centre.

Map on page 206

finished, the proud citizens of Antwerp, who had invested a good part of their fortune to pay for it, could gaze up at the largest Gothic church in the Low Countries, with a graceful spire rising over 123 metres (403 ft) and dominating Antwerp's skyline, as it still does today.

Recently, both the exterior and the seven-aisled interior of the cathedral have undergone a remarkable renovation, restoring Our Lady to her former beauty. The intricate, lace-like, sculpted façade cannot fail to impress, but it is only when you enter the cavernous, brightly lit interior that the immense grandeur of the cathedral is felt. Over the centuries, the decoration has suffered from fires and regular pillaging from Calvinists and French revolutionaries, but it is still a treasure trove of artworks.

What everyone comes to see, though, are the four massive works by Pieter-Paul Rubens (1577–1640), inspired by religious allegory: *The Raising of the Cross*, *The Descent from the Cross*, *The Resurrection* and *The Assumption*. The latter is above the altar, while *The Descent from the Cross*, a moving triptych painted just after the artist's return from Italy, where he had been influenced by the realism of Caravaggio, is to the right of the central crossing.

## Groenplaats

The pedestrianised Handschoen-markt continues from the cathedral, past a tacky array of fast-food outlets and souvenir shops, and opens up into the vast open space of **Groenplaats** ❽, once the city cemetery. This square is bigger than the Grote Markt, but there is little to detain a visitor here, unless it is picking up a tram from the transport hub in the centre, paying an extortionate price for *moules frites* at one of the scores of touristy restaurants whose terraces fill the square, or listening to the buskers who perform beneath a statue of Rubens. There is, however, a beautiful 1920s Art Nouveau building on one side, which used to be the Grand Bazar department store, Antwerp's version of Harrods, but has now been transformed into an American-owned hotel and modern shopping mall.

*The cathedral houses treasures from Rubens masterpieces to fine stained-glass panels.*

**LEFT:**
Antwerp's cathedral is one of the finest Gothic churches in Belgium.
**BELOW:** reflective mood by the cathedral.

*If the Groenplaats used to be a cemetery, it is nowadays very much alive.*

**BELOW:** "doing the Meir" is Antwerpans' favoured pastime.

Groenplaats is the dividing line between the city's very different neighbourhoods. To the north lies the route into Het Eilandje, Antwerp's old docklands; to the east is the great shopping boulevard, the Meir; the west is the waterfront of the Schelde River; and to the south lies the oldest part of the city, dating back to the Middle Ages.

## The Meir

On Saturday morning the **Meir** ❾ is jam-packed with local residents out shopping, taking a family stroll, walking the dog, meeting friends for coffee – it is called "doing the Meir". This long, straight boulevard has been Antwerp's main artery for the past four centuries, although it has changed character many times. It was the preferred residential address of the aristocracy and wealthy merchants, then became the business quarter, but today has lost some of its gloss, as the majority of shops are the same multinational names that are present on every high street across Europe. Fortunately for shoppers-in-the-know, there is a

host of side streets that have a far more creative and original selection of boutiques.

It is impossible to miss the beginning of the Meir, as it is marked by a soaring skyscraper, the **Torengebouw** ❿, which wouldn't look out of place on Manhattan's skyline. It was built in the late 1920s, after its architects travelled to America for inspiration, their aim being to build the first skyscraper in Europe to commemorate the 1930 World Exhibition that was to be held in Antwerp. It has weathered well with time, and certainly fits in far better with the surrounding architecture than an equally tall office block on nearby Oudaan, which towers over the elegant spire of the cathedral. Officially, this ugly 1960s skyscraper is called the Administrative Centre of Antwerp, but it is known to locals by the more sinister pseudonym of the Police Tower. But as all architectural trends seem to go through ups and downs – remember how Parisians detested the Pompidou Centre before taking it to their hearts – so, after being hated for years, the Police Tower has now become a location for art exhibitions and installations, and is almost becoming appreciated.

Those interested in shopping should turn off right at the beginning of the Meir into the pedestrian-only Wiegstraat. In between the dozens of fashion and design boutiques, food enthusiasts will recognise the strong smell wafting out of No. 28, Kaashandel Vervloet, a cheese and dairy shop that is the ideal place to buy excellent Belgian and regional cheeses, such as Witte von Rotseloon, made from goats' milk, and the city's very own Antigoontje, which is aged in beer.

Wiegstraat continues into Korte Gasthuisstraat, whuch is lined with an eclectic array of shops. Hip fashion stores fill the retro 1950s shopping arcade, the Nieuwe Gaanderij,

opposite the premises of the avant-garde jeweller, Nico Taeymans, and the delightfully old-fashioned Burie, the most famous artisan chocolate-maker in town. Here you will also find Goosens, a bakery and patisserie that inevitably has a long queue stretching out of the door, and be tempted by the irresistible, freshly baked cakes and biscuits displayed in Philip's Biscuits.

## Mercantile past

While one side of the Meir is dedicated to modern consumer culture, the other leads back into the history of the city. Antwerp was one of the world's most important financial and economic centres, and the **Handelsbeurs** ⓫, on Twaalfmaandenstraat, can claim to be the oldest commodity exchange in the world. Here merchants created the concept of "shares" to trade in, and it was used as a model when the London Stock Exchange was created. The original medieval exchange, dating back to 1521, was long ago destroyed by fire, but the present 19th-century building, which is based on

the original plans plus some extravagant neo-Gothic additions, remains impressive, and has been used as a venue for temporary art exhibitions and fashion shows. The interior courtyard is quite splendid, and although the premises are closed at the moment, while their future is decided, it is still possible to get a glimpse of the courtyard at a side entrance gate on Israelienstraat.

## Hendrik Conscienceplein

It is just a short walk from the Handelsbeurs into Antwerp's prettiest square, the **Hendrik Conscienceplein**, an oasis of calm and tranquility hidden away in the heart of the frenetic city centre. The atmosphere here is more like that of a laid-back Italian piazza than a formal Flemish square, and there are usually street musicians playing an array of tunes to entertain passers-by. A trendy new wine bar, called Raga, offers fine vintages from around the world; an Iranian restaurant, Persepolis, serves delicious Persian cuisine; and the shady terrace of the friendly 't Brantyser bistro is invariably full.

Map on page 206

**TIP**

For a cutting-edge hair style, go to the Hair & Styling Salon, at 17 Steenhouwersvest, and see if they can fit you in among their fashionable young clients.

**LEFT:** laundry day on the Meir.
**BELOW:** resistance is futile at Confiserie Burie.

In the centre of the square stands a statue of the well-loved 19th-century Flemish writer, Hendrik Conscience, after whom the square is named, and it is fitting that he should have been placed right outside the public library.

Wherever you stand in the square, your eyes will be drawn to the sumptuous baroque façade of the **Carolus Borromeus Kerk** ⑫ (Carlo Borromeo Church; Mon–Sat 10am–12.30pm, 2–5pm; free). Built in 1614 by the Order of Jesuits at the height of the Counter-Reformation, the church is named after one of the leaders of that movement, Carlo Borromeo, Archbishop of Milan. There is some controversy over the claim that Rubens was involved in designing the façade, but whatever the truth, it is exceptionally beautiful. No one disputes the fact that the great master and his students completed 39 ceiling paintings to decorate the interior, which must have been an amazing sight, but sadly they were all destroyed by fire in 1718. It is still worth going inside, as the church is embellished in a classic

baroque style, with a particularly fine chapel on the right of the central aisle. It also has an important collection of antique lace, which is open to the public every Wednesday. Although it is not visible from Hendrik Conscienceplein, as it is obscured by the church's imposing façade, there is also a tall belfry at the back. This has been under renovation for many years, hidden under scaffolding, but is due to be re-opened again during 2006.

## Around Hoogstraat

The road leading directly from the Grote Markt into the south of the city centre is **Hoogstraat** ⑬, a pedestrian thoroughfare that is one of the liveliest spots in Antwerp, with busy bistros open for morning coffee and a cheap dish-of-the-day at lunchtime, with funkier bars like Mata Mata & Pili Pili opening for cocktails in the early evening and carrying on till the early hours. One of the oldest buildings on the street is at No. 70, which is now a cutting-edge contemporary art gallery, De Zwarte Panter. The premises are part

*Hendrik Conscience's national epic,* De Leeuw van Vlaanderen *(The Lion of Flanders, 1838), recounts the victories of the Flemish over the French occupiers.*

**BELOW:** the hip and exotic Mata Mata & Pili Pili restaurant.
**RIGHT:** the elaborate altar inside Carlo Borromeo Church.

of a 16th-century charitable institution, the Sint-Juliangasthuis, which once offered food and lodging to passing pilgrims, and the paintings are exhibited in what was once the chapel. Any of the side streets off Hoogstraat are worth exploring, to discover bars, restaurants and boutiques. Look down the two narrow streets, Grote and Kleine Pieter Potstraat, to be transported back into medieval Antwerp, with religious statues in high corniches dating back to the 15th century.

For antiques hunters, the appointment not to be missed is Friday morning, when, just nearby, the **Vrijdagmarkt** ⓮ is held. Be prepared for quite a spectacle, as this flea market, which has been held in the square for more than 500 years, operates as a public auction. Although Flemish is the principal language, foreigners have no problems joining in the bidding, and everything from silver cutlery to armchairs and sofas, oil paintings and porcelain is sold. The square was designed in the 16th century for this kind of market, and in the centre stands a statue of St Catherine, the patron saint of rag-and-bone men. The market has spread out into dozens of warehouses around the square, and for visitors, these may be less intimidating places to get involved in the bidding.

Throughout the week, there are numerous specialist antiques shops open in this neighbourhood, especially in Steenhouwersvest, such as Phenix (No. 20), an Aladdin's cave of Art Nouveau and Art Deco design objects. As Steenhouwersvest is just on the border with the fashion district, there are also some hipper places to check out, such as Bazar Bizar (No. 18), an exotic Oriental fabrics and interiors emporium.

## Plantin-Moretus Museum

This part of the city centre holds one more attraction, the **Plantin-Moretus Museum** ⓯ (Tues–Sun 10am–5pm; admission charge). Housed in a grandiose 16th-century mansion that is worth seeing just for itself, the museum takes up almost one whole side of Vrijdagmarkt square. Try not to be put off by the

Map on page 206

**TIP**

Where Hoogstraat comes out at Sint-Jansvliet, there is a small grassy square which is transformed every Sunday morning into an irresistible antiques and bric-à-brac market; here you can spend some time sifting through what is often a load of rubbish looking for a brilliant bargain.

**BELOW:** the magnificent courtyard in the Plantin-Moretus Museum.

rather dry official description of the museum – "An overview of printing from the 15th–18th century" – as this is one of the hidden jewels of Antwerp, a rare experience for visitors of all ages. The name Plantin-Moretus refers to two of the most influential printers in Europe, Christoffel Plantin, a Frenchman who settled in Antwerp in 1548, originally as a bookbinder, and his son-in-law, Jan Moretus. In 1555, Plantin established one of the earliest commercial book printing and publishing houses, the grandly titled, Masters of the Golden Compass. Wealthy printers in those days installed their printing works and libraries in their homes, so the museum provides a snapshot of patrician daily life alongside some of the oldest printing presses in the world. The museum offers an informative explanation of the step-by-step process of producing a book, and there is a splendid collection of antiquarian books and prints on display in a series of fascinating libraries, and a recreated 17th-century bookshop. The house itself is beautifully decorated with

original furnishings and artefacts, including works by Rubens, who worked with the printing house on book illustrations.

There is an extraordinary feeling that time has stood still here and at the end of a tour around this perfectly preserved environment you will come away with a real insight into what living and working conditions were like five centuries ago. The mansion is constructed around a truly delightful courtyard and is surrounded by a landscaped garden, a peaceful place in which to relax before setting off again.

## The Left Bank

The historic centre of Antwerp grew up hugging the bank of the River Schelde, and the city's past wealth and present position as one of the most important ports in the world owe everything to its proximity to the river, so a walk along what is known as "the blue stone" is crucial to get a real feel for the city.

At one corner of Sint-Jansvliet square you will see the entrance to the **Sint-Anna Tunnel** ⑯. This is a quaint, 1930s pedestrian tunnel that runs for 500 metres/yards under the river till it comes out on the Left Bank. Although the tunnel is pedestrianised, bicycles are allowed, so watch out as cyclists whizz back and forth. Nothing has been altered from the tunnel's original Art Deco design, including the wooden escalator, from which you emerge at the ultimate position for a panoramic view of Antwerp, particularly at sunset.

There isn't much to see on the Left Bank, a residential area of unexciting modern architecture, but if you want to escape the city, there is a sandy beach, the Sint-Anna Strand, just a 15-minute walk from the tunnel. This is a popular spot for sunbathing – swimming is not allowed in the river – or a lazy lunch at one of the waterside brasseries.

*Antwerp is still very much an active port, for both cargo ships and yachts.*

**BELOW:** the Sint-Anna tunnel takes you from the Right Bank to the Left Bank of the river.

## The Steen

Back at the Sint-Anna Tunnel, on the city side of the river, walk up towards a majestic fortress castle that looks as if it came either from the Middle Ages or Disneyland. This is the **Steen**, the oldest building in Antwerp. It is the only construction that escaped massive demolition to clear space for the docks when they were built in the 19th century, which explains why it looks rather out of place today. This was one small part of a massive fortification set up on this strategic bend in the Schelde around 1200 to protect the growing city of Antwerp.

Although it has had a colourful history, including once being used as a prison, the Steen is now home to the **Scheepvaartmuseum** ⓱ (National Maritime Museum; Tues–Sun 10am–5pm; admission charge; for guided tours, contact the tourist office on Grote Markt, *see margin tip page 207*), an immensely popular venue for children, naval enthusiasts and anyone who just likes looking at boats. Apart from the permanent collection of maritime memorabilia

there are also some real ships to explore, stored down below under giant sheds on the quayside in the **Maritime Park** (Easter–Oct Tues–Sun 10am–4.45pm; free). Just by the Steen there is a pontoon where a small flotilla of pleasure boats are moored. Although many people opt for a full-day trip, either to Brussels or into the nearby picturesque Dutch countryside, you can also embark on a 2½-hour cruise round the modern port of Antwerp, which is inaccessible by any other means. Even local people come away, after one of these tours, totally impressed by the sheer size of the tankers, cruise ships, cranes and containers that are continually on the move in the high-tech docks.

The waterfront area around the Steen has undergone a great deal of redevelopment over the past few decades, and the result is a contrasting mix of architectural styles. Some solid Victorian buildings, like the Entrepôt du Congo, where Antwerp's residents once flocked to witness the unloading of exotic cargo from Belgium's far-flung colonies, have been

The Maritime Museum contains many original artefacts from the *Belgica* expedition, led by Adrien de Gerlache de Gomery, the first expedition to make winter camp at the South Pole (1897–99).

**BELOW:** the impressive Steen, once a prison, now houses the Scheepvaartmuseum.

*Flemish architect Bob van Reeth's Van Roosmalen House, on the Scheldekaai, was nominated in 1990 for the Mies van der Rohe Architectural Prize.*

**BELOW:** the Vleeshuis used to be the city slaughterhouse.
**RIGHT:** the extravagant entrance to Sint-Pauluskerk.

meticulously renovated and turned into a succession of trendy lofts and designer cafés, bars and restaurants. Other reminders of Antwerp's glorious past have been summarily torn down and replaced with arresting avant-garde apartment buildings, desirable residences for the town's resolutely fashionable crowd. This has made a big change after dark, when the neighbourhood used to be all but deserted, and the waterfront has now become a popular nightlife meeting place.

## Transformations

The area north of Antwerp's historical centre is one of contrasts, beginning in a maze of cobbled, medieval alleys, and ending in the wide open spaces of the old docklands, where an ambitious urban regeneration project is rapidly transforming a melancholy, abandoned industrial zone into the city's newest exciting neighbourhood.

Take the narrow lane, Braderijstraat, that disappears behind the town hall out of the Grote Markt, and a spectacular red-brick Gothic building immediately towers over the smaller private houses. This is the ancient city slaughterhouse, built in 1501 by the influential Butchers' Guild. At present it is the premises of the Museum Vleeshuis which was originally the town's archaeological museum, with an eclectic collection. But the Vleeshuis is now closed for renovation and will reopen in the spring of 2006 as **Klank van de Stad** ⑱ (City Sounds), a brand-new museum dedicated to music and musical instruments. Although there is a mix of old and modern buildings in this area it is still quite easy to imagine the gory scenes that must have taken place here hundreds of years ago, when the side streets where filled with animals, which were slaughtered out in the open, then sold off on the ground floor of the Vleeshuis.

## Sint-Pauluskerk

The atmosphere is far more tranquil at the nearby **Sint-Pauluskerk** ⑲ (St Paul's Church; Easter and May–Sept daily 2–5pm; entrance by donation), a church with the richest art

collection in Antwerp – more than 50 paintings and 200 sculptures. St Paul's is not open such long hours as other churches in the city, so it is important to schedule a visit here in the afternoon. Although built not long after the Vleeshuis, the original Gothic architecture has been somewhat overshadowed by extravagant baroque additions. The magnificent interior is also a shrine to baroque art. The most interesting Rubens paintings on display here are *Disputation of the Holy Sacrament* and *The Adoration of the Shepherds*. Other works to look out for are by Van Dyck and Jordaens, as well as the intricate wooden carvings of Verbrugghen on the confessionals and choir stalls. Free explanatory leaflets are available in English.

## Red-light district

The atmosphere changes markedly north of Sint-Pauluskerk, as you enter one of the less-attractive parts of the city. For centuries it has been the haunt of sailors, a raunchy red-light district that operates round-the-clock. The attitude of the local

authorities has been to clean up the area but to tolerate the continuation of a thriving system of prostitution, following the Dutch model. The area is essentially restricted to a triangle of three streets – Vingerling Straat, Ververspui and Schippers Straat – and allows women to work independently and safely, renting out "windows" on the street in the same way as in Amsterdam's more famous red-light zone, and with a visible police presence. Unlike Amsterdam, though, this is never likely to become a tourist attraction. Parents travelling with children are best advised to make a detour.

## Change of tone

The streets lying just behind Sint-Pauluskerk could not be a bigger contrast, transporting the visitor right back to the city's Golden Age. This was where wealthy merchants built themselves sumptuous mansions. Begin at Kleine and Grote Godaard, one of the oldest streets in the city, then wander through Wolstraat and Wijngaardstraat, before ending up in the elegant Keizer-

Map on page 206

*The delightful Sint-Pauluskerk was built for the Dominicans in 1517 and survived a series of lootings, notably from the Calvinists in 1578.*

**BELOW:** the fine interior of Sint-Pauluskerk.

Map on page 206

*As President of the Arquebusiers' Guild, Nicholaas Rockox commissioned Rubens in 1611 to paint the famous* Descent from the Cross *triptych (see page 209).*

**BELOW:** fine dining and pumping engines at Het Pomphuis.

straat. Wijngaardstraat boasts some of the city's best restaurants, alongside chic boutiques specialising in designer jewellery and accessories; while Wolstraat is lined with great art and antiques galleries, as well as the lively Café de Kat, the ideal spot for a lunchtime snack or an afternoon beer *(see page 221)*. In the 16th and 17th centuries, Keizerstraat was the preferred address for wealthy bankers, powerful merchants and influential politicians.

One notable resident was Nicholaas Rockox, who was mayor of Antwerp and perhaps Rubens' most important friend and patron. His home has been impeccably preserved, and the **Rockoxhuis** ⓴ (Tues–Sun 10am–5pm; admission charge) is one of the hidden gems among Antwerp's many museums. The foundation that runs the museum has enlarged the mayor's own magnificent art collection to include nearly all the great 17th-century Flemish painters, whose works are tastefully exhibited alongside period furniture and objets d'art. There is also a lovely, landscaped garden in the mansion's enclosed courtyard, planted with dozens of different herbs. All the information on the exhibits is in Flemish, but there are multilingual audio-guides available.

## Redeveloped docklands

Antwerp's sprawling docklands were pretty much off-limits for tourist sightseeing until recently, but now **Het Eilandje** ㉑, a sprawling complex of docks, quays, warehouses, locks and industrial metal bridges that separates the city from the port, is the latest up-and-coming neighbourhood. Nineteenth-century solid brick entrepots, that were once used for storing coffee, wine and cotton, have been transformed into luxurious lofts, designer shops and galleries. Antwerp's most famous local fashion stylist, Dries van Noten, has set up his workshop and offices in the Godfried warehouse, which stands on the section of the docks originally built by Napoleon.

Over on Bordeauxstraat, a grain storehouse has been transformed into a pirate island theme park for children. It is worth making the effort to walk right to the end of the longest dock, Kattendijkdok, in order to see the most impressively restored building, **Het Pomphuis**, on Siberiastraat, once an industrial pump house for the dry docks and today a chic restaurant *(see opposite page)*. And if the return walk seems too long, you can always get a bus or taxi back to the centre.

There is still a lot of room for development in Het Eilandje, and it can be easy to get lost and feel as if you are in the middle of an abandoned city. But new bars and restaurants, theatre projects and art galleries, are starting up all the time, so it won't be long before the docklands get a much more lived-in feel, and become completely integrated into the city centre. ❑

# RESTAURANTS, BARS & CAFÉS

## Restaurants

Choices for eating out run from expensive gourmet restaurants to inventive fusion cuisine and traditional bars serving simple Flemish home-cooking. Avoid the "tourist menus" in Grote Markt and Groenplaats and head down a nearby backstreet to find friendly, inexpensive bistros just waiting to be discovered. The new area to open up for eating out is Het Eilandje, the old docklands, which is now filled with inviting brasseries, restaurants and bars, many with waterfront locations.

### Brasserie Appelmans
1 Papenstraatje. Tel: 03-226 20 22. Open L & D daily. €€
Most restaurants around Groenplaats have nice, sunny terraces but offer overpriced, unexciting tourist menus. Appelmans doesn't have tables outside but its three-storey 19th-century interior has been lovingly renovated. Expect classic brasserie fare, with great seafood platters. Its cocktail bar, Absinthe, has its own DJ and is packed till the early hours.

### Caribbean Inn
22 Korte Nieuwstraat. Tel: 03-231 03 77. Open D only Tues–Sun. €€
An anonymous medieval door on a narrow side street barely prepares you for this delightfully offbeat place. The door leads into a 16th-century chapel, but the decor is brightly Caribbean, and the Jamaican food features jerk chicken and lobster reggae.

### Da Giovanni
8 Jan Blomstraat. Tel: 03-226 74 50. Open: L & D daily. €
On the street between Groenplaats and Grote Markt, you can't miss the kitsch red-and-white checks of this bustling Italian trattoria. Don't expect the best Italian cuisine, but prices are very reasonable and the location for a quick lunch could not be better.

### Den Rooden Hoed
25 Oude Koornmarkt. Tel: 03-233 28 44. Open L & D daily. €–€€
The oldest restaurant in Antwerp, dating from 1750, Den Rooden Hoed is opposite the cathedral. The Flemish cuisine is of a high standard; the atmosphere and service are relaxed and friendly. The owners have recently renovated their 16th-century wine cellar.

### Folies d'Anvers
13 Reynderstraat. Tel: 03-231 71 15. Open D Wed–Mon. €€
Reynderstraat is lined with interesting restaurants, but only the Folies d'Anvers has the delightful surprise of a roof terrace with a view of the cathedral. The menu is "Belgian fusion", but all this means is a few exotic spices sprinkled in traditional dishes like beef carbonade.

### Hangar 26
94 Rijnkaai. Tel: 03-233 25 07. Open L & D Sun–Fri, D only Sat, closed Sun in winter. €€
As its name implies, Hangar 26 is an industrial warehouse in the old docks that has been converted into a funky bar and restaurant that each weekend transforms itself into a salsa dance club after 10pm.

### Hell's Kitchen
2 Wisselstraat. Tel: 03-290 00 62. Open L & D Thur–Tues. €€€–€€€€
In a side-street at the back of the Grote Markt, this small but elegant restaurant has just opened, and the young chef, trained in Marseilles, presents an innovative menu that changes every day. Although the basis of the cuisine is French, expect influences from Italy and Asia, while the wine list is equally international.

### Het Pomphuis
Siberiastraat z/n. Tel: 03-770 86 25. Open L & D daily. €€€
You'll need to catch a bus ot take a taxi to get out to Het Pomphuis but it is worth the effort, as this is quite the most visually stunning restaurant in the city. North of the old docks, with splendid waterside views, this Art Nouveau pumping station, complete with giant engines, has been converted into a bustling brasserie. It looks very French but the menu features innovative Pacific Rim cooking.

### Het Vermoeide Model
2 Lijnwaadmarkt. Tel: 03-233 52 61. Open D only Tues–Sun. €€
The medieval backstreets between the cathedral and Groenplaats are a labyrinth of bars and restaurants, many plain and overpriced. This is one exception, hence why there are just as many locals eating here as tourists. With ancient paintings and tapestries covering every inch of the walls, the dining room resembles an art gallery. For a quieter meal, it is better to reserve a table upstairs. The cuisine is firmly Flemish: *lapin à la Gueuze* (rabbit cooked in beer), or a simply grilled Coucou de Malines, the famous Belgian free-range chicken.

### PRICE CATEGORIES

Prices for three-course dinner per person with a half-bottle of house wine:

€ = under €25
€€ = €25–40
€€€ = €40–60
€€€€ = over €60

### Hofstraat 24

24 Hofstraat. Tel: 03-225 05 45. Open L & D Mon, Tues, Thur, Fri, D only Sat **€€€–€€€€**

Another recent addition to the Antwerp fine-dining scene, this very elegant restaurant has a small but delicious menu, and diners can choose to eat in an airy modern salon decorated with modern paintings, or a cosy room with glittering chandeliers and gilt mirrors.

### In de Gloria

8 Kleine Koraalberg. Tel: 03-232 59 08. Open L & D daily. **€**

Antwerp's traditional *estaminets* are not just great places to sample Belgian beers, but also cheap and cheerful diners where you can feast on hearty Flemish cooking. Situated in an old merchant's house, this one is always packed out for lunch or dinner,

and serves great seasonal dishes like *faisan a la brabançonne*, (pheasant braised with endives) or steak with chunky chips.

### La Riva

52 Londenstraat. Tel: 03-225 01 02. Open L & D Mon–Sat. **€€€**

A stunning building in Het Eilandje, this cool funky restaurant is a fashionable venue for lunch or dinner. During the summer, when the evening meal is over, tables miraculously disappear and the restaurant is transformed into a dance club.

### Lenny's

47 Wolstraat. Tel: 03-233 90 57. Open L & D Tues–Fri, D only Sat. **€**

Only a short walk from Groenplaats, Lenny's is an immensely popular and cheerful diner. The decor is bright, fun and funky, there are maga-

zines and newspapers to read, friendly staff and a young studenty clientele drawn in by the very reasonably priced menu of huge salads and tasty *plats du jour*.

### Le Zoute Zoen

15–17 Zirkstraat. Tel: 03-226 92 20. Open L & D Sun & Tues–Fri, D only Sat. **€€**

In a quiet street just off the Grote Markt, the Zoute Zoen is a romantic place for dinner, serving delicious French dishes like pan-fried foie gras. Quite pricy, but invariably booked so it is advisable to reserve in advance.

### Lux

13 Adriaan Brouwerstraat. Tel: 03-233 30 30. Open L & D Sun–Fri, D only Sat. **€€€**

The most fashionable restaurant to open so far in the up-and-coming Het Eilandje neighbourhood. It is set in a beautifully renovated 18th-century warehouse, whose ancient façade contrasts greatly with the cool, modern decor inside. Similarly, the cuisine is a mix of Flemish fare, especially strong on local fish like sole and cod, and more exotic Asian fusion dishes.

### Marinade Bistrant

8 Zirkstraat. Tel: 03-227 15 95. Open D only Wed–Sun. **€€**

Old-fashioned Belgian bistro, one of the few strictly non-smoking restaurants in town. Cosy interiors and big portions of *coq au vin*, saddle of lamb and the traditional *waterzooi*

stew. Impossible to miss because of the tailor's dummy sitting outside.

### Mata Mata & Pili Pili

44 Hoogstraat. Tel: 03-213 19 28. **€€**

In the middle of one of Antwerp's liveliest streets, this hip restaurant and late-night bar features exotic African cooking, while the barmen are renowned for mixing even more exotic cocktails. The chef takes you on a tour of the African continent, with dishes like *poulet à la moambe* from the Congo and *bobotie*, a delicious South African recipe of minced lamb with apples, bananas and a spicy tomato sauce.

### Neuze Neuze

19–21 Wijngaardstraat. Tel: 03-232 27 97. Open L & D Mon–Fri, D only Sat. **€€€**

Wijngaardstraat is lined with smart restaurants, and Neuze Neuze is perfect for a splash-out meal. It stretches like a maze through five tiny 16th-century houses, and has been one of the city's top addresses for gourmet Belgian cuisine for the past 25 years.

### Pazzo

12 Oudeleeuwenrui. Tel: 03-232 86 82. Open L & D Mon–Fri. **€€€**

A favourite hangout for locals, this renovated warehouse is both a restaurant and late-night wine bar. The menu is eclectic to say the least, offering risotto and couscous, tempura and tapas.

### P'Tit Paris Services

41–45 Lange Lobroekstraat. Tel: 03-272 52 72. Open L & D Mon–Fri, D only Sat. €€
One of the best places for fish and seafood, with everything delivered daily from Europe's prime market, Rungis, outside Paris. Huge *plateaux de fruits de mer* with oysters, clams and prawns, fresh tuna and lesser-known fish like *capitaine* and *serran chevrette*. Bustling, friendly atmosphere around an open kitchen.

### Sir Anthony van Dyck

16 Oude Koornmarkt. Tel: 03-231 61 70. Open L & D Mon–Sat. €–€€
One of the gourmet landmarks of Antwerp, this elegant restaurant is perfectly located on the corner of the Grote Markt. French cuisine served in tasteful surroundings.

### 't Brantyser

7 Hendrik Conscienceplein. Tel: 03-233 18 33. Open L & D daily. €
The square in front of the baroque Carolus Borromeus Church is the prettiest in Antwerp, and the sunny terrace of this old-fashioned bistro is always full. Inside is a cosy bar with a huge crystal chandelier. The daily menu features delicious home-made soups, salads and a traditional Flemish dish-of-the-day.



### Bars & Cafés

Belgians love to go out for a drink, and the centre of town is perfect for a pub crawl where you can choose from a host of bars, cafés, cocktail lounges and wine bars. On the Grote Markt, stop off for a drink any time of the day or night at Antwerp's most famous bar, **Den Engel** (3 Grote Markt). As long as there is a customer, The Angel never closes, and the colourful regulars ensure a lively atmosphere. Don't make the mistake of going into the bar next door, which tries to confuse people by calling itself Den Bengel. Over towards Groenplaats are two great bars almost side by side, **Paters Vaetje** (1 Blauwmoezelstraat), which serves over 100 different beers, and **Witzli Poetzli** (8 Blauwmoezelstraat), a bohemian, literary hangout which has live bands at the weekend. On Groenplaats itself, don't miss an Antwerp institution, **Max** (12 Groenplaats), a simple *frituur* (chip shop) that has been serving the best *frites* in town since 1836. The oldest bar in Antwerp is the **Quinten Matsijs** (17 Moriaanstraat), but it is a bit of a tourist trap, and a better bet is the more authentic **Café de Kat** (22 Wolstraat), on the next corner. The barmaids and regular customers couldn't be friendlier and you'll immediately feel at home. There is a similar convivial atmosphere at both **Café Pelikaan** (14 Melkmarkt) and **Cafe 't Parlement** (15 Hoogstraat) which are genuine "brown cafés", perfect for an ice-cold beer or a coffee traditionally served with a free *speculoos* biscuit. The **Elfde Gebod** (10B Torfbrug), "The Eleventh Commandment", should win a prize as the weirdest bar in Antwerp, resembling a medieval church with hundreds of painted wooden statues of saints, but although it is a popular stop for tour groups, later in the evening it is still a favourite haunt of locals too. Live jazz is on the menu every night at **De Muze** (15 Melkmarkt), which not only has a marvellous, laid-back atmosphere but serves cheap drinks, too. And no one should miss **De Vagant** (25 Rendersstraat), which serves over 100 types of genever. This one could be of most interest to women readers: take a break from shopping to have afternoon tea in the original **High Tea & Hoeden Passen** (62 Oude Koornmarkt, tel: 03-233 52 98). This is actually a couture hat boutique, but every day from 4–6pm they serve afternoon tea. It is necessary, though, to call ahead to make a reservation.



### PRICE CATEGORIES

Prices for three-course dinner per person with a half-bottle of house wine:
€ = under €25
€€ = €25–40
€€€ = €40–60
€€€€ = over €60

**LEFT:** cocktail time at Absinthe, in Brasserie Appelmans.
**RIGHT:** the lights are on at trendy Lux.

# SOUTH OF THE GROTE MARKT

The area south of the Grote Markt is home to some of the city's most dynamic museums as well as cutting-edge fashion and innovative restaurants – and sometimes you'll find all three together

The area south of the Grote Markt, known as **Het Zuid** ❶, is an immediate change from the busy city centre. It has undergone a remarkable change over the past few years, transforming itself from a run-down district into the liveliest, most vibrant part of the city. This is the fashionable new face of Antwerp, the birthplace of its creative fashion industry that has put the city firmly on the world map of hip destinations. But Het Zuid is not just about design stores and the couture business. This is also where the biggest concentration of museums is to be found, along with some of the best restaurants and bars, and chic designer bed & breakfasts, all set against a backdrop of well-preserved turn-of-the-20th-century belle-époque architecture.

The frontier street between the historical centre and the south is Steenhouwersvest, but its traditional antiques shops and bistros are being replaced by trendy fusion restaurants and clothes stores. Steenhouwerswest emerges at a busy crossroads on the corner of Nationalestraat, which could be renamed Antwerp's Fashion Boulevard. Of all the designer boutiques lined on Nationalestraat, the highlight is **Het Modepaleis** ❷, an imposing 19th-century building that showcases the undisputable king of Antwerp fashion, Dries van Noten.

## Dynamic museums

Just down the road from Van Noten's shop is the newest of the city's museums, which is totally devoted to the fashion industry. **MoMu** ❸ (Tues–Sun 10am–5pm; admission charge, *see also page 247*) is not just the most creative and dynamic museum in Antwerp, but one of the most important museums of decorative arts in Europe. MoMu is renowned for its permanent collection, dedicated to the history of fashion, for its influential educational role on new generations

Map on page 224

**LEFT:** Het Modepaleis is one of the fashion temples of Antwerp. **BELOW:** Art Nouveau on a street corner.

*The MoMu collection consists largely of exhibits from the former Textile and Costume Museum.*

of designers, and for innovative temporary exhibitions that draw on the talents of some of the most famous haute-couture designers in the world. MoMu's permanent collection is divided into contrasting sections: from the conventional lace, embroidery and haute-couture to more off-beat themes like the art of the replica and clothing for children. Items are only displayed when they are relevant to the current temporary exhibition. The bookshop, Copyright, is excellent and the seriously trendy Brasserie National is a favoured meeting spot for the local fashion world.

The boutiques on Nationalestraat are not restricted to famous names like Véronique Branquinho and Dirk Bikkembergs, and it is worth checking out some of the lesser-known outlets: The People of the Labyrinths (No. 42), Boulevard of Broken Dreams (No. 45) and Maison Close (No. 139). They may be cheaper and even more original.

Halfway down Nationalestraat you reach Sint-Antoniusstraat, where fashionistas will head straight for the cutting-edge showroom and gallery of the bad-boy of Belgian fashion, Walter van Bierendonck,

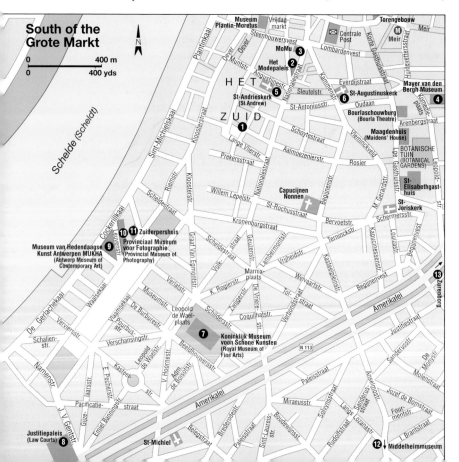

housed in a renovated industrial garage. Continue down Sint-Antoniusstraat, which leads to one of the city's excellent hidden museums.

The exquisite private collection of Low Countries art amassed by a wealthy merchant is exhibited in the **Mayer van den Bergh Museum ❹** (Tues–Sun 10am–5pm; admission charge). Only a vast private fortune could have bankrolled this eccentric and priceless collection and Antwerp is thankful that Van den Bergh's mother turned over her son's gallery to the state on his premature death. The collection includes masterpieces like *De Dulle Griet* by Pieter Brueghel the Elder, along with tapestries and porcelain, medieval sculptures and stained-glass windows. The two floors of exhibition space are not enormous, and convey a feeling of intimacy. The fireplaces in each salon, for example, look as if they could have been used recently rather than being part of a museum.

## A mixed area

On the other side of Nationalestraat, Sint-Andriesstraat leads into a quieter residential area and to **Sint-Andrieskerk ❺** (St Andrew's Church; May–Sept 2–5pm; entrance by donation). The church is the only surviving part of a large monastery founded by Saxon Augustinian monks. Although it is best known for its monumental high altar and pulpit, there is much else to admire, including a rather unexpected epitaph to Mary, Queen of Scots, and an even stranger statue of the Madonna, dressed by fashion designer, Ann Demeulemeester.

Right next to the church, running parallel to Nationalestraat, is yet another tempting shopping oasis, Kloosterstraat. This time forget about clothes for a while, as this is the antiques mecca of Antwerp, lined with colourful stores stocking inexpensive bric-à-brac as well as highly priced collectors' items.

At the end of Nationalestraat is **Sint-Augustinuskerk ❻**, a deconsecrated baroque church that now hosts a busy schedule of cultural events, concerts and exhibitions.

If Nationalestraat is all about shopping, then its continuation, Volkstraat, is dedicated to the pleasures of eating and drinking. The atmosphere is peaceful during the day because many bars and restaurants do not open before the cocktail hour of 6pm. Do not expect too many old-fashioned bistros and cafés in this area, as this is the cosmopolitan face of Antwerp, where fashionistas flock to dine at Moroccan or Turkish eateries, at a Mexican cantina or a Spanish tapas bar, at Asian or Indian restaurants. To get a feel for the neighbourhood, look for a seat on a café terrace in one of two key places. One is the peaceful Marnixplaats, which is dominated by a rather over-the-top 20-metre (65-ft) high monument in the centre. The other is Leopold de Waelplaats, which offers a perfect view across to the immense, neo-Classical Royal Museum of Fine Arts.

Map on page 224

*MoMu is an eye-catching museum, using every modern visual medium.*

**BELOW:** high-street fashion and haute-couture mix in perfect harmony in Antwerp.

## Royal Museum of Fine Arts

The **Koninklijk Museum voor Schone Kunsten Antwerpen** ❼ (Royal Museum of Fine Arts; Tues–Sun 10am–5pm; admission charge) was built in 1890 as a showcase "temple of culture" on the site of the Zuidkasteel, one of the medieval defensive fortresses similar to the Steen *(see page 215)*. The collection began with works of art that were confiscated when the city was under French revolutionary rule, with the altruistic aim of using them as study material for students. Today, this outstanding museum contains more than 7,000 works, and a regular calendar of temporary exhibitions complements the permanent display; it can rightfully claim to be in Europe's premier league, and the quality of the collection makes it an essential stop for all visitors, as well as for true art lovers, for whom it will be the highlight of a trip to Antwerp.

Most important of all, it is an extremely user-friendly museum. Although the organisation of some of the rooms may not seem to follow the most logical order, each work is well captioned and documented. The spacious, well-lit galleries never seem crowded, and there is always enough room to view the paintings properly. On entering, walk straight up the majestic staircase to the first floor to begin with the earlier part of the collection, as for some peculiar reason it is the modern paintings that occupy the entire ground floor. To confuse matters even more, the museum's exquisite series of works by Brueghel the Younger, together with contemporary Dutch paintings, are exhibited on the ground floor, along with another small section devoted to James Ensor and artists of his generation.

On the first floor, the first significant works date back to the 15th century, including two exceptional pieces by Van Eyck – *St Barbara* and *Virgin and Child at the Fountain* – and an evocative painting by Fra Angelico. Pride of place obviously goes to Pieter-Paul Rubens, who has two whole rooms devoted to his canvases, mainly extremely large religious paintings. His 17th-century contemporaries, particularly

*The lobby of the Fine Arts Museum was designed entirely around Nicaise De Keyser's series of paintings.*

**BELOW:** the Royal Museum of Fine Arts also does quirky.

Map on page 224

Anthony van Dyck and Jacob Jordaens, are also well represented.

The museum benefits from a second breath of fresh air as visitors move downstairs into the bright and colourful sections dedicated to 19th- and 20th-century art. Although there are obviously paintings by the great Belgian surrealist, René Magritte, this is the place to appreciate lesser-known figures, especially Paul Delvaux, James Ensor, and most of all, Rik Wouters, whose emotive, powerful work falls between the Impressionist and Fauvist movements. Although the Fine Arts Museum is the ideal place to chronicle Flemish paintings, there are also important works by a number of internationally renowned European painters, from Titian and Cranach to Modigliani and Chagall. There are free audio guides available in a variety of different languages.

## Regeneration

Standing in the middle of Leopold de Waelplaats, with the Fine Arts Museum on your left, you will find that a very strange sight catches your eye. Right at the end of the boulevard is what looks like a tall, white-sailed ship. The only thing wrong with this illusion is that the River Schelde is on the other side of the square. The explanation lies in the miracles of modern architecture, as this phantom ship is actually the futuristic **Justitiepaleis ❽** (Law Courts). Five years in the making, the new Law Courts is due to open in March 2006 and is already being lauded as one of the most iconic buildings in Belgium. The architect is Britain's Richard Rogers, who has already changed Europe's urban landscapes with projects such as the Pompidou Centre in Paris and the Lloyds Building and the Millennium Dome in London.

Until now, this part of Het Zuid hadn't benefited from the gentrification centred around MoMu and the Fine Arts Museum, and it is hoped that the new Law Courts will regenerate the surrounding neighbourhood. The heart of the building will be an immense, transparent public space on the second floor, which may delight enthusiasts of

**BELOW:**
the white "sails"
of the Law Courts.

*The MuHKA stages four large-scale exhibitions per year, following the rhythm of the season.*

architecture, but as it is called the Salle des Pas Perdus (Room of Lost Footsteps) it may not be so welcoming for those forced to attend the Law Courts for official reasons.

The town planners made a positive decision not to allow construction on a more attractive site on the nearby bank of the Schelde, thereby avoiding a potential clash with local residents. The old quays down by the river, along Vlaamsekaai, Waalsekaai and Cockerillkaai, were the earliest part of the Het Zuid district to be redeveloped, with the opening of two contemporary museums, a world-culture centre, and a host of popular nightlife locales.

## MuHKA

This neighbourhood really began to change character back in the early 1980s, when an abandoned grain silo, housed in a distinguished 1922 warehouse, was transformed into the **Museum van Hedendaagse Kunst Antwerpen** ❾ (Antwerp Museum of Contemporary Art; Tues–Sun 10am–5pm; admission charge). Because it has such an unpronounce-

able name, everyone refers to this innovative museum by its acronym, MuHKA. Although its official brief is to present contemporary art from the 1970s onwards, what the museum really concentrates on are the very latest developments in the modern art world.

The MuHKA collection has only reached 700 works so far (which hardly compares with the 7,000 works to be found in the Fine Arts Museum) but that is not important. The permanent collection is rarely displayed, and the strength of the museum is its radical temporary exhibitions, which are organised at a great pace compared to the usual museum bureaucracy, which invariably requires shows being planned and organised years in advance.

MuHKA's first collaboration was with the American conceptual artist, Gordon Matta-Clark, and after his death the museum based its permanent collection around the 150 pieces lent to it by the Gordon Matta-Clark Foundation. Over the years it has been adding not just the latest works to emerge from the

**BELOW:** colourful exhibition at the MuHKA.

Belgian avant-garde art scene, but from contemporary international artists, too. On the fourth floor of the museum you will find that the bright, airy café and restaurant is a great place to take a break for lunch or a drink; it also has a sunny roof-top terrace. Visitors with children should also check out the first floor of the museum, called MUST for Kids, where there is a playground area with art-inspired toys and games.

## Photography

Shortly after MuHKA was opened, work began on renovating another turn-of-the-20th-century warehouse, the Vlaanderen, in an adjoining street, to create a museum dedicated to the art of photography. The **Provinciaal Museum voor Fotografie ⑩** (Tues–Sun 10am–5pm; admission charge), opened in 1986, and it was such a resonating success that 17 years later, in 2004, a new wing was inaugurated. This added not just more exhibition space, but also a popular café, a bookshop, and ateliers for budding photographers.

You really don't have to be a camera enthusiast to enjoy a tour round the museum, because apart from an exhaustive historical collection of photographic equipment, there are also some stunning images by the likes of New York photographer Paul Strand (1890–1976); his contemporary, the Illinois-born Edward Weston (1886–1958); and the eminent French photographer Robert Doisneau (1912–94); as well as major temporary exhibitions that usually present the work of young, contemporary photographers. The extension is still not quite complete, so the permanent collection will only be displayed from 2006.

## Docklands come to life

The process of renovating parts of Antwerp's old docklands continues apace, and the latest building to get a makeover has been the **Zuiderpershuis ⑪**, which is situated at the corner of Waalsekaai and Timmerwerfstraat. This structure was originally a 19th-century power station, with two massive towers that were filled with water which had to be pumped at high pressure round the docks to operate cranes, locks and bridges. Looking back to Belgium's somewhat murky colonial past, the authorities have made a gesture by creating the Centre for World Cultures here, presenting a mixed programme of music, dance, drama and exhibitions.

All these much-needed cultural initiatives have reinvigorated the neighbourhood, encouraging the opening of art galleries and boutiques. Vlaamsekaai has been turned into one long boulevard of bars and restaurants occupying renovated warehouses. There is still an ugly car park in the no-man's-land between Vlaamsekaai and Waalsekaai, but with ambitious plans to build luxury housing and smart business premises, such urban eyesores will hopefully soon be a thing of the past.

Map on page 224

*In addition to its cutting-edge exhibitions, MuHKA also engages in more modest, but no less important, projects with artists who are invited to "intervene" in the presentation of the collection and to engage in a dialogue between their own work and works from the gallery.*

**BELOW:** the Photo Museum sets out to emphasise the diversity of the photographic image.

**TIP**

You can reach
Zurenborg by tram
No. 11 or bus No. 34,
which both have stops
at the Cogels-Osylei,
Draakplaats and
Dageraadplaats.

## Open-air sculpture

Sculpture enthusiasts can pick up a taxi back at Leopold de Waelplaats and take a 10-minute ride to visit Antwerp's respected open-air sculpture park and museum, **Middelheimmuseum** ⑫ (June–July Tues–Sun 10am–9pm; May and Aug 10am–8pm; Apr and Sept 10am–7pm; Oct–Mar 10am–5pm; free). Situated in a grassy space just the other side of the city's busy ring road, in the suburb of Middelheim, this is a family-oriented place that local residents tend to use as an ordinary park for picnics, football matches and walking the dog.

These are all pleasant activities, but the focus of the park is the 300-piece sculpture collection, which has been regularly expanded over the past 50 years or so. It is of a rather high international standard and ranges from a classic work by Auguste Rodin through pieces by Henry Moore (1898–1986), and his contemporaries Alexander Calder and Ossip Zadkine, to works by present-day artists like Luciano Fabro and Didier Vermeiren.

**BELOW:** enjoying the summer street music.

## Zurenborg

Although it is outside the Het Zuid neighbourhood, there is another small district in the southern part of the city that is worth exploring. **Zurenborg** ⑬ can be described as a village hidden away inside the urban landscape of Antwerp, a peaceful hideaway that was created by Antwerp's wealthy merchant class, who built grand mansions here to show off their wealth. It is now the preferred neighbourhood for the city's artistic and bohemian population. Zurenborg was created in the 19th century as an escape from the booming city centre, at least for those who could afford it. The sumptuous belle-époque mansions and apartment blocks built here are some of the finest examples in Belgium of the architecture of that period, and several are the work of one of Europe's most influential Art Nouveau architect, Victor Horta. Ironically, though, they barely escaped demolition in the 1960s when the area had become quite dilapidated and town planners set their sights on creating a modern, luxury residential complex.

But ideas on urban planning have changed, here as all over Europe, and today these historic houses have been declared protected monuments, and the whole neighbourhood has been reborn as one of the most attractive parts of the city. For the visitor, this is a most agreeable place for an afternoon stroll, to admire, among other things, the neo-baroque "white palaces" at Circus Cogels-Osylei. This quartet of monumental apartment buildings boast façades so impressive that local people go as far as comparing them with the French châteaux on the Loire. The place to relax for a drink is the Dageraadplaats, the hub of the quarter, lined with cafés, and very lively on Thursday morning when a street market takes place. ❑

# RESTAURANTS, BARS & CAFÉS

## Restaurants

Ever since MoMu, the Museum of Fashion, opened its doors on Nationalestraat, this part of town, south of the centre, has been transformed into the cutting-edge frontier for dining out in Antwerp – be it in terms of the cuisine, decor, music or atmosphere. Things move fast here, and as often as a hip new locale opens up, another quietly closes down. Right now, the buzz word is definitely fusion food, with local residents loving every couscous, sushi and taco restaurant that appears on the scene.

### Bizzie Lizzie
16 Vlaamsekaai. Tel: 03-238 61 97. Open L & D Tues–Fri, D Sat. €–€€
Vlaamsekaai boasts half-a-dozen good restaurants and cafés to choose from, and this is one of the most popular with locals. There is a comfortable bar used both for early-evening aperitifs and post-dinner digestif, while in the dining room, you can sample inventive Belgian cooking.

### Cantina Buena Vista
37 Volkstraat. Tel: 03-293 79 91. Open L & D Mon–Tues, Thur–Fri, D only Sat–Sun. €

Fun South American restaurant, serving authentic Mexican and Peruvian cuisine. Quite reasonably priced and hearty helpings. Although the kitchen only serves up until 10pm, the cantina stays open afterwards when latecomers arrive for margaritas and caipirinhas, salsa and samba.

### Chilli Club
43 De Burburstraat. Tel: 03-248 90 90. Open D daily. €€
This Asian version of a French brasserie is bright, fun and friendly. A dozen chefs work their woks non-stop in an open kitchen, and despite the name, not every dish is chilli-hot. Ingredients could not be fresher, and you can choose between a quick, low-priced lunch or a splash-out dégustation dinner in the evening. Their adjacent Hotshop sells woks as well as their home-made spicy sauces.

### De Wok en 't Tafeldier
1 Gentplaats. Tel: 03-248 95 95. Open L & D Fri–Sat, D Sun–Thur. €€
This bright Asian restaurant is well-known for its "wokbuffet" and "wok-a-soup", all-you-can-eat feasts of Oriental dishes at a bargain price. At the weekend the chefs carry on cooking at their woks until 1am, making it a popular stop-off for the city's late-night crowd.

### El Mundo
13 Marnixplaats. Tel: 03-237 27 77. Open D only Wed–Mon. €€
Marnixplaats is a quiet square in the fashion district, just off Volkstraat, and has several hip bars and restaurants. This great Spanish tapas bar and restaurant is the most recent to have opened here. El Mundo opens for drinks at 4pm, and while some clients prefer to sample New World wines and light tapas at the bar, the creative Mediterranean cuisine served later on is well worth trying.

### Funky Soul Potato
76 Volkstraat. Tel: 03-257 07 44. Open L & D daily. €
This fun diner is a great spot for a cheap, no-frills meal, and the location, looking out over the Fine Arts Museum, could hardly be better. The menu is limited to a vast variety of jacket potatoes and salads, and the generous size of the portions will ensure that you don't leave the premises feeling hungry.

### Grand Café Leroy
49 Kasteelpleinstraat. Tel: 03-226 11 99. Open L & D Mon–Fri, D only Sat. €€
Hidden away in a quiet, residential part of town, this smart but friendly restaurant is situated in a grand mansion

with a delightful garden at the back. Invariably packed out at both lunch and dinner, it doubles up as a wine bar and has a particularly irresistible selection of chocolate desserts.

### Gusto
29 Steenhouwersvest. Tel: 03-239 23 90. Open L & D daily. €€
A newcomer set in a side street behind the Fashion Museum, Gusto has quickly become the spot to be seen in. The decor is serious Sixties: bright orange walls and retro plastic tables. But at the long bar, clients can sample an extensive contemporary selection of wines that stretches to Chile and Argentina, South Africa and New Zealand, while the food is a fusion of Mexican, Italian, French and Japanese flavours.

### Hippodroom
10 Leopold de Waelplaats. Tel: 03-248 52 52. Open L & D Mon–Fri, D only Sat. €€€
This busy busy Leopold de Waelplaats is

dominated by the imposing neo-Classical architecture of the Royal Museum of Fine Arts and a host of lively bars and restaurants – and Hippodroom is definitely one of the best. Its long dining room is decorated with huge, striking, black-and-white photographs. Although it can be described as a French restaurant, the chef often adds exotic spices, and also prepares a choice of vegetarian options. There is also a long cocktail bar, specialising in a host of different vodkas, and a pleasant garden courtyard at the back.

**Huis de Colvenier**

8 Sint-Antoniusstraat. Tel: 03-226 65 73. Open L & D Tues–Fri, D only Sat, L only Sun. €€€€

Set in a cosy, 19th-century merchant's house, this establishment is one of the gastronomic landmarks in Antwerp, and chef-owner Patrick van Herck has been attracting a loyal clientele for the past 15 years with his gourmet French cuisine. Before being seated in one of the romantic salons, start with an aperitif in the subterranean wine cellar, and don't miss the verdant winter garden in the glass atrium.

**L'Entrepôt du Congo**

42 Vlaamsekaai. Tel: 03-238 92 32. Open L & D daily. €

One of the first places to open up in what is now Antwerp's fashion district, the Entrepôt du Congo is as popular as ever. This friendly café and restaurant occupies a wonderfully renovated industrial space that reflects Belgium's colonial past, and the ever-changing menu of simple bistro fare is always reasonably priced, while portions are enormous.

**Mezze**

31 Volkstraat. Tel: 03-238 75 91. Open D only Wed–Sun. €€

There are many traditional North-African eateries dotted around Antwerp, but Mezze stands out from the rest. The Moroccan owners have capitalised on its perfect location on fashionable Volkstraat to create a hip venue that attracts as many people who want to hang out in their cool lounge bar sipping mint tea or cocktails as diners who are drawn here for the copious servings of couscous and tasty tagines.

**Museumcafé**

17 Verviersstraat. Tel: 03-248 49 78. Open L & D daily. €–€€

Situated in the avant-garde Photography Museum *(see page 227)*, this is no ordinary museum café, despite its name. It is open for lunch, but also in the evening for dinner when the museum itself has shut down. The design is modern, bright and white, and the cuisine is a mix of Belgian and French influences. Daytime visitors to the museum can rest assured though: the café also bakes a delicious array of cakes available at any time of the day.

**National**

32 Nationalestraat. Tel: 03-227 56 56. Open L & D Tues–Sun. €€–€€€

Situated in the same building as the Fashion Museum, MoMu *(see page 221)*, the National is the unofficial canteen for the fashion world of Antwerp, and is definitely the place to dine and be seen dining. You'll eat well here, but frankly, the food in this "Italian brasserie" is only a complement to the cutting-edge interior design and the chic clothes worn by the clientele. The National is also a great place for an early-evening aperitif, sitting outside in front of all the fashion boutiques.

**Non Solo Tè**

1 Museumstraat. Tel: 03-248 49 54. Open 8am–6pm Tues–Sun. €

Recently opened, this

**LEFT:** the clean, minimalist decor of the Museumcafé makes for an elegant dining experience.

minimalist Italian deli-catessen-diner is open all day and serves cappuccino and pastries for breakfast, followed by brunch, home-made pasta for lunch and a welcome aperitif for those coming out of one of the numerous surrounding museums.

### Soeki
21 Volkstraat. Tel: 03-238 75 05. Open D only Tues–Sun
**€–€€**
Only open in the evening, Soeki is a favourite hang-out for the Antwerp fashion and design crowd. On first appearances, it looks like a psychedelic seventies-style lounge bar where the customers are drinking sangría and chilled sparkling wine while listening to the DJ's selection of mambo, reggae and flamenco. But it is actually a great place to eat too, with the tiny kitchen turning out an excellent variety of Mediterranean tapas and salads. Prices are inexpensive and food is served later than is usual in a normal restaurant.

### Zuko
21 Museumstraat.
Tel: 03-238 76 01. Open L & D Tues–Sat, D only Sun. **€€**
In a narrow road just opposite the Royal

Museum of Fine Arts, Zuko is a zen diner that looks like a trendy sushi bar but actually serves light Mediterranean cuisine. The bar is always packed out in the early evening, and after the dinner service is over, the crowds come back for the in-house DJ.

---

### Bars & Cafés

In a neighbourhood that is dominated by fashion boutiques, designer bed & breakfasts, and avant-garde museums, it should come as no surprise to discover that trendy bars are more the norm here than old-fashioned *estaminets*. First stop for a cool cocktail has to be the minimalist black-and-white bar, **Mogador** (57 Graaf van Egmontstraat). Then move on to the main square looking out over the Royal Museum of Fine Arts, and choose between one of the most popular bars in town, the **Hopper** (2 Leopold de Waelstraat), which often has live jazz concerts; or grab a table outside the stylish **Bozart – Café** (32 Leopold de Waelplaats), one of the best spots in town for people-watching. The next place to move on to is the

Waalsekaai, which is lined with lively bars and restaurants. **Nick's Café** (18 Waalsekaai) is a laid-back bar to begin your evening, with great music, followed by a caipirinha cocktail in the **Café Local** (25 Waalsekaai). As the night wears on you'll see most people heading in the direction of **The Heming Way** (19 Waalsekaai), which has an incredible selection of rums. Alternatively, for reggae and African music, there is the exotic **L'Ile Afrik** (13 Aalmoenzenierstraat) or the ultra-fashionable bar, **Velvet Lounge** (6 Luikstraat),

modelled on the famous Buddha Bar in Paris. To enjoy a quieter last drink, why not end up at another little-known locale also serving late, **Chez Fred** (83 Kloosterstraat), which is hidden away in a narrow street that most people visit in the daytime for its numerous and wonderful antiques shops.

**RIGHT:** the Elixir d'Anvers liqueur has been in existence since 1863. It is prepared from 32 plants and herbs from the four corners of the world which impart it its unique taste.

# RUBENS' HOUSE AND THE DIAMOND DISTRICT

The east of the city is characterised by variety, whether it is the people who reside here or the attractions, which range from the ever-popular Rubens' House, to the fascinating diamond district and the zoo

**A**s the Meir heads out of the old city centre in the direction of the monumental Centraal Station, Antwerp takes on a very different personality. Although there are still ancient churches and religious buildings and some significant cultural sights, notably the house where Rubens lived, this part of the city is, architecturally, the fruit of the financial boom of the 19th century. The colourful ethnic mix, ranging from a big Jewish quarter, a Chinatown and a significant African community, owes more to 20th-century immigrants making their home here.

## Rubenshuis

Along the Meir there is invariably a steady stream of people heading off to the right into a pedestrian square called the **Wapper**. Although the Wapper is lined by elegant baroque buildings, there is a rather unattractive modern pavilion in the middle – a "reception centre" that is more a glorified ticket booth – and there are usually throngs of tourists outside, queueing up to enter Antwerp's most popular attraction, the palatial **Rubenshuis ❶** (Rubens' House; Tues–Sun 10am–5pm; admission charge). Rubens purchased this house in 1610 and it served as his home and studio for the rest of his life. The great majority of his masterpieces that are

now spread around the fine arts museums of the world were produced here, and the house provides a rare, fascinating glimpse into the 17th-century life of a man who was not only recognised in his day as the most famous painter in northern Europe, but was also a diplomat, humanist, businessman and art collector. The rich decor and furnishings of the house also illustrate Rubens' passion for collecting, from paintings, drawings and sculptures by his contemporaries to objects from classical antiquity.

Map on page 236

**LEFT:** the magnificent domed café inside the Bourlaschouwburg.
**BELOW:** this district is Rubens territory.

Even if Rubens had not made his home in this gorgeous 16th-century mansion, it would still be worth visiting. He was forever expanding the original house and although the façade is rather sober, this is contrasted by the sumptuous baroque of the interior, portico and gardens. The overall impression is more of an Italian palazzo than a solid Flemish burgher's house. Rubens needed to impress his steady stream of visitors, which included prospective patrons for his art, royalty, cardinals and military commanders connected with his influential diplomatic missions. Much of the furniture and artworks were not here in Rubens' lifetime – most of his own collection was dispersed among relatives or sold off soon after his death – and the aim of the museum is to evoke the artist's environment rather than create an exact historical reproduction. Although there are few actual paintings by Rubens himself, with the notable exceptions of a rare self-portrait and a touching portrait of his preferred pupil, Anthony van Dyck, the museum does possess an interesting collection of oil sketches, which give a feeling of how the emi-

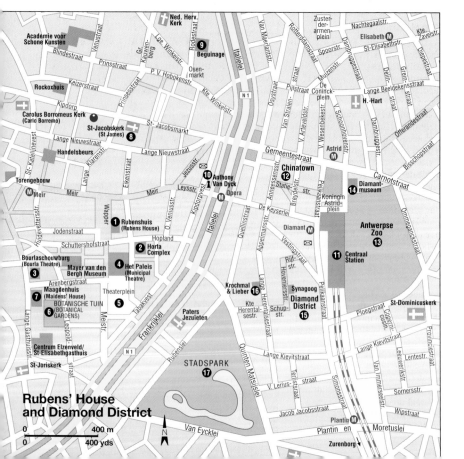

**Rubens' House and Diamond District**

nent artist created his larger works, beginning with these experimental drafts sketched in oil onto wood.

You can best appreciate the genius of Rubens outside in the courtyard, on the baroque portico and in his new Italian wing, where he established his studio. Here, he paid tribute to the glories of Greek and Roman art, painting friezes illustrating Greek artists, and decorating the façades with a riot of classical statues depicting Roman philosophers and mythical creatures. The landscaped garden, recreated from original 16th-century drawings, is a wonderful place to relax from the crowds.

## The Horta Complex

At the end of the Wapper there is another eye-catching building, from a totally different era. The **Horta Complex** ❷, on the corner of Hopland, looks at first just like another gleaming glass and metal shopping complex. But it is not named after Belgium's most famous Jugendstil architect for nothing, and inside the modern shell is a perfectly preserved masterpiece of Victor Horta's inimitable design that has been incorporated into the Grand Café Horta, a vast, bustling brasserie with an arresting glass floor. The area round the Café Horta is one of the most attractive districts in town, and is popularly known as Antwerp's Quartier Latin. This is the place to while away an afternoon discovering creative boutiques showcasing local fashion designers and jewellers among the elegant mansions that line Schuttershofstraat, or window-shopping in the Gucci, Hermès, Louis Vuitton and other haute-couture boutiques along the Komedieplaats. And rather than shop-till-you-drop, why not drink in the atmosphere of two of Antwerp's most traditional *estaminets*, the Oud Arsenal on Maria-Pijpelincxstraat, or Den Arme Duivel, just round the corner in Arme Duivelstraat?

For a glass of Chardonnay rather than a pint of beer, a bio-salad instead of a plate of *frites*, join the chic crowd congregating in the cafés and bistros around the **Bourlaschouwburg** ❸ (Bourla Theatre). Built in the 1830s as a theatre and opera house, the building fell into disrepair and only just escaped being razed to the ground in the redevelopment frenzy of the 1960s. It was not only saved but completely renovated and restored to its former glory in time for Antwerp to begin its reign as Cultural Capital of Europe in 1993.

## Theaterplein

If the Bourla Theatre is a much-loved local institution, the same cannot be said for its close neighbour, the **Het Paleis** ❹ (Municipal Theatre). This immense concrete structure, inaugurated in 1980, may have every state-of-the-art stage device imaginable, but it doesn't blend in with the surrounding landscape. Het Paleis looks out over the **Theaterplein** ❺, a vast square that didn't escape the demolition men. During the week, this abandoned-looking space resembles

*After his trip to Italy, Rubens decided to expand his house and opted for an Italian palazzo feel, which is in sharp contrast with the façade.*

**BELOW:** the elegant Bourlaschouwburg.

**BELOW:** Mediterranean flavours at the aptly-named Exotishe Markt.

an urban wasteland, but it is totally transformed at the weekend, when it is the venue for Antwerp's Saturday and Sunday markets, and is squatted by hundreds of colourful stands, noisy stallholders hawking their wares and thousands of local residents who come here both for the shopping and the vivid spectacle.

The Exotische Markt on Saturday is essentially a food market that sells not only local Flemish products but an "exotic" range of fruits, vegetables, spices and olives from North Africa and the Mediterranean. There are great fast-food stalls selling sticky-sweet Moroccan pastries accompanied by mint tea, or Vietnamese spring rolls and piping-hot plates of wok-fried noodles and rice. The Sunday market is even bigger, spreading out into the surrounding side streets. This is the traditional **Vogelenmarkt**, the Bird Market. These days you can find just about everything here from clothes and household items, to plants and furniture, a cheap bric-à-brac section, and naturally there is a section devoted to birds. The Vogelenmarkt

used to sell many other live animals and domestic pets, but apart from the birds, all the rest have now been banned, either through the rigours of European Union hygiene regulations, or the lobbying of animal-rights campaigners. There must be over 20 bars and bistros dotted around the market, where shoppers stop off for an early-morning beer or, in winter, a steaming glass of *vin chaud*.

### Gardens and philanthropy

Before heading back in the direction of the Meir, take time to explore the backstreets off the Theaterplein, particularly the quiet residential Leopoldstraat. This is the location of another of the city's hidden oases of calm, the **Botanische tuin** ❻ (Botanical Gardens; 8am–6pm). Although there are 2,000 different plants and herbs in these 19th-century gardens and greenhouses, this is no Kew Gardens, but rather a peaceful spot to sit and relax. There is also a stylish café-restaurant, Het Gebaar, serving creative gourmet cuisine at lunchtime.

This area is a mine of upmarket antiques stores, especially Leopoldplaats, a beautiful square dominated by the majestic National Bank building. Ask in the bank for a leaflet published by the Foundation of Antwerp Antique Dealers; it outlines a pleasant walk through the neighbourhood, from one antiques shop to another.

Just behind the Botanical Gardens, on Lange Gasthuisstraat, is one of the more eccentric museums in Antwerp, the **Maagdenhuis** ❼ (Maidens' House; Mon–Tues, Thur–Fri 10am–5pm, Sat–Sun 1–5pm; admission charge). In the mid-14th century, a local philanthropist, Hendrik Suderman, established a refuge for destitute women. Over the centuries, wealthy benefactors donated art treasures and the buildings expanded to include an orphananage, a

hospital and a school for "poor maidens". The present buildings date back to the 17th century. Although owned by Antwerp Social Services, the original Maiden's House is solely a museum. The collection is not really outstanding, but this is an appealing place just to wander around, especially the austere but pretty red-brick courtyard. On the way out, on the left, there is a small, unmarked chapel which contains a poignant exhibition of the orphans' porridge bowls made of traditional Antwerp majolica.

A little further down the street is the Centrum Elzenveld. The sign above the archway reads Sint-Elisabeth Gasthuis, which is the name of a modern hospital that lies at the back of the Centrum. This was a medieval convent that has been transformed into a congress centre, hotel, artists' residence and venue for concerts and exhibitions. There is a lovely shady garden with two strange sculptures, apparently of ghosts, and it is possible to visit the peaceful Gothic chapel, which is often used for art exhibitions.

## Rubens' resting place

While the Rubenshuis side of the Meir is full of sights, shops and restaurants, there is not so much to see in the other direction. Rising up high above the houses, though, is the tall, unfinished, spire of **Sint-Jacobskerk** ❽ (St James' Church; Apr–Oct Mon–Sat 2pm–5pm; admission charge). During the 16th century the aristocratic residents of this parish wanted to demonstrate their riches by building a spire even higher than that of the cathedral, but they ran out of money before it was finished. The anonymous-looking entrance to the church is rather hard to find, on a narrow back street, but be prepared for the lustrous baroque interiors. There is always a steady flow of tourists heading to this church, the reason being that it is where Rubens is buried. The great master meticulously prepared his own burial chapel, directly behind the high altar. The chapel's altar is adorned with one of Rubens' last works, *Our Lady Surrounded by Saints*, in which Rubens himself appears as

*Sint-Jacobskerk is Rubens' chosen resting place.*

**Map on page 236**

**BELOW:** the 17th-century Maagdenhuis.

St George, alongside images of his two wives as Martha and Mary, and his father as St Jerome.

Sint-Jacobskerk was the preferred final resting place for Antwerp's powerful nobility and wealthy merchants, so there are a good many other reasons to visit this opulent church. There are dozens of richly decorated chapels, including the family chapel of Nicholaas Rockox, Rubens' great friend and patron.

Before moving on from this part of town, walk over to Rodestraat, and push open the inocuous arched doorway marking No. 39. This is the entrance to a labyrinth of courtyards, a tiny church, gardens and cottages that form the **Beguinage ❾** (10am–5pm; free). Nearly every town in the Low Countries has at least one beguinage, originally built to house the Beguines, a community of pious women who lived and dressed as nuns, but never took Holy Vows *(see also page 84)*. Antwerp's beguinage has become a chic place to live, although most of the houses remain the property of the church. You are allowed to wander round

*More than 100 different kinds of marble were used to make the opulent tombs inside Sint-Jacobskerk.*

**BELOW:** the Beguinage's peaceful grounds.

the cobbled passageways of the complex, which has a beautiful inner courtyard with an orchard and pond, but remember that people live here and expect visitors to act quietly and respectfully.

## Bold boulevards

At the beginning of the 20th century, the town council decided that, with the arrival of the railway, it was time to extend Antwerp's original grand boulevard, the Meir, as far as the newly built Centraal Station, by constructing two new streets, Leysstraat and De Keyserlei. The aim was to demonstrate the prosperity and financial power of the city, by designing the most imposing buildings imaginable. This is especially noticeable in the twin Art Nouveau towers at the beginning of Leysstraat. The only figure that seems out of place against this backdrop is a lonely looking **statue of Anthony van Dyck ❿**, Antwerp's second most celebrated artist, right in the middle of the sreet. Unlike Rubens, Van Dyck was born in Antwerp, but although he had his own studio here as well as working with Rubens, Van Dyck actually found fame and fortune overseas, and is buried in London's St Paul's Cathedral.

The final run-up to the magnificent Centraal Station, De Keyserlei, is something of an anticlimax. Both sides of the boulevard are lined with bars and restaurants, but the atmosphere is not always salubrious, and there are more attractive parts of town in which to have a meal or a drink. At present, the whole area resembles a huge building site, as works are in progress to allow the high-speed TGV and Eurostar trains to arrive beneath Centraal Station, which is also being extensively renovated. Restoration of the station itself is scheduled to be completed at the end of 2006, with the train link operational from 2007.

Despite all these incoveniences, **Centraal Station** ⑪ remains one of Antwerp's grandest buildings, and is definitely worth a visit. Built in 1905 by architect, Louis Delacenserie, this "railway cathedral" is as impressive as any of its contemporaries that were going up at the same time in all Europe's leading cities. Even before the renovations began, the station had been well maintained, and the immense entrance hall with its stunning glass and steel interior and majestic staircase still takes the breath away. The opulent station café, located by the platforms, which was originally the waiting room for first-class passengers, is now a genteel venue to have a coffee and croissant.

Among the building works surrounding the station there are still several attractions to seek out. Antwerp's compact but colourful **Chinatown** ⑫ centres on Van Wesenbekestraat, easily recognisable by two stone lions standing guard. There are dozens of Chinese and Thai restaurants here, serving authentic and reasonably priced meals, and several exotic supermarkets stacked with Asian products. At one corner, by Koningin Astridplein, there is Aquatopia, an underwater world that is a favourite with children. Right at the other end of Van Wesenbekestraat, you come out in De Coninckplein, a popular rendezvous for members of African communities living nearby.

## The zoo

In a corner of Koningin Astridplein is the imposing entrance of the **Antwerpse Zoo** ⑬ (July–Aug daily 10am–7pm, Mar–June and Sept–Oct 10am–5.30pm, Nov–Feb 10am–4.45pm; admission charge). The zoo, opened in 1843, is one of the oldest in the world, and has a global reputation not just for the number and variety of animals, but for concentrating as much as possible on their living conditions and participating, through the Royal Society for Zoology, in international breeding projects to safeguard threatened species. There are more tham 6,000 animals here, representing 750 different species, but the zoo never feels

Map on page 236

*Pink flamingos at the Antwerpse Zoo.*

**LEFT:** the flamboyant clock inside Centraal Station. **BELOW:** the zoo's impressive entrance.

overcrowded as it resembles a huge, verdant garden, with plenty of space for animals and visitors alike. All over Europe, 19th-century architects exercised their fantasies for the surreal in city zoos, and Antwerp is no exception. Here you'll find giraffes living in an Egyptian temple, cute penguins sliding around in Freeze Land, while the massive hippos inhabit a shocking pink villa. For those who really want to spend a whole day at the zoo, there are several restaurants and picnic areas, an aquarium, planetarium, and a regular "nocturama", when animals can be viewed after dark.

### Diamonds for ever

Next door to the zoo entrance is a contrasting contemporary building, which was opened in 2002 as the new premises of the **Diamantmuseum** ⑭ (Feb–Dec Thur–Tues 10am–5pm; admission charge). Antwerp and diamonds are synonymous. The city has been the world's capital of the diamond trade for more than 500 years, and nowhere else offers so many opportunities to discover the mysteries of this business. The Diamond Museum is the ideal place to trace the history of diamond trading and the technical processes involved in cutting the world's most precious stone. Then it is the time to window-shop in glittering jewellers or mingle with the dark-suited traders with black attaché cases cuffed to their wrists, rushing to-and-fro between safety vaults and diamond exchanges.

The Diamantmuseum is an interactive, three-floor museum, where visitors are given an audio-guide, and there are numerous computer terminals. The first part of the guided tour concentrates on the history of diamond trading and the tests and processes that transform a rough stone into a priceless diamond *(see also below)*. Visitors can examine a diamond under a magnifying glass and decide how it should be cut. Then a series of armoured doors are opened, revealing high-security vaults containing a treasure trove of diamonds, a historical collection that begins with a Renaissance ring from the 15th century and ends with contemporary designer jewellery.

A great majority of the world's diamond production is traded in the **diamond district** ⑮. A tour of the district begins round the corner from the museum, the other side of Centraal Station, along Pelikaanstraat. On one side of this street, in a series of arches under the station, shops brim not just with diamonds, but gold and silver jewellery, too. One of the city's four diamond exchanges is on Pelikaanstreet, but this is not yet the heart of the diamond district, as these shops are a recent phenomenon. The diamond district proper begins at Rijfstraat, and it is impossible to miss the entrance as the road is blocked with armed guards. Rijfstraat runs into Hovenierstraat, which is where the action really is, with the most important

**BELOW:** diamond expert at work.

exchange situated just opposite a small, beautiful Portuguese synagogue. Despite the massive security, this synagogue, serving the Sephardic Jewish community, was the target of a terrorist bomb 20 years ago, and is still not open to the general public.

Do not come come to the diamond district expecting to see a great deal. The few shops tend to be selling either technical instruments for specialist diamond cutters or a host of threatening security material to protect traders. But what you do get on a tour of the district is a sense of the palpable tension in the air, as these narrow, pedestrian-only streets are packed with traders from the 1,500 different diamond companies based here. It is impossible to resist the temptation of imagining just how much wealth must be stashed away in their briefcases when the annual turnover of diamonds traded here is over US$25 billion.

For a long time, this was a business run almost exclusively by different Jewish communities, but that has changed a great deal today, and there are just as many Indian, Lebanese and East European traders doing business as traditionally black-clad Jews with their homburg hats and flowing locks of curly hair.

## The Jewish quarter

The square kilometre that constitutes the diamond district ends where Schupstraat comes out into Lange Herentalsestraat, and this street marks the beginning of the city's extensive **Jewish quarter**. There is also a traditional diamond factory here, **Krochmal & Lieber** ⓰ (29 Lange Herentalsestraat; admission charge), which organises guided tours that show visitors the process of how rough diamonds are transformed into brilliant precious stones. This represents a far more authentic experience than you get at the Diamantmuseum.

There has been a significant Jewish presence in Antwerp since the Middle Ages, inextricably tied to the diamond trade. What you see now in this quarter depends very much on which day you choose to visit. On a Saturday, the Sabbath, every shop is closed, but the streets are packed with families heading off to the synagogue or visiting friends and relatives. During the week, a walk along Simonsstraat takes you past a good many religious shops, selling traditional ritual objects, side by side with colourful kosher restaurants and food stores.

At the bottom of Lange Kievitstraat is the **Stadspark** ⓱, the town's biggest park. Antwerp is not a city with an abundance of green spaces, so the Stadspark is much-loved by locals and is a meeting place and melting pot for all the diverse communities that live in the city. This triangular park was laid-out in the mid-19th century on what was once part of the city's fortifications, when it was under Spanish rule, and the pretty lake follows the route of the fortress's original moat. ❏

Map on page 236

*Diamonds are definitely a girl's best friend in Antwerp.*

**BELOW:** street scene in the Diamond District.

# RESTAURANTS, BARS & CAFÉS

## Restaurants

The area around Rubens' House, the Bourla Theatre and the Meir shopping district abound in reasonably priced restaurants serving Flemish cuisine. But the nearer you get to the diamond district and Centraal Station, the less appealing the bars and restaurants become. It is worth noting, however, that to the side of the station a mini Chinatown has grown up around Van Wesenbekestraat, full of excellent, cheap eateries.

### Antwerps Kaaps Degustatiehaus
25 Breydelstraat. Tel: 03-231 39 54. Open L & D Wed–Sun. €€

Offbeat diner that showcases the exotic cuisine of South Africa – but not the place for wildlife-lovers, with a menu featuring ostrich, antelope and crocodile. The extensive South African wine list is excellent.

### Den Abbatoir
65 Lange Labroekstraat. Tel: 03-271 08 71. Open L & D Tues–Fri, D only Sat–Sun. €€
As its name suggests, this restaurant is near the town's old abbatoir, and it is a meat-lovers' paradise. Portions are huge, prices reasonable, and on top of their famous entrecôte and T-bone steaks, you can choose from sweetbreads, veal liver and grilled kidneys. Due north from the diamond district.

### De Markt
6 Graanmarkt. Tel: 032-33 03 41. Open L & D Tues–Sun. €€
Opposite the theatre, this welcoming brasserie is warm and cosy inside and has a bright courtyard terrace covered by a glass atrium so you can eat outside all year round. The menu is reasonably priced, featuring hearty Flemish cuisine.

### Del Rey
9 Appelmansstraat. Tel: 03-470 28 61. Open L Mon–Sat €
The diamond district lacks in interesting places to eat, but this artisan *chocolatier* is one exception. Irresistible aromas of cocoa waft out of the kitchen-atelier, and attached to their boutique is a *salon de dégustation*, where lunch and afternoon tea are served.

### Den Arme Duivel
1 Armeduivelstraat. Tel: 03-232 26 98. Open L & D Mon–Fri. €
One of the most beautiful traditional *estaminet*, this is also a great place to eat. The menu is short but every dish is freshly cooked, and the homemade soups are fabulous.

### Grand Café Horta
2 Hopland. Tel: 03-232 72 13. Open L & D daily. €€–€€€
Named after Art Nouveau architect Victor Horta, this place is worth a visit as much for its stunning design as for its food. Next door to Rubens' House, this building looks like just another gleaming glass and metal shopping mall, but inside the original Horta design has been left untouched. A good place to sample hearty Belgian specialities.

### Guylian
15 Komedieplaats. Tel: 03-232 18 58. Open L only Mon–Sat.
The Komedieplaats is where shoppers come for designer clothing. The perfect spot for a light lunch of salad and gourmet sandwiches, this café is run by one of Belgium's most renowned chocolate makers.

### Het Gebaar
24 Leopoldstraat. Tel: 03-232 37 10. Open L only Tues–Sat. €€
Het Gebaar describes itself as a "lunch lounge" and although this may sound a little pretentious, the place is a great discovery. The owners have taken over an idyllic red-brick Victorian mansion at the bottom of the Botanical Gardens and turned it into an ideal place for lunch after a visit of the gardens. The menu has plenty of vegetarian dishes, light Mediterranean cuisine, and home-made desserts.

**LEFT:** the superb and airy Grand Café Horta.
**RIGHT:** kosher restaurant Hoffy's in the Jewish quarter.

**La Luna**
177 Italielei. Tel: 03-232 23
44. Open L & D Mon–Fri, D
only Sat. €€€€
Located on a busy
boulevard, La Luna is a
chic minimalist restaurant
where fashionistas book
a table hoping to catch
a glimpse of the town's
famous designers. The
chef uses classic Flem-
ish products like endives
and Zeebrugge shrimps
in eclectic Thai, Japan-
ese and Italian recipes.
Good selection of vege-
tarian and low-calorie
dishes. A bit expensive,
but worth it for a splash-
out gourmet meal.

**Lambik**
16 Lange Leemstraat. Tel:
03-226 01 32. Open L & D
daily. €
An Antwerp institution,
the Lambik is named
after one of Belgium's
most famous beers, but
this lively local is not just

for drinking in. The fare
includes old-fashioned
dishes like *moules
marinières* and tasty
sausages. There is also
a bargain dish-of-the-day.

**The Foodmaker**
52 De Keyserlei. Tel: 03-767
07 70. Open L & D daily. €
The busy boulevard up to
Centraal Station is lined
with brasseries, but the
most popular spot for
hungry commuters is
this high-tech, modern
café that offers fast-food
– salads, sandwiches
and pastas – made with
high-quality produce.

## Bars & Cafés

**The Taverne Rubens** (18
Wapper) may not be the
most authentic *esta-
minet*, but its sprawling
outdoor terrace opposite
Rubens' House is a
great place to relax after
a bout of cultural sight-

seeing. Just nearby,
tucked down a sidestreet
by the Café Horta, is the
far more old-fashioned
**Estaminet Oud Arsenal**
(4 Maria-Pijpelincxstraat),
where tourists sit outside,
but the real action takes
place in the smoky bar
where local people play
cards, and loudly discuss
politics and sport. For
a completely different
atmosphere, but equally
popular with Antwerpans,
head for the psychedelic
**Lombardia** (78 Lombar-
denvest). This health-food
bar and café is caught in
a 1970s time-warp, but it
still attracts the crowds,
drawn in by the organic
salads, fruit juices and
delicious home-made ice
creams. On market day,
each Saturday and Sun-
day, the bars around
Theaterplein are packed
out and make a great
place to watch the crowds

shopping. Serving the
best food is the brightly
coloured **Lunchbox** (8–10
Nieuwstad). Tourists
nearly always make a
detour to visit the land-
mark Sint-Jakobskerk,
but most walk straight
past the nearby **Café De
Hovenier** (26 Sint-Jakob-
smarkt). Run by the same
family for nearly 40 years,
this welcoming bar is
similar to an Amsterdam
Brown Café, where
everyone knows each
other. You can either
have a beer, a glass of
wine, a genever or just
a coffee or tea.

### PRICE CATEGORIES

Prices for three-course
dinner per person with a
half-bottle of house wine:
€ = under €25
€€ = €25–40
€€€ = €40–60
€€€€ = over €60

# DESIGNER ANTWERP

**Antwerp is a shop window for the work of some of Europe's most innovative designers**

Antwerp is indisputably a major fashion centre. Its reputation has gone from strength to strength, thanks largely to the Fashion Department of the Royal Academy of Fine Arts. It all began with the so-called Antwerp Six, a group of young designers who graduated from the college in the early 1980s and are now established names in the fashion circles of Paris, Milan, London and Japan. Ann Demeulemeester, Marina Yee, Dries van Noten, Walter van Beirendonck *(above)*, Dirk van Saene and Dirk Bikkembergs (with Martin Margiela joining them later as the seventh member) paved the way for a new generation of young designers – among them Kaat Tilley and Stephaan Schneider – whose collections were much admired on the Paris catwalks in the 1990s.

Among the original Antwerp Six, Van Beirendonck is definitely the most anarchic, giving his collections names like "Bad Baby Boys", but he is also a switched-on business-man, head of a flourishing fashion empire.

Prominent among those who have made a splash on the international fashion scene in the 21st century are Véronique Branquinho, Christian Wijnants and Bruno Pieters – all proof that the city nurtures creativity and the Antwerp Six were not an anomaly.

## Where to find fashion in Antwerp

Nationalestraat and its surrounding area are the places to head for: you'll find established names such as Dries van Noten and a host of outlets showcasing lesser-known, cutting-edge designers. If you want guidance, you can join a two-hour fashion walk, organised by Tourism Antwerp (Grote Markt 13, 03-232 01 03) or do it yourself by buying a booklet from the same office.

**ABOVE:** Ann Demeulemeester is famed for her slick yet sensual designs.
**ABOVE LEFT:** Walter van Beirendonck, one of the Antwerp Six.
**LEFT:** Nationaale-straat is lined with famous names but also boasts highly original boutiques, which you'll also find on Volkstraat.

## MOMU AND THE FASHION INSTITUTE

Antwerp's growing importance as an international fashion centre was endorsed by the inauguration, in September 2002, of MoMu (Mode Museum), whose curator, Linda Loppa, is a lecturer at the Royal Academy of Fine Arts.

It is housed in the newly renovated ModeNatie, a large modern building in the heart of the city. Architect Marie-José van Hee's light and airy structure was designed to reflect Antwerp's status as a major European fashion centre. This dynamic museum has a renowned permanent collection on the history of fashion – inherited from the Provincial Textile and Costume Museum in Vrieselhof – supplemented by a succession of innovative temporary exhibitions of work by Belgium's top designers.

The ModeNatie complex is also home to the Flanders Fashion Institute (FFI), initiated in 1997 by Linda Loppa who stated "It is not enough to foster fashion talent, it also needs to be structured". Every year, at the end of September, the Institute organises a 10-day event known as Vitrine (Shop Window), which showcases the latest Antwerp fashions. New and established designers present their creations to the press, public and international fashion buyers through exhibitions, installations and other fashion-related events, and students are encouraged to express themselves in any way they wish.

The major highpoint of the fashion year, however, is without a doubt the Antwerp Fashion Show, organised by the Royal Academy and held each year in mid-June in the Oude Beurs, the old commodity exchange in Twaalfmaandenstraat. The innovative and highly successful show attracts thousands of visitors flying from all over Europe, the USA and Japan.

# AROUND ANTWERP

**Close to the city lie two ancient towns – one the 16th-century capital of the Burgundian Netherlands – and a stretch of lovely countryside, where forests, fields and waterways are well worth exploring**

Halfway between Antwerp and Brussels, Mechelen is often overshadowed by its two neighbours. Today it is the preferred residential suburb of businessmen based in Brussels, but 500 years ago, it was the capital of the Burgundian Netherlands. The royal court that ruled here in the 15th century was not just a political power base, but a centre of learning that attracted the likes of Erasmus and Thomas Moore. There is a direct train service from Antwerp (journey time 20 minutes). The sleepy rural town of Lier, which dates from the 8th century, is only 17 km (10 miles) from Antwerp and easily reached by train or local bus.

## Mechelen

Visitors to the well-preserved city centre of **Mechelen ❶** discover many reminders of its golden past, including a towering cathedral, magnificent churches, and grand mansions and palaces. As in every major Flemish town, the heart of Mechelen is the **Grote Markt**, where lavish guildhouses surround the town hall. But in Mechelen's case, the 14th-century Stadhuis, which resembles a wedding-cake, is overshadowed by an older monument, the **Sint-Rombout Cathedral**. Dating back to the 12th century, it has an imposing Gothic tower that rises almost 100

metres (325 ft). Inside are two sets of carillons, each with 49 bells. Mechelen calls itself the world's capital of carillon music, and the cathedral bells ring out at 11.30am on Saturday and 3pm on Sunday. In summer (June–early Sept), there are concerts every Monday at 8pm. The city also has its own prestigious carillon school.

The city resembles a small island, virtually surrounded by the River Dijle and its canal. Although you can just jump on a boat excursion, the ideal way to get a feel for Mechelen

Map on page 250

**LEFT:** Mechelen's cathedral looks down on the Grote Markt. **BELOW:** you can take a horse-drawn carriage from the Grote Markt.

is by foot. The best places for lazy waterfront walks are the Grooteburg, a four-arched medieval bridge, the Vismarkt, an ancient fish market, and the Haverwerf, lined with 16th-century merchants' houses and cafés. These are the perfect places to try one of the town's locally brewed beers .

Three museums are worth seeking out: the **Schepenhuis** (Tues–Sun 10am–5pm; admission charge) is filled with 15th–16th century Flemish art treasures; the **Hof van Busleyden** (Tues–Sun 10am–5pm; admission charge), the 16th-century home of Charles V's tutor, is devoted to local traditions and culture; and the **Speelgoedmuseum** (Toy Museum; Tues–Sun 10am–5pm; admission charge), with everything from antique toys to comic-strip characters and modern games. The most beautiful palace in the city is the **Paleis van Margareta van Oostenrijk**, a romantic red-brick edifice built in 1507 for Margaret of Austria, and it now

*Mechelen's locally brewed beers are Carolus Triple or Cuvee van de Keizer, both named after Emperor Charles, who moved to Mechelen from Ghent as a child.*

**BELOW:** the astronomical clock in Lier.

houses the city's law courts. Plan to visit the churches after lunch, as they are only open to the public from 1.30–4.30pm (closed Mon). Both St Jan Church and St Pieter en St Paulus have important paintings by Rubens.

Of even more interest than its churches are the splendid beguinages hidden away in Mechelen's back streets. Enter the **Groot Begijnhof** through the narrow Jezuspoort (Jesus Gate), on Nonnenstraat, and you find yourself in a compact, mini-village of narrow streets, well-tended gardens and perfectly restored houses. This is a UNESCO World Heritage Site, and has its own baroque church, with a splendid interior. A few minutes' walk away is the older, and smaller, **Kleine Beguinage**, and the **Refugie van de Abdij van Sint-Truiden**, a 15th-century refuge for the poor that has been beautifully renovated and now is home to the De Wit Royal Tapestry Manufacture, where tapestries are woven and restored.

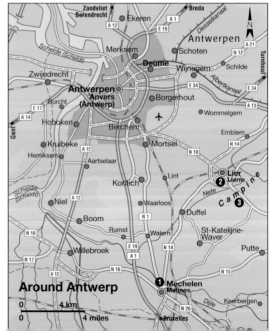

**Around Antwerp**

0    4 km

0    4 miles

## Lier and the Campine

Spend a day wandering around sleepy **Lier ❷**, or use it as a starting point to hire a bike and discover the beautiful countryside, known as the **Campine ❸**. Attractions range from a Trappist brewery at Westmalle to the medieval Abbey of Tongerlo, from canoeing on the River Nethe to windsurfing on the Zilvermeer lake at Mol.

One eye-catching building in Lier's **Grote Markt** is the **Zimmer-toren** (Apr–Sept daily 10am–noon, 1–6pm; Oct–Mar 10am–noon, 2–4pm; admission charge). Named after Lodewijk Zimmer, a wealthy merchant and astronomer, the tower, once part of the city ramparts, has a wonderful clock, similar to Prague's famous astronomical clock, that indicates not just the time – it has 13 dials – but the zodiac signs and phases of the moon among other wonderments. Although the tower dates from the 14th century, it was almost in ruins until it was restored in 1930 to become Zimmer's atelier. His clocks and dials are on display inside.

The **Stadhuis** is not officially open for visits, but you will usually be allowed in to have a look at the flamboyant rococo interiors and elaborate, free-standing oak staircase. The unassuming museum **Municipal Wuyts** (Apr–Oct Tues–Thur, Sat–Sun 10am–noon, 1.30–5.30pm; admission charge) is something of a surprise with its pieces by Brueghel the Elder and his two sons, one by Rubens, and some of lesser-known Flemish artists like David Teniers and Jan Steen. There is a typical beguinage, off the Grote Markt, and the one church to see is the Gothic **Sint-Gummarustum**, which underwent extensive renovation 25 years ago.

Lier is also reputed for its gastronomy. Its reasonably priced restaurants specialise in regional dishes like *konijn van 't begijn* (beguinage-style rabbit), *paling in 't Groen* (eels in a green sauce), and *lierse vlaaike* (cakes). In summer, go on a Koninkijke Moedige Bootvissers boat trip. The name means the royal courageous fishermen, an association of eel fishermen who use their traditional boats to ferry tourists around the canals (reservations: Taverne t' Schaeckbert, 12 Zimmerplein). ❏

Map on page 250

*The multi-turreted clocktower of the Stadhuis (town hall) in tranquil Lier.*

---

# RESTAURANTS & BARS

## Restaurants

### Mechelen

**De Kok en de Proever**
43 Adegemstraat. Tel: 01-534 60 02. Open L & D Tues–Fri, D only Sat. €€€
The latest fashionable place to open, this busy restaurant mixes a bold modern decor with creative fusion cuisine. Best to book in advance.

**Gulden Anker**
2 Brusselsesteenweg. Tel: 01-542 34 99. Open L & D Mon–Fri, D only Sat, L only Sun. €€
This romantic restaurant serves delicious regional dishes like *Mechelse koekoek*, free-range, pot-roasted chicken. Portions are generous.

### Lier

**De Fortuin**
7 Felix Timmermansplein. Tel: 03-480 29 51. Open L & D daily. €€
This old merchant's house has been transformed into a popular restaurant. The menu extends from local cooking to vegetarian and seasonal dishes. Lovely river terrace.

**Zuster Agnes**
16 Schapenkoppenstraat. Tel: 03-288 94 73. Open L & D daily. €€
A relaxed place to eat, next to Lier's beguinage, this has an informal, tavern-like atmosphere.

## Bars

In Mechelen, **Eetkafe et Nieuwwerk** (11 Nieuwwerk) is a popular watering-hole. Try the locally brewed beer. **De Cirque** (8 Vismarkt) is more a bar to be seen in, with modern design and an extensive international wine list. In Lier, **Sint-Gummarus** (2 Felix Timmermansplein) is a classic Belgian *estaminet*. **'t Sterk Water** (9 Berlaarsestraat) specialises in lethal genever.

● ● ● ● ● ● ● ● ● ● ● ●
*Prices for three-course dinner per person with a half-bottle of house wine. € under €25, €€ €25–40, €€€ €40–60, €€€€ over €60.*

## ANTWERP TRANSPORT

# GETTING THERE AND GETTING AROUND

Antwerp is relatively easy to reach by rail, road or air. The city is about 30 minutes by car or train from Brussels and approximately 40 minutes from both Bruges and Ghent.

## GETTING THERE

### By Air

Antwerp Deurne is a small city airport used by the Belgian carrier VLM Airlines. There are direct flights to London City airport, with connections from Manchester and Liverpool (www. flyvlm.com). Located on the edge of the city, Deurne is linked with Centraal Station in the city centre by an inexpensive shuttle bus. The main Belgian airport is at Zaventem, east of Brussels (see page 124). The train journey to Antwerp Centraal station takes about an hour and involves changing at Bruxelles Nord station. An airport shuttle bus operated by SN Brussels Airlines runs to the centre of Antwerp. Those who fly with Ryanair will land at Charleroi Airport, they will have to take the airport bus to Bruxelles Midi station and then change onto a train to Antwerp. The total journey time is approximatley two hours.

### By Car

Antwerp is reached from Brussels on the E19 motorway and the E17 from Ghent. The city has two main ring roads. The outer ring is a busy motorway outside the city limits, sign-posted Ring, while the inner ring follows a line of 19th-century boulevards built along the site of the ancient city wall. Follow signs to Antwerpen Centrum for town centre addresses.

### By Train

Recently restored to its original splendour, Antwerpen Centraal is one of the most sublime railway stations in Europe. Buit in 1905 in a monumental neo-baroque style, it has a soaring, domed booking hall and a splendid station buffet with a huge clock. It is located in a cosmopolitan quarter of the city with various attractions just a few steps away, including hotels, cafés and the zoo. The city's Chinatown and the main cinemas are also in this neighbourhood, making it exceptionally lively at all hours.

Intercity trains (IC) run directly to Antwerpen Centraal from Brussels, Ghent and the Belgian coast. Trains from Brussels take about 30 minutes to reach Antwerp. Travellers who take the Eurostar from Britain should change at Bruxelles Midi station. The Eurostar ticket is valid on the Brussels to Antwerp section, as long as you continue the journey within 24 hours of the Eurostar train time, so there is the possibility of doing a quick tour of Brussels before heading on to Antwerp. The Eurostar ticket can also be used on the return journey without buying a separate one.

High-speed Thalys trains run to Antwerp from Paris, Brussels and Amsterdam. There are also conventional international trains from Brussels and Amsterdam to Antwerp. Seats have to be reserved in advance on Thalys high-speed trains, but this can be done online. Thalys tickets are normally more expensive than for conventional trains, although you can sometimes secure a special last-minute deal by booking online at www.thalys.com.

A brand new underground station especially built for high-speed trains opened in early 2006 at Centraal Station.

### By coach

The cheapest way to get to Antwerp is by coach. Eurolines runs a daily service from Victoria Coach Station in London, taking 6–8 hours. In the UK, tel: 08705 143219; www.eurolines.com

## GETTING AROUND

### Trams and buses

Antwerp has an extensive network of trams and buses, operated by the Flemish public transport operator De Lijn. Some trams run through the centre of the city on an underground network called the pre-metro. From Centraal Station, underground trams run to Meir and Groenplaats. A single ticket bought on the bus or tram costs €1. Cheaper options include a day pass, which costs €3, or a 10-journey pass, which can be used on public transport throughout Flanders, at a charge of €7.50. Tickets have to be inserted in the orange scanner located near the doors every time you board public transport.

### Taxis

Taxis can be flagged down in street, though it's more usual in Belgium to pick up a cab at a taxi rank or by dialling the central switchboard (tel: 03-216 16 16). The fares are set by the city council, and depend on the distance, time and zone. The rate is double between 10pm and 6am, or if the destination is in Zone II (beyond the city ring road). On longer taxi journeys, it is always advisable to agree on the fare in advance.

### Car parks

Parking is difficult in Antwerp, but not impossible. There are often spaces along the waterfront, but the easiest option is to leave your car in one of the large car parks close to the city centre.

### On foot

The scale of Antwerp makes it possible to reach most destinations on foot. Most hotels are within walking distance of the centre, although a tram may be necessary for addresses in southern Antwerp. There are some seductive places for strolling, such as the Meir (which is car-free), the Grote Markt and the narrow cobbled lanes around the Cathedral. But the most appealing urban ramble is along the Schelde waterfront, where two raised promenades were built in the 19th century above the quaysides. While transatlantic Red Star liners no longer berth here, there are still occasional visits by luxury cruise ships or military gunboats.

The tourist office publishes a series of booklets describing various walks in Antwerp. Even without a booklet, it's fairly easy to pick up a route by following the hexagonal walking tour signs dotted throughout the city.

### Bike hire

While the centre of Antwerp is easily covered on foot, it may be worth renting a bike to explore the waterfront, the Cogels-Osylei neighbourhood, the northern docklands and the left bank (reached by the Sint Annatunnel, reserved for cyclists and pedestrians). Traffic in Antwerp is fairly dense compared to Ghent or Bruges, so cyclists need to be extra cautious. Potholes are also a problem in some of the older districts. Bikes can be rented by the hour or for a full day at Cyclorent, Sint Katelijnevest, tel: 03-226 95 59; or De Windroos, Steenplein 1a, tel: 03-480 93 88.

## ORIENTATION

The main historic sights are clustered around the Grote Markt, a cobbled square in the centre of town. The Cathedral spire provides a useful landmark for anyone trying to get to the heart of the city without a map. Reached by a series of grand streets, Centraal Station is the focal point for a cosmopolitan district that includes the zoo, the Jewish district and Chinatown. The Het Zuid district, to the south of the centre, is where many of the city's art museums and galleries are found. Further out, Cogels-Osylei is a district of flamboyant architecture, best reached by tram.

The St Paulus quarter, spreading to the north of the Grote Markt, was once dominated by the red light district, but it is gradually losing its rough edge. Yet it still has the feel of an old maritime quarter, with music cafés, seamen's missions and shops selling ships' supplies. Beyond this district, Het Eilandje is an old docklands area that is gradually being turned into a chic residential quarter – but it hasn't quite made it yet.

When looking for an address, it is helpful to know that a *plaats* is a square, a *straat* is a street and a *lei* is an avenue.

### Day trips

Antwerp makes a good base for exploring historical small towns. There are direct trains to nearby towns such as Mechelen and Lier. The countryside around, although flat, has a few interesting places that can best be reached by car, including nature reserves and abbeys that brew beer.

For a more industrial experience, the tourist office has created a route for motorists that runs through the port of Antwerp, north of the city, past oil refineries, power plants, container ports and car factories. The strangest feature is an isolated church tower left over from a demolished village.

## PHONE NUMBERS

The local phone numbers given in this guide include the Antwerp local area code (03). When dialling from abroad, omit the first 0 of the code.

BRUGES

GHENT

ANTWERP

# ANTWERP ACCOMMODATION

## SOME THINGS TO CONSIDER BEFORE YOU BOOK A ROOM

### Choosing a Hotel

Despite being one of the world's coolest cities, Antwerp has long suffered from a dearth of decent hotels. The building boom of the 1970s and 1980s resulted in a succession of large modern hotels along the Keizerlei, but these hotels now seem rather dated (although they are still popular with business visitors and diamond dealers). However, the situation is slowly improving. The first signs of change came in the early 1990s, as Antwerp prepared for its year as Cultural Capital of Europe.

Several small hip hotels opened up in converted buildings, providing fashion designers and culture tourists with interesting boutique hotels brimming with style. Some of these are located in attractive 17th-century buildings. The choice of lodgings expanded further as enterprising young people turned huge 19th-century town houses into Bed & Breakfasts.

### Location

The overwhelming majority of the most interesting hotels are to be found in central Antwerp, close to the cathedral and the Grote Markt. Often set in historic buildings, these hotels are ideally located for the city's restaurants and bars, although it has to be said that these neighbourhoods can be noisy on a Saturday night.

Modern hotels are mainly located around Centraal Station, close to Chinatown, the zoo and the diamond district. While conveniently located and efficiently run, these hotels have very little charm or character. For cheaper accommodation, some travellers choose one of the older hotels on the Koningin Astridplein, next to Centraal Station and the zoo, but these can be shabby and noisy.

It is worth considering one of the small hotels in the residential quarters to the south. You will need to use a tram to get around, but these hotels often have more spacious rooms and gardens.

### Timing and Booking

Antwerp is lively throughout the year, but it is at its best in the summer, when various festivals bring music and dance to the city's streets and squares. The busiest times of year are Easter and from July to mid-September, although it is usually possible to find a room at short notice.

With more than 2,000 bars and one of the most vibrant nightlife scenes in Europe, Antwerp is a fairly noisy city. Saturday is the main night for partying, and you may want to book a hotel in a quiet neighbourhood, or ask for a room at the back of the building, if you are staying at the weekend.

The Antwerp Tourist Office offers a free accomodation booking service, which is useful for last-minute reservations. You can check out room availability and make a booking via their website (www.visitantwerpen.be) or by phone (from abroad, tel: +32 9-225 36 41). For more competitive rates, try one of the internet booking sites, but it can take several days to process an application. Resotel (tel: 02-779 39 39, fax: 02-779 39 00, www.belgiumhospitality.com) is a free accommodation booking service for the whole of Belgium offering competitive hotel rates.

### Cost and Quality

Hotels are graded from one to five stars, according to the facilities they offer, but this gives no indication of factors such as helpful staff or character. You can sometimes find an atmospheric one-star hotel for a fraction of the price of a dull four-star establishment. With a bit of searching, you should be able to track down a room with a view of a lovely Renaissance garden, or tucked under the eaves of an old mansion. Room rates normally include a buffet breakfast.

ACCOMMODATION LISTINGS

# THE OLD CENTRE

## Expensive

**De Witte Lelie**
16–18 Keizerstraat
Tel: 03-226 19 66
Fax: 03-234 00 19
www.dewittelelie.be
This truly beautiful hotel occupies three white-washed 16th-century gable houses. Located in the city's most exclusive Renaissance street, the hotel has just 10 rooms, all tastefully decorated with pale furnishings, stone fireplaces and wooden beams. A firm favourite with hip fashion designers, De Witte Lelie is often fully booked for weeks ahead.

**Hilton**
Groenplaats
Tel: 03-204 12 12
Fax: 03-204 86 88
www.hilton.com
The new 211-room Hilton is discreetly concealed behind the fin-de-siècle façade of the former Grand Bazar department store in the heart of the old town. Bedrooms are spacious and comfortable, while the vast lobby has become a popular place

for striking business deals over afternoon tea. But the real strength of the Hilton lies in the highly attentive and efficient staff.

## Moderate

**Diamond Princess**
2 St Laureiskaai
Tel: 03-227 08 15
Fax: 03-227 16 77
This Norwegian mail boat built in the 1950s was turned into a hotel in 1993. The docklands location is striking, but the hotel has a few drawbacks, such as cramped bedrooms and low-tech administration. Moored in the Bonapartedok in the heart of the fashionable Het Eilandje district. A 10-minute walk along the waterfront brings you to the Grote Markt.

**Julien**
24 Korte Nieuwstraat
Tel: 03-229 06 00
Fax: 03-233 35 70
www.hotel-julien.com
A boutique hotel located in two restored houses. The 11 rooms are furnished in a cool minimalist style.

**Prinse**
63 Keizerstraat
Tel: 03-226 40 50
Fax: 03-225 11 48
www.hotelprinse.be
This small hotel lies off the beaten track in a handsome 17th-century street. A cobbled coach entrance leads into the building, which is decorated in a crisp modern style. The 35 rooms are comfortable and bright, and some have views of the secluded garden. Quietly elegant and close to the main sights and shops.

**Villa Mozart**
3 Handschoenmarkt
Tel: 03-231 30 31
Fax: 03-231 56 85
A small hotel located in the heart of the old town, with 25 rooms recently refurnished in Laura Ashley style. Most have a view of the cathedral. Sometimes a bit noisy.

## Inexpensive

**Cammerpoorte**
38–40 Nationalestraat
Tel: 03-231 97 36
Fax: 03-226 29 68
A friendly hotel located

in the heart of the fashion district, close to stylish boutiques and hip cafés. The rooms are comfortable and elegantly decorated, if a bit less hip than the shops. There is parking next door.

**Postiljon**
6 Blauwmoezelstraat
Tel: 03-231 75 75
Fax: 03-226 84 50
For those who like to wake up to the sound of cathedral bells, this is a perfect budget hotel, with 23 clean and bright rooms (12 with bathrooms), and double-glazed windows. Located in an old cobbled lane next to the cathedral, which makes it the perfect base for exploring the old town. The only drawback is that the neighbourhood can get noisy on Saturday night.

# SOUTH OF THE GROTE MARKT

## PRICE CATEGORIES

Price categories are for a double room with breakfast:
**Expensive**: €200–300
**Moderate**: €100–200
**Inexpensive**: under €100

## Moderate

**Firean**
6 Karel Oomsstraat
Tel: 03-237 02 60
Fax: 03-238 11 68
www.hotelfirean.com
An impressive Art Deco mansion situated in a

quiet residential neighbourhood, this small, family-run hotel has enormous charm and character. All rooms are decked out with Art Deco lamps, thick carpets and vases of fresh flowers.

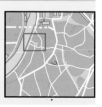

**'t Sandt**
17–19 Zand
Tel: 03-232 93 90
Fax: 03-232 56 13
www.hotel-sandt.be
Formerly occupied by a fruit-importing company, this 19th-century building has been converted into a stylish 29-room boutique hotel. The bedrooms are spacious and minimalist, and each one has its own personality. An Italianate garden and a rooftop terrace help make it one of the most seductive little hotels in the city.

### Inexpensive

**Industrie**
52 Emiel Banningstraat
Tel: 03-238 66 00
Fax: 03-238 86 88
www.hotelindustrie.be
Despite the name, there is nothing industrial about this hotel, which is located in a beautiful Antwerp town house decorated in pale pastel colours. The 13 rooms are furnished in a contemporary style and breakfast is served in a bright dining room. The staff are friendly, and the location is ideal for exploring the handsome 19th-century Lambermontplaats district.

**Rubenshof**
115–117 Amerikalei
Tel: 03-237 07 89
Fax: 03-248 25 94
www.rubenshof.be
This friendly hotel is located in a former cardinal's residence in the fashionable, vibrant Zuid district. Dating from 1860, the hotel has a comfortable lounge and an astonishing Art Nouveau breakfast room decorated with carved wood and stained-glass windows. The 22 guest rooms come in various sizes, with the larger rooms sleeping three or four people. The owners are friendly and serve a generous breakfast.

# RUBENS' HOUSE AND THE DIAMOND DISTRICT

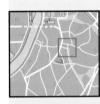

### Expensive

**Hyllit**
28–30 De Keyserlei
Tel: 03-202 68 00
Fax: 0-3202 68 90
www.hyllit.be
This modern hotel on the edge of the diamond district has 127 spacious bedrooms with comfortable beds and large desks. The hotel has guarded underground parking, a health club, a pool, a sauna, a Turkish bath and a solarium. An extensive buffet breakfast is served on the rooftop restaurant, which offers great views over the Keyserlei, arguably the most prestigious avenue in Antwerp. Rates often drop sharply on Friday and Saturday.

**Radisson SAS Park Lane**
34 Van Eycklei
Tel: 03-285 85 85
Fax: 03-285 85 86
www.radissonsas.com
This modern eight-floor hotel offers the most comfortable rooms in Antwerp, some with lovely views of the city park. Guest can enjoy a sleek health centre complete with an indoor pool, a Turkish bath and a sauna. All the rooms are equipped with wireless internet access. Drawbacks are the brisk 20-minute walk from the centre, and the hefty surcharge for breakfast.

### Moderate

**Astrid Park Plaza**
7 Koningin Astridplein
Tel: 03-203 12 34
Fax: 03-203 12 51
www.parkplaza.com
A funky 228-room hotel that looks as if it were designed for a Disney resort (not so surprising when you know that the architect, Michael Graves, also built the Hotel New York at Disneyland Paris). Located on the square opposite Centraal Station and the zoo, it adds a touch of colour to an otherwise grey district. Guests can enjoy the impressive urban view from the Astrid Lounge, use the indoor pool and "wellness" centre, or just chill out in their room with a Nintendo game. Breakfast is extra.

**Golden Tulip Carlton**
25 Quinten Matsijslei
Tel: 03-231 15 15
Fax: 03-225 30 90
www.carltonhotel-antwerp.com
This large modern hotel overlooking the romantic city park is divided into 127 spacious rooms. The staff are friendly and the location is ideal for strolling through the atmospheric diamond district. Wireless internet access is provided in all the rooms, the bar and the restaurants. There are some parking places in front of the hotel.

**Plaza**
43–49 Charlottalei
Tel: 03-287 28 70
Fax: 03-287 28 71
www.plaza.be
A friendly hotel with a distinctive green façade located on a leafy boulevard close to the park. Guests can linger over a beer in the Victorian-style bar, or arrange a meeting in the comfortable lounge. The bedrooms are spacious with walk-in wardrobes, good-sized bathrooms and huge beds. Breakfast is served in a bright orangerie. Caters to business executives during the week, and rates drop considerably at the weekend. The Plaza also offers studios and spacious apartments. Private underground parking.

### PRICE CATEGORIES

Price categories are for a double room with breakfast:
**Expensive:** €200–300
**Moderate:** €100–200
**Inexpensive:** under €100

## BED & BREAKFAST

There are some attractive bed and breakfasts in Antwerp, although fewer than in Bruges or Ghent. It has to be said that they are not particularly cheap, but they offer guests a far more friendly experience than many of the large Antwerp hotels. Most are run by local people who can point you in the direction of new restaurants and interesting events. Some hosts will even pick you up from the railway station or let you park your car in their garage. The easiest way to book is through the website of the Antwerp Guild of Guest Houses, which lists 17 approved addresses in the city (www.bedandbreakfast-antwerp. com). It is worth checking when you book that the B&B accepts credit cards, as most do not.

**Bed, Bad & Brood**
43 Justitiestraat
Tel: 03-248 15 39
www.bbantwerp.com
"Bed, Bath & Bread" is a favourite with artists and musicians. This grand *belle-époque* 1905 town house close to the law courts offers three comfortable rooms named Sissi, Gustav and Victoria. The elegant, spacious rooms have wooden floors, huge marble fireplaces and tall stucco ceilings. Special rates for longer stays. Organic Belgian-style breakfasts.
**Molenaar's Droom**
35 Molenstraat
Tel: 03-259 15 90
www.bedandbreakfastdream.com

Greta Stevens offers three stylish rooms in a sumptuous 19th-century mansion close to the city park. The vast rooms (all with en-suite bathrooms) are tastefully decorated, with interesting works of modern art. Two rooms look out on the garden, while the third has a balcony facing the street. Each room has a refrigerator stuffed with food for making breakfast in your room. The neighbourhood is quiet, but the heart of the city is within easy walking distance. A double room at this B&B costs no more than a tiny one in a grim hotel near Centraal Station. No smoking or credit cards.
**Slapen Enzo**
20 Karel Rogierstraat
Tel: 03-216 27 85
Fax: 03-216 28 65
www.slapenenzo.be
A stylishly minimalist B&B located in a townhouse in the fashionable Het Zuid district. There are just three monochrome rooms, named The White Room, The Dark Room and the Mocca-Rocca Room. Not the cheapest B&B in town, but very fashionable. The breakfast is superb, and fresh pineapple flambéed with cream and honey is the speciality.
**The Big Sleep**
4 Kromme Elleboogstraat
Tel: 04748 49565
www.intro04.be
The owners offer a single large loft space covering the whole ground floor of a warehouse close to the River Schelde. There is a living area and even a wood-decked terrace

where you can have breakfast in the sun, and beds for up to four people. The Big Sleep is located in a quiet lane in the heart of the trendy Het Zuid district.
**Vandepitte**
49 Britselei
Letterbox 6
Tel: 03-288 66 95
The Vandepitte B&B is located on the top floor of a nondescript office building on a busy ring road. Ignore the drab surroundings and take the lift to the top floor. There are three rooms available, two of them relatively small (and not too expensive). But it is worth splashing out on the huge penthouse apartment, which provides you with a sublime living space with stone floors, state-of-the-art sound system and a rooftop terrace with views of the Antwerp skyline. The location is not ideal, but the accommodation is great.

## YOUTH HOSTEL

**New International Youth Hostel**
256 Provinciestraat
Tel: 03-230 05 22
Fax: 03-281 09 33
www.niyh.be
A bright modern hostel with singles, doubles and dorms. A 10-minute walk south of the station, in a quiet street next to the eclectic Cogels-Osylei quarter. Book ahead in the summer.

## SELF-CATERING

You might consider booking an apartment or house, often much cheaper than staying in a hotel, especially as you can eat at home. Flats and houses must be booked for at least two days. Some properties are listed on the tourist office website.

**BELOW:** Antwerp has many boutique-style B&Bs.

## ANTWERP ACTIVITIES

# THE ARTS, FESTIVALS, NIGHTLIFE, SHOPPING AND SIGHTSEEING

### THE ARTS

To find out what's happening locally in Antwerp, pick up the free weekly listings magazines *Week-Up* or *Zone03*, both in Flemish but you should be able to make out what's on and where. They can be found at the tourist office, in cafés and theatre foyers. Some information is also available online at www.weekup.be/antwerpen. *The Bulletin*, an English-language weekly published in Brussels, lists a selection of events.

#### Booking and Discount Cards

**Prospekta** (13 Grote Markt, tel: 03-203 95 85; www.prospekta.be; open Tues–Fri 10am–5.45pm, Sat noon–5pm) is the central booking office for concerts, ballet, opera and theatre.

#### Concerts and Opera

The **Vlaamse Opera** (8 Van Ertbornstraat; www.vlaamseopera.be) is the main venue in Antwerp for opera. Performances of baroque and contemporary opera are staged in a sumptuous neo-Classical building, with great acoustics, on a boulevard close to the station. It was built in

1907 following pressure from the Flemish composer, Peter Benoit, to provide the city with a Flemish opera house that would rival the French-language Bourla Theatre. The Vlaamse Opera (Flemish Opera) schedules other performances in a second opera house in Ghent *(see page 195).*

**De Singel** (25 Desguinlei; www.desingel.be) is the main venue for classical concerts. Performances by major international orchestras are given in the Blue Hall, while smaller ensembles play in the intimate Red Hall.

#### Carillon Concerts

Crowds gather on Monday evening in the squares and cobbled lanes around the cathedral to listen to the carillon concert (May–Sept, Mon from 8– 8.45pm). Most people try to grab a table on one of the café terraces on Groenplaats or Handschoenmarkt, but connoisseurs claim that the best place is in one of the lanes of the Vlaeykensgang.

#### Cinema

Antwerp used to have a flourishing cinema quarter near Centraal Station, but most of the old downtown cinemas went out of business when the 24-screen **Metropolis** complex opened (394 Groenendaallaan, tel: 05-44 36 00; www.kinepo-

lis.be). This enormous centre has a huge car park, shops and restaurants. The UGC group responded by creating the modern 17-screen **UGC Cinema** close to Centraal Station (17 Van Ertbornstraat, tel: 0900 10 440; www.ugc.be), which offers a varied programme of international hits and European films. Close to Grote Markt, **Cartoon's** (4–6 Kaasstraat, tel: 03-232 96 32; www.cartoons-cinema.be) offers a serious selection of European films; while the **Filmmuseum**, now attached to the Museum of Photography (47 Waalsekaai, tel: 03-233 85 71; www.muhka.be) screens cinema classics. The website www.cinebel.be lists all films in Antwerp cinemas.

#### Dance and Theatre

The **De Singel** arts centre (25 Desguinlei; www.desingel.be) is the most important venue for international dance and theatre groups. Opened in 1980, it is the main venue in Flanders for performing arts of all kinds.

The **Zuiderpershuis** (14 Waalsekaai, www.zuiderpershuis.be) in southern Antwerp is a major venue for international theatre, dance and film. Companies are invited from all over the world to perform in a striking 19th-century building that once contained a pump house.

## FESTIVALS AND EVENTS

### May

**Sinksefoor** A five-week fun fair takes over a huge square in southern Antwerp every year, beginning on Whit Saturday. Attractions include wild rides, ghost trains and stalls selling *smoutebollen* (apple doughnuts).

### June

**Beer Passion Weekend** More than 100 distinctive beers can be sampled at this friendly annual festival.

### July

**Festival of Flanders** A major festival of classical music with performances taking place in various Antwerp venues.
**Zomer van Antwerpen** International summer festival with a huge programme of events held in unusual locations. Activities include street theatre, open-air cinema, and jazz concerts in city squares. Lasts till August. For more information on this event visit www.zomervanantwerpen.be.

### August

**Laundry Day** A massive, free street festival with great Flemish DJs, street-fashion stalls and washing hanging on lines. The festival was launched in trendy Kammenstraat and moved in 2005 to Het Eilandje, the up-and-coming docklands district.

### September

**Open Monument Day** Historic buildings that are not usually accessible are open to the public.

### December

**Kerstmarkt** A Christmas market with wooden stalls selling *glühwein* and wooden toys takes place every year on the Grote Markt. The main attraction is an open-air ice-skating rink, with hip dance music played by local DJs borrowed from Café d'Anvers.

## NIGHTLIFE

Even on the wettest nights of the year, hordes of people wander the streets of Antwerp in search of a good time. As well as approximately 2,000 bars, the city has many specialised beer cafés, DJ lounges, wine bars and a cluster of karaoke bars just off the Grote Markt. While beer is the main draw, local people are also attracted by the decor, which can be anything from an array of plaster-cast saints to the barest Zen Minimalism.

Before you set out, bear in mind that the Flemish dress to look good. Baggy trousers and rude T-shirts are a definite no-no in this sleek maritime port. Likewise with the decibels. The Flemish character is essentially quiet and contemplative, so keep the noise down if you want to blend in with the bar scene.

For most local people, an evening in a restaurant followed by a drink in a bar makes a perfect night out. But Antwerp has recently acquired a reputation as a cool northern city of gay bars and hard clubbing. The fashionable venues keep changing, so you need to do some rapid research on arrival, checking out the agenda of parties and festivals in the free city magazine *Zone/03* or by consulting the website www.noctis.com, and then filling your pockets with the flyers that lie around in cafés, clothes shops and theatre foyers.

### Grote Markt

The streets around the Grote Markt are packed with intimate bars and cafés where locals rub shoulders with tourists in a genial, beer-fuelled crush. Start the night in **Den Engel** (5 Grote Markt), next to the flamboyant town hall, where local politicians mingle with sharp Flemish journalists, and gruff retired dockworkers grumble about just about everything. If

that's full, squeeze into the café next door, order a *bolleke* of De Koninck (the delicious local beer), and ask the barman why the café is called **Den Bengel**. From here, it's just a brief stroll to the **Irish Times Pub** (52 Grote Markt), but don't expect to find any Irish drinkers. It's probably full of Belgians, while the Irish are sitting in somewhere like **De Elfde Gebod** (10 Torfbrug), admiring the kitsch religious decor, or grappling with the choice of beers on offer at the **Paters Vaetje** (Blauwmoezelstraat). For another change of scene, head to **De Vagant** (25 Reyndersstraat), a bar that serves more than 200 types of genever (the Flemish version of gin) in various colours and vintages.

### Het Zuid

When the old docks in southern Antwerp were filled in, the neighbourhood lost most of its charm, but it has recently been revived as an arts scene and nightlife zone. Start the evening at **l'Entrepôt du Congo** (42 Vlaamse Kaai), once a quayside warehouse where the spoils of the Belgian Congo were unloaded from steamships. Now with stripped-down floorboards and bare walls, it attracts a serious crowd of artists and designers. End the evening in relaxed style at **Hopper** (2 Leopold de Waelstraat), where earnest fans listen to sophisticated jazz. Or head down the Schelde waterfront to the desolate garbage-sorting depot (21 d'Herbouvillekaai) where **Petrol** holds rave events on Friday and Saturday nights. Click on www.5voor12.com/petrol for the current agenda and a map to get there.

### Schipperskwartier

The Schipperskwartier was once a shabby red-light district, but most of the brothels have gone and abandoned buildings have been converted into design shops and trendy lofts. The seedy atmosphere has long gone, and the area now attracts crowds of clubbers heading for the legendary **Café d'Anvers** (15 Verversrui; www.cafe-d-anvers. com), a former 16th-century church converted into a scintillating techno venue in 1991.

## SHOPPING

### What and Where to Buy

Antwerp is one of the most stylish shopping cities in Europe, with fashion magazines regularly dispatching journalists to trawl its cobbled lanes in search of emerging designers and cool new trends. Although Brussels has tried in recent years to imitate Antwerp, it just can't seem to capture the Flemish city's nonchalant chic and sheer whacky enthusiasm. Fashion seekers first began to notice Antwerp in the late 1980s when six graduates from the Royal Academy of Fine Arts made their mark in London, where they were dubbed the Antwerp Six. Despite their difficult styles and even more difficult names, designers such as Walter van Beirendonck, Dries van Noten and Ann Demeulemeester have consistently wowed the fashion press with their mixture of melancholy elegance and wild excess.

The main international stores are located on the **Meir**, an elegant, traffic-free street lined with impressive 18th- and 19th-century buildings, but more interesting designer boutiques and contemporary jewellery shops are found in **Huidevetterstraat** and **Schutterhofstraat**.

The really avant-garde shops are clustered in a dense quarter of narrow streets called **De Wilde Zee**. Stand outside MoMu, the modern fashion museum, and you are in the heart of Antwerp's fashion district. The streets radiating out from here such as **Nationalestraat**, **Lombardvest** and **Kammenstraat** offer a

mixture of achingly cool clothes stores, stylish jewellers and plain old launderettes. You can dig for old flares in one shop and then plunge into designer heaven one door further on, never quite sure of whether you are looking at Fifties kitsch or high fashion.

For the experience of a Jewish *shtetl*, or village, head to the district close to Centraal Station, where you are likely to see schoolchildren in uniform and Hasidic Jews in traditional costumes. Start in **Pelikaanstraat**, where the diamond shops are concentrated. Here you will find kosher butchers' shops, family-run grocery stores, restaurants and delicatessens. Shops are closed on Saturday, the Jewish Sabbath, but open all day on Sunday.

### Antiques

The most elegant antique shops are located along **Minderbroedersrui**, **Leopoldstraat** and **Mechelsesteenweg**, where dealers sell Flemish paintings and baroque cabinets in sublime settings. But cheaper antiques and odd collectables are found in shops along **Kloosterstraat**, not far from the Plantin-Moretus Museum. Look inside **Fiftie-Fiftie** (156 Kloosterstraat) for candy-coloured objects from the 1950s and stop off for a coffee in **'t Findingrijk** (8 Muntstraat), a cluttered coffee shop where everything you see is for sale.

### Art

A centre for art since the 16th century, Antwerp has a flourishing contemporary art scene, with local artists such as Panamarenko, Jan Fabre and Luc Tuymans regularly exhibiting in the city's galleries. The main gallery district is in **Zuid**, close to the Museum of Fine Arts. The most prestigious shows take place close to the Schelde waterfront in **Ronny van de Velde**'s modern gallery (3 Ijzerenpoortkaai), where the Antwerp artist Panamarenko occasionally exhibits weird invented aircraft. **Zeno X**

(16 Leopold de Waelplaats) is another well-established gallery, where Luc Tuymans regularly exhibits his highly regarded portraits. Near the centre, the **Zwarte Panter** gallery (70 Hoogstraat) displays works in a former Gothic chapel.

### Bakery

**Steinmetz** (64 Lange Kiewitstraat) is a kosher bakery in the heart of the Jewish quarter *(see previously)*. Established in 1967, it is famed for its traditional and succulent cheesecake.

### Beer

Antwerp has several specialised beer shops where you can pick up a selection of sublime Belgian beers to take home. One is the **Bierparadijs** (9 Handschoenmarkt), which sells 250 types of bottled beers, along with beer-related T-shirts and posters. **Belgium Beers** (2 Reyndersstraat) is another reliable address for the beer lover.

### Books

The French multimedia chain **FNAC** (31 Groenplaats) has a large store on the main square with a good selection of guidebooks and fiction in English.

### Chocolates

The city is dotted with shops selling Léonidas and Godiva chocolates, but those in the know make a bee-line for **Hans Burie** (3 Korte Gasthuisstraat, tel: 03-232 36 88), a tiny chocolate shop renowned for the hand-made chocolate art displayed in the window.

### Diamonds

Antwerp has been dealing in diamonds since the 16th century, but the trade really took off in the 19th century. The 1,500 dealers and four exchanges are now concentrated in a small and heavily policed area close to Centraal Station, some shops located below the railway viaduct that runs along Pelikaanstraat. The biggest store is **Diamondland** (33 Appelmansstraat), but there are hundreds of smaller shops to check out. Be sure to stick to dealers that belong to the Antwerp Diamond and Jewellery Association (look for the ADJA sign in the window).

## Fashion

The Antwerp fashion trail meanders around the narrow streets near the Modemuseum, passing landmark shops such as **Het Modepaleis** (16 Nationalestraat), where Dries van Noten sells his sublime creations in an old department store filled with antique furniture and splendid chandeliers. Another essential halt is the vaguely menacing **Walter** (12 Sint-Antoniusstraat, where Walter van Beirendonck showcases his wild clothes and eccentric installations in a vast space remodelled from a city garage.

**Inno** (80 Meir) is the last of the grand department stores in Antwerp. It's good for basic clothes and many other items, but a bit uninspiring.

## Food

The Chinatown district close to Centraal Station has several stores stocked with Chinese specialities. The huge **Sun Wah** supermarket (16–18 Van Wesenbekestraat) has the biggest choice of food from China, Korea and Japan. **St Anny Food** (23 Van Wesenbekestraat) is the best address in town for sweet Hong Kong cakes.

## Jewellery

As well as fashion designers, Antwerp is home to many of Belgium's top jewellery designers, some of them based in tiny workshops in unexpected locations. The acclaimed Flemish designer **Nadine Wijnants** (26 Kloosterstraat and 14 Nationalestraat) creates inspired works using unusual materials, which she strives to sell at affordable prices. **Christa Reniers** (8 Vrijdagmarkt)

sells more upmarket works in both gold and silver. For a selection of interesting works by up-and-coming young designers, take a look at the small shops in **Wijngaardstraat**.

## Lace

Located opposite Rubens' House, **Kanthuis Dupon** (14–16 Wapper) is a specialised lace shop selling genuine Flemish hand-made lace.

## Markets

The **Vogelenmarkt** (Bird Market), is a sprawling street market held every Sunday morning on the Oude Vaartplaats and Theaterplein. Originally a bird market, these days the dealers sell just about everything. An international food market is held in the same location every Saturday. On Wednesday and Friday morning, a public auction of old furniture and bicycles is held on the **Vrijdagmarkt**, right outside the dignified Plantin Moretus Museum. Prices tend to drop as the dealers pack up their stuff and offload everything they can. It's fun to haggle, even though you almost always end up paying too much.

# OTHER ACTIVITIES

## Guided Tours

**Antwerpen Averechts** has been offering intelligent guided tours of the city since the 1980s. Aimed at revealing the city's social and cultural history, the tours cover topics such as the new city library, Antwerp by night, the Jewish quarter and the Chinatown district (tel: 03-248 15 77; fax: 03-248 50 71; www.antwerpenaverechts.be). The Antwerp Tourist Office organises walking tours, with commentary in English, of the historical quarters at 11am on Saturday and Sunday throughout the year, and every day in July and August.

# SIGHTS AND ATTRACTIONS

## Children's Activities

Take your kids to **Antwerp Zoo** (Koningen Astridplein) to look at rare okapi and Congo peacocks in a beautiful 19th-century setting. Located next to Centraal Station, the zoo is one of the world's oldest and most respected. The 6,000 animals are kept in a series of exotic buildings, including an Egyptian temple for the elephants and a bright pink villa for the hippos. Facing the zoo, a futuristic complex of 35 aquariums called **Aquatopia** (Koningen Astridplein) lets kids (and adults) get up close to sharks, piranhas and octopuses. The **elevated terraces** along the Schelde waterfront are perfect places for kids who need to run around.

# SPORTS

Antwerp's brief moment of sporting glory came in 1920 when it hosted the Olympic Games. The main sporting event now is the 10-day **Proximus Diamond Games**, when the world's top tennis players compete in the **Sportpaleis** for a tennis racket studded with 1,000 diamonds. "I'll be coming back until I have that racket," swore Venus Williams after the 2005 competition.

The city has several **swimming pools** but, until the historic Veldstraat reopens, they are all in the suburbs. The **Olympia Bad Wezenberg** (17–19 Desguinlei) is a modern pool for serious swimmers, in southern Antwerp, not far from the ring road.

St Anna Beach on the left bank of the Schelde is where people go to play **beach volleyball**, but swimming in the river is strictly prohibited because of fierce currents, not to mention industrial pollution.

# A–Z

## A HANDY SUMMARY OF PRACTICAL INFORMATION, ARRANGED ALPHABETICALLY

### A dmission Charges

Most museums have an admission charge of about €3–5, with reductions for children, students and people over 65. Some have free entry on a fixed day of the week or month, or on special museum open days and heritage days. Churches are normally free, although some take a charge to visit the treasury or crypt.

### B udgeting for your Trip

Bruges, Ghent and Antwerp are not particularly expensive cities to visit. Prices for hotels are generally lower than in Paris, Amsterdam or London. While eating out can be expensive in traditional Belgian restaurants, you can easily find inexpensive "ethnic" restaurants in Antwerp's Chinatown, or in Ghent's student quarter. Even in Bruges, there are several alternative cafés with inexpensive menus. Transport costs in the cities are likely to be negligible, as most places can be reached on foot. The cost of a coffee, even in the most stylish café, is rarely more than €2.50, and a good Belgian beer will cost about the same.

### Business Hours

Shops are usually open from 9am–6.30pm. Most are closed on Sunday, except for bakeries and flower shops. Office hours are normally 9am–6pm, with a lunch break, usually from 1–2pm. Churches have variable opening hours, but most are open for a few hours every day. Museums throughout Flanders are usually closed on Monday.

### C limate & Clothing

Flanders has a changeable maritime climate similar to that of southern England, so it is worth packing an umbrella at any time of the year. Temperatures in winter rarely drop below zero, although Bruges can occasionally turn bitterly cold when the wind is blowing off the North Sea. Spring weather is variable, with mild sunny days when you can sit out on a café terrace, alternating with dank rainy spells that drive you into the nearest museum. Summers are fairly cool, although you should survive most days without a sweater or

LANGUAGE & FURTHER READING

## CLIMATE CHART

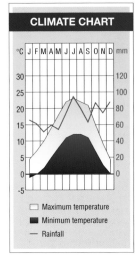

☐ Maximum temperature
■ Minimum temperature
— Rainfall

jacket. Once autumn arrives (normally in mid-September), the weather becomes less reliable, but you might still hit upon a glorious late-autumn spell.

There are no strict dress codes in Flanders, although most people tend to dress in smart-casual clothes in restaurants, theatres and concert halls.

### Crime & Safety

Bruges, Ghent and Antwerp are safe places to visit, although there is a small amount of petty street crime in Antwerp. Do not leave any valuables in your car overnight, and always watch out for pickpockets in crowded railway stations, in markets and on public transport. Road traffic is more dangerous than in Britain or the US, so you should take care when crossing busy roads, even at pedestrian crossings. Cars are allowed to turn right even when pedestrians have a green light to cross, so be extra cautious.

### Customs

There is no limit to the amount of foreign currency that can be brought in or taken out of Belgium. Items for everyday use and those frequently transported by tourists, such as cameras and sporting equipment, may be brought into the country duty-free.

Visitors over 17 travelling between EU nations are not subject to restrictions on goods and consumable items for personal use. Duty-free shopping is no longer available to travellers within the EU. For travel within the EU, customs restrictions on alcohol, cigarettes and many other items no longer apply, although there are guide levels designed to prevent illegal trading.

Visitors entering Belgium from a non-EU nation are permitted to bring the following items duty-free: 200 cigarettes or 50 cigars or 250g tobacco; 2 litres still wine; 1 litre spirits or 2 litres sparkling or fortified wine; 50g perfume and 0.25 litres *eau de toilette*.

### **D**isabled Travellers

Belgium has only recently adopted policies on access for the disabled, and the country still lags far behind Scandinavia and the Netherlands. Most railway stations, museums and cinemas have lifts offering access for the disabled. Getting around on public transport can be difficult, as the old models of city trams in Antwerp and Ghent have narrow doors and steps. The transport

### **EMBASSIES IN BRUSSELS**

Australia, rue Guimard 6
Tel: 02-286 05 00
Canada, ave. de Tervuren 2
Tel: 02-741 06 11
Ireland, rue Wiertz 50
Tel: 02-235 66 71
New Zealand, square de Meeus 1
Tel: 02-512 10 40
South Africa, rue de la Loi 26
Tel: 02-285 44 00
UK, rue d'Arlon 85
Tel: 02-287 62 11
USA, boulevard du Regent 27
Tel: 02-508 21 11

authority is currently introducing new models with low floors, but it will be some time before the old stock has been replaced.

### **E**lectricity

The standard in Belgium is 220 volts AC. Visitors bringing appliances from countries where the standard is 110 volts may need to bring or buy a voltage transformer and perhaps also a plug adaptor before using them. Hotels may have a 110-volt or 120-volt outlet for shavers.

### Embassies and Consulates

The main national embassies and consulates are located in Brussels *(see box opposite)*. They can provide help if you lose your passport, and offer advice in the case of medical emergencies.

### Entry Regulations

Citizens of EU countries require a valid personal identity card (or passport for countries that have no identity card). Citizens of some other European countries require only a passport; others need a visa also. Visitors from the United States, Canada, Australia, New Zealand, Japan and most other developed countries need only a valid passport; no visa is required. Citizens of other countries may need a visa, obtainable in advance from Belgian Embassies or consulates in their country of residence. Children under the age of 16 must be in possession of a child's identity card/passport if their names have not been entered in one of their parents' cards. Everyone over the age of 12 is required to carry either a passport or identity card at all times.

### **G**ay & Lesbian Travellers

Belgium is one of the most tolerant and progressive regions in Europe for gays and lesbians. The situation regarding same-sex

- **Emergency number** tel: 112
- **Police** tel: 101
- **Fire, Ambulance** tel: 100
- **Belgian Red Cross 24-hour ambulance service** 105
- **Poison Control** 070-24 52 45 or www.poisoncentre.be

couples is closely modelled on the Netherlands; gay marriage was legalised in Belgium in 2003 and same-sex couple now enjoy virtually the same rights as heterosexuals. The main Flemish gay scene is in Antwerp: it is dotted with gay hotels, bars and clubs.

### ealth & Medical Care

No health certificates or vaccinations are required for citizens of the EU and many other countries. EU citizens with a European Health Insurance Card are entitled to free treatment by a doctor, excluding a small patient charge at private practices, and free prescribed medicines. This card is not comprehensive and will not cover you, for example, for holiday cancellation or the cost of repatriation. For full cover, you are advised to take out separate private medical and travel insurance. As long as you are insured, treatment will be given and the cost recovered later.

### Pharmacies

After regular business hours and during holidays you will find the name and address of the nearest pharmacy *(apotheeke)* on night-duty posted at all pharmacies (easily identified by a green neon cross). If you are seriously ill, call the emergency number 112 and explain your problem, or go to the casualty department *(spoedgevallen)* of the nearest hospital *(ziekenhuis)*.

### nternet

The majority of large hotels have internet connections in rooms. The following cafés offer broad-band internet access.
**Bruges**. The Coffee Link, 38 Mariastraat, tel: 050-34 99 73.
**Ghent**. The Globetrotter, 180 Kortrijksepoortstraat, tel: 09-269 08 60.
**Antwerp**. 2Zones, 15 Wolstraat, tel: 03-232 24 00.

### ost Property

Crime is rare in Bruges and Ghent, but more frequent in Antwerp, especially around Centraal Station. Report any loss or theft of property to the police immediately and ask for a police report in writing, as most insurance companies insist on this formality. For items lost on buses or trams in Flanders, contact the De Lijn central helpline, tel: 070-220 200. For items lost on Belgian trains, contact the national railways, tel: 02-555 25 25. Loss of passports should be reported immediately to the police and to your nearest consulate or embassy.

Main police stations:
**Bruges**: 7 Hauwerstraat, tel. 050-44 88 44.
**Ghent**: 4 Belfortstraat, tel: 09-266 61 30.
**Antwerp**: 5 Oudaan, tel 03-202 55 11 (open continuously).

### aps

Tourist offices in Bruges, Ghent and Antwerp will provide you with a free map, highlighting all the main sights. Some hotels give out adequate free maps, and paid-for maps are available from bookshops, newsagents and souvenir shops. Free public transport maps are available from the main train stations, as well as on the metro network in Antwerp.

### Media

**Print Media**: Newsagents in Flanders carry most international newspapers and magazines. The Flemish press has some outstanding titles including the dailies *De Morgen* and *De Standaard* and the weekly *Knack*.

The main English-language publication is *The Bulletin*, a weekly magazine published in Brussels, which has good coverage of Flemish politics and culture as well as an extensive listings section. Other useful information sources are found on the internet, including the expatriate sites www.xpats.com and www.expatica.com. You can also pick up free listings magazines at tourist offices, cultural venues and some cafés in each of the three cities.

**Radio and Television**: The state-owned Flemish television stations Een and Canvas screen some high-quality programmes, often in English, while VT4 is a more downmarket commercial station. Most hotels have cable television, which usually offers a choice of more than 30 channels, including BBC1 and BBC2, CNN, EuroNews, and a selection of Dutch, German, French, and Ital-

ian stations. While most Flemish programmes are in Dutch, the stations often screen British and American serials and documentaries, along with English-language films. *The Bulletin* magazine publishes a useful weekly television guide that covers the main channels.

## Money

The unit of currency in Belgium is the euro (€). A euro is divided into 100 cents. Euro notes come in denominations of 5, 10, 20, 50, 100, 200 and 500; coins are 1 cent, 2 cents, 5 cents, 10 cents, 20 cents and 50 cents, €1 and €2. When changing money, ask for banknotes in small denominations, as many shops refuse to accept €200 and €500 notes.

The country has an extensive network of Bancontact and Mister Cash cashpoints (ATMS) where you can obtain money using a credit card or bank card equipped with a pin code and Maestro chip. Most machines have instructions in English. Major credit cards are accepted by hotels and most restaurants and large shops, but the majority of hotels do not accept travellers' cheques. Always check in advance in order to avoid any embarrassment.

## Changing money

All banks in Belgium exchange foreign money, and they generally give the best rates. Banks open Mon–Fri, from 9am–4pm or 4.30pm, but some branches close for lunch from 1–2pm. Banks are closed at weekends and on public holidays. When a public holiday falls on a weekend, banks are normally closed on the following Monday.

Foreign-exchange offices are located near most large railway stations and in town centres; they are open for longer hours than banks but often give a less-favourable rate of exchange. If you lose your bank card or credit card, you should call 070-34 43 44 as soon as possible to stop it being used. You should also contact your bank at home straight away to report the theft. Beware of high commission rates at hotels.

## Tipping

Tips are included in taxi fares and prices in restaurants and bars, so all that is required is to leave some small change if you think the service warrants it – but service personnel will not object to receiving a tip and have become used to the fact that many visitors (in contrast to their fellow citizens) do tip. In most restaurants, a tip of 10 percent will be considered generous, or at least adequate. In public toilets and establishments with a toilet attendant, it is customary to leave between 20 and 50 cents.

## P ostal Services

Post offices (*post* or *posterijen*) are normally open Mon–Fri 9am–6pm, but smaller branches may close for lunch, usually from 1–2pm. The main post offices in the three cities are listed below.
**Bruges**. 5 Markt,
tel: 050-47 13 12.
**Ghent**. 55 Lange Kruisstraat,
tel: 09-269 27 50.
**Antwerp**. 43 Groenplaats,
tel: 03-202 69 11.

### PUBLIC HOLIDAYS

**1 January** New Year's Day
**1 May** Labour Day
**21 July** National Day
**15 August** Assumption
**1 November** All Saints' Day
**11 November** Armistice Day
**25 December** Christmas Day
In addition, there are "moveable" holidays: Easter Monday, Ascension Day and Pentecost Monday. If any holidays should fall on a Saturday or Sunday, the following Monday is taken off instead.

## R eligious Services

Most churches in Belgium are Catholic, but there are weekly, English-speaking Protestant services in Bruges and Antwerp.
**Bruges**: the English Church of Sint-Pieterskapel, Keerstraat, tel: 050-55 24 92, has services every Sunday at 6pm.
**Antwerp**: the Anglican Church of St Boniface, 39 Grétrystraat, tel: 03-239 33 39, has three services on Sunday at 9am, 10.30am and 3.30pm.

## S tudent Travellers

Students and young people may be entitled to reduced-rate admission to many museums, but a passport or student identity card may be required as proof of age and validity.

## T elephones

The national phone operator is Belgacom. Phone boxes, which are increasingly scarce because of the rise of mobile phones, are normally found in railway stations, metro stations and shopping malls. Most public telephones only accept phonecards (sold at post offices and some supermarkets) or Proton bank cards, but some accept international credit cards. Only a few public phones accept coins. Many cafés have a public phone, often next to the toilets.

Telephone numbers in Belgium consist of the area code followed by a six- or seven-digit number. When calling from within Belgium, dial the area code followed by the number. When calling Belgium from abroad, first dial the country code (**32**), followed by the area code minus the initial zero, then the suscriber number.

Belgacom runs an English-speaking service for directory enquiries, tel: 1405. This covers both domestic and international calls. For online information on telephone numbers: www.infobel.com.

## Toilets

Public toilets are few and far between in Belgium, but can usually be found at railway stations and in large department stores. Other useful locations are museums and cafés. You can normally use the toilets in large hotels or fast-food restaurants. Most Belgian cafés will also let you use their toilets, although some expect you to pay a small charge (normally about 50 cents).

## Tourist Information

### Bruges
The main tourist office is located at 34 't Zand, tel: 050-44 86 86; www.brugge.be. Open daily 10am–6pm (Thur 10am–8pm).
### Ghent
The tourist office is located at 17A Botermarkt (in the crypt of the belfry), tel: 09-266 52 32; www.gent.be. Open April–Oct 9.30am–6.30pm, Nov–March 9.30am–4.30pm.
### Antwerp
The main tourist office is close to the town hall at 13 Grote Markt, tel: 03-232 01 03; www.visitantwerpen.be. Open Mon–Sat 9am–5.45pm, Sun and public holidays 9am–4.45pm. A second tourist office is located at 26 Koningin Astridplein, next to the main railway station and the zoo.

## *Offices Abroad*
### Belgian Tourist Office
**USA**
220 East 42nd Street, Suite 3402, 34th Floor, New York 10017
Tel: 212-758 8130
Fax: 212-355 7675
E-mail: info@visitbelgium.com
www.visitbelgium.com
**Canada**
Same mailing address as USA.
Tel: 514-457 2888
Fax: 212-355 7675
E-mail: info@visitbelgium.com
www.visitbelgium.com
**United Kingdom**
Brussels and Flanders: 1A Cavendish Square, London W1G 0LD
Tel: 0906-302 0245
Brochure line: 0800-954 5245
Fax: 020-7307 7731
E-mail: info@visitflanders.co.uk
www.visitflanders.co.uk

## **W**ebsites

### Transport
www.eurostar.com
Information and booking for Eurostar train.
www.brusselsairport.be
Brussels airport information, including flight details.
www.b-rail.be
Information on Belgian Railways, including online ticket booking.

## TIME ZONE

Belgium is on Central European Time (CET), which is Greenwich Mean Time (GMT) plus one hour. When it is noon in Bruges, Ghent and Antwerp, it is also noon in Paris, Rome and Berlin; 11am in London; 6am in New York, Montreal and Boston; 5am in Chicago; 3am in Los Angeles and San Francisco; and 9pm in Sydney. From the last weekend in March to the last weekend in October, clocks are advanced 1 hour – this corresponds to Daylight Saving Time in the UK and North America.

www.eurotunnel.com
Eurotunnel shuttle service for cars between Folkestone and Calais.
www.snbrusselsairlines.com
Flights to Brussels from major European cities.
www.ryanair.com
Budget flights to Charleroi airport, which is located in southern Belgium.
www.thalys.com
Information and booking for Thalys high-speed train network, which links Paris, Brussels, Antwerp and Amsterdam.
www.delijn.be
Information on bus services in Flanders.
www.fqlyvlm.com
Flights to Antwerp from London City airport.
### Tourism
www.visitflanders.com
Official site of the Flanders tourist office.
www.brugge.be
Bruges city information, including tourism.
www.gent.be
Ghent city information, including tourism.
www.visitantwerpen.be
Antwerp tourist information in English.
### Hotel Reservations
www.bookings.be
Useful site which has special offers on business hotels, small, family hotels and budget accommodation.
www.hotelclub.com
Efficient site dealing mainly in business hotels with customer reviews and last-minute deals.
### News
www.xpats.com
Expat site for the English-speaking community in Belgium.
www.expatica.com
Expat site in English with news and tourist information.
### Entertainment
www.cinebel.be
Cinema listings for whole of Belgium. French and Flemish.
www.noctis.com
Interesting independent site with full information on all aspects of Belgium after dark.

# **L**ANGUAGE

## UNDERSTANDING THE FLEMINGS

### Flemish vs Dutch

The people of Flanders speak Dutch. Behind this simple statement lies a thicket of complication. There is no such language – the word reflects the historical English inability to distinguish between the languages of Germany (Deutsch) and the Low Countries (Nederlands), and their lumping of them together and corrupting it to Dutch.

To English speakers, Dutch is the language of Holland and Flemish is the language of Flanders: simple. But to the 'Dutch', Nederlands is the language of Nederland (the Netherlands), of which Holland is but a part, and they are Nederlanders, not Dutch at all. To Flemings, Vlaams (Flemish) is not a separate language, and certainly not a dialect, with its connotation of second-class status – but an equal variant of Nederlands.

The language academy of Flanders calls this 'Netherlandic', but is willing to live with Dutch as an internationally accepted substitute, provided no one falls for the implication that it belongs to the Netherlands alone.

While most people are happy to speak English or German, some people may be less friendly when addressed in French.

### Dutch pronunciation

This Germanic language regularly uses a guttural consonant similar to the "ch" in the Scottish word "loch". In Dutch terms this is known as the "soft g", although the "hard g" sounds similar – if you look at Dutch words that begin with a "g", then you can reasonably assume the word starts with that infamous "ch". Here are a few tips on Dutch pronunciation:

### *Consonants*

As a rule, the "hard consonants" such as t, k, s and p are pronounced almost the same as in English, but sometimes softer.
*j* is pronounced as a *y* (*ja* meaning yes is pronounced *ya*)
*v* is pronounced as *f* (*vis* meaning fish is pronounced *fiss*)
*je* is pronounced as *yer*
*tje* is pronounced as *ch* (*botje* meaning little bone is pronounced *botchyer*)

### *Vowels*

*ee* is pronounced as *ay* (*nee* meaning no is pronounced *nay*)
*oo* is pronounced as *o* (*hoop* meaning hope is also pronounced as *hope*)
*ij* is pronounced as *eay* (*ijs* meaning ice cream is pronounced *ace*)
*a* is pronounced as *u* (*bank* also meaning bank is pronounced as *bunk*).

### Dutch Words & Phrases

**How much is it?** *Hoeveel is het?* (or) *Hoeveel kost dit?*
**What is your name?** *Wat is uw naam?*
**My name is...** *Mijn naam is ... Ik heet ...*
**Do you speak English?** *Spreekt u Engels?*
**I am English** *Ik ben Engels*

**...American**...*Amerikaan*
**I don't understand** *Ik begrijp het niet*
**Please speak more slowly** *Kunt u langzamer praten, alstublieft*
**Can you help me?** *Kunt u mij helpen?*
**I'm looking for...** *Ik zoek...*
**Where is...?** *Waar is...?*
**I'm sorry** *Excuseer/Pardon*
**I don't know** *Ik weet het niet*

**No problem** *Geen probleem*
**Have a good day!** *Prettige dag nog!*
**That's it** *Precies*
**Here it is** *Het is hier*
**There it is** *Het is daar*
**Let's go** *Kom/We zijn weg*
**See you tomorrow** *Tot morgen*
**See you soon** *Tot straks!*
**At what time?** *Hoe laat?*
**When?** *Wanneer?*
**What time is it?** *Hoe laat is het?*

**yes** *ja*
**no** *neen*
**please** *alstublieft*
**thank you** *dank u*
**...(very much)** *...(wel)*
**you're welcome** *graag gedaan*
**excuse me** *excuseer/pardon*
**hello** *hallo*
**goodbye** *tot ziens*
**good morning** *Goede morgen*
**good evening** *Goeden avond*
**here** *hier*
**there** *daar*
**today** *vandaag*
**yesterday** *gisteren*
**tomorrow** *morgen*
**now** *nu*
**later** *later*
**right away** *direct/onmiddellijk*
**this morning** *vanmorgen*
**this afternoon** *deze namiddag*
**this evening** *vanavond*

## On the Road

**Where is the spare wheel?** *Waar is het reservewiel?*
**Where is the nearest garage?** *Waar is de dichtstbijzijnde garage?*
**Our car has broken down** *Onze auto is in panne*
**I want to have my car repaired** *Ik wil mijn auto laten herstellen*
**the road to...** *de straat naar...*
**left** *links*
**right** *rechts*
**straight on** *rechtstreeks*
**far/near** *ver/nabij*
**opposite** *tegenover*
**beside** *naast*
**car park** *de parking*
**over there** *daar*
**at the end** *aan het eind*
**on foot** *te voet*
**by car** *met de auto*
**town map** *het stadplan*
**road map** *de (wegen) kaart*
**street** *de straat*
**square** *het plein*
**give way** *geef voorrang*
**dead end** *doodlopende straat*
**no parking** *verboden te parkeren*
**motorway** *de autosnelweg*
**toll** *de tol*
**speed limit** *de snelheids-beperking*
**petrol** *de benzine*
**water/oil** *water/olie*
**puncture** *een lekke band*

## Shopping

***Where is the nearest bank?*** *Waar is de dichtstbijzijnde?*
***...post office?*** *postkantoor?*
**I'd like to buy...** *Ik zou graag* (or) *kopen*
**How much is it?** *Hoeveel is het?* (or) *Hoeveel kost het?*
**Do you take credit cards?** *Neemt u crediet kaarten?*
**Have you got?** *Hebt u...?*
**I'll take it** *Ik neem het*
**What size is it?** *Welke maat is het?*
**Anything else?** *Iets anders?*
**cheap** *goedkoop*
**expensive** *duur*
**enough** *genoeg*
**too much** *te veel*
**a piece** *een stuk*
**each** *per stuk*
**bill** *de rekening*
**chemist** *de apotheek*
**bakery** *de bakkerij*
**bookshop** *de boekhandel*
**department store** *het warenhuis*
**fishmonger** *de viswinkel*
**grocery** *de kruidenier*
**tobacconist** *de tabakwinkel*
**market** *de markt*
**supermarket** *de supermarkt*

## Sightseeing

**town** *de stad*
**old town** *de oude stad*
**abbey** *de abdij*
**cathedral** *de kathedraal*
**church** *de kerk*
**hospital** *het ziekenhuis*
**town hall** *het stadhuis*
**tower** *de toren*
**walk** *de tour*
**country house/castle** *het kasteel*
**museum** *het museum*
**art gallery** *de galerie*
**exhibition** *de tentoonstelling*
**swimming pool** *het zwembad*
**tourist information office** *het bureau voor toerisme*
**free** *gratis*
**open** *open*
**closed** *gesloten*
**every day** *elke dag*
**all year** *het hele jaar*
**all day** *de hele dag*
**to book** *reserveren/boeken*

## Emergencies

**Help!** *Help!*
**Call a doctor/an ambulance** *Bel een dokter/een ziekenwagen*
**Call the police/fire brigade** *Bel de politie/brandweer*
**Where is the nearest telephone?** *Waar is de dichtstbijzijnde telefoon?*
**Where is the nearest hospital?** *Waar is het dichtstbijzijnde ziekenhuis?*
**I am sick** *Ik ben ziek*
**I have lost my passport/purse** *Ik ben mijn paspoort/portemonnee kwijt/verloren*

## Telephoning

**How do I make an outside call?** *Hoe krijg ik een buitenlijn?*
**I want to make an international (local) call** *Ik wil naar het buitenland bellen*
**What is the dialling code?** *Wat is het zonenummer/landnummer?*
**The line is busy** *De lijn is in gesprek*

## Eating Out

**breakfast** *het ontbijt*
**lunch** *lunch/middageten*
**dinner** *diner/avondeten*
**meal** *de maaltijd*
**first course** *het voorgerecht*
**main course** *het hoofdgerecht*
**drink included** *drank inbegrepen*
**wine list** *de wijnkaart*
**the bill** *de rekening*
**fork** *het vork*
**knife** *het mes*
**spoon** *de lepel*
**plate** *het bord*
**glass** *het glas*
**napkin** *het servet*
**ashtray** *de asbak*
**I am a vegetarian** *Ik ben vegetarier*
**I am on a diet** *Ik volg een dieet*
**What do you recommend?** *Wat beveelt u aan?*
**I'd like to order** *Ik wil bestellen*
**That is not what I ordered** *Dit is niet wat ik besteld heb*
**Is service included?** *Is de dienst inbegrepen?*

# FURTHER READING

## General

**Antwerp** by Nicholas Royle, 2004, Serpent's Tail.
A stylish thriller set in contemporary Antwerp
**Bruges-la-Morte** by Georges Rodenbach, 1892, English translation 1993, Atlas Press.
Classic fin-de-siècle novel set in a foggy Bruges.
**The Sorrow of Belgium** by Hugo Claus, Viking (1990).
A novel charting the effects of the Nazi occupation of Flanders through the eyes of a young boy.

## History

**The Fair Face of Flanders** by Patricia Carson, 1992, Lannoo.
Authoritative account of the history of Flanders.
**Flemish Cities Explored** by Derek Blyth, 2003, Pallas Athene.
Walks in the historic Flemish cities of Bruges, Ghent, Antwerp, Mechelen, Leuven and Ostend, concentrating on the beautiful, the historical and the quirky.

## Art

**The Flemish Primitives: The Masterpieces** by Dirk De Vos, Princeton University Press (2003).
More than 200 colour illustrations of works by the likes of Jan van Eyck, Rogier van der Weyden and Petrus Christus, are a feast for the eye.
**From Van Eyck to Bruegel** by Max J Friedlander, Phaidon (1969).
Definitive account of the *œuvre* of the great Flemish Masters.
**Peter Paul Rubens: A Touch of Brilliance**, by Mikhail Piotrovsky, Natalya Gritsay, Alexey Larionov, Vegelin van Claer, Stephanie-

Suzanne Durante, James Cuno, Peter Paul Rubens, Joanna Woodall, 2004, Prestel Publishing.
Two important collections of Rubens' oil sketches and drawings are brought together in this revealing look at the artist's inspiration, technique, and place in history.

## FEEDBACK

We do our best to ensure the information in our books is as accurate and up-to-date as possible. The books are updated on a regular basis, using local contacts, who painstakingly add, amend and correct as required. However, some mistakes and omissions are inevitable and we are ultimately reliant on our readers to put us in the picture.
We would welcome your feedback on any details related to your experiences using the book "on the road". Maybe we recommended a hotel that you liked (or another that you didn't), as well as interesting new attractions, or facts and figures you have found out about the country itself. The more details you can give us (particularly with regard to addresses, e-mails and telephone numbers, the better.
We will acknowledge all contributions, and we'll offer an Insight Guide to the best letters received.

Please write to us at:
Insight Guides
PO Box 7910
London SE1 1WE
United Kingdom
Or send e-mail to:
insight@apaguide.co.uk

## Food & Drink

**Cheese** by Willem Elsschot, 1933, English translation 2002, Penguin.
Laconic Flemish novella involving an unsuccessful Antwerp businessman who lands a massive consignment of Dutch cheese to sell.
**Everybody Eats Well in Belgium Cookbook** by Ruth Van Waerebeek-Gonzalez and Maria Robbins, Workman Publishing (1996).
A lovingly detailed Belgian cookbook which includes 250 recipes from around the country.
**The Great Beers of Belgium** by Michael Jackson, Running Press (1998).
The author has drunk his way devotedly through the beer rosters of many a land. He came away from his Belgium investigations convinced that it is the proud bearer of one of the world's greatest beer-brewing traditions.

## Other Insight Guides

**Insight Guide: Belgium** covers every aspect of the country: history, culture, people and places with insightful text and superb photography. **Insight City Guide: Brussels** concentrates on the ever-changing capital city: entertaining features recount how it grew from modest beginnings to become the powerhouse of the European Union. For those on a tight schedule, **Insight Pocket Guide: Brussels** sets out carefully crafted itineraries designed to make the most of your visit, and comes with a full-size fold-out map. **Insight Pocket Guide: Bruges** does a similar job for the medieval gem of Flanders. Separate **Insight Compact Guides** to Brussels, Belgium and Bruges are ideal on-the-spot reference guides.

# BRUGES, GHENT AND ANTWERP
# STREET ATLAS

The key map shows the area of Bruges, Ghent
and Antwerp covered by the atlas section. An index of
street names and places of interest shown on the maps
can be found on the following pages. For each entry
there is a page number and grid reference.

## Map Legend

| | |
|---|---|
| Autoroute with Junction | |
| Autoroute (under construction) | |
| Dual Carriageway | |
| Main Road | |
| Secondary Road | |
| Minor road | |
| Track | |
| International Boundary | |
| Province/State Boundary | |
| National Park/Reserve | |

| | |
|---|---|
| ✈ ✈ | Airport |
| ✝ ✝ | Church (ruins) |
| ✝ | Monastery |
| 🏰 🏯 | Castle (ruins) |
| ∴ | Archaeological Site |
| ∩ | Cave |
| ★ | Place of Interest |
| 🏠 | Mansion/Stately Home |
| ※ | Viewpoint |
| 🏖 | Beach |

| | |
|---|---|
| | Autoroute |
| | Dual Carriageway |
| | Main Roads |
| | Minor Roads |
| | Footpath |
| | Railway |
| | Pedestrian Area |
| | Important Building |
| | Park |

| | |
|---|---|
| Ⓜ | Metro |
| 🚌 | Bus Station |
| ❶ | Tourist Information |
| ✉ | Post Office |
| ✝ | Cathedral/Church |
| ☾ | Mosque |
| ✡ | Synagogue |
| ⚐ | Statue/Monument |
| ▯ | Tower |
| ⌖ | Lighthouse |

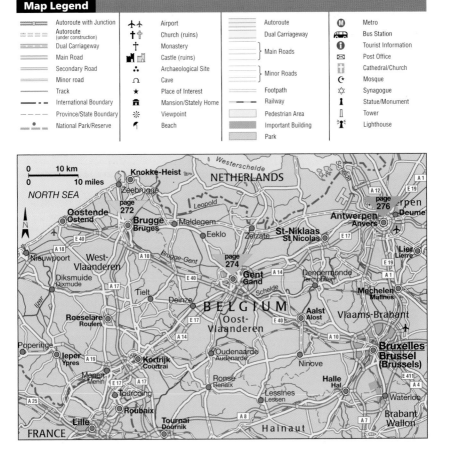

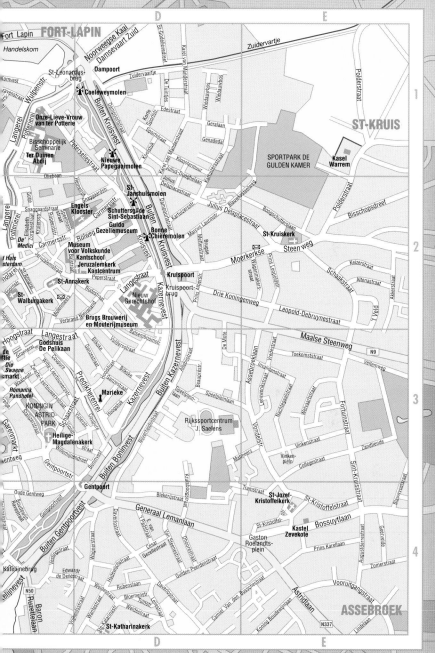

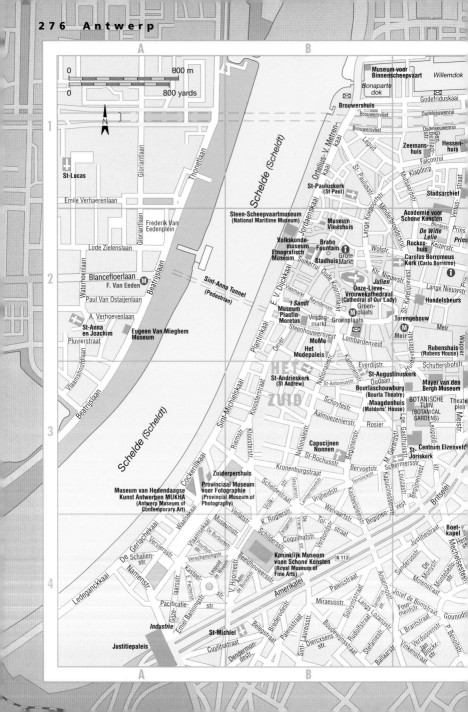

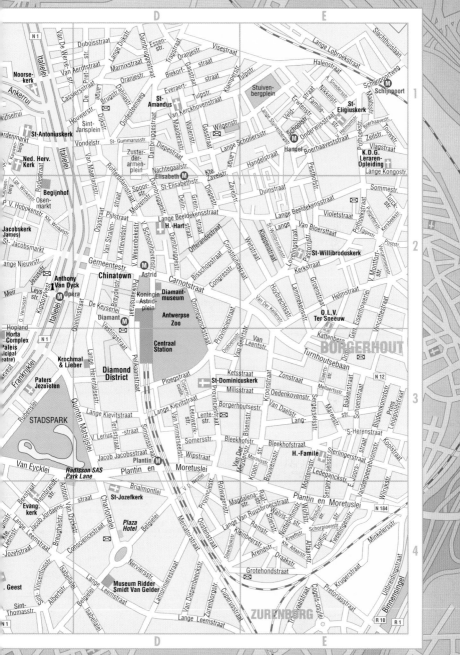

# GHENT

# ANTWERP

# ART & PHOTO CREDITS

# GENERAL INDEX